READER'S DIGEST

# THE PC PROBLEM SOLVER

PUBLISHED BY THE READER'S DIGEST ASSOCIATION LIMITED
LONDON • NEW YORK • SYDNEY • MONTREAL

A READER'S DIGEST BOOK

Published by The Reader's Digest Association Limited
11 Westferry Circus
Canary Wharf
London E14 4HE
www.readersdigest.co.uk

We are committed to both the quality of our products and the service we provide to our customers. We value your comments, so please feel free to call us on 08705 113366, or via our web site at www.readersdigest.co.uk. If you have any comments about the content of any of our books, you can contact us at gbeditorial@readersdigest.co.uk

Copyright © Eaglemoss Publications Ltd 2006

All rights reserved. No part of this publication may be reproduced, stored in a retrieval system or transmitted in any form or by any means, electronic, mechanical, photocopying, recording, or otherwise, without the permission of the copyright holder and publisher.

ISBN-13: 978 0 276 42697 1
ISBN-10: 0 276 42697 5

A CIP data record for this book is available from the British Library

This book was designed, edited and produced by Eaglemoss Publications Ltd
in association with VNU Business Publications Ltd,
based on the partwork *PC KnowHow*

Printed in Singapore

410-593-0

® Reader's Digest, The Digest and the Pegasus logo are registered trademarks of
The Reader's Digest Association, Inc., of Pleasantville, New York, USA

# Contents

**1 Getting Started** ... 5
- Buying a PC ... 7
- Starting up ... 22

**2 Solving Problems** ... 39
- Getting help ... 41
- Troubleshooting basics ... 59
- DIY fixes ... 73
- Curing viruses ... 99

**3 Preventing Problems** ... 109
- Housekeeping basics ... 111
- Backing up ... 121
- Data protection basics ... 131
- Restricted access ... 143

**4 Improving Performance** ... 151
- Speeding up ... 153
- Using utilities ... 163
- Enabling technology ... 171

Glossary ... 183

Index ... 190

# 1
# Getting Started

## Buying a PC ....................7
Which PC?
Read the label
Look and feel
Software bundles
Buyer beware
Shopping list
Buying a printer
Which printer?
Choosing a printer
Back-up & storage
Peripherals
Portables

## Starting up ....................22
Inside your PC
Starting out
Windows
Going soft
Choosing software
Office and business software
Getting hooked
Serving up the Net
World Wide Web
Games

# Buying a PC

**Before you even start looking for a PC you should decide which type of shop fits your needs.**

There are more places than ever to buy a PC. They all have advantages and disadvantages, depending on what you need. You can find places where you'll get a rock bottom price – as long as you know what you're looking for. Other places offer better service at a premium. You can pick up the phone and order a computer by credit card from a magazine, or buy one over the Internet, made to your exact specification. Follow these guidelines to see what's best for you.

## The high street

High street electrical stores and department stores are easy places to buy a PC, and you'll find well-known brands like Compaq and Packard Bell. But often the prices are not competitive, and the models may not be the latest ones. In smaller stores, there may not be anyone to answer your questions.

## The supermarket

Although there aren't many supermarkets selling computers yet, those that do are offering very good value for money. But you'll probably find that there isn't a choice of models, and there may not be anyone to demonstrate the system or answer questions. It really will be just the same as buying anything else from your local supermarket.

## PC superstores

If you want to try out a PC before buying it, a PC superstore, such as PC World, is the best place to shop. You'll find a wide range of PCs, and plenty of staff to answer questions. If you decide to buy, you'll be able to take whatever you've chosen with you right away.

You may be able to arrange a credit deal to save you paying for everything in one go. But, as with high-street stores, the prices aren't as competitive as those of mail-order companies.

## Mail order

Pick up a PC magazine and you could be forgiven for thinking that it's all adverts. Ordering a PC off a magazine page is one of the best ways to do it. You'll find the latest technologies, and at the keenest prices. In many cases, the PC will be put together to order.

You won't be able to try before you buy, and you'll have to wait. It's unlikely that there will be any sort of credit facilities available and you'll need a credit card.

## Online shopping

Large companies such as Dell offer online shopping, as do smaller mail-order PC makers. You can't try before you buy, but there will often be lots of information about different systems. The disadvantages are much the same as for mail order, and you'll need a credit card.

## Second hand

You can buy PCs second hand, but remember you won't get a warranty, and you could end up with a PC that isn't powerful enough to run the latest programs. Unless you're on a really tight budget, it's not recommended.

# Which PC?

**Choosing a new PC is not easy. Follow these steps to simplify the process.**

Buying a new PC can be hard, particularly if you have never owned or used one before. Here are four sample configurations. Just follow the questions and you'll have a better idea of the sort of system that will suit you best.

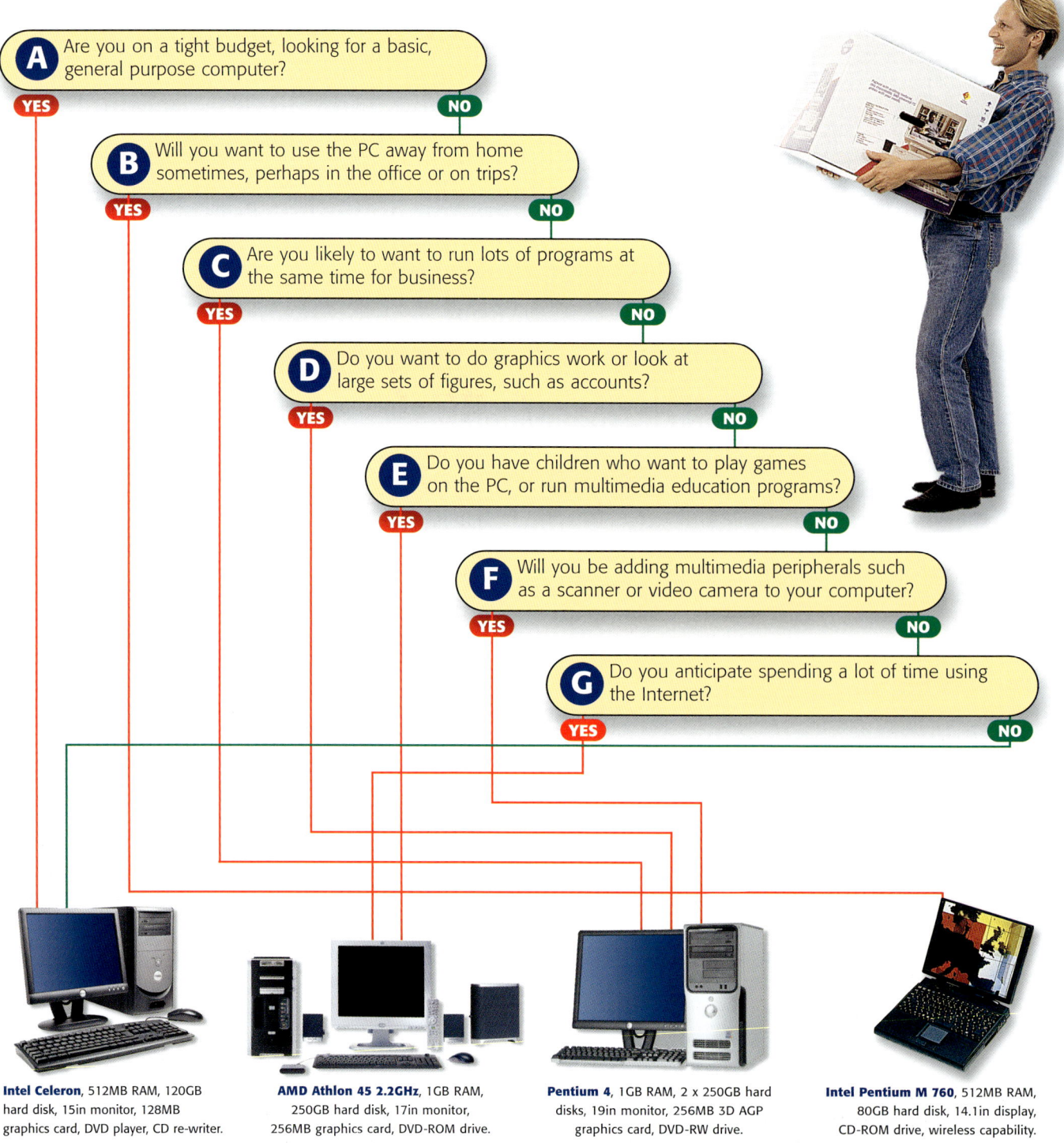

**A** Are you on a tight budget, looking for a basic, general purpose computer? YES / NO

**B** Will you want to use the PC away from home sometimes, perhaps in the office or on trips? YES / NO

**C** Are you likely to want to run lots of programs at the same time for business? YES / NO

**D** Do you want to do graphics work or look at large sets of figures, such as accounts? YES / NO

**E** Do you have children who want to play games on the PC, or run multimedia education programs? YES / NO

**F** Will you be adding multimedia peripherals such as a scanner or video camera to your computer? YES / NO

**G** Do you anticipate spending a lot of time using the Internet? YES / NO

**Intel Celeron**, 512MB RAM, 120GB hard disk, 15in monitor, 128MB graphics card, DVD player, CD re-writer.

**AMD Athlon 45 2.2GHz**, 1GB RAM, 250GB hard disk, 17in monitor, 256MB graphics card, DVD-ROM drive.

**Pentium 4**, 1GB RAM, 2 x 250GB hard disks, 19in monitor, 256MB 3D AGP graphics card, DVD-RW drive.

**Intel Pentium M 760**, 512MB RAM, 80GB hard disk, 14.1in display, CD-ROM drive, wireless capability.

# Read the label

**Learn to recognise the parts that make up a PC before a salesman tries to blind you with science.**

A PC is the sum of many parts, and each one has a specific purpose. Knowing what they do, and why, means you can make more sense of the different options you'll be bombarded with when you go to buy one.

You may see a package that looks great and seems to include everything, but by cutting out the things you don't need and spending more money on those you do, you will end up with a system better suited to your needs.

If you're not too bothered about playing games, why have a superfast 3D graphics card or special speakers? You might be better off opting for a faster modem to give you a better connection to the Internet; or you might want the best possible quality when you print out letters, even if it does take a little longer, and opt for a different type of printer, rather than a bigger screen.

To help you make the right choices, here are what some of the parts of a modern computer do, and what you might need to consider when you're choosing your system.

## Graphics card
Graphics cards produce the picture on your PC's display. A card with more memory built into it will display more colours and more information at the same time. If you want to play games, make sure your card has 3D capability. If your card supports TV output, you can display DVDs or video streamed over the Internet from your PC on a television set.

## Soundcard
Soundcards are used to play back music and sound effects. A wavetable card is the most realistic; it has samples of real instruments used to create music, rather than a synthesiser.

## Modem
A modem links your PC to the phone line, so you can send and receive e-mail, surf the Internet or exchange faxes with other people. An internal modem fits inside your PC, while an external one sits on your desk and has lights to let you know what's happening. A modem's speed is measured in bits per second (bps). The faster the speed, the better.

## Speakers
Some PCs rely on a speaker inside the case, but for better quality look for external ones. See if you can find some that clip on to the side of your monitor. A sub-woofer is an extra speaker which enhances bass sounds.

## CD-ROM or DVD drive
Many programs come on CD-ROMs so you can install them quickly and easily; you can also use a CD drive to play music. Faster CD drives allow you to install programs quicker. Most PCs also have DVD drives. These can read CDs as well as DVD discs, which means, with the right software, you can watch feature films on your PC. A more powerful PC also lets you write your own files to DVDs.

## Processor
The processor does all the work of a PC. The speed is measured in Megahertz (MHz) and the bigger the number, the faster the PC. A Pentium 4 chip is faster than a Pentium III, which in turn is faster than the Celeron.

## Memory
The memory (or RAM) chips are where your computer stores the information it's working on at the moment. More memory helps it run faster. Today a system with less than 128 megabytes (MB) is underpowered.

## Hard disk
Computer programs and the documents you create are stored on the hard disk. The size varies from 120 gigabytes (GB) to 500GB, but under 100GB is not enough for a PC with most modern applications.

# Look and feel

**If you are going to spend a lot of time using your PC, it's important to feel comfortable with it.**

PCs aren't just uniform boxes. That may have been true a few years ago, but now they come in lots of shapes and sizes, and with different add-ons. You can spend almost as much time thinking about what you want your PC to look like as you can deciding what type of system it should be.

## The PC

There are, with the rare exception of all-in-one boxes that include the monitor as well, two main types of PC – the tower case and the desktop case. As the name suggests, a tower case is tall and narrow, while a desktop case sits on top of your desk, usually with the monitor on top of it. A tower case has to go either on the floor or beside the monitor. Sometimes, you'll find that a tower case has more space to add extra expansion cards or disk drives than a desktop but, on the whole, you can make your choice based on which is the more convenient shape. It might also be worth looking for a case that's easy to open if you think you might want to upgrade later – with some you have to undo dozens of screws; others come apart at the flick of a lever.

## The monitor

The monitor is the face of your computer, so it's worth making sure you get a good one. Although you'll find some systems with a 15in monitor, a 17in one isn't much more expensive and will give you a much better display. If you want to do lots of graphical work or often use large spreadsheets, consider a 19in model.

You can also buy monitors that have speakers built in, which will save you having to clutter up your desk. For the ultimate in size, flat-panel liquid crystal displays (LCDs) take up very little desk space, but they're expensive.

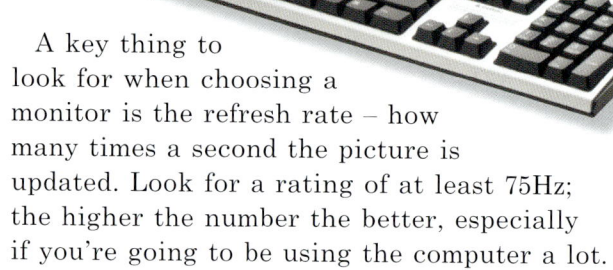

A key thing to look for when choosing a monitor is the refresh rate – how many times a second the picture is updated. Look for a rating of at least 75Hz; the higher the number the better, especially if you're going to be using the computer a lot.

## The keyboard

If you buy a cheap PC, it'll come with a cheap keyboard. That may be fine for occasional use but it's a false economy for anyone planning to use the computer regularly. A bad keyboard, together with a bad seat, can end up causing you lots of problems, including RSI (repetitive strain injury).

It's worth spending a little extra for an ergonomic keyboard. These usually include a wrist rest to help you keep the right position. With some, the keyboard is split in two, which makes typing even more natural though it feels awkward if you can't touch type. If cables are a problem, you can buy a cordless keyboard; you just have to point it at the computer.

## The mouse

There are different types of mouse and there are also alternatives. With most PCs you get a standard two-button mouse, but you can buy a cordless mouse or one with more buttons. The third button can be configured to do whatever you want. There's also a mouse with a wheel between the buttons. The wheel can be used to scroll through documents without having to move to the side of the screen. Or how about a pad? It's a small plastic sheet that you write on with a special pen, so you can draw on screen just as easily as you would on a piece of paper.

# Software bundles

**Think carefully about software bundled with a new computer: will it do exactly what you want?**

Without software PCs can't do anything useful. Windows usually comes with new PCs but the software with it only enables you to write basic documents, send e-mail and connect to the Internet. To do anything else, you need extra software. The best solution is a software bundle, a collection of programs sold as a package or included free with a new PC. Free software is enticing, but what appears to be a great deal because it includes so many programs might be a bit of a con. The first thing to consider is what you want to do with your PC. For most people a word processor is essential; plus a spreadsheet that can be used to do calculations or organise information. You might also want a personal organiser and a program to create pages on the Internet. If you're planning to use your PC for business, a database program is useful too.

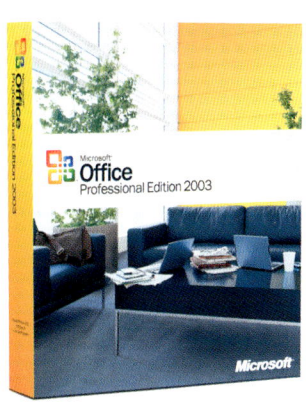

## Office suites

These are the most common bundles. Office suites usually contain a spreadsheet, a word processor, a personal organiser and sometimes extra programs like a Web page editor. The most popular suites are Microsoft Office, Lotus SmartSuite and Corel WordPerfect Suite.

If you're planning to buy one of these suites, shop around. Prices vary, and you may be able to upgrade the software that came with your PC at a discount.

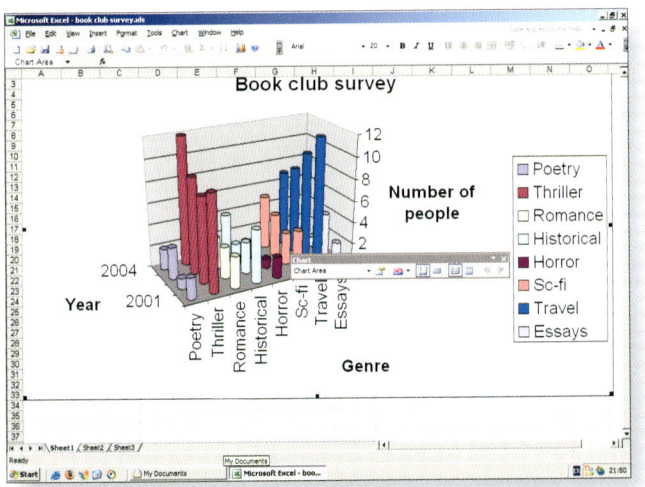

**Excel** is one of the most popular programs. It's a spreadsheet, which means it can be set up to perform calculations on numbers, and even turn them into instant graphs.

## Integrated software

Cheaper PCs are likely to come bundled with an integrated package – a single program that incorporates a word processor, spreadsheet, database and so on. The most popular integrated package is Microsoft Works. It is more than adequate for most home computing.

But if you plan to bring work home from the office, find out whether you can save files in a format that is compatible with your home system. There's no point planning to bring your work home only to find your computer can't read it.

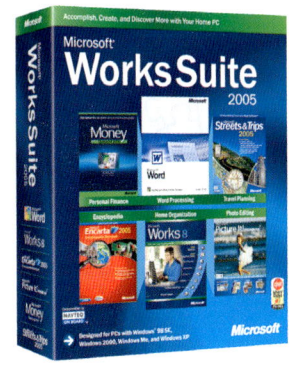

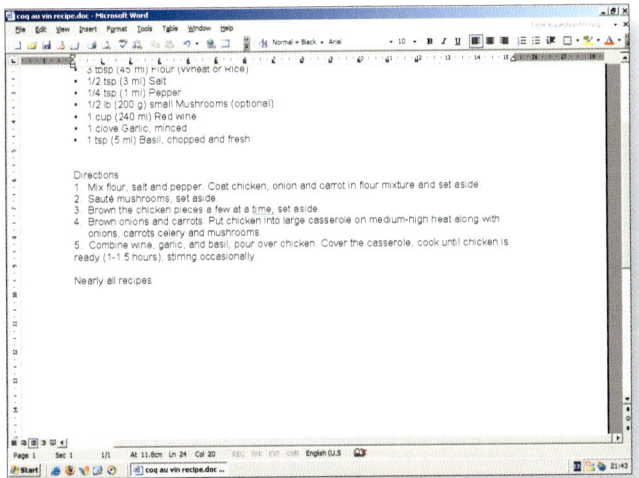

A **word processor** such as Microsoft Word is essential for business tasks such as letter writing or desktop publishing.

# Buyer beware

**Know your rights and you should be able to avoid being cheated by an unscrupulous supplier.**

Understandably, people can be apprehensive when they are thinking of spending a lot of money on something like a PC. What if it goes wrong? What if it's not delivered? How should you pay? Who can help solve problems?

Fortunately, there are straightforward answers to all these questions, and the list on the next page will help you to compare PCs from different suppliers without too much difficulty. Fill in the details of different systems as you go.

### Don't forget

It's easy to compare basic specifications such as the amount of memory, the size of the hard disk and so on, but you can forget other things that are just as important. For instance, will you have to take the PC back to the manufacturer if it goes wrong or will someone come to your home to repair it? If you work from home, that could be vital. Check the warranty (see pages 42–3). Fill in all the spaces on the list for each PC you're considering, and if the answer isn't obvious, don't be afraid to ask. It's your money; you're entitled to know what you'll be spending it on.

There is no correct answer to which computer to buy because everyone's requirements will be different. You'll have to weigh up the different factors yourself.

## Watch out!

It can sometimes seem like the odds are stacked against you when you're faced with a computer salesperson who seems to know it all, but here are some points to bear in mind:

### BEFORE YOU BUY

● If you can, pay by credit card, especially for telephone and mail-order purchases. The credit-card company is legally liable as well as the supplier, so if the PC doesn't arrive, you will get your money back.

● Always write down the names of people you deal with in person or on the phone. If there are any problems later, it'll make them easier to sort out.

● If you need a computer by a certain date, write 'Time Is Of The Essence' on the order form; otherwise you won't have any grounds for complaint if it doesn't arrive on time or turns up months late.

● If you need to do a specific task with your computer, make that clear to the salesperson. Whatever you end up buying must be fit for any task you told the salesperson you wanted to do with it.

● Remember to confirm that a price includes taxes, delivery and all the options you want with the computer.

● In-store credit agreements can seem attractive, but read the small print carefully. Buy now, pay later, interest-free credit can turn out to be expensive if you miss the payment date. A store must give you a written quotation for credit if you ask. Compare it with a bank loan or credit-card loan for the same amount.

### WHEN YOU'VE BOUGHT YOUR COMPUTER

● Don't just sign for a delivery without checking the boxes to make sure that the contents are undamaged. If there is damage to the packaging, you should note that clearly on the courier's receipt, and contact the supplier immediately.

● Check all the parts of your system as soon as you can. If you don't use your scanner for a month, and then discover it doesn't work, you'll have a harder time having it replaced.

● If something goes wrong, complain promptly, but stay calm. You won't win any support by being rude to people.

● You are entitled to demand your money back within a reasonable time if the PC doesn't work. You don't have to accept a credit note or a replacement from the supplier.

● If a supplier isn't dealing with your complaint properly, contact your local Citizens' Advice Bureau for help. If you still can't get your money back and you feel you're entitled to it, contact the credit-card company that you used to buy the computer.

**BUYING A PC**

# Shopping list

**Fill in a list like the one below as you look around, to help you compare computer systems.**

|  | Computer 1 | Computer 2 | Computer 3 |
|---|---|---|---|
| Supplier | | | |
| Brand and model | | | |
| Sales telephone number | | | |
| Contact name | | | |
| Quote reference | | | |
| Processor type and speed | | | |
| Memory | | | |
| Disk size | | | |
| CD-ROM/CD-RW | | | |
| DVD-ROM/DVD-RW | £* | £ | £ |
| Video card type and memory | | | |
| Soundcard | £ | £ | £ |
| Speakers | £ | £ | £ |
| Modem | | | |
| Mouse type | | | |
| Keyboard type | | | |
| Monitor size | | | |
| Desktop or tower case? | | | |
| Windows XP Home or Professional? | | | |
| Software included | | | |
| Type of warranty | | | |
| Will someone come out to repair? | | | |
| Who pays for returning PC for repair? | | | |
| Length of warranty | | | |
| Cost to extend warranty | | | |
| Is telephone support included? | | | |
| Can the system be set up for you? | £ | £ | £ |
| Total cost of system (incl. tax or VAT) | £ | £ | £ |
| Delivery charges | | | |
| Time to deliver system | | | |
| Payment method | | | |
| APR if credit is being offered | | | |
| Total cost of credit | £ | £ | £ |
| Length of credit period | | | |

\* Some add-ons are optional and will increase the price of your system. Fill in the extra cost here.

# Buying a printer

**After your PC itself, a printer is probably the most important piece of equipment you can buy.**

Sooner or later you'll need to print things out, which means, of course, you'll need a printer. Originally there was really only one type of printer you could buy: the dot matrix (see page 16). Anything that offered high-quality printing was far too expensive for a home user. Today, computer stores stock a good range of printers to suit a variety of needs at accessible prices.

The most popular type of printer is an inkjet (below). It works by firing dots of ink at a sheet of paper – rather like squeezing the cartridge in a fountain pen but more precise. Basic inkjet printers are inexpensive but top-of-the-range models can cost much more. Nearly all will print in colour. Inkjet printers are often quite compact and, if you're buying a portable PC, you'll be able to find a portable inkjet to match it. The latest models can print on special paper to give photographic quality, which is ideal if you are using a digital camera.

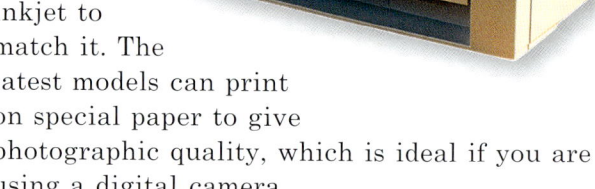

## See the light

The second common type of printer is a laser (above), which works in a similar way to photocopiers, using a fine black powder called toner to make up the images. They rely on your PC to do a lot of the work of transferring the page onto paper, so a slow PC will print slowly. Personal laser printers are compact and not too expensive (though more than inkjets). They usually print in black and white. Colour laser printers are available, although they are usually more expensive.

## Jargon buster

**Cartridge** The part of the printer that you replace when it runs out of ink or toner. Find out how many pages you can expect from each cartridge. More pages and a cheap cartridge means the printer is cheaper to run.

**CMYK** Cyan magenta yellow and key (or black), the four colours used in an inkjet printer to make up any other colour.

**Dpi** This stands for dots per inch, the number of dots the printer puts on the page in each inch. High numbers mean better quality.

**Gsm** This stands for grammes per square metre and is often used to refer to the thickness of paper a printer can handle. Bigger numbers mean thicker paper or card; typical photocopier paper is 80gsm, while a business card is about 120gsm.

**MFD (multi-functional device)** These offer printing, copying, scanning and sometimes faxing facilities in one machine, and are widely available.

**Parallel port** The traditional way of connecting a printer to a computer. Most modern printers connect via the USB port. It's faster and the printer can be connected or disconnected without switching off the PC.

**Photo-realistic** This describes a printer that can produce near-photo-quality prints, but you'll need a special ink cartridge and special paper for the best results.

**Ppm** Pages per minute, the speed at which a printer prints. Colour printers may quote one speed for colour and another for black and white.

**Sheet feeder** A device or part of the printer that takes a sheet of paper from a stack and feeds it through. On printers without this facility (usually portable, or very cheap ones) you'll have to put each sheet in yourself at the right time.

**Toner** The fine powder used by a laser printer.

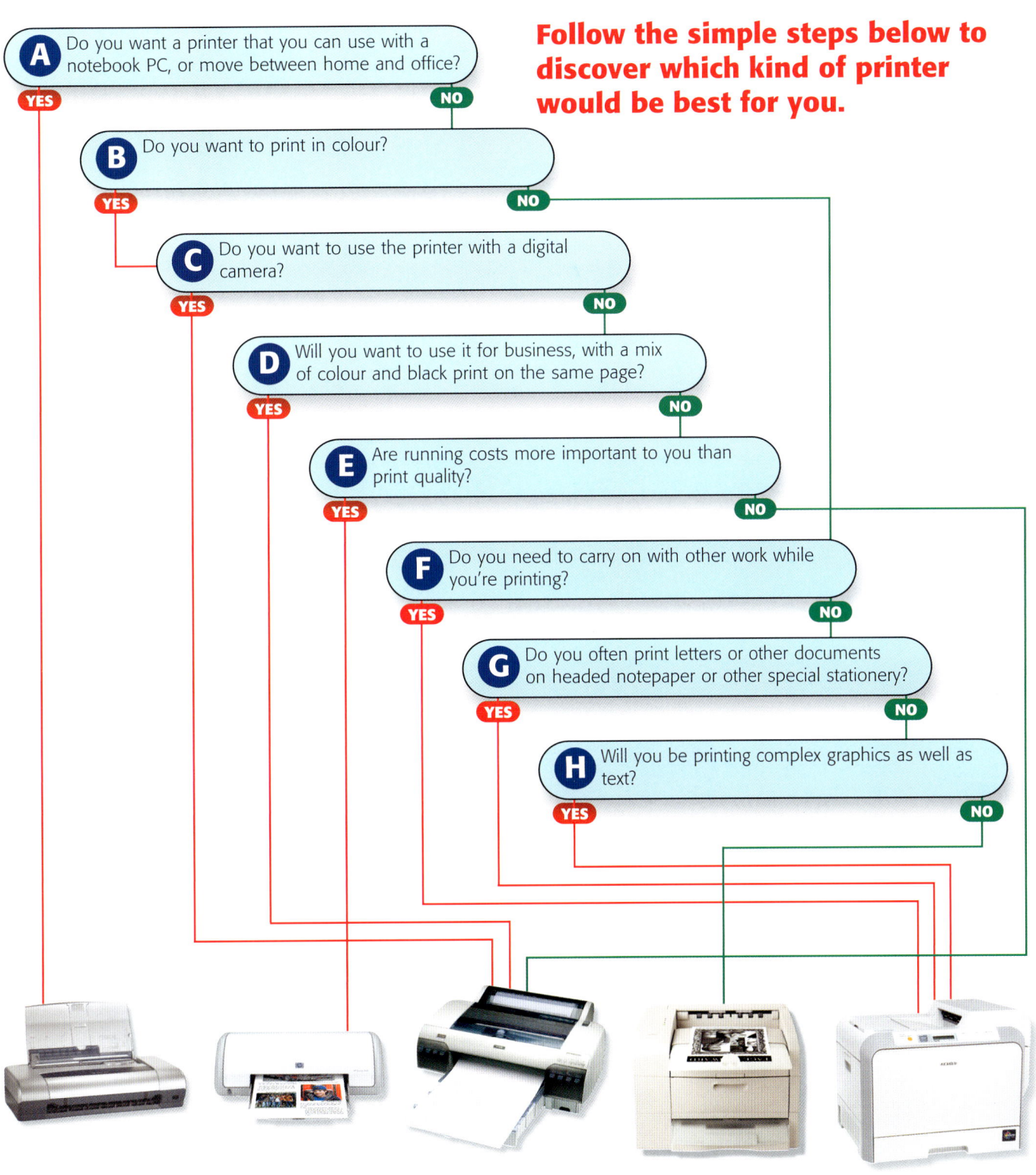

# Choosing a printer

**Most people opt for an inkjet printer, but for special needs consider a laser or dot matrix.**

Understanding more about the different types of printer will help you make the right decision.

### Dot-matrix printers
These were once very common, but today they are hard to find. Dot-matrix printers (below) work just like the printer in cash registers, making letters up out of dots created by pins pressing against a ribbon. Look for a 24-pin printer if you want to buy one.

There's really just one reason to buy a dot-matrix printer: they're the only type that can print on carbon paper. So if you want carbon copies, or you have special stationery that has carbon in it – invoice forms, for instance – you'll need one of these. For anything else, they're too old-fashioned and not of good enough quality.

### Inkjet printers
For most home users, this is the best sort of printer to buy. An inkjet (top right) can produce both colour and black and white printing, and the quality is good. A modern inkjet will produce print-outs with a resolution of 4800 x 1200 dots per inch (dpi). On average it will also typically be able to print out pages of text at between 8 and 16 black-and-white pages per minute (ppm). Some larger models can print on paper as big as A3, while for people on the move, there are printers small enough to fit in a briefcase.

Many inkjet printers work much more slowly when printing in colour, and the colour resolution may also be less than in black and white. Most inkjet printers rely on your computer to do most of the work, and so you may find the PC goes slowly when you're printing.

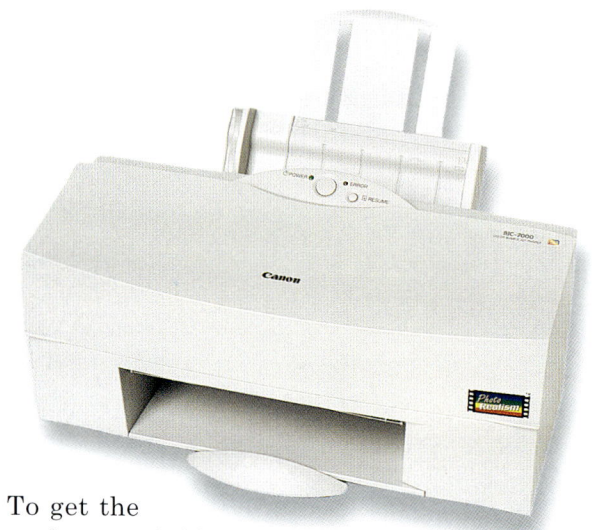

To get the best from an inkjet printer you need to be careful about the paper that you use. While almost all will print on cheap photocopier paper, look closely and you'll see the difference between brands of paper. Since the printer works by firing wet ink at each sheet, if the paper's too absorbent, images smudge. For the best results, you need special paper, which can be expensive. Some printers claim to give photo-quality output, but for those you may need to buy a special ink cartridge as well as the paper, making it expensive. Stick with ordinary paper and ink for all your day-to-day printing.

### Laser printers
These are also sometimes called page printers or LED printers. Unlike inkjets, which create the image of a page one row of dots at a time, lasers build up an image of a whole page on a special drum, just like a photocopier.

Once the whole page is created the image is transferred to paper using toner, again like a photocopier. The only difference is that instead of being scanned with a bright light, the image is made by a computer controlling a laser, or a series of LEDs (light-emitting diodes).

To create an image of a page, laser printers need memory, just like your PC. A printer with more memory can create more complicated pages. You can program some to do things like add your own letterhead to each page that's printed.

# BUYING A PC

Low-cost laser printers generally have a resolution of 600dpi, although more and more models manage 1200dpi at a reasonable price. Bear in mind that, because many printers have some form of enhancement, a salesperson may claim a resolution of 1200dpi (with enhancement). A real resolution is more important than an enhanced one.

Laser printers usually come with more sophisticated options for handling paper than other types of printer. You may be able to have two stacks of paper so you can have headed notepaper and ordinary paper in it at the same time, saving you having to swap.

Laser printers can be fast. If you're prepared to pay, you can buy one that will print out up to 28 pages per minute, but very detailed pages print more slowly. Colour lasers have become much more affordable in recent years.

## Specialist printers

Although colour laser printers are faster than colour inkjets, the quality of the colour printing is often not as good. Lasers use four toner colours – cyan, magenta, yellow and black – and create the other colours by mixing these together. Although they're becoming more popular, they're still not common and as a result they're expensive to run. They are best suited to producing documents on which it's not crucial that the colours are accurate.

For high-quality results you should consider other types of colour printing. The most accurate colours are achieved by printers that use a process called dye sublimation, but these are not for the casual user. These printers cost much more than a computer, the running costs are substantial and special paper is required.

Another type of colour printer is the hot wax printer. These heat blocks of coloured wax to the point where the melted wax will print on the paper. The advantage is that any paper the wax will stick to, including photocopier paper, can be used, making them much cheaper to run than dye sublimation printers. However, they are very expensive to buy and are not easily available.

Thermal transfer printers use a special ribbon and produce good-quality prints. The printers cost very little but they are not a cheap option. The ribbons can be used just once, and you could find printing each sheet of paper costs a fortune.

## Multi-function devices

If you are short of desktop space, you can choose a multifunction device that is printer, scanner, copier – and sometimes standalone fax – in one. You have to balance convenience against quality to a certain extent.

The printer in a multi-function device is usually of reasonable quality. It can be either an inkjet or a black and white laser.

## Consumables

When you buy a printer, remember that you're making a commitment to continue paying out money. You will need to keep your printer stocked with paper and ink or toner.

Choose the wrong model and you could end up spending a fortune, so check out how much it will cost you to run before making your decision. The first thing is to find out how easily you can obtain supplies. If the printer's not a well-known make, or it's an end-of-line special, will you be able to get supplies for much longer? Will you have to go back to just one shop, or can you shop around?

With inkjet printers, remember that most of your printing is likely to be in black, so can you replace the black ink on its own, or will you have to throw away perfectly good colour ink just because the black section of a cartridge is worn out? Remember that the stunning printouts in the shop may well have been done on expensive paper. Ask to see colour printing on ordinary paper.

With a laser printer, find out how much toner cartridges cost and be prepared for a shock. On some models, it could be more than a cheap inkjet – and you need to multiply that by four for colour. You can buy recycled units more cheaply, but find out first whether or not that will invalidate your warranty.

# Back-up & storage

**Give yourself more room for storing files and back up the precious data on your PC.**

Your PC has a hard disk (right), which stores the programs you use as well as the work you create. In order to keep your computer working smoothly, you should always have a minimum of 1GB of free space on your hard disk. No matter how much free space you think you have, you will soon find that you're running short, and that's the time to think about storage.

There are other good reasons to add storage to your PC. It's a good idea to keep a copy of vital information away from your computer, in case the computer is stolen or destroyed by fire, or your data is accidentally deleted. You might want to take work to and from your office or school.

What types of storage are there, and when should you use them? How easy is it to integrate them with your PC? There are three main storage systems: expansion, to allow you to add space to your PC; removable, which you can unload and swap round easily; and back-up, for keeping information safe. Adding storage to your PC is not difficult. In some cases, you'll need to take the PC's case off and plug in a new disk drive, but it's usually straightforward, and you'll soon be up and running with much more capacity than before.

## Expansion storage

The main type of expansion storage is an extra hard disk drive; your computer will already have a main disk drive referred to as drive C. Add an extra one and it becomes drive D. If you want to experiment with editing videos on your PC, it's worth having a drive just for that; you should consider a fast SCSI audiovisual drive, which is designed to save information quickly enough for video. A slower drive just means jerky pictures.

Most PCs are sold with a hard drive and a CD/DVD drive already fitted, which means you are limited to two more hard drives using the connectors built into the PC. If you want to add anything more, you'll have to look for one of the other types of connector. If you just need more space, adding an extra hard disk is the cheapest option.

## Removable storage

Older PCs have a floppy disk drive for transporting small amounts of data but you'd need thousands of floppy disks to make a copy of the typical PC's hard disk drive. Instead, there are other forms of removable storage which are larger versions of a floppy disk drive. With a removable drive, you can eject one disk, and load another one. If you can afford more disks, you have an effectively unlimited amount of storage space.

Removable storage drives start with the Iomega Zip drive, which is available in 250MB and 750MB versions. Most of the drives will come with either a USB or Firewire connection. Iomega also produce the REV drive which is a removable hard disk system, and uses disks that hold 35GB of data (perhaps as much as 90GB if compressed).

If you use your computer for a variety of tasks, a removable drive could be a good choice. You could have, for instance, one with all your office work on it, and another full of games, and just swap them over when you need to. But remember that you'll have problems if you want to access files or software from the different disks at the same time.

Bear in mind, too, that although removable disks give you unlimited amounts of storage, you'll have to pay a lot of money for disks, and it may often be cheaper to buy a single large hard drive for your PC. However, if you need to move large files from one computer to another, and you can easily separate out different types of information that you don't need at the same time, then a removable drive is a great option. You can also use the disks to back up data that you want to keep safely somewhere else.

For smaller amounts of information that you want to transfer between PCs, you could burn the data to a CD-R or CD-RW (up to around 700MB) or a DVD-R or DVD-RW (around 4.7GB). However, you need to have a separate CD or DVD writer, if one is not installed on your computer, and the appropriate software.

## Back-up storage

Computers are pretty reliable, but things do go wrong with them. It's important, therefore, to have a back-up copy.

Back-up storage is available in a number of forms. You can use Zip disks, CDs or DVDs to save information, although these are not a cheap option. Traditionally, the cheapest way to back up your data is with a tape drive. This is a unit that connects to your computer and takes a small cassette of tape, copying all the information from your hard drive to the tape. If something goes wrong with the hard drive, you can copy all the data back, but make sure you have a copy of the disks you need to access the tape drive. The drive is expensive compared to an external DVD writer, for example, but a tape used to store data is considerably cheaper than buying the same amount of space in the form of DVDs. The tape can also be reused, whereas the data on a DVD cannot be erased, and a full DVD cannot be used again.

There are many kinds of tape drive available, ranging from units that can store a couple of hundred megabytes per tape and plug into your computer's EIDE connector, just like a new disk, to high-capacity models that use DAT (Digital Audio Tape) and can store the contents of a few hard disks on a single tape.

On the down side, however, if you want just one thing from a tape, you'll have the same problem as when you want to watch a single program in the middle of a video tape – it may take some time to find it. As a result, many people also use some type of removable storage to back up information that they might want to access quickly.

An alternative is to have an external hard drive (or a removable hard drive such as the Iomega REV) that enables you to locate the information you want as simply as if you were searching the hard disk of your PC. For smaller amounts of information, you can also back up critical files to a mini drive (also called a USB drive as it plugs directly into the PC's USB port).

## Jargon buster

**ATA** A common interface for storage devices which is also sometimes known as EIDE.

**CD-R** This stands for CD-Recordable – a CD that you can save information on once. You can't erase things that you've already copied to the disc.

**CD-RW** This stands for CD-Re-writable. This type of CD can be used just like an ordinary disc; you can delete and re-record data.

**DVD-R** A re-writable form of DVD. An alternative format, DVD+R, is designed to hold 8.5GB (up from 4.7GB) of information.

**DVD-ROM** Read only DVDs, similar to CD-ROMs, but with a much higher capacity.

**EIDE** The standard way of connecting hard disks and CD-ROMs in modern PCs. Most computers can have up to four EIDE devices installed, including removable disks, tapes and CDs.

**Firewire** This is a type of high-speed connector, also called 1394, that is common on digital camcorders and may also crop up on some hard disks designed for multimedia use. It's faster than USB 1.1, and you can add it to your existing set up with the appropriate expansion card.

**IDE** The standard way of connecting hard disks on PCs. Now superseded by EIDE, but the terms are often interchanged.

**SCSI** One of the older standards for connecting disk drives and other storage devices to a computer. You'll usually need a special SCSI controller (also called an adapter card) to add SCSI to your computer. SCSI drives can be very fast, but are more expensive than EIDE types.

**USB** This stands for universal serial bus, a type of connector found on most new PCs. It can be used for a number of things, including connecting Zip drives.

# Peripherals

**You can get more from your computer if you buy specialised add-ons or peripherals.**

Peripherals are extra goodies you can buy to make your PC more versatile and more powerful. For some people they're just gadgets, but for others they are the factor that makes it worth buying a computer.

Before you buy, find out what connectors you have on your PC. A modern PC will have several USB ports, and most of the gadgets listed here are available in versions to plug into them. USB versions are straightforward to set up – you just plug the new peripheral into the socket of the last one and the PC will install the software for you. If you don't have USB connectors, you can still buy peripherals, but setting them up will be harder. You may have to fit extra parts in the PC.

## Joystick

PCs can be great for playing games, but if you want fast shooting action, using a keyboard and mouse lacks a certain something. A joystick or other type of game controller will get you higher scores and give you a more realistic gaming experience.

## Digital camera

Take pictures with a digital camera and you can transfer them to your computer in minutes. Send a picture of the new baby via e-mail to relatives in Australia, or add party snaps to a Web page. With a good colour printer, you can make proper prints.

Almost any camera will do if you just want to e-mail pictures or put them on the Internet. But if you want to print them, buy a camera with as many megapixels as you can afford. Your pictures will be higher quality; otherwise snaps will always look grainy. And remember that while a screen built into the camera looks good, it uses batteries quickly, so if possible choose one with an old-fashioned viewfinder.

## Scanner

A scanner lets you turn anything on paper into a computer document. With a modem, your PC becomes a fax machine. With a printer, it can be used as a copier.

A flatbed scanner looks like a small photocopier and takes up a lot of space, but you can scan almost anything with it. Other options are portable scanners, such as the Visioneer Strobe, that pull a sheet of paper through automatically. They're compact, but you can't scan a book unless you cut it up. Photo enthusiasts can buy special film scanners that give high quality.

## Web camera

Add a web camera to your PC, hook up to the Internet, and you have an instant video phone. With appropriate software, the computer will save pictures of everyone who comes into the room!

Cameras come in two types. USB cameras plug in to the USB port, while others come with a capture card which can also be used with a video recorder or camcorder, allowing you to save holiday clips, or other videos on your hard disk.

For serious video work, like editing films, buy a dedicated capture card and use your camcorder. If it's just chatting to people online, a USB camera will give hours of fun.

## Art pad

An art pad is the best way to create PC art. You can draw as if you are using a pen and paper on a plastic tablet. They come in different sizes, so you can find one that's the right size for your desk and the type of drawings you want to do. Check whether the pad replaces your mouse or can be used alongside it. You may have to keep swapping connectors if the pad's not convenient to use when you're not drawing.

# Portables

**Notebook computers offer all the functions of desktop computers in a portable case.**

Notebook computers – older terms like laptop are rarely used any more – can do pretty much anything desktop computers can do. However, their small size means they don't use many off-the-shelf components and this makes them more expensive than desktop PCs of a similar specification. Consider your requirements carefully before you buy. It's essential to choose the notebook that's right for you because you can't change the screen, keyboard or pointing device if you don't like them.

Notebook PCs come in all shapes and sizes, from tiny sub-notebooks to briefcase-size models with big screens. All of them run Windows and have the same set of applications as a desktop PC. If the licence permits it, you can install your desktop applications on a notebook, to avoid having to buy two copies of everything.

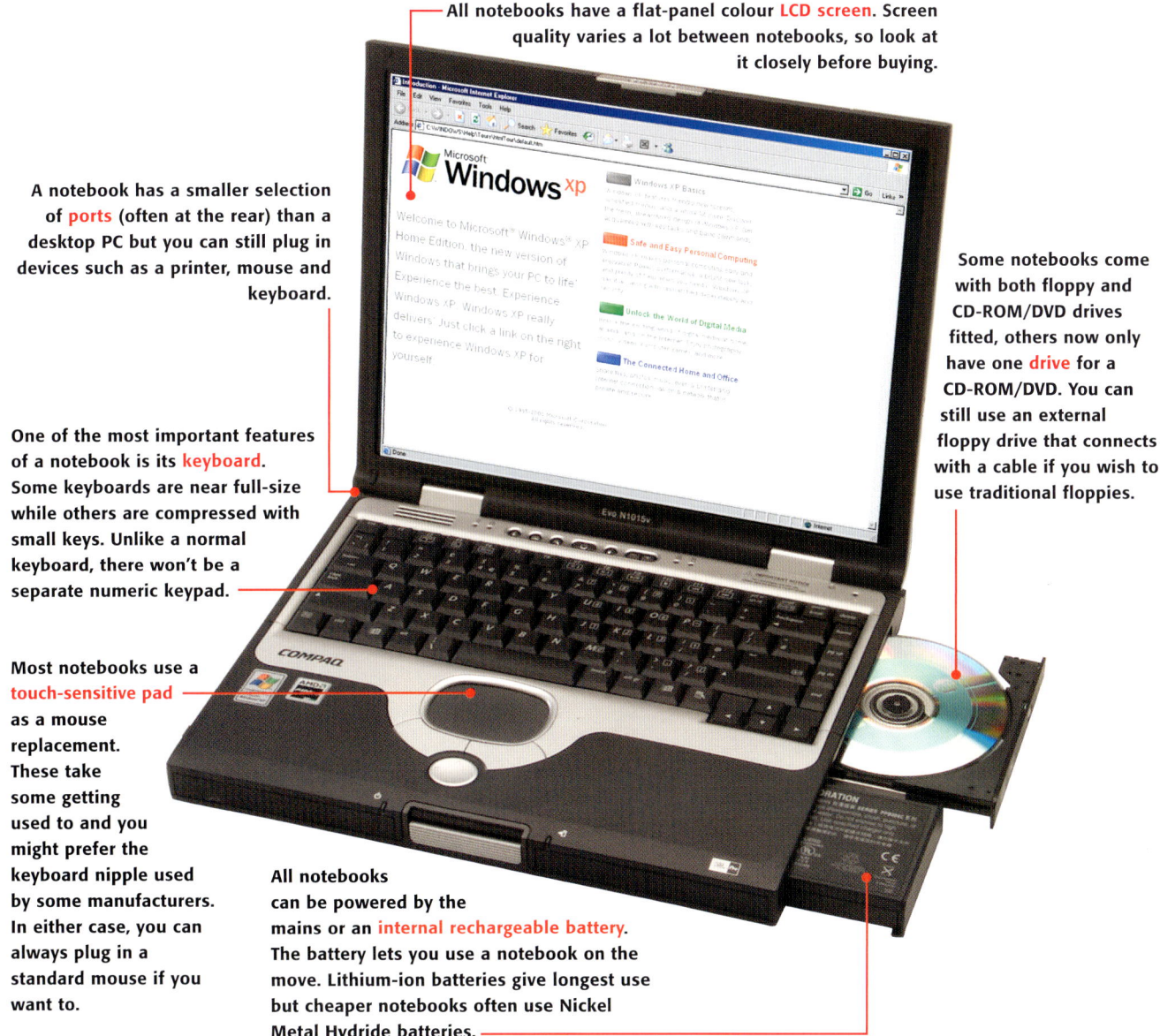

All notebooks have a flat-panel colour LCD screen. Screen quality varies a lot between notebooks, so look at it closely before buying.

A notebook has a smaller selection of ports (often at the rear) than a desktop PC but you can still plug in devices such as a printer, mouse and keyboard.

Some notebooks come with both floppy and CD-ROM/DVD drives fitted, others now only have one drive for a CD-ROM/DVD. You can still use an external floppy drive that connects with a cable if you wish to use traditional floppies.

One of the most important features of a notebook is its keyboard. Some keyboards are near full-size while others are compressed with small keys. Unlike a normal keyboard, there won't be a separate numeric keypad.

Most notebooks use a touch-sensitive pad as a mouse replacement. These take some getting used to and you might prefer the keyboard nipple used by some manufacturers. In either case, you can always plug in a standard mouse if you want to.

All notebooks can be powered by the mains or an internal rechargeable battery. The battery lets you use a notebook on the move. Lithium-ion batteries give longest use but cheaper notebooks often use Nickel Metal Hydride batteries.

# Starting up

## Take a quick look at all the bits and pieces that make up a computer system.

A PC depends on software to function. Most PC software comes on CD-ROMs or DVD-ROMS, which look like audio CDs but contain encyclopaedias, games, accounts programs, word processors and so on. The programs are displayed on a monitor and controlled via a keyboard and mouse, both of which are used to send commands to the main system. Thus far a PC has something in common with a video recorder with its cassettes, TV screen and remote control. Where a PC is different is that its processor – its brain – is not pre-programmed for the specific tasks of recording and playing tapes. It's adaptable. Among other things, it can calculate taxes, answer the phone and check your spelling.

You don't need to know about engines to drive a car, and you don't need to know how a PC works to use it effectively. However, you do need to be familiar with the controls and accessories described here.

The **monitor** displays what a PC is doing and it does so in millions of vivid colours. Screen sizes range from 14in, which is rather small, to 21in, which is excessively generous. Most are 15in, 17in or 19in. The larger models are not only expensive, they're too bulky for the average desk. Some monitors incorporate speakers and microphones and a small number have built-in cameras for video conferencing.

**PC speakers** come in all shapes and sizes. Some are internal, others external. They have to be able to generate all the sounds that a PC is capable of producing, including CD-quality stereo, speech, telephone messages and exploding space ships. The best way of judging speakers is to listen to them playing different kinds of sound at different levels of volume.

The standard computer **keyboard** uses the Qwerty layout, a name derived from the first six letters on the top row. A rectangular keyboard is suitable for learners but some may prefer a moulded keyboard that uses the same layout in a more ergonomic case. Non-Qwerty layouts, including Braille, are also available.

The **mouse** controls a pointer on the screen. As you move the mouse on the mouse mat, it moves the pointer accordingly: push it away from you and pointer moves to the top of screen; pull it towards you and the pointer moves down. You may also move it from side to side and in any direction in between. The buttons on the mouse determine whether the pointer is used to draw objects, access pull-down menus or to select and move items.

## STARTING UP 23

An **internal modem** is a device that turns computer signals into a form that can be sent down an ordinary telephone line. It must have a socket for a phone cable and may also have jacks for a telephone handset, microphone and speaker. External modems are also available.

The **soundcard**, which processes sound and music, plugs into a socket inside the PC. Its connectors are on the back panel. The small jack plugs are for speakers, microphone and line connections to other equipment. The larger socket accepts either a joystick or a MIDI instrument.

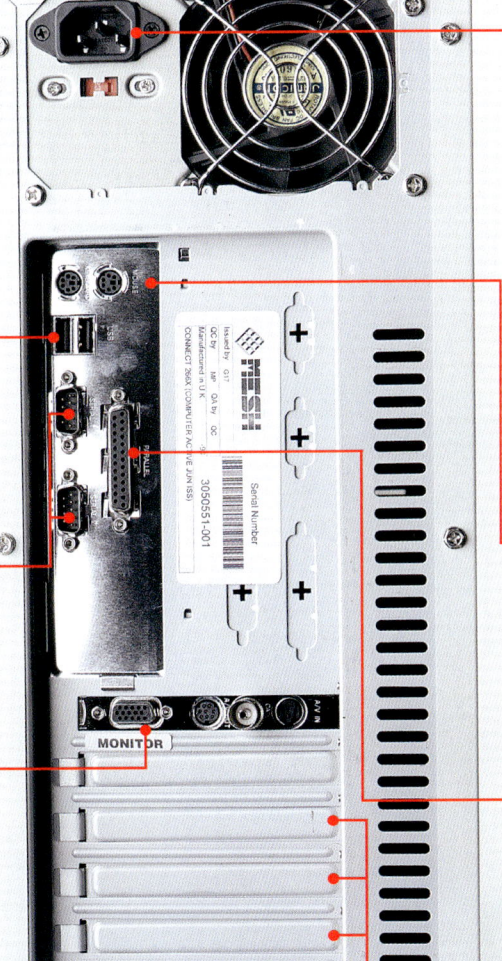

**Joysticks** are for playing games. The buttons can be programmed according to the game being played, and may be used to fire guns, launch missiles or operate the brakes of a car.

**USB ports** can be used like parallel and serial ports but really come into their own when used with more complicated equipment, such as scanners and digital video cameras, where a lot of information has to be transferred very quickly.

Your computer's **power lead** and the socket it plugs into are identical to the lead you use to power a kettle or other domestic appliances.

**Serial ports** are for connecting mice, external modems and some types of printer. You can also connect two PCs by a cable between their serial ports.

This PC has two almost identical **PS2 ports**. One is for a keyboard and the other for a mouse. Not all PCs have these ports, in which case there'll be a DIN socket for the keyboard and the mouse has to be plugged into a serial port.

The **monitor port** connects your PC to a monitor so you can see what it is doing.

The **parallel port** was originally designed for printers, but other devices, such as a scanner or Zip drive, can be connected at the same time as a printer using a piggy-back arrangement called a pass-through adapter.

If you plan to play games with your PC you will need to connect a joystick to the **joystick port** which is connected to a soundcard. The soundcard will also have sockets for external speakers and a microphone.

Your computer should incorporate several **expansion slots** for devices such as an internal modem or a soundcard (see above).

# Inside your PC

## Lift the lid off your computer and you should find that it is not as complicated as you thought.

The inside of a PC looks complicated, but the modular design means that most parts are easy to change; it is just a question of unplugging one component and slotting in another.

Computers generally come in two types of case: desktops and towers. Although there are some slight internal differences, a tower case is essentially no more than a desktop case turned on its side. There is usually more room inside a tower case. Removing a computer's case is usually a matter of undoing a few screws or bolts and sliding off the cover. Make sure that the computer is turned off when you do it and take care not to snag any loose wires.

The **power supply** is a transformer that converts the 240V mains supply into a voltage that the PC can use. The red and yellow cables supply power to all parts of the system.

The **graphics card** is responsible for displaying images on the monitor. Special graphics cards called 3D accelerators can speed up sophisticated three-dimensional graphics, making games look better and play more smoothly.

Sometimes called the CPU (central processing unit), the **processor** is the brain of any PC. The faster and more powerful it is, the faster and more powerful the PC. Most PCs have processors made by Intel, but there are other types made by companies such as AMD and Cyrix.

**Expansion slots** are narrow plastic slots with electrical connectors that let you add expansion cards to a PC. Some expansion cards are essential like graphics cards, while others are useful extras like a modem. Most new PCs have several PCI expansion slots and a single AGP slot. Some older PCs may also have ISA slots (see Glossary).

**Random Access Memory** (RAM) is a PC's short-term memory. When a PC is switched on, it stores parts of the operating system, running applications and any work you are doing. The more RAM a PC has, the faster it will be. RAM loses its contents when a PC is switched off.

The chips on a PC's motherboard (main circuit board) are called the **chipset**. These control some of the most important parts of a PC and allow the processor to communicate with the other components.

The **hard disk** provides long-term storage for software and your work. It looks like a metal box but inside are several magnetic disks rotating at very high speeds. Hard disks store data even when a PC is switched off unlike RAM.

A **modem** lets a computer communicate with another computer over the telephone line, for such things as accessing the Internet and sending e-mail. Most modern PCs come with an internal modem (on an expansion card) but external modems are also available.

A **soundcard** is essential if you want your PC to make noises. Some soundcards are built onto the motherboard, some fit into an expansion slot but all convert computer data into sound that you hear through your speakers.

# Starting out

**The online Help systems that come with the latest versions of Windows make it easy to get up and running.**

In the past, when you bought an operating system for your PC, it came with copious documentation – much more than is typically supplied with today's software. However, while software and operating systems were accompanied by huge manuals, their content wasn't particularly easy to digest. They were often written by experts for experts, and so were not much help for first-time users.

### XP experience

Times have changed and both software and operating systems are more complex. Even compared with its immediate predecessors, Windows 98 and Me, Windows XP is a much more complicated operating system. Most new PCs for the home come with the latest version of Windows – Windows XP Home Edition. Paradoxically, although it is more powerful than earlier versions of Windows and can do more, it is also easier to use because it has a more intuitive user interface. Also, Windows XP can perform tricky operations, such as installing and configuring soundcards, or even linking up a home network, without requiring any technical knowledge on the part of the user. In short, you should experience far fewer problems using XP.

When you buy Windows these days, the only manual supplied with it is likely to be the slimline *Getting Started* book. This will not attempt to tell you everything there is to know about Windows, just enough to get you up and

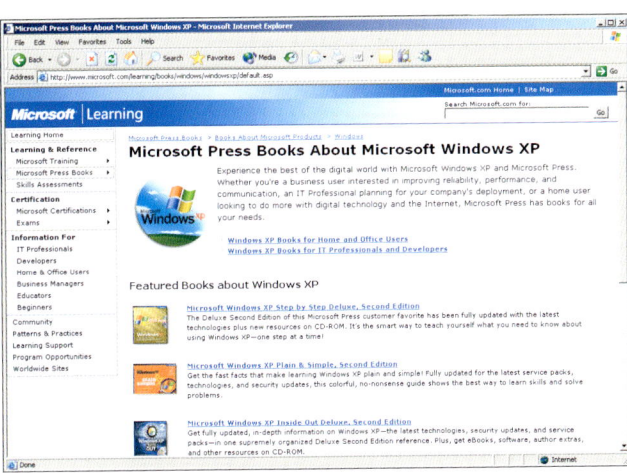

There are many **useful books** available on Windows XP. Go to Microsoft Press's Web site for information.

## Get started with Windows XP

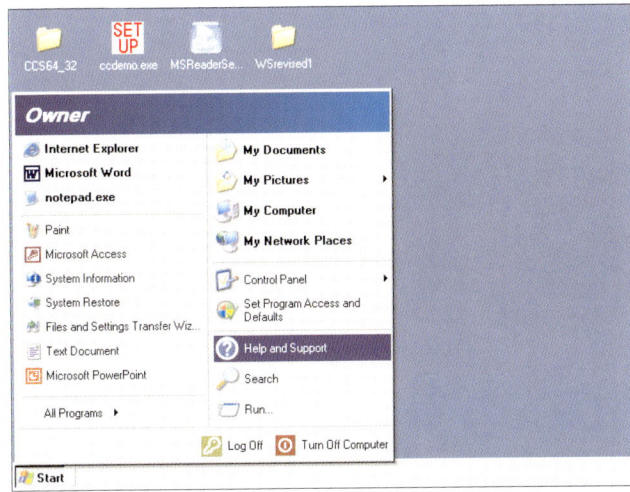

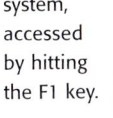 Whatever version of Windows you have, there's plenty of learning material for novice users. All the material is supplied on disk, which makes it much easier to use – it's always available while you are using your PC; it's searchable, which means you don't have to dip into an index to find information; and it's also interactive, so you can click on buttons or text in the online material to launch a program or a troubleshooter wizard.

Windows online Help is your first port of call whenever you want more information on a particular Windows feature. This is always available, no matter what you're doing. Simply click on Start, then Help and Support (just Help in Windows Me and 98), to bring up the main **Windows Help** index. Note that applications, such as Word or Excel, have their own Help system, accessed by hitting the F1 key.

running. It will cover the basics such as using and customising your desktop, controlling a mouse and using the Internet. It is also likely to cover the differences with earlier versions of Windows. If you want more detail, you'll have to buy a book. Most good bookshops have plenty of titles on Windows XP, at various prices. If you have Internet access, visit http://computer-manuals.co.uk or www.amazon.co.uk to buy books online. Microsoft Press has a web site at http://mspress.microsoft.com/ which has a comprehensive list of Windows XP titles and other Microsoft books. You can also find other computing titles published by Reader's Digest listed at www.readersdigest.co.uk.

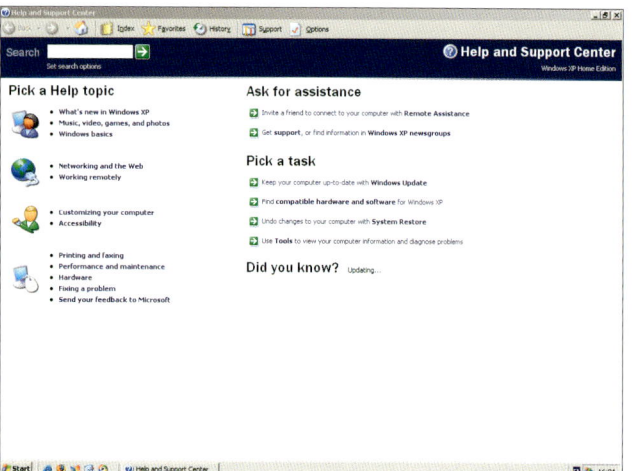

**2** Help is organised into various topics (indicated in Windows 98 by tiny purple book icons). To open a topic, simply click on the link. A description of the topic's contents is displayed on the right. A list of the subject areas covered in the topic appears on the left. If you want to find something not listed there, enter a one or two word description in the Search field above. Another important source of learning material is the online tutorial. In Windows XP and Me this can be run from Help. For PCs using Windows 98, place your Windows 98 CD-ROM in the CD-ROM drive and click on Start, Run. In the Open dialogue box, type in TOUR98 and click on OK.

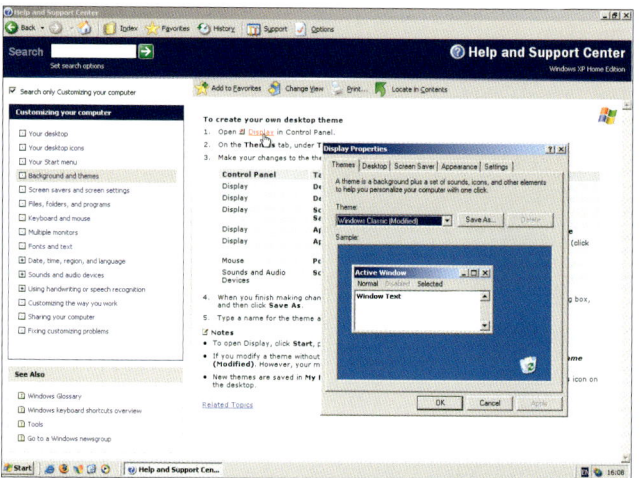

**4** If you're not sure how to carry out an on-screen instruction, a **Show Me button** shows you how. Simply click on the link, usually indicated by an icon of a pointing hand, and it will carry out the action for you — such as here, opening the Display Properties control panel.

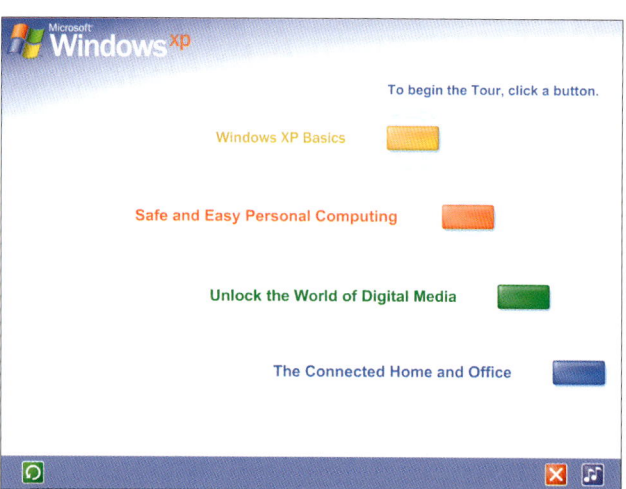

**3** In Windows XP click on What's New in Windows XP, then Taking a Tour or Tutorial. You can then select Take the Windows XP Tour on the right-hand side. This tour offers four subject areas, catering for absolute beginners as well as those upgrading from earlier versions of Windows. The lessons are in **multimedia** form, so you get animated graphics and spoken instructions, making it easier to absorb than reading from a page.

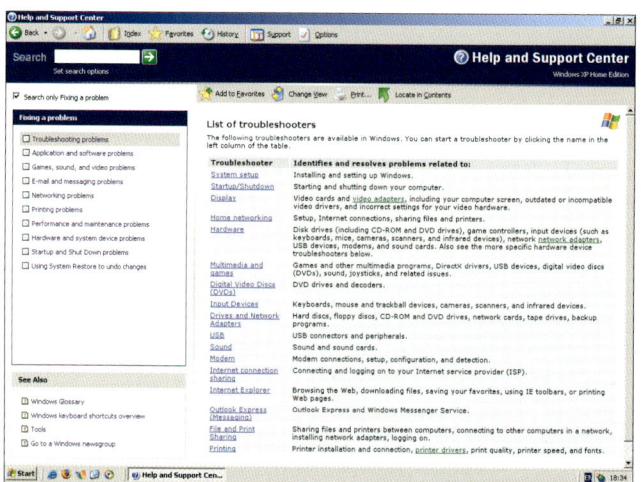

**5** Also included with Windows as standard are a number of **Troubleshooter programs**, which can help to solve common problems. For example, Print Troubleshooter can take you through the steps needed to determine why your printer isn't working. You can access troubleshooters from the Windows Help system as well as from the Microsoft web site at www.microsoft.com/. They take the form of a number of questions that you have to answer before you can proceed to the next question. By a process of elimination, the possible cause of the problem can be isolated and a course of action to fix it suggested.

# Windows

**Windows is the software that allows all your other applications and hardware to work together.**

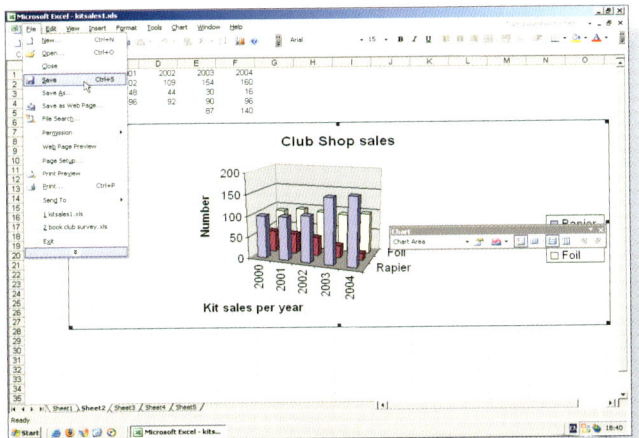

Like all good Windows programs, the **Excel spreadsheet** has a Save command on its File menu.

Programs have to work with the hardware in a PC and the devices plugged into it. They have to respond to instructions from the mouse and keyboard; they have to be able to generate pictures on any monitor; and they have to be able to produce text and pictures on different types of printer. Some years ago, Microsoft came up with a program called Windows that provides these background services for all other programs. It understands how a PC's monitor, mouse, keyboard and printer work, so that the other programs don't have to.

The technical name for a computer's supporting software is its operating system. Windows is not the only operating system for PCs, but it's the most popular one. When you buy a piece of software, whether it's a business tool or a game, it's written for a particular combination of computer and operating system. The majority of programs are written for Windows, so if you don't use Windows you limit your choice of programs.

Microsoft continues to develop and improve Windows despite its dominance in the market. Windows 98, in both its editions, introduced new features – wizards, programs and utilities – to improve both the speed and reliability of the

## Classic style display

The look and feel of Windows XP has changed substantially from earlier versions of the operating system. XP allows different user accounts, and these user accounts allow each user to adapt the display to suit their own taste. The default desktop theme is called Windows XP. In this book we are using the Classic Windows theme, which is blue and grey and resembles the style of earlier versions of Windows. To change the appearance, go to the Start button and select Control Panel. Double-click on Display. Click on the Appearance tab in the Display Properties control panel, and choose Windows Classic style from the drop-down list in the Windows and Buttons field.

operating system compared with Windows 95. It was also designed to integrate your desktop with the Web more closely. Windows Me added to this. With Windows XP, the operating system was redesigned completely to cope with more demanding and complex tasks.

## Consistent system

Each version of Windows is consistent. For instance, the Windows Print command is always in a program's File menu which is always in the same place in a window. Before Windows there was no conformity between programs and every time you bought a new one you had to learn what all the different commands were from scratch.

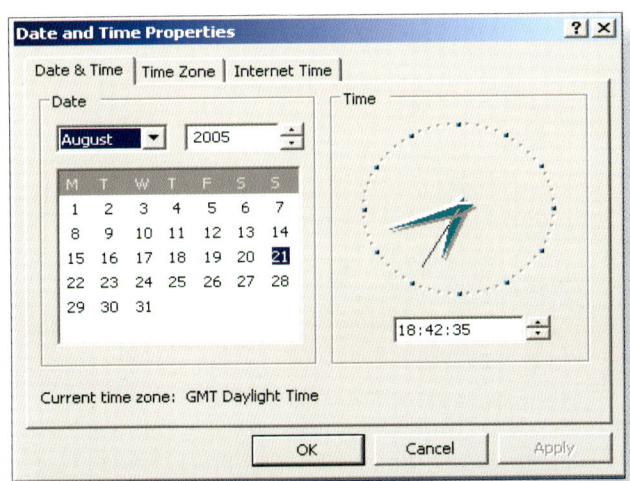

The **Date and Time Properties** box is typical of the point-and-click approach of Windows. Dates and times are displayed as screen clocks and calendars that look just like the real things.

# Going soft

**Master the art of Windows software in an instant: get to grips with GUIs, identify with icons and wise up to WYSIWYG.**

Software programs, the collective name for all types of computer programs, are simply a huge set of instructions which make your PC do something useful. They tell your PC what to do with the information you are feeding into it, what to show on screen and what to print. There's no point in having a PC without any software. It would be like having a television that didn't receive any channels, buying a CD player but no CDs, or refitting your kitchen but not bothering to buy any food to cook in it. One without the other is no use to anybody.

Software is supplied on a set of CD-ROM discs, or DVDs for bigger programs, and is then transferred onto your PC's hard disk. When you buy a PC, you will find the operating system, usually Windows, has already been loaded onto it. Once on your PC's hard disk, programs are represented by a small picture or icon on the screen. When selected, the PC finds the program on the hard disk, loads it into the PC's memory bank and gets it ready for you to use.

## Windows operating system

This book concentrates on software that works with Microsoft Windows because, as already discussed, this is the operating system used by most PCs today. Windows presents you with graphics, images, icons and lists of choices called menus, which make it easy to use.

Windows is called a graphical user interface or GUI (pronounced gooey). It's also an example of what's become known as a WYSIWYG program because 'what you see (on the screen) is what you get' when you start printing.

Once you have mastered the way Windows works, you can work your way around any Windows-compatible program, no matter how new it is to you.

# Choosing software

**Whatever you want to do with your computer, you'll probably find a software package to suit.**

Software programs are divided up into separate categories, depending on what they are being used to do. System software (the operating system) controls how the computer works. It incorporates utilities, such as Disk Cleanup and Disk Defragmenter, to help improve the speed and reliability of your PC. Applications are used to produce something, such as word processing programs for writing a letter, a graphics program for designing a poster, or a spreadsheet for calculating how much your computer has cost you!

Another category you may come across is network software which enables groups of computers to communicate with each other and share peripherals, such as a printer.

### CD-ROMs
Nearly all PC software comes on CD-ROMs or DVDs. They store the instructions that make a program work. When you buy a new program you have to install it – that is copy it to your PC – before you can use it. Usually all you have to do is put the disc in the CD-ROM or DVD drive and it will start its installation program automatically. Then you simply follow the instructions that appear on the screen.

The range of available software is extraordinary. The chances are you'll be able to find a program that will help you do anything you want to do. There are programs for writing letters, sending faxes, designing room interiors, laying out gardens, running household accounts, budgeting for a loan repayment, planning meals, creating a family tree, designing greetings cards, learning a foreign language, planning a journey and so on.

### Software for free
New PCs usually come with several programs (sometimes dozens) to get you started. Typically these will include a word processor, a spreadsheet, perhaps a home-finance program, a multimedia encyclopaedia and a few games. You can buy new software from a high-street computer shop or by mail order. You can save a lot of money if you take the time to compare prices when you buy.

### Cover discs
There are several ways in which you can check out a program before you buy it. Many computer magazines include a free CD-ROM containing demonstrations of a number of programs – sometimes it's a full version of an earlier edition of the program – and you can download demonstrations from the Internet, but there will be restrictions. They may stop working after a set number of days, for example, or they won't let you save anything you've done. Visiting a computer exhibition is another way of getting a look at new software.

When you buy a program, fill in and return the registration card that comes with it. When you register you become eligible for extra information about the program, free updates when small changes are made to it, and news of new versions. Registration is free.

# Office and business

**Check your cash flow, draft your correspondence and keep up with contacts – all from your PC.**

Using a PC to run a business, no matter how small, makes good sense but software is only worth buying if it saves you time and lets you conduct your business more professionally.

## Word processing
If all you ever do is scribble the odd letter, you don't need to buy any software at all, just use WordPad or Notepad which come with Windows. For anything more sophisticated, you need a word processor. Word processors can handle different sizes of text as well as coloured, underlined, bold and italic text. You can count how many words you've written, get the program to check your grammar and so on.

## Spreadsheets
Spreadsheets act rather like a sophisticated calculator. They look like large grids made up of rows and columns; the numbers you want to calculate are typed into the grids. Spreadsheets use various formulae to make complex calculations and are perfect for analysing cash flow, working out repayments or setting up a family budget.

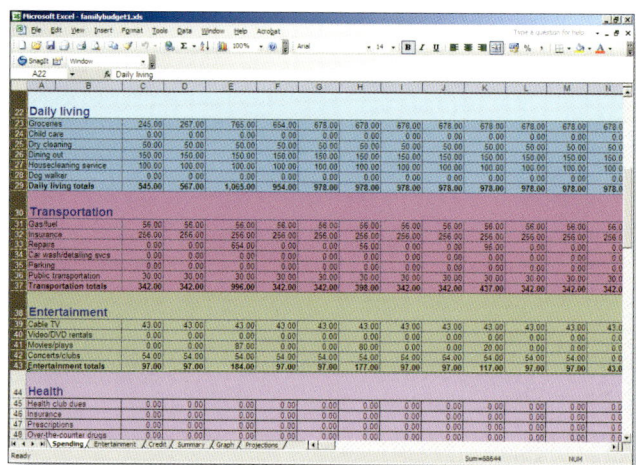

**Spreadsheets** like this one in Excel are useful for keeping track of your household expenses.

## Databases
Databases are used to store information in such a way that you can find it again quickly. In an address database, for example, you simply go to the search feature, type in the name you want and the details appear on screen.

## Organisers
PC organisers usually include a calendar program for appointments, a to-do list of tasks, a name and address list, a notepad and sometimes an expenses manager. You can set audible alarms to remind you to do something.

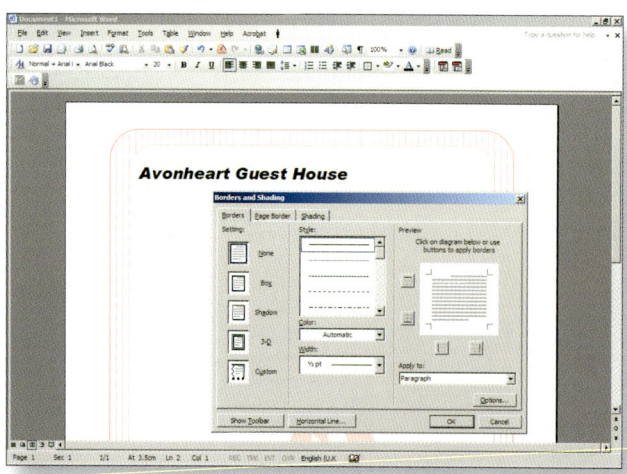

**Because word processors** can also display and print out pictures, they're useful for creating letterheads. This is being designed with Microsoft Word.

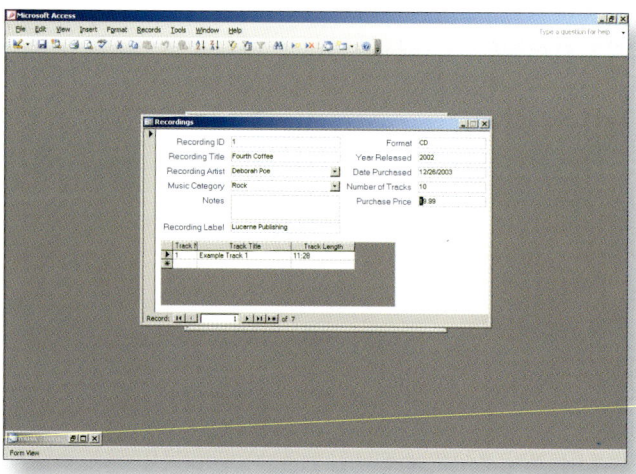

**Databases** sound complicated, but they needn't be. This database, created in Access 2003, lets you keep a record of your music collection.

# software

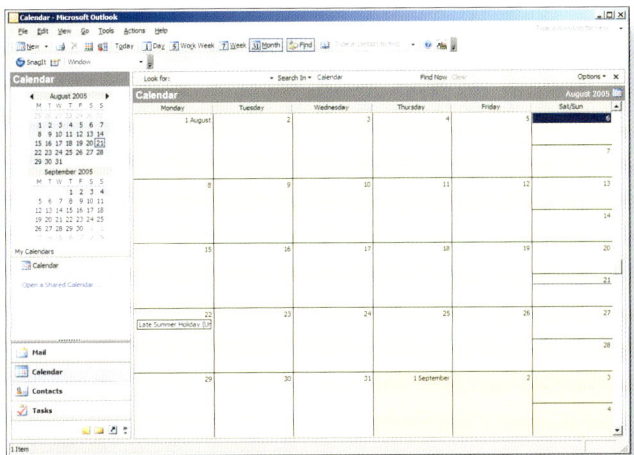

**Organisers**, such as the calendar in Outlook 2003, are a good way of keeping track of appointments and lists of things to do.

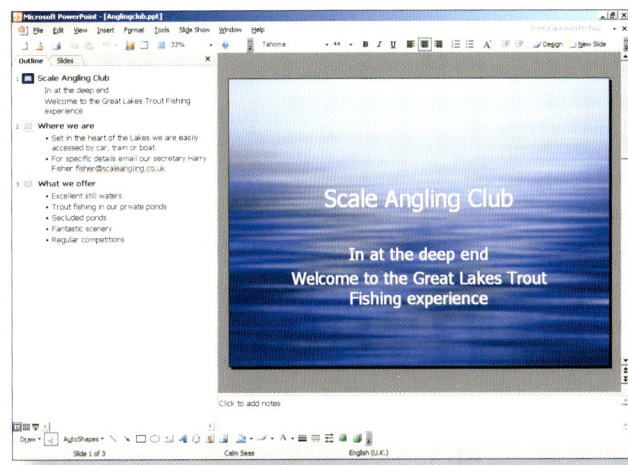

**Presentation** programs like Microsoft PowerPoint can be used to create compelling slide shows.

## Desktop publishing

These programs are excellent for creating club newsletters, invitations, cards, adverts, business cards, stationery, posters and so on. You can incorporate colour pictures and photos and use many of the same layout techniques that you see in magazines and newspapers.

## Presentation software

Remember the school overhead projector? Presentation programs are their modern equivalent. Use them to assemble slide shows, creating each slide with colourful graphics, text, and perhaps some background music, or a short video clip that will also play on the computer screen. These programs are great for presenting to any kind of group, whether it's a club or society, or a parents' evening.

## Suites

The office suite is a collection of programs (usually a word processor, a spreadsheet and a database) designed to go together. When you've worked out the basic functions (saving, printing, copying, moving and so on) in one, you know how the others will work. The programs in office suites are also good at swapping information between each other.

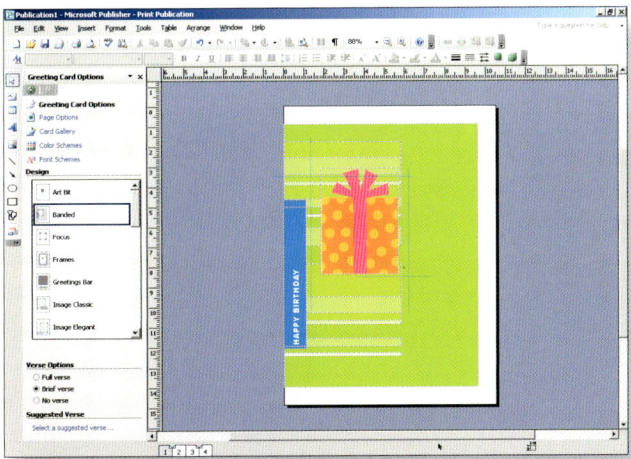

**Desktop publishing** programs, such as Publisher, can produce effective results, such as this birthday card.

There are many kinds of **graphics program**. Here Paint Shop Pro is used to adjust the perspective in a digital photograph.

# Getting hooked

**Before you can explore the Net you need to buy a modem and link up with a service provider.**

A modem is simply a piece of hardware that plugs into your PC and connects you to the Internet. There's no magic, no messing about and no hi-tech wizardry needed.

There are two types of modem – external and internal. As the names suggest, the external one plugs into a socket at the back of your computer and sits on your desk, while the internal one is a small card that fits into a slot inside your computer. If you don't have an internal modem already fitted, an external one is the easier option because you don't have to fiddle around inside the computer to get started. It really is just a matter of plugging it in. However, internal modems are cheaper.

## How it works

The modem connects your computer to the Internet by way of the telephone line. It converts the information sent out by a computer, which comes in digital code, into a form that can be sent over the phone – beeps, whistles and other noises. If you listen to a modem making a connection and a fax machine dialling a line, you'll notice they sound similar.

When you make a connection to the Internet, for example to send a message to your grandmother in America, your computer software lets you type 'Hello Granny' as a message. This simple message is made up in digital code in the computer. When you send the e-mail, your modem converts the code into noise. The noises are packaged and sent out along the telephone line until they reach your Internet service provider (the company, a bit like the phone company, which provides you with your Internet connection). The service provider has a number of modems and these convert the noise back into computer code and send it across the Internet until it reaches its destination, your grandmother's Internet service provider in the United States.

## Mail box

When Granny next collects her e-mail, the message will be waiting for her in her mailbox with her service provider. Its modems convert it back into beeps and whistles, pump it down the telephone line, through Granny's modem where it is put back together as computer code again and it appears as 'Hello Granny' on her computer screen. So, all a modem really does is turn your information into noise.

## Into the fast lane

The Internet can be a bit slow, but it doesn't have to be. A few years ago, the standard modem used to connect to the Internet ran at only a quarter of the speed of the latest models. Now ADSL (asymmetric digital subscriber line), or broadband, offers a way to speed down the information superhighway. Broadband works over your existing telephone lines and can routinely connect at 2Mbps – roughly 20 times faster than the best dial-up modem. You can get connections up to 8Mbps with 25Mbps in development.

Cable is available to most homes now, and can deliver the Internet at high speeds, similar to those achievable with ADSL, than a traditional modem.

In more remote, rural areas you can join up to the Internet using satellite links. For these, you still need a modem to request the information you want. The modem connects to the Internet and receives information via your satellite dish. At the moment getting the Internet via satellite is not a cheap option, since different companies use different, incompatible equipment. But once there's a standard you should be able to buy a high-speed connection as easily and almost as cheaply as you can buy a modem today.

# STARTING UP

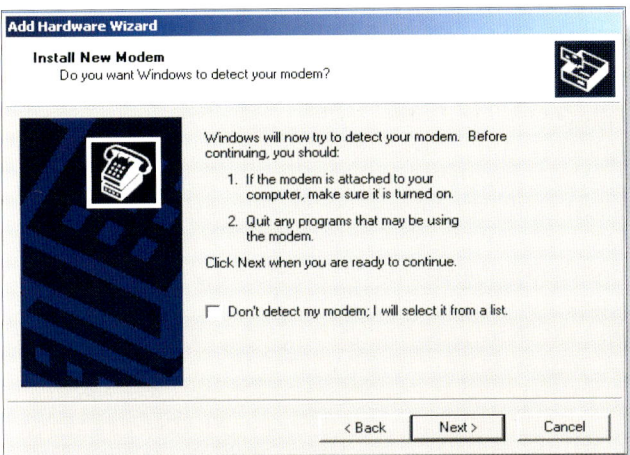

**Windows** makes it easy to install your new modem. Not only does it ask you questions in plain English, but it will even quiz the modem itself to find out exactly which model you have got, and ensure it is installed correctly.

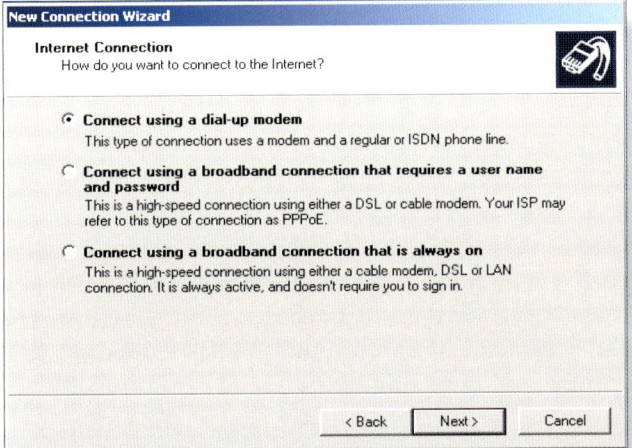

When you come to make your first connection to the Internet, select the type of connection you want in the **New Connection Wizard**. Here we are using a traditional dial-up modem.

Buy the modem that offers the best value, taking into account its speed. The speed of your connection with the Internet is decided by the speed of the modem together with the quality of the phone connection and the amount of traffic through your ISP.

The modem's speed is shown on the box – 28.8, 33.6 or 56. The fastest modems for an ordinary dial-up connection are 56K, that is 56,000 bits per second (bps). In fact, they can only receive data at that speed; the maximum speed for sending information is 36,600bps.

Some modems are flash upgradeable, which means they have a special type of memory that can be upgraded to the latest, or standard, version by downloading a program from the manufacturer's Web site. This was how many people using the two different versions of 56K modems – x2 and K56flex – were able to switch to the new standard, V.90.

## Internet consoles

You don't have to have a computer to connect to the Internet. You can use a special Internet console, which plugs into your TV and lets you access the Web and e-mail. They're much cheaper than a PC and there's no complicated setting up to do. But there are drawbacks. A console can't be used to do tasks such as word processing or household accounts for which you could use a computer.

With the popularity of online gaming, you can also get games consoles that link up to the Internet. While the consoles provide Internet access – and can usually play DVDs as well – they don't have any of the processing powers of a PC to handle other applications.

Most modems can also be used to send and receive faxes, although generally at slower speeds (up to 14.4bps). If the modem has voice features, it can be used for setting up your PC as an answering machine or with a voicemail system.

The faster the modem the better, as the quicker it can move information between your PC and the Net, the less time you will spend waiting for pages to appear on screen, and the cheaper your telephone bills will be (because you won't be connected for so long).

Some software, including a start-up program, comes with the modem. Load this onto your PC as instructed, plug in the modem, and the next time you turn on your PC it will notice that there is a new modem attached and install it for you. In just a few minutes you will be ready to get connected.

## Jargon buster

**Dial-Up** The method by which you connect to the Internet. You dial your Internet service provider using a modem attached to a phone.

**Download** To transfer information – a picture or message, for example – from the Internet onto your PC. Sending data from your computer onto the Internet is known as uploading.

**Handshake** The noise you hear modems and fax machines making when they connect with each other.

**ISDN** Prior to broadband, the fastest method of connecting to the Internet. It stands for Integrated Services Digital Network and can be a lot faster than an ordinary modem.

**Kbps** Kilobits per second, the speed at which information is sent using your modem.

**Login** The act of connecting to your Internet service provider when you want to use the Internet.

**Modem** The box that connects your computer to the Internet. The name comes from MOdulator/DEModulator.

# Serving up the Net

**Choose an Internet service provider that will give you exactly what you want from the Internet.**

Internet service providers, or ISPs, are the vital link between you, your PC, your modem and the rest of the Internet.

## Get connected

An ISP uses the phone lines to connect your PC, via the modem, to its modems at the nearest ISP exchange point, which is nearly always a local phone call away. From here you get connected directly to the ISP's computer network which has a permanent link to the Internet.

Choosing an ISP depends on what you want to do on the Net. Competition is fierce to get your business, and everybody's at it – banks, stores, publishers, supermarkets. As a result the services they offer, and the cost, are changing all the time. Some ISPs, such as AOL or BT Internet, use their exclusive content to encourage you to choose them. Others, such as Pipex or Demon, emphasise the quality and reliability of their service. So what to look for?

Free Internet Access – this used to mean no monthly subscription fee, but you still had to pay telephone charges. Now there are unmetered access schemes with no subs and no phone charges. Beware though, not all of these

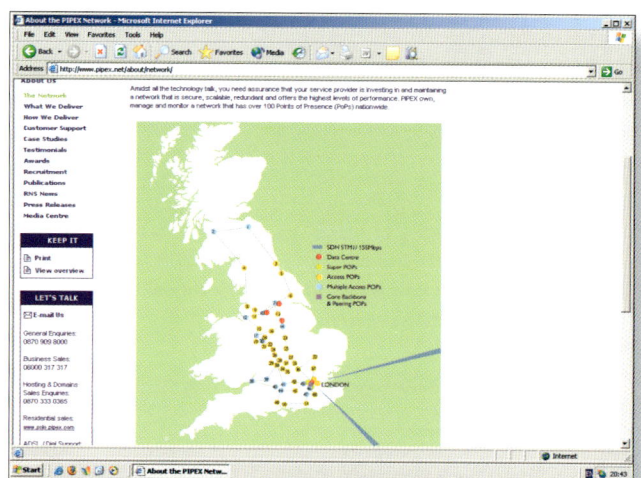

**PIPEX** is one of the biggest ISPs in the UK, and its wide network means it is easy to get a dial-up connection.

'free' offers are totally free. Some involve an upfront administration charge. With others you may have to use a specified telephone service and guarantee a minimum monthly amount in non-Internet phone calls.

Broadband Access – this uses rapidly developing technology that operates at a different frequency from voice calls, enabling you to access the Internet over your existing phone lines but at speeds routinely 40 times faster. It's always on – so there is no lengthy dial-up to connect to the Internet – for which there's a monthly flat-rate charge. So it's useful if you want a video piped quickly to your PC.

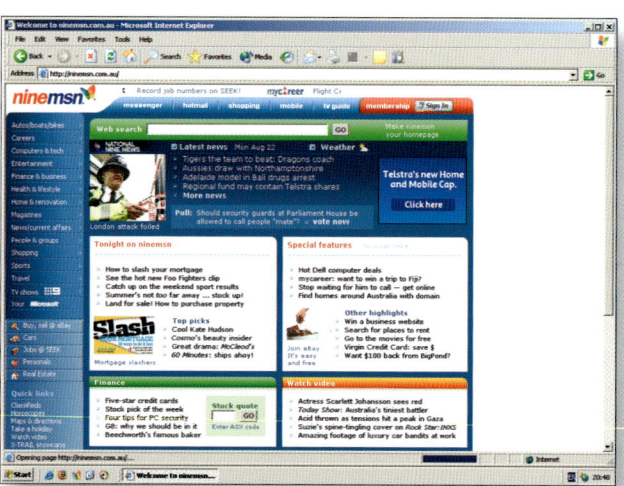

**MSN Australia** is just one of the global services offered by Microsoft's ISP, the Microsoft Network.

**Demon Internet** was the first in the UK to bring Internet access to home users and is now one of the UK's biggest ISPs.

## STARTING UP

WAP – Wireless Application Protocol-enabled services allow you to access Web sites or send information and e-mail via your mobile phone. This is useful if you need to trade shares or book a restaurant while on the move. Several ISPs are now offering WAP-enabled services.

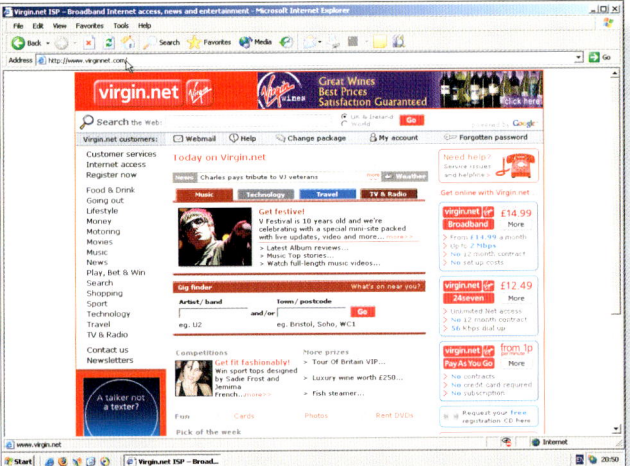

**Well-known brands are now starting to appear as ISPs, such as Richard Branson's VirginNet, for example.**

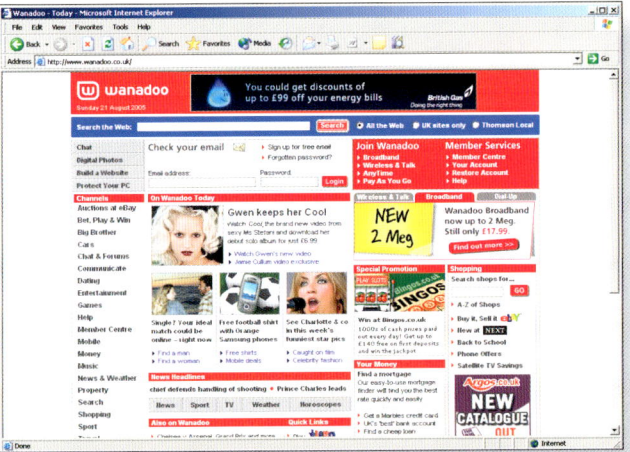

**In 2000, Wanadoo took over FreeServe, the first of the free UK Internet service providers and still one of the biggest.**

**AOL, the world's biggest ISP by quite a large margin, is easy to use and offers all kinds of extras before you even start exploring the Internet.**

Ask about technical support. If things go wrong, you need to know your ISP will be there to help. Is it free, 24 hours a day, seven days a week? Test the phone number it gives.

Every ISP should offer a number of e-mail addresses and Web space where you can create your own site. In addition each ISP has its own particular services (see below). Ask about software. Your ISP should provide everything you need, for free and in a package that makes it easy to install and get started.

If you choose a free ISP, you have nothing to lose if you don't like the service, and most of the ISPs that charge let you try out the service for a month before you commit yourself.

### The top ten providers

● **AOL** This is an online service rather than just an ISP, which means you get extras like members-only chat areas, magazine areas and so on. AOL is the world's biggest Internet service provider, with millions of customers.

● **BT Internet** An ISP operated by British Telecom. It is easy to set up and get running, with straightforward software. For home customers it has teamed up with Yahoo! to create BT Yahoo! Internet, where members can personalize a number of features such as the news they access.

● **Demon** The first Internet service provider to bring Internet access to the home in the United Kingdom, and one of the UK's largest. No fancy extras are offered, just simple Internet access, without hassle, for a low monthly cost.

● **MSN** Microsoft Network is Microsoft's online service provider, although the connection is provided in partnership with British Telecom. There's plenty to see and do here, with possibly the widest range of online entertainment.

● **NTL** Broadband access is offered by this cable television company. NTL services do not use telephone lines and are only available in areas where its cables have been installed.

● **PIPEX** With a long tradition as an ISP, Pipex's Dial service was a popular choice for home users seeking dial-up access in the years of the Internet boom in the 1990s. It has now been joined by a broadband service.

● **Tiscali** Part of a major European network, Tiscali offers extra value in access to special family entertainment areas, as well as Internet access itself.

● **VirginNet** Richard Branson's Virgin brand has extended into the Internet access market. VirginNet trades on its ease of use, for even the most inexperienced of computer users.

● **Wanadoo** This was formerly known as FreeServe, the first ISP to offer access to the Net for free. FreeServe was set up originally by Dixons, a retailer of computers and other electrical goods. Like many ISPs, it now promotes high-speed broadband access to the Web as much as, if not more than, traditional dial-up connections.

# World Wide Web

**The World Wide Web is your window onto the Internet and all the information it contains.**

An Internet without pictures, lacking in links and requiring you to master a whole host of obscure commands to get anything done would be no use to anyone. But that's what it was like until the early 1990s when the World Wide Web burst into the picture.

## Hyperactive

The Net can trace its origins back to the 1960s, but the Web was only conceived in 1989 when a British scientist at a nuclear physics laboratory came up with the idea of linking pages on the Net. The idea was that you could be reading one page, say about Elvis Presley, and if there were any highlighted words (hyperlinks), you could click on them to open another page that delved further into the subject. Clicking on the word Graceland, for example, would open a document about Elvis's home.

The clever bit is that these documents don't need to be stored in the same place. They can be stored on any computer connected to the Internet. The main thing is that when you click on a highlighted link on a Web page the

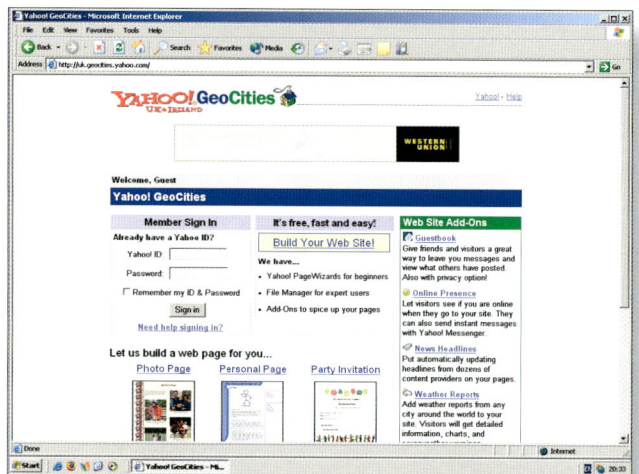

**Web page communities have started to grow. The biggest of all is Yahoo! GeoCities, made up of thousands of individuals with Web pages. Like-minded people get together to form streets and avenues that have Web pages covering similar topics.**

information you request appears on your screen. It doesn't matter where it comes from.

At first the World Wide Web consisted of pages of plain text but it didn't take long for pictures and sound to appear. Now few people would dream of using anything but the Web to get what they want from the Internet.

Anyone can have a home page on the Web. ISPs give free Web space when you join, that is from 5 to 50MB or more on a hard disk connected to the Net on a Web server – a

**The Web is composed of links. Almost everything on this page for kids is a hyperlink. If you move your mouse pointer over it and the pointer changes into a hand shape, you can click on that link and get more information.**

**You can even do your shopping using the Web. Amazon.co.uk, is part of one of the world's biggest bookshops, Amazon.com, but it only exists on the Web. Ask it to find the book or CD you are interested in and order with your credit card.**

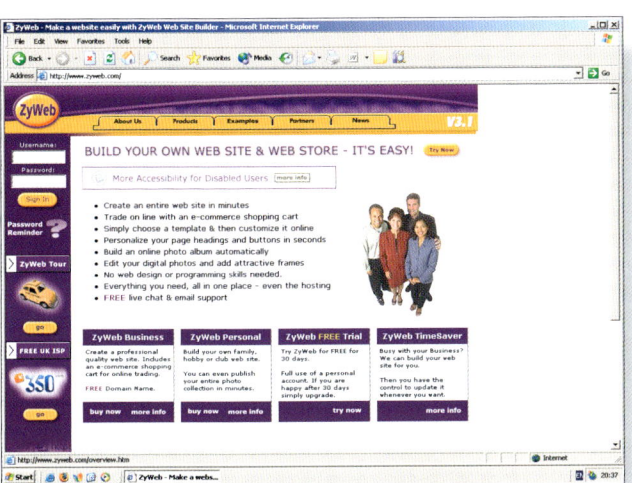

**Using resources like ZyWeb, creating a Web page is as simple as making a few selections from the screen, and that includes fancy graphics, buttons and fonts.**

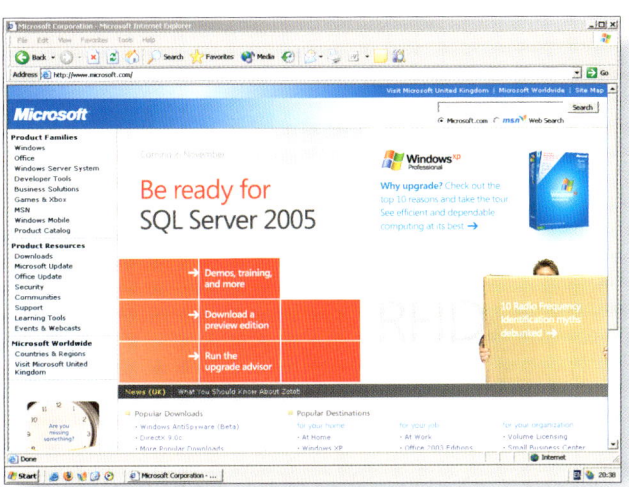

**The Microsoft Homepage, viewed using Microsoft's Internet Explorer Web browser. If you've used any Microsoft product, you'll feel at home with Internet Explorer.**

computer that stores Web pages. Designing a Web page isn't difficult. Some ISPs offer software that will turn the process into a straightforward question-and-answer session.

## Room for everyone

Schoolchildren, housewives and business people are all on the Web these days. Web pages are used as an outlet for your writing or artistic talents; to tell the world about your hobby; to sell handicrafts; or as an online fan club for your favourite pop star.

## Browsing

The Web is not much use to you unless you have a way of viewing it, which is where Web browsers come in. Browsers are programs that enable you to view Web pages easily.

Choosing a Web browser isn't difficult. Originally there were two that led the field by a margin: Netscape and Microsoft. Netscape had its Navigator browser and Microsoft had Internet Explorer. They are both big, fully functional programs, and they are free. They were subsequently joined by other free browsers, such as Opera or Firefox, which are smaller yet as powerful as their rivals.

Stick with the browser your ISP supplies. It will offer technical support if you have problems, and it will be installed on your computer as part of the ISP package. This is likely to mean you will use Microsoft Internet Explorer, as most ISPs use this.

## Finding stuff

Nothing on the Web is any good unless you know where to find it. The answer is search engines. These are like phone books. If you want to find a site, let a search engine look for it. Type in a word that describes what you want and the search engine will scan its directory and return a list of sites that contain relevant information.

### TOP THREE SEARCH ENGINES

● **Yahoo! (www.yahoo.com)** The first Web search engine, and one of the biggest. Search by entering a keyword, or just browse through categorised directory listings.

● **Google (www.google.com)** One of the most powerful search engines. It's easy to use and works quickly.

● **Ask Jeeves! (www.askjeeves.com)** Rather than suggesting you enter a single word to start a search, Ask Jeeves (below) insists you ask in plain English.

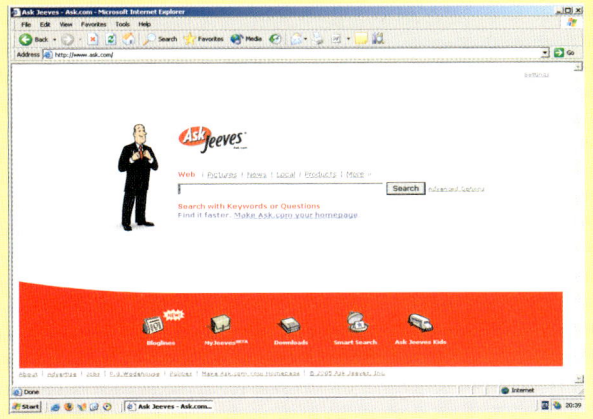

# Games

**Enjoy your hard-earned free time with a quick shoot 'em up, a murder mystery or a whist drive.**

Avoid the bloodthirsty games and those in poor taste by checking the box for the ELSPA rating; it's like a film certificate. Most games can be played with the mouse and/or keyboard, although some need a joystick, which is like a pilot's flightstick.

## Action
The range is enormous. There are realistic flight simulators and first person shoot 'em ups, where your character hurtles down corridors, shooting everything that moves. There are some good car-racing games (often using real circuit layouts), platform games (in the style of Sonic the Hedgehog) and space fighting games; plus games for most sports.

## Strategy
These games, often with themes of trade and conquest, are more thought-provoking than their action counterparts. Typically the game will give you an aerial view of a city, a country or the ocean floor, and your job is to make your side prosper. Detective games are fun too, where you solve a crime by interviewing suspects and gathering clues.

**You control a dungeon full of monsters in Dungeon Keeper 2 and it take lots of planning to keep adventurers out.**

**Aliens vs Predator adds a new twist to the first person shoot 'em up by letting you play as an alien, predator or marine.**

## Card and board
There are loads of these games, from the two that come free with Windows to curious hybrids like Star Wars Monopoly which is the original game reworked with Star Wars locations and characters. Versions of Chinese games are popular, as are bridge and chess, jigsaws, solitaire, poker and whist.

## Online
On the Internet, you can play games against other people. You both connect at the same time and instead of playing against the PC, you race against each other, or try to defeat each other's armies, or test your chess skills.

**Sports management games such as the highly popular Championship Manager rely on plenty of statistics to help players with the decision-making process.**

# 2
# Solving Problems

## Getting help 41
- PC warranties
- Extended support
- Online support
- User groups and utilities
- Consult the manual
- Fault finders
- Windows Help
- The Knowledge Base
- Online help

## Troubleshooting basics 59
- Use back-up
- First aid
- Software tools
- Peripheral problems
- Anti-virus tools
- Error messages

## DIY fixes 73
- Managing devices
- Monitoring your PC
- Safe Mode startup
- Startup troubleshooter
- Shutdown troubleshooter
- Net doctor
- Running MS-DOS
- Retrieving lost files
- Fine-tune settings

## Curing viruses 99
- What is a virus?
- PC doctor
- Which type of virus?
- Don't panic
- Safety first

# Getting help

**When things go wrong with your computer the most important thing is to know where to go for help.**

Everyone needs a little help with their computer from time to time – not just total beginners and those who want to learn more, but also the most experienced power users. The hardware and software inside a computer are far too complex for any one person to have a complete mastery of them, and of course not all computers and certainly not all software are alike.

## Hard even for the experts

It's a rare person who can take a car to pieces and put it back together again. It's rarer still to find someone who can do it with a PC. In both cases even the experts need to resort to product manuals and installation guides. The same goes for you. But thankfully there is no need to have years of expertise behind you before you know where to look for assistance. One great feature of the computer business is that you never have to look very far to find sources of help.

A culture of support, technical helplines and online advice has grown up around computers. Even if you sometimes feel that you're out on your own with your PC, nothing could be further from the truth. PCs, peripherals and software go wrong for even the most experienced users – usually at the worst time. So read on to learn how to prepare yourself for the worst. When PC illness strikes, knowing who to call for help is as important as understanding how to administer the remedy.

## You will need

**ESSENTIAL**

**Software** Current software versions. Few software vendors and publishers offer technical help with obsolete software. An upgrade to the latest version may solve your problem anyway.

**Hardware** A modern PC. As with cars, it gets increasingly difficult and expensive to obtain assistance as the age of your kit increases.

# PC warranties

### Warranty tip

When you first buy a computer product, check to see whether there are circumstances under which the warranty is rendered void. Many manufacturers will not fix a broken peripheral device, for example, if they think you have been fiddling unnecessarily with the internals. Watch out for labels that read 'Warranty Void If Removed'.

### Jargon buster

**E&OE** Many adverts for PCs and peripherals carry this expression in the small print. It stands for Errors and Omissions Excepted. It's a standard disclaimer to cover the advertiser in case there are printing mistakes in the advert, which means it's up to you to ensure that generous warranty promises are not one of the errors.

## The law is on your side if any computer kit you buy breaks down – but only for a limited period.

Whenever you buy a non-consumable product in the UK the law covers you for a limited period in case your purchase turns out to be faulty. The rules are particularly strict in the case of electrical goods, which the law expects to work well for up to a year as proof that they were manufactured properly and sold honestly. If a product breaks down within a year, the law regards it as a faulty product and expects the manufacturer to fix or replace it. If it breaks down a year after purchase the law regards it as bad luck.

### Return to base

There is every reason to take PC warranties seriously. If your PC or peripheral is covered by a standard one-year warranty and anything goes wrong, you will have to return the PC in its huge packing box. This is known as a return to base warranty: you return it at your expense, and the manufacturer fixes it and sends it back to you at its expense.

### Save time

If you live within driving distance of the place where you bought the product, you can save time and expense by delivering it in person rather than arranging couriers or parcel collection. Naturally, if the product is small, you should be able to send it back in the post as long as it is well padded and marked 'Fragile' in huge lettering. Just remember that in all cases, and without exception, it is essential that you call up the company first to tell it that the product is faulty. The company will issue you with a returns number which must be printed clearly on the outer packaging and on a covering letter inside. This will speed up the process considerably.

## Collect and return

If having to foot the return bill on a faulty product irritates you – as it should – buy from companies which offer enhanced warranties. A popular alternative is a collect and return warranty, which is basically the same as return to base except that the company arranges and pays for all transport or postal costs involved in returning the product for fixing. Better still is an on-site warranty, which means that a representative from the company will come to your home or office to fix the product in situ. This person should be a qualified PC engineer, but if the faulty product is a printer, monitor or other peripheral device, what usually happens is that a delivery person turns up with a replacement and simply takes your broken one back with them. This system is known as on-site swap out.

## Mechanical faults

You also need to consider how warranties affect software, because the situation can be very different. The floppy disks or CD-ROMs provided in a software package will be covered for mechanical faults, but only for a short period such as 90 days. This is considered to be enough time for you to discover that the disks aren't working. However, trying to convince a software company that the software itself does not work will be futile. There may be internal conflicts and other rare reasons why a software package might not function properly on your PC but these are not normally considered in law as the fault of the software seller. You cannot return a software product for an instant refund once you break the seal.

## Online support

You may be offered assistance by phone or online. Many PC manufacturers take a holistic view of computing and offer hotline support for their PCs and the software installed on them. Take time to find out if the company you are buying from is going to provide this kind of help. When you are buying kit, it is easy to get carried away with slick advertising. Keep reminding yourself that computer products can go wrong unexpectedly, no matter who you buy them from, so it's up to you to make sure you obtain the best warranty cover available.

**Watch out for E&OE disclaimers when you buy computer equipment from mail-order adverts.**

### Watch out!

When looking at warranties, be sure to check the small print. Many manufacturers offer generous sounding five-year warranties, but this may cover replacement parts only: after the first year or two, you might have to pay for the labour charge which can be high. Look for genuine parts and labour cover. Also, with collect and on-site warranties, find out how quickly the company will respond to your call for help. Will you get a replacement the next day, the next week or when?

# Extended support

## Jargon buster

**Remote diagnostics** Some support companies may offer this as a hi-tech method of providing help inexpensively without having to send an engineer to your doorstep. With your permission, they will call up your PC over the phone line and use specialist software tools back at their office to work out what the problem is and identify corrupt files, missing drivers and so on. You may need to install some remote diagnostic software as part of the deal, and you will certainly need a modem.

**For real peace of mind it is worth extending the short-term warranties offered by most manufacturers.**

Long, generous warranties are a new phenomenon in the UK. When you buy computer kit you are much more likely to get a simple or short-term warranty included in the product price, with the option of extending the cover as required. This is the same kind of deal offered to consumers when they buy hi-fi equipment or kitchen appliances. But TVs, hi-fis and microwave ovens are much less likely to go wrong over time than a computer, and much less expensive to fix or replace when they do.

## Buy early

There is a lot to be said for extending a warranty on PCs and peripherals – depending on the cost, of course. Often the price of upgrading a standard warranty to an on-site warranty or extending an on-site warranty by an extra year is very little. Such upgrades will always be cheapest if you pay for them when you buy the product to start with, and will increase exponentially each year if you put them off until later.

A useful alternative to consider is employing a third-party support company to look after your kit. When you purchase on-site warranty extensions from PC manufacturers, you may well find that this cover is provided by a specially appointed third-party support company anyway. This arrangement is cheaper for a manufacturer than having to staff its own in-house support team, and offers good service to buyers because they get expert help from a dedicated support engineer every time.

## Piecemeal

As with any service and support deal, you need to compare the cost with that of getting something fixed yourself. If your PC's power supply fails, for example, it can cost a fair amount for a new one and you will have to fit it yourself or pay someone to do it for you. Then you will probably start wishing you had paid for one year's on-site support, covering all parts and labour.

It is worth calling a few companies to check prices and coverage deals. Some companies require a small monthly retainer and then offer cut-price call-out charges in an emergency. Third-party support companies offer a sliding scale of prices according to response time, whether you want an engineer at your door in two or four hours, or whether you are happy to wait until the next day or the day after.

## Call-out charge

Smaller companies, such as local PC shops, simply charge for each call-out just like a plumber or electrician. You might even be able to find someone who can fix small problems cheaply and who knows where to turn if there is a major problem.

Two other support methods worth considering are training and PC audits. By attending a training course run by experts you will learn to head off and resolve many non-critical PC errors yourself, so you can save a lot of money. An audit is rather like a car service or health check. It's worth having one to keep your PC in top form.

## Hotlines

You can find numbers for support companies in PC magazines, on the Internet and at the library. As well as checking out what they have to offer, you might want to try their emergency hotlines for size if you can get hold of the telephone number. If it turns out to be permanently engaged, consider yourself warned off. This goes for manufacturers offering extended warranties too: if you can't get through to the support line, the warranty is worthless.

Manufacturers often say that if a piece of hardware is going to go wrong, it will do so within the first three months after purchase, but things can go wrong at any time. If you rely on your computer for work, an extended support deal is well worth the money.

### Ten per cent rule

When trying to gauge the value of extended and third-party support, apply the ten per cent rule. For full on-site support, many companies charge an annual fee of ten per cent of the purchase price of the products being covered. Naturally this charge depends on the quantity and age of the equipment, but it gives you an idea of prices. If you don't need fast response call-out, the cost will be much less.

### Internet tip

To get the most from the Internet it helps if you can see exactly how fast data is being transferred between the Internet and your PC, and if any errors are getting in the way. Use software that will monitor your connection, such as DUN Monitor, which is available free on the Net. Connect to the Net and use your browser to find http://jongrieve.net. Select the link that says Dial Up Networking Monitor and download the software as instructed.

You can configure DUN Monitor to run as you want it to. You can change the colours used on the graphing feature, and choose when and how the DUN Monitor window should appear. Setting it to show statistics when a call is established and hiding them when you disconnect is the best bet.

Now every time you connect to the Internet a pop-up window shows you how fast data is being sent and received. As you tweak your PC and modem configurations you should be able to monitor the improvements. The higher the figure next to Current, the faster your connection is running. While originally made to work with Windows 98, DUN Monitor also works with later versions of Windows and with ADSL connections.

# Online support

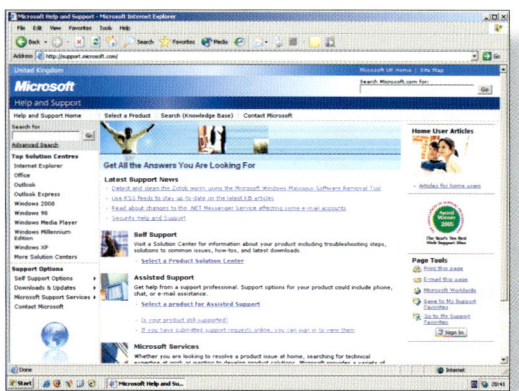

**All the major software companies offer technical assistance on their Web sites, from simple lists of common problems all the way to interactive Help databases like Microsoft's dedicated support site.**

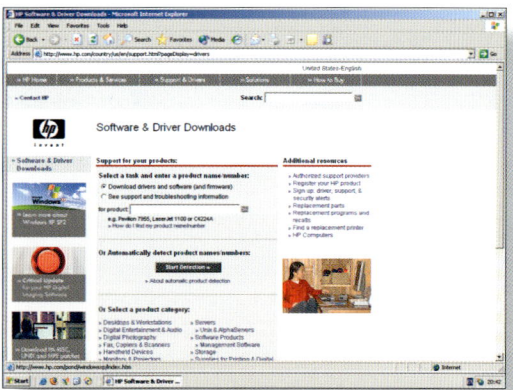

**Instead of wasting time being put on hold on a telephone support hotline, browse your hardware manufacturer's Web site. It may have the driver, update or fix you need for immediate download.**

### Netiquette tip

When asking for advice in an Internet newsgroup or online forum, bear in mind that these areas are not always run by the company which manufactured the product you are having trouble with. Those most likely to come to your aid are people like you who just happen to own the same product, and are offering their knowledge for free. For this reason, be polite in your request. Simple netiquette phrases like please and thank you, and not typing your message in capital letters will increase your chances of a speedy and equally polite response.

## The Internet is an enormous and valuable resource for anyone having trouble with their PC or peripherals.

One of the biggest benefits the Internet has brought to the everyday PC user is instant support. When you go online, you don't have to wait in a queue or answer a set of predetermined, irrelevant questions to find what you want. The volume of information and advice that can be obtained online often goes well beyond the scope of mere product manuals, and can go into far greater detail than an operator on a telephone help desk.

### Weak link

The weak link in the chain is that you need a working PC and modem plus an online service provider to get online to start with. If you are having problems with any one of these three, you will have to resort to other sources of help. But if the problem is with another peripheral, a software application or a non-critical PC component, you will be surprised at how much support information is available to you for free.

Hardware and software companies all over the world have established sites on the Web and with online services such as AOL for this purpose. It is, after all, cheaper for them to provide support this way too. In the first instance, if you are having trouble with a product, a quick visit to the company's Web site may reveal the answer in the form of an FAQ (frequently asked questions) or troubleshooting page. It could well be that other users are having the same problem as you, so the company may have published the solution on its site for all to read.

### Available for download

Many hardware problems are caused by drivers, the little software utilities which enable each computer component to work with each other. Hardware manufacturers generally ensure that their latest drivers are always available for download from their online sites. Perhaps you have recently upgraded your operating system or are reinstalling the components (graphics card, soundcard, Zip drive for instance) in another machine, but have lost your original driver disks. All you need to do is go to the company's online site, locate its support section and download the drivers you want.

Software works in much the same way. Many companies provide free updates to their programs between major upgrades, and make them available for immediate download. If you are having trouble with a brand new product version 1, always check the relevant site for an update to version 1.01 or 1.02. It will often be the answer to your troubles.

## Up to date

Some software products will update automatically, providing a menu command or a button which accesses an Internet site and checks to see if a newer version of the program is available, downloading it as necessary. Many anti-virus programs let you do this, ensuring that you always have an up-to-date list of viruses. Windows owners can also ensure that they have the latest updates by running the Windows Update program near the top of the Start menu.

## Forums

You can take advantage of more interactive online help by posting your questions in specific Internet newsgroups and relevant forums hosted by online services (see pages 57–8). Post a cry for help one day and by the next day you should have at least half a dozen responses, any of which may have the right answer. The respondents will generally be people with some measure of expertise in – or at least experience with – the product you are having difficulty with. And the clever solutions they give might not even be known to the manufacturers.

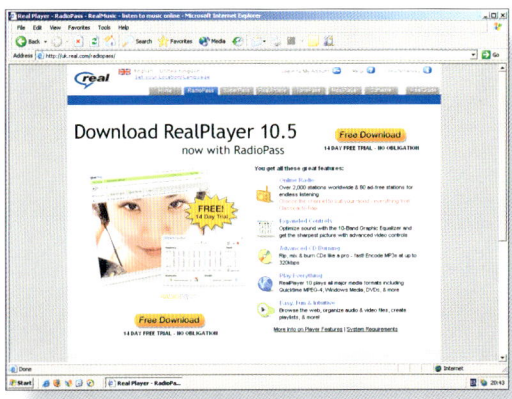

**Check the company Web site to see if any free upgrades are available. If so, take advantage of them because it may be that the problem you are having has been solved in the upgraded version.**

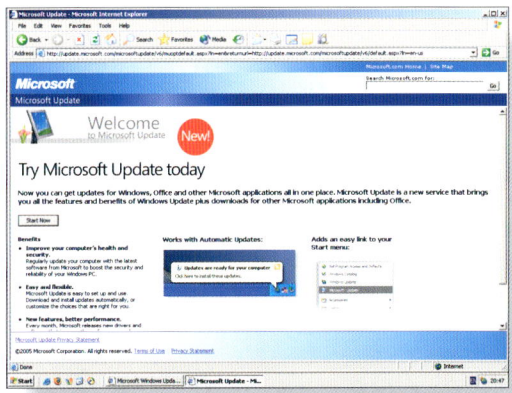

**MIcrosoft's SmartUpdate Web site allows you to access the latest versions of relevant software quickly, easily and even automatically.**

### Favourites tip

When you first visit an Internet site run by the manufacturer of a product you own, or a user organisation associated with it, remember to add the site to your Bookmarks (Netscape) or Favorites (Internet Explorer). Even if you only discovered the site by accident, you never know when you will need to hunt it down again to obtain help or contact information. Keep a portfolio of these sites ready for emergencies.

### Jargon buster

**Patch** This is a small piece of software which fixes errors or bugs in a program that were discovered after it was put on the market. These days, the sticking-plaster imagery of the term is considered unfortunate and most software companies now refer to patches as updates. This new term implies that you are getting extra value for no expense, but updates are generally devised for fixing errors and bugs just the same.

### Jargon buster

**FAQ** Stands for frequently asked questions. An FAQ is a list of common problems raised by PC users about a particular product, along with the solution. It's always worth checking an FAQ for an answer before taking your support query further up the ladder.

# User groups and

**Some software applications are so complex yet so popular that they encourage the formation of self-help associations online, such as the Access User Group which organises training courses, seminars and competitions.**

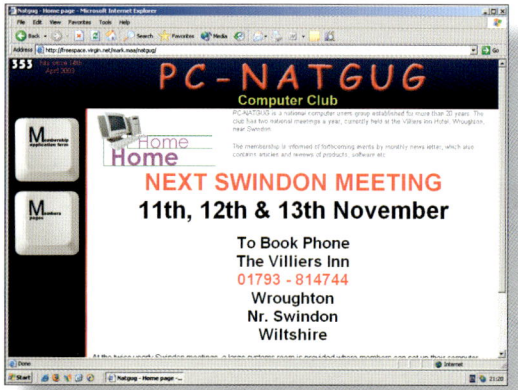

**Hardware-specific user groups are less common than software clubs and more regional. But they can still be a valuable source of hands-on help when it really matters – and inexpensive too.**

## Think small

Often the biggest problems are caused by the smallest things. The term bug was originally coined when an insect flew into the valves of an early computer and caused an entire program to go wrong. Recurrent serious PC crashes may be due to nothing more than a corrupt driver file (easily reinstalled), a broken processor fan (very cheap to replace) or a badly seated memory chip (just press it back in). Only when you have checked the small items should you concentrate on the bigger suspects.

### Often the best place to look for help with hardware or software is an online group of fellow users.

Once you have obtained help from an online source, such as a fellow PC user in an Internet newsgroup, you will appreciate the potential of these users' knowledge when pooled. Even the best products have been known to be indifferently or expensively supported by their manufacturers at times, and this has led to the creation of user groups. These are self-help organisations which specialise in a specific product area, from something as general as computers to individual software programs.

### Members benefit

The essence of a user group is to distil the expert knowledge from dedicated users of a product to benefit all its members. Typical groups organise training courses, negotiate discounts on computer products, and provide a pool of support resources for those in need of help. Software user groups are generally national or international, and may even obtain a little bit of funding from the software company itself. Hardware user groups, especially those focusing on PCs rather than peripherals, tend to be regional and meet up on a regular basis.

User groups were much more popular in the 1980s when desktop computing was still new. Since then, manufacturers have a better understanding of what buyers expect and offer their own support services. People these days do not perceive such a great need for organised self help. However, a user group has no compulsion to toe a corporate line: if it has discovered a problem in its chosen product, it is hardly going to keep quiet about it. As a user group member, you will hear about problems before anyone else, and also be party to the first solutions.

### Geeks galore?

User groups have a public image of being populated by geeky fan-club types. Ignore the image. If you take your computing seriously, getting involved in a user group could well save your neck one day, and will almost certainly help you achieve more with your PC. Even if you're not keen on joining

# utilities

clubs, a local user group get-together twice a year is no great effort considering what can be obtained in return. User groups can be located by searching the Web or checking at your local library.

## Utilities

Getting organised is not the only self-help option open to those in need of expert support. In addition to the various disk and file utilities on the market, there is a wealth of problem solving and disaster prevention software available shrink-wrapped on the shelves. These range from anti-virus programs to full hardware troubleshooting utilities. In principle, everyone should own an anti-virus package, especially if they are connected to the Net. For the sake of a cheap utility, it would be a foolish way to lose your files.

## Useful utilities

Another popular type of software troubleshooting utility is the kind designed to identify the cause of a PC problem rather than promise a solution for it. For example, if your PC keeps crashing and you don't know why, these utilities will try to analyse your PC components and perhaps prompt you with a series of interactive tasks before identifying the problem. With this knowledge, you can confidently fix the problem yourself, go out and buy a new component, call up a support company or do whatever is necessary. It may not save you money, but it will save time by accelerating the process of getting things fixed.

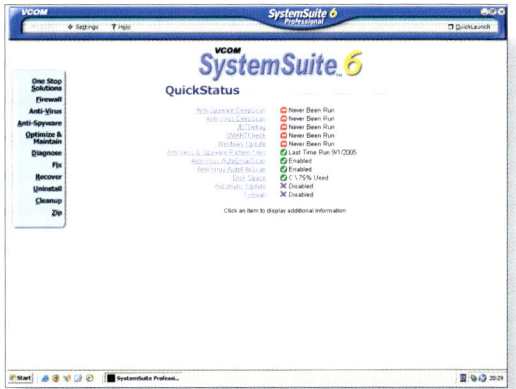

**Some utility software**, such as VCOM's SystemSuite, will attempt to check your hardware and software components for problems and suggest appropriate solutions, ending any uncertainty you may have of what's gone wrong.

### Jargon buster

**UGNETs** User groups use the product's initial followed by UG (user group). If the user group is online, it often tags the word NET on the end. WUGNET is the Windows User Group.

### Watch out!

No-one is infallible in their judgement and it can happen that interference with the internal workings of your PC, peripherals or software can cause more problems rather than solve the original fault. When you call in a support engineer there will at least be some kind of guarantee that if it all goes wrong, the company will make every attempt to put things right at its own expense. But if you are on your own or taking advice from a user group, you have no-one to put the blame on.

This isn't a reason for not trying to solve computer problems yourself, but a warning that fiddling can do more damage than good unless you know exactly what you are doing, or at least know how to restore everything to its original state. Take notes when offered help by a user group and read them back to the helper to check you have understood the method and not missed anything. When reconfiguring or reinstalling hardware or software, take a note of each step you have completed, along with sketches and listings. This way, it'll be easy to retrace your steps if necessary. These notes may also be invaluable if the problem ever crops up again, or if someone else asks you for help.

# Consult the manual

## Hunt the .pdf

An increasing number of hardware and software companies provide simple installation manuals on paper, but supply the complete product guides as electronic documentation on a disk or CD. Invariably it will be in Adobe Acrobat .pdf format, which can be opened and printed only by the Acrobat Reader program. This can be downloaded for free from Adobe's Web site at www.adobe.co.uk.

**When something goes wrong with your PC, you could always try reading the manual.**

There is an old curse in the computing world which is often quoted in its short form: RTFM. It stands for 'read the friendly manual' – or close enough – and is intended to remind PC users that the answers they are looking for are right at their fingertips. This is more applicable now than ever, as intuitive software and plug and play hardware give the impression that any lack of instant functionality is an insurmountable problem that can be solved only by contacting product support staff.

### Keep the manual safe

Most PC kit can be installed and used without wasting time poring over the instructions, but make sure you keep the manual safe just in case. One day you may need to move a hardware device from one PC to another, and will appreciate having the instructions. Dull and obscure documents like a motherboard manual suddenly become valuable the day you decide to upgrade your processor or RAM. Net forums are full of queries about motherboards, posted by people who threw away their manuals.

Software manuals are fat and off-putting, but if you look, the solution to your problems could be in there. Some software companies help by providing troubleshooting chapters, and many products come with separate user and reference manuals. The first gets you up and running, while the second contains details if you ever get stuck.

### Look at books

Check out the computing shelves at your local book store or an online bookshop. Flicking through hundreds of pages of paperback books is probably not the best method of obtaining a solution to your computer hassles, but it remains the most convenient way of training yourself on a topic in far greater depth than a product manual ever could. If you come to rely heavily upon a particular product, especially software, having a huge tome of detailed documentation at hand is as practical as it is reassuring.

# Fault finders

**Even if your PC is displaying no obvious symptoms, it's still a good idea to give it a regular checkup.**

It's rare for a PC to develop a mechanical fault. When a computer goes wrong it's often because an item of software has been added or removed, disturbing an otherwise stable system. It is less likely that a hardware component has worn out or broken down. Usually the first indication of a problem is that a file won't load properly or a procedure that used to work perfectly now produces unpredictable results.

## Fault finders and fixers

Diagnostic software should be able to do more than simply find faults. It should determine whether the PC's hardware is working properly and identify any problems with the applications software or operating system. And it should correct or repair the faults it finds, except where the problem is a hardware malfunction.

It's quite easy for a computer to carry out the second and third tasks of putting its own software system in order, but working out whether a fault is caused by hardware or software can be problematic. Take, for example, not being able to send or receive e-mail. If you have a hardware fault, it could be that the modem is broken or that the phone line

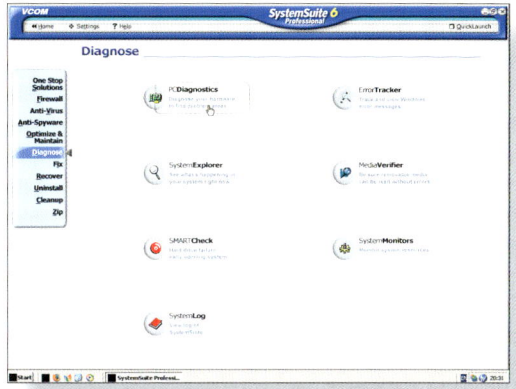

To test any component in a PC using **SystemSuite**, all you have to do is click on the relevant item on the virtual Desktop. You may instruct SystemSuite to run a full diagnostic check of your PC, as here.

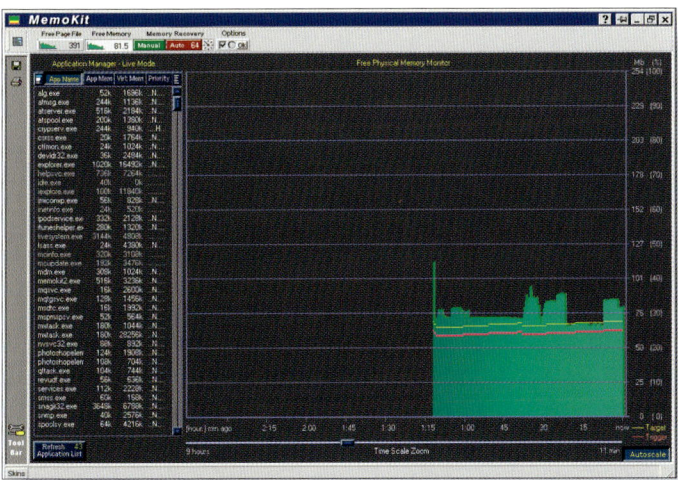

**Programs such as MemoKit not only show how your memory is used, but also manage it for you.**

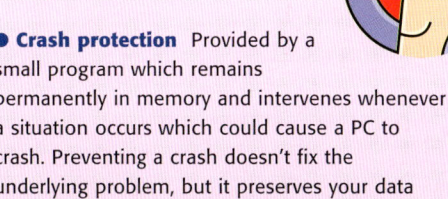

## Fact file

● **Crash protection** Provided by a small program which remains permanently in memory and intervenes whenever a situation occurs which could cause a PC to crash. Preventing a crash doesn't fix the underlying problem, but it preserves your data and gives you a chance to correct things yourself.

● **Background monitoring** Differs from crash protection in that it doesn't assume responsibility for your PC, it merely warns when potentially dangerous situations occur. Most warnings are about low memory, shortage of disk space or overburdened system resources. If you ignore the warnings, your computer might crash.

● **Recovery disk** A CD-ROM containing enough to start your PC plus copies of key system files from the hard disk and some simple recovery tools to get Windows working again. You can create your own if your optical drive has the ability to burn CD-ROMs.

● **SMART disk** A type of hard disk that can warn you that its condition is deteriorating before it actually fails. Don't dispose of your existing hard disk just to fit a SMART one, but ask for a SMART disk on your next computer. The acronym stands for Self-Monitoring, Analysis and Reporting Technology. You can also get software that will monitor the health of your non-SMART disk.

# SOLVING PROBLEMS

## Buying tips

● AMIDiag, Micro-Scope and Eurosoft's PC-Check are diagnostic software programs that will test your PC to identify problems rather than fix them.

● VCOM's SystemSuite and Symantec's Norton Utilities are typical of Windows-based diagnostic programs suitable for casual users. Both programs include preventive modules to monitor a PC and detect problems before they develop. SystemSuite is easy for absolute technophobes to master but the Norton Utilities offer more features for those with the expertise to use them.

● Don't buy any diagnostic tools until you've looked at what's already on your PC. There are several utilities that come with Windows. Diagnostic programs in Windows XP can be reached by going to the Start menu, selecting All Programs and opening Accessories, highlighting System tools and choosing the software you want from the list. Among the maintenance tools found here are Disk Cleanup for clearing space and troublesome files left behind after browsing the Net, and Disk Defragmenter, which physically optimizes the way files are stored on your hard disk. You can also manage your disk using Computer Management, found by going to Control Panel in the Start menu, and then selecting Administrative Tools.

itself is dead. Perhaps the modem is working fine, but it has come loose in its mounting slot. Maybe the family pet has chewed the phone cable between the socket and the back of the PC.

Diagnostic software can tell you if your e-mail software isn't getting a signal from the modem, but it can't tell you why there's no signal. For this reason, the most appropriate diagnostic software for non-technical users is interactive – at least to the extent that when it can't diagnose a problem by itself it enlists your help rather than giving up.

## Disaster recovery

Software designed to run under Windows is the easiest to use. But what do you do if your computer is so badly damaged that Windows won't even start? Some diagnostic programs, such as AMIDiag, will work under both Windows and DOS so either can be run. Working in DOS, though, is not as easy as Windows, with its point-and-click style of operating. (See pages 89–92 to learn more about using MS-DOS.)

## Early warning systems

The ideal diagnostic software for non-professional users should work in both Windows and MS-DOS. It should include preventive maintenance and background monitoring. And it should be able to back up important Windows system files and reinstate them when required. Look for a graphical program that can run a system test automatically. And bearing in mind that there will always be situations which require human intervention, it's worth choosing a program that can show you what it expects you to do using explanatory video clips.

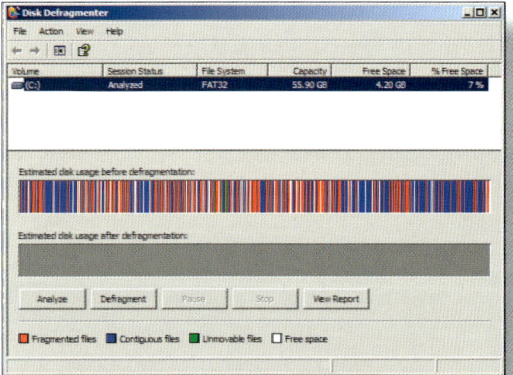

**Disk Defragmenter** will check your PC's hard drive to see if performance could be improved by reorganizing the way its files are stored.

## Top five brands

● **AMI** www.amidiag.com
● **Eurosoft** www.eurosoft-uk.com
● **McAfee** www.mcafee.com
● **Micro2000** www.micro2000.com
● **Symantec** www.symantec.com

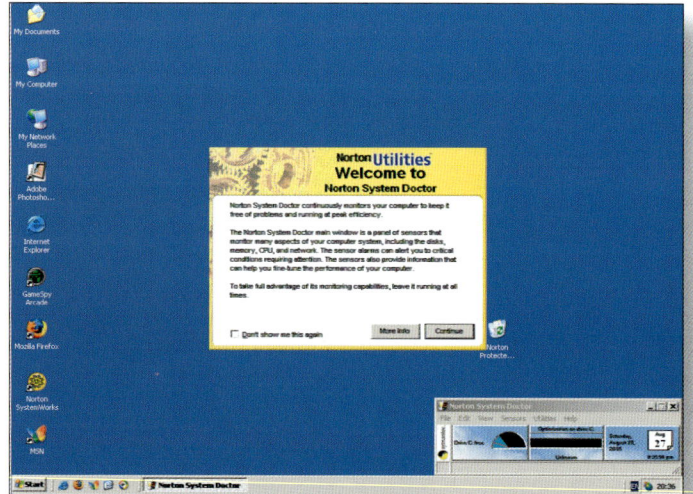

**Norton's System Doctor** runs in the background. If it identifies any problems there's a good chance they can be fixed by a companion program called WinDoctor.

# Windows Help

**If you run into trouble using Windows, Help is the best place to look for a solution.**

Windows is a sophisticated system with a large number of features. It's easy to use, but that doesn't mean that when you want to do something, the way to do it is always going to be obvious.

Windows is too complex for you to learn or remember everything you will ever need to know about the system. Even experts sometimes have to think twice about how to go about a task. So don't become discouraged if you have to as well.

The Help system not only gives you information on making the most of Windows, it also links you to troubleshooters, tours and tutorials and other Internet-based help resources.

### Help tip

Windows also offers context-sensitive help. This means that the Help box gives you information about the specific task you are trying to do. For example, if you are selecting an option, it will offer details of what this does.

## Getting Windows to help you

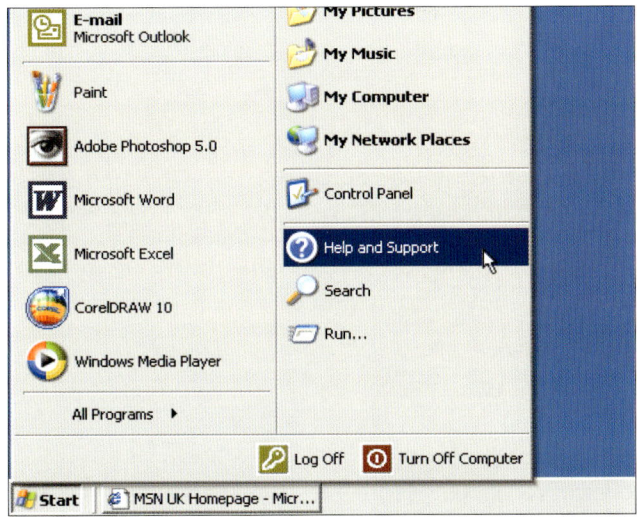

**1** You can access the on-line help for Windows from the **Help and Support** option on the Start menu (or simply Help in other versions of Windows). Click on this and you'll see the Help topics dialogue box. Another way to start Windows Help and Support is to click on the Desktop and press the F1 key. Pressing F1 will nearly always load the Help file of whatever program you're working in.

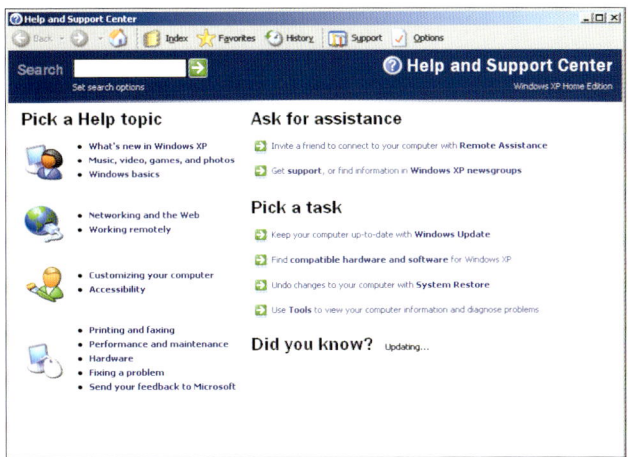

**2** In Windows XP, the Help and Support window lists the **Help topics** on the left. These topics include Networking, Customizing your computer, and Printing. Each topic contains more topics and when you click one, they will appear. Some topics are nested several layers deep. Depending on how complex the Help file is, you might have to navigate several levels to get to the information you want.

With other versions of Windows, a list of Help topics appears on the left and a welcome message on the right.

# SOLVING PROBLEMS

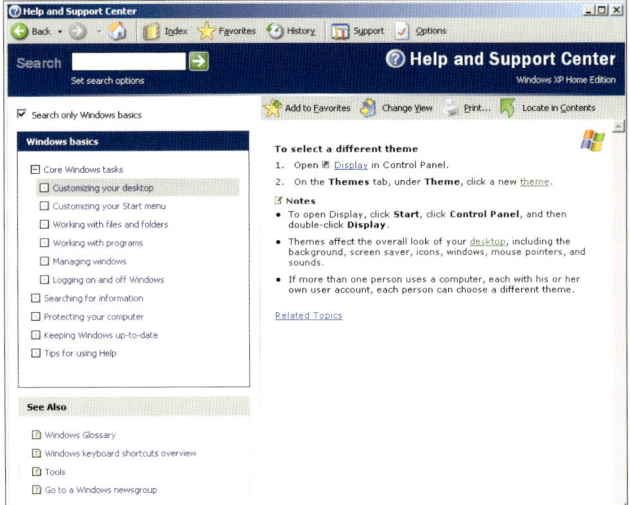

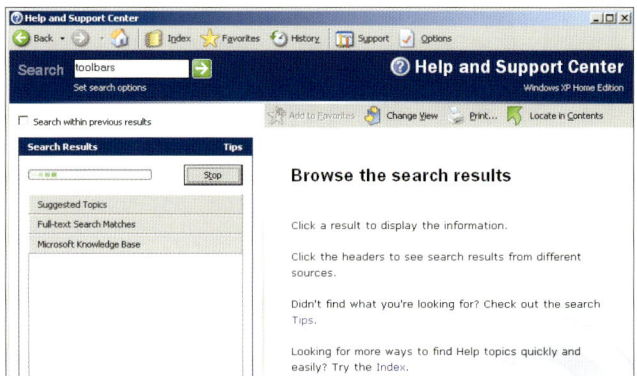

**3** In all versions of Help, if you click on one of the subjects on the left, its **contents** appear in the right of the window. Most help pages make extensive use of hyperlinks – words or phrases that are underlined – to link together pages containing related data. If the underlining is solid, clicking the hyperlink will take you to another page. If it is broken, or green, a small pop-up window will appear above the page to give you further information.

**5** The **Search box** (a tab in earlier versions of Windows) lets you do a search on the whole of the text in the Help file, not just keywords. In Windows XP's Help, you enter a list of words that you want found in the database. Earlier versions of Windows handle this automatically and search the database when you press Enter or click the green arrow or List topics button.

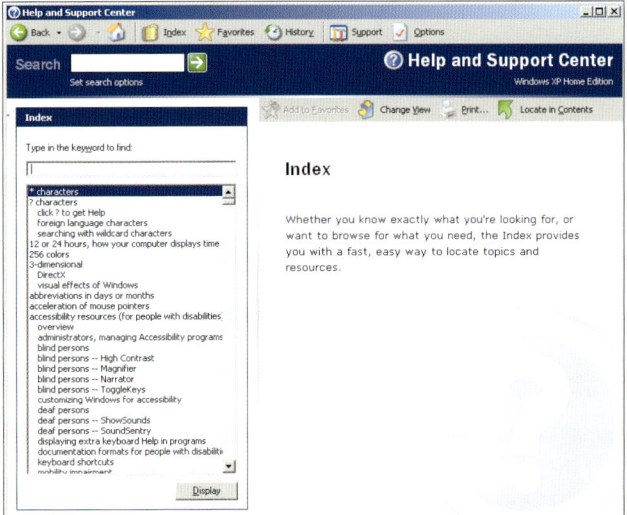

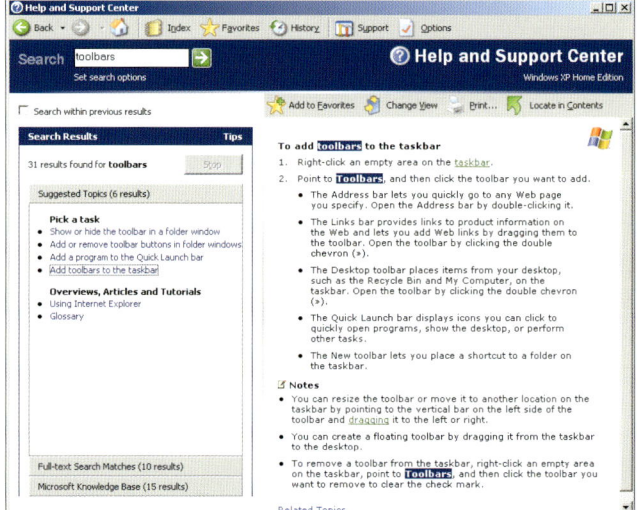

**4** A general list of topics is useful for browsing through a book or a Help file, but if you're looking for something specific it's better to use an **index**. If you click on the Index button in the top toolbar (a tab in earlier versions) you will see the index for the Help file. Scroll through the list of keywords until you find what you want, then double-click on it. Alternatively, you can start typing the word you are interested in, and the list will automatically select an entry.

**6** Type a phrase that describes what you want to find and Help displays the topics that contain words you searched for. Double-click on a **topic** and its contents appear in the right of the window with the matched words highlighted. Windows may not always use the same terms as you, so if a text search doesn't locate the data you want, try using different words.

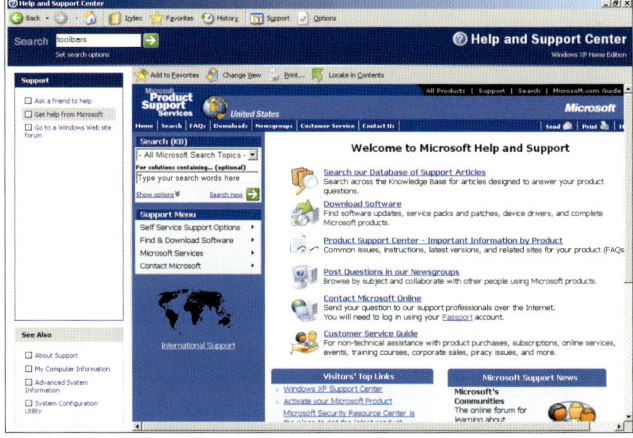

## Help tip

Sometimes the Windows Help program can tell you exactly how to solve a problem. However, occasionally you may need to load a different program to get you out of trouble. If you click on the curved arrow in Help, it will automatically take you to that program.

**7** Some of the Help and Support available is provided via the Web. Clicking on some topics will display Microsoft's on-line **Help site**. This may contain more comprehensive and up-to-date information on the subject you're looking for.

# The Knowledge Base

**You can find answers to even the most obscure questions about Windows on the Internet.**

Your first stop in answering any query should be the Help and Support Center that comes with Windows. However, this only holds answers to commonly asked questions.

If you have a more advanced question, or an unusual problem, and you find the Help and Support Center doesn't offer enough information to give you a solution, you can turn to sources of help on the Internet. The biggest of these is the Knowledge Base on the Microsoft Web site. This searchable database covers known problems with all Microsoft applications, including Windows, and contains troubleshooting wizards and program updates.

## Accessing the Knowledge Base

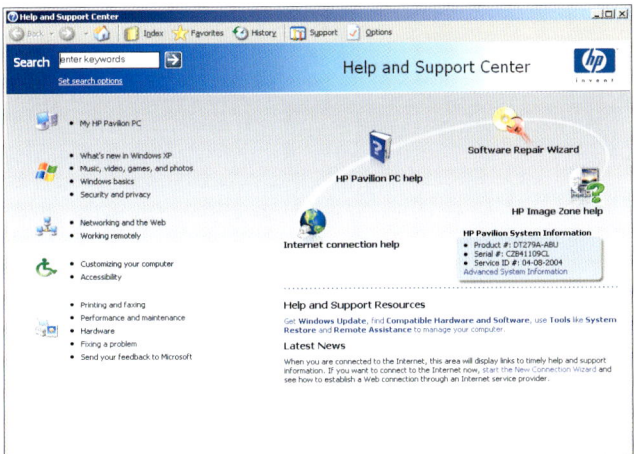

**1** Before going online to search the Knowledge Base, make sure that you can't find the answer to your question in the **Help and Support Center**. You can access this direct from the Start menu on your PC. In Windows XP, the center may even have been customised by the manufacturer of your PC so that help and information about the hardware and software of that particular model is provided. In this example, HP Pavilion system information has been included in the Help and Support Center.

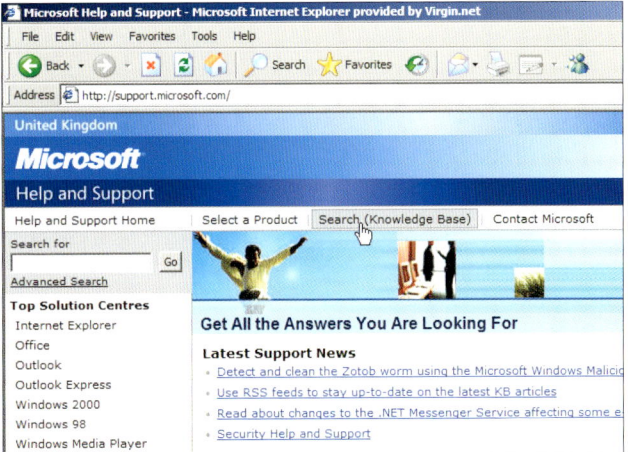

**2** If the Help and Support Center doesn't answer your question, access the Technical Database by going to the **Microsoft Help and Support home page** at http://support.microsoft.com. From here you can get information on how to use the support site, and also obtain information about what support services are available. Click on the link to Search (Knowledge Base) to go to a database of technical information about every Microsoft product available.

# SOLVING PROBLEMS

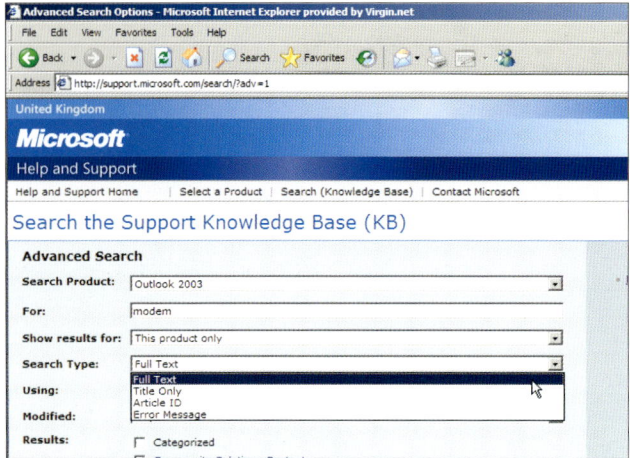

**3** The main Knowledge Base page is a **search engine**. You can narrow the search to a specific Microsoft product by selecting one from the Search Product dropdown list, then typing keywords or a question in the For field to help the search engine find what you want. Click on the arrow pointing to the right to start the search. It can sometimes take a minute or two to get an answer, because the Knowledge Base is heavily used.

If you know the name of the article or download file that you want (perhaps because you read about it in an article), enter the details – for example, the number of the article – in the For field. Then, in Search Type select where to search – through Full Text (as here), by title or by article ID – and click on the arrow.

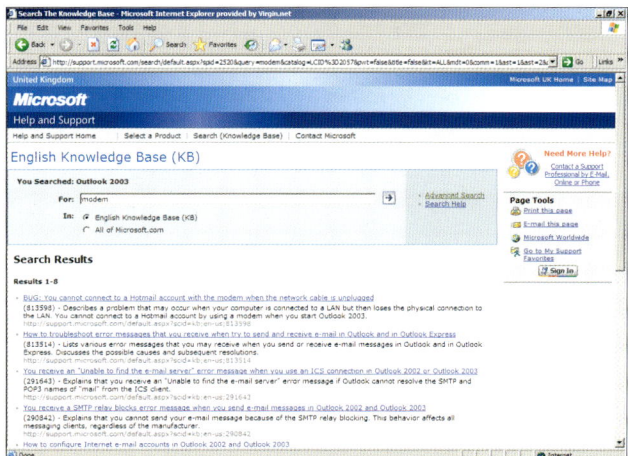

**4** For general searches, such as 'modem', your question will return a **number of articles**. You'll be given the title of the article and a short extract so that you can see what it relates to. To view the complete text of any article of interest, click on its hyperlink.

If the article is relevant, print it from your browser, since you'll almost certainly want to refer back to it later. Before closing the browser, skim through the article to see if it contains links to other, related articles that might also be relevant to your problem.

**5** It's worth visiting the Support site and Knowledge Base even if you don't have a technical problem. The site has a series of **how-to articles**, with advice on each Microsoft product, which can save you time by showing you easier or quicker ways of doing things. From the Support home page click on the product you want to know more about from the list under Top Solution Centres on the left. Here it's Windows XP. If your product is not listed, click on More Solution Centers and you will be taken to a new page containing a list of products. The products on this page are organised by theme. The Encarta Encyclopedia, for example, is found under the heading Reference and Educational. Click on the product and you'll be taken to a new page with a list of articles dealing with common problems.

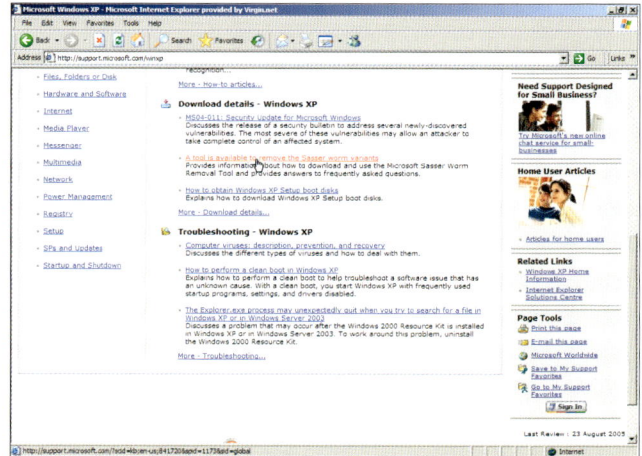

**6** When you've located the relevant product page you'll find a list of how-to and troubleshooting articles. If you scroll further down the page to the **Download Details – Windows XP** section, you can download updates and patches for that product. Even if your computer is working well, you may still find improved versions of utilities and fixes for bugs that will make your programs run even better. Here, for example, there's a tool to remove a particularly nasty virus.

## Search tip

You can access Knowledge Base information direct from the Help and Support Center in Windows XP. To do so, type in the keywords you want to search for in the Search box and click on the button with the green arrow. At the bottom of the Search Results box that appears on the left of the screen is a grey tab marked Microsoft Knowledge Base, with the number of results it has found displayed in brackets next to it. Click on this and you will see the links to the relevant articles.

# Online help

**If you run into trouble using Windows, there are plenty of people online who can assist.**

In the rare event that you can't find a solution to your problem from the Windows XP Help and Support Centre or at the Microsoft Knowledge Base Web site, you'll want to turn to a knowledgeable friend. It's disconcerting if you have a problem with a PC and you don't know what to do.

Even if you don't know any PC experts, you can use the Net to get help from people with immense experience of running Windows on similar hardware to yourself. They may have suffered in the past from the same difficulties as you — and discovered a solution. They'll have plenty of friendly advice to offer when you get in touch.

Microsoft has recognized that the best help can often come from its customers and has consequently set up special newsgroups. You can access them via the Communities link on www.microsoft.com. Look for the Newsgroups link on the Technical Communities page. There are several other on-line services — such as AOL — that also provide technical support forums. Online exchanges — for example, Experts Exchange at www.experts-exchange.com — also give expert advice, although such sites sometimes charge a subscription fee.

## Getting support from other users

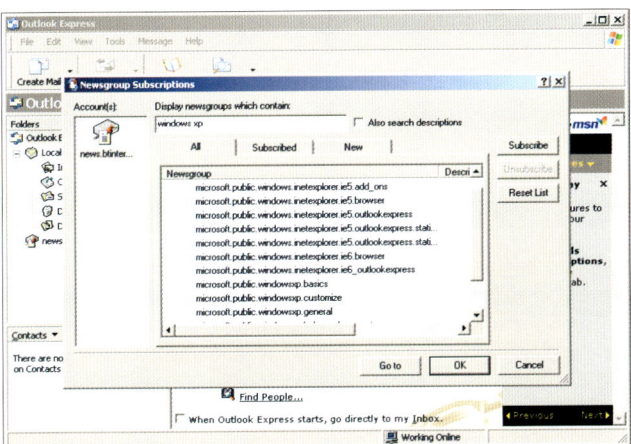
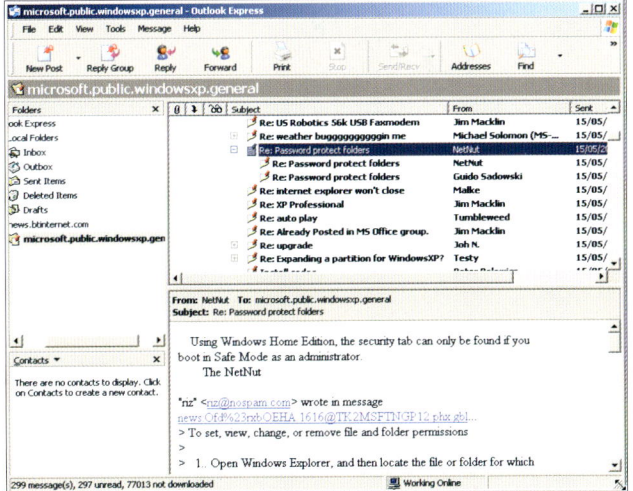

**1** If you have an Internet connection, your ISP should provide access to a **news server**. You can use Outlook Express to read and post newsgroup messages. If you haven't already set it up to do so, go to Tools, Accounts, click on the News tab and select the Add button then News. Follow the Internet Connection Wizard and Newsgroups will be added to the Tools menu.

To find some newsgroups to subscribe to, go to the Tools menu, select Newsgroups, and type the text you wish your newsgroup name to contain – for instance, 'Windows XP'. Outlook Express will give you a list of suitable newsgroups. Among the thousands of newsgroups, there are many that are devoted to Windows.

Microsoft.public newsgroups are the premier forum for getting help with problems, as the information posted there is monitored by Microsoft itself. Newsgroups have been set up for just about every area of computing, from disk management to printing – simply subscribe to the one that seems most likely to have a solution for your problem.

**2** Most of the newsgroups devoted to Windows issues have plenty of messages posted to them so, to save download time, when you connect to the news server it's best to download only the **message headers**, not all the messages. Right-click on the newsgroup name and select Synchronization Settings, then Headers only. When this action has completed you will be given a list showing only the subject headings of each message. To see the text of any message, just select it from the list and Outlook Express will download the message body.

It's considered bad form to ask a question without first checking to see if the same question hasn't already been asked in the recent past, so spend a few minutes browsing the list of headers. Messages that have replies to them are shown with a plus sign alongside them. Quite often these replies are useful and may answer your own question.

# SOLVING PROBLEMS

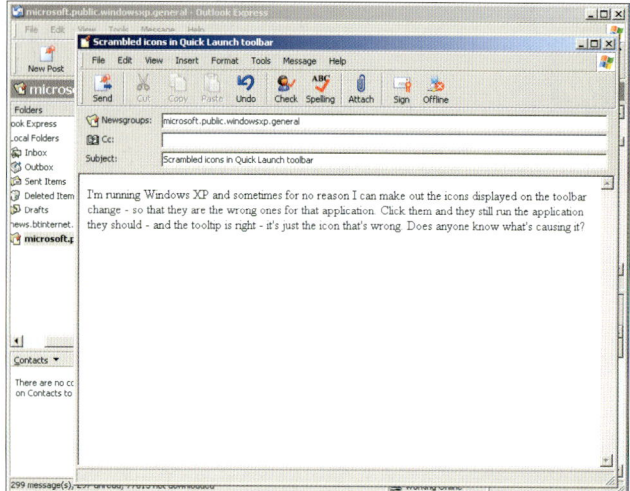

**3** If you can't see any messages that answer your question, you'll have to post a message yourself. It's much like sending an e-mail. Click on the **New Post** button to open a window into which you can type your message. When you've finished, click on the Send button to send it.

Do everything you can to help the person who has the answer to your question find your message. First, choose the most appropriate newsgroup to post your message. Next, make the subject header a concise description of your problem – subject headers such as Windows Problem or Help Needed aren't very useful. In the message body keep to the point – ask your question or describe your problem as clearly as you can. You should also make sure you provide any technical information that might be relevant, such as the version of Windows, the type of graphics card, how much memory your computer has, what other programs are running when the problem occurs, and so on.

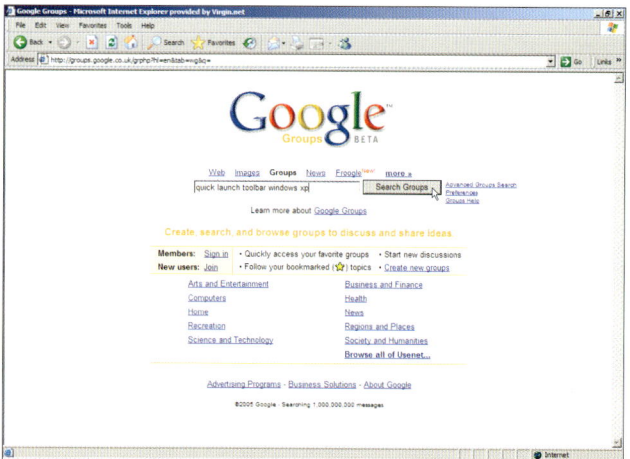

**4** One of the disadvantages of newsgroups is that messages aren't held on the news server for very long. To make sure you don't miss the answer to your question, you must check back regularly. Fortunately, Google Groups at http://groups.google.com offers a **searchable database** of Internet news messages, and this is a great way to find out if your question has ever been asked or answered previously.

Go to the Google Groups site and in the Google Search field enter some keywords that you would expect to see in messages relating to your problem. Then click on the Search Groups button. Google will present you with a list of newsgroup threads containing the words you specified. From the subject headers you should be able to get an idea of how relevant they are. To read the full messages, just click on the hyperlinks.

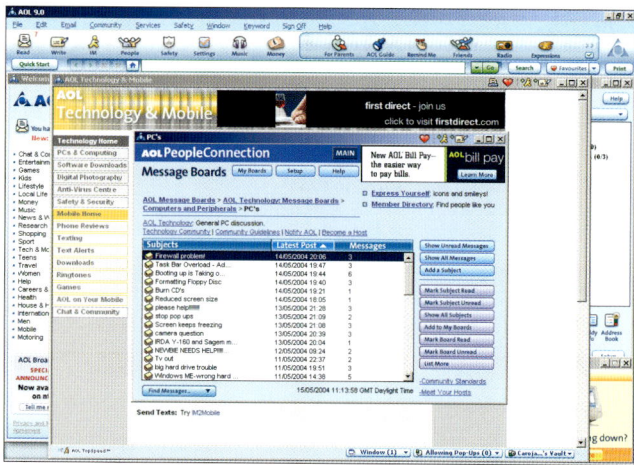

**5** If you subscribe to **AOL**, the service has its own online forums that are available only to subscribers. As the number of participants is restricted, there's a better chance that your question will be read and answered than in some of the busier newsgroups and, if you want to see what topics have already been discussed, you won't have to trawl through quite so many messages.

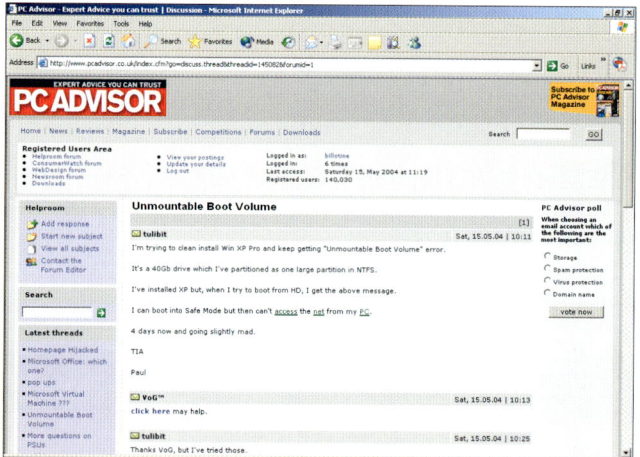

**6** Another place to look for help is the **FAQs** on magazine and manufacturers' web sites. A simple way to locate them is to search on a web search engine such as AltaVista, including the keyword 'FAQ' in your query. Alternatively, you can look on the site of your favourite computer magazine. Most magazine sites carry a wealth of information, including how-to articles and advice from the readers' help pages. Some sites, such as PC Advisor shown here, even have online message boards where you can post your questions in the hope of receiving a reply.

## Fact file

While there's more flexibility in accessing the newsgroups via an e-mail program such as Outlook or Outlook Express, the Microsoft newsgroups can also be accessed via the Web – so you can log in from any PC. Go to the Microsoft Support home page (http://support.microsoft.com) and select Self Support Options from the Support Options on the left. Then select Microsoft Newsgroups, and choose the language you use. You can then click on the group that interests you from the categories on the left and you can read the postings online.

# Troubleshooting basics

**Skilled computer engineers are thin on the ground, but DIY computer maintenance is an alternative.**

The twin themes of troubleshooting and disaster recovery make computing at home sound much more dangerous than it really is. The dictionary defines a troubleshooter as an expert detector and mender of any trouble, mechanical or otherwise, but it's also true to say that a good troubleshooter should be able to anticipate and prevent disasters as well as recover from them.

### Never fails
Most PC failures have nothing to do with mechanical problems, so if you're unlucky enough to have bought defective equipment there's little you can do apart from claiming a repair under warranty or paying for a replacement. Most manufacturing defects come to light when a PC is almost new, and if a computer doesn't fail in the first three months of intensive use the chances are it never will.

In order to keep your PC working properly you must be sure to install its software correctly, follow the rules about starting and closing it down safely, and run regular maintenance checks. Nevertheless, faults are bound to occur.

### Do it yourself
If it's a software or configuration problem you can fix it yourself. If it's a hardware problem you might prefer not to open up your PC to replace the defective component, especially if the system is still under warranty. But being able to identify a hardware fault means you can request repairs knowing exactly what you're letting yourself in for and what they should cost.

### You will need

**ESSENTIAL**
**Software** Windows includes a number of diagnostic and repair tools, but those from third parties such as McAfee and Symantec offer additional features and ease of use. Two programs everyone should have are a better back-up utility than the one included with Windows and an up-to-date anti-virus program.
**Hardware** Some form of removable storage with a capacity of at least 100MB and preferably more. This could be a Zip, REV or disk-based drive or a tape drive (with cartridge) designed specifically for backing up hard disks.
**Other** Basic household cleaning materials such as lint-free rags or dusters and an all-surface cleaning spray.

# Use back-up

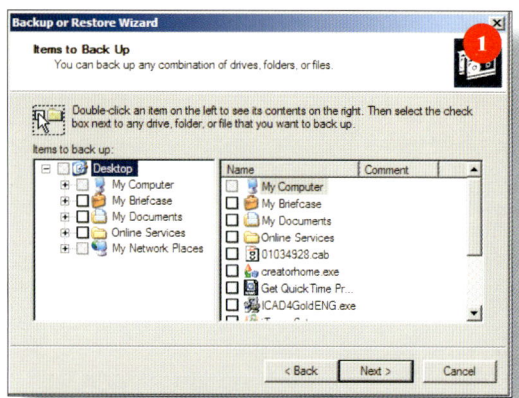

Launch **Backup** by going to the All Programs menu, selecting Accessories then System Tools. In Windows Me and 98 Backup was called Microsoft Backup, and might have to be installed first using Add/Remove Programs. Backup lets you make back-ups of an entire disk or of selected files.

## When changing hardware or software, making a back-up first can save time and trouble.

When it comes to keeping your PC in first-class order, prevention really is better than cure, if only because when your computer goes down it always seems to do so at the most inconvenient time. Keeping your PC in good shape needn't take more than a few minutes a week, but do remember to find extra time to make a back-up before changing any of the software or hardware in your system.

### Back up your troubles

Backing up a hard disk is boring and most people tend not to do it, even when they know they should. But while you have to be dedicated to stick to a regular back-up regime, it's not too much of a chore to make a precautionary back-up before installing a new piece of software or hardware (1).

A new piece of software may replace existing files with more recent ones. The new program may work fine but programs you've been using without problems for years may suddenly stop working. Removing the offending software won't fix the problem because the old files have been

### Installation tips

- Install one item of software or hardware at a time.

- Make a full back-up (or a copy of your system configuration files) before installing new software.

- Make a note of everything you do, while you're doing it. Don't rely on your memory.

- Don't replace existing files with older versions if, when installing software or drivers, you get a warning that the files on your hard disk are newer than those being installed.

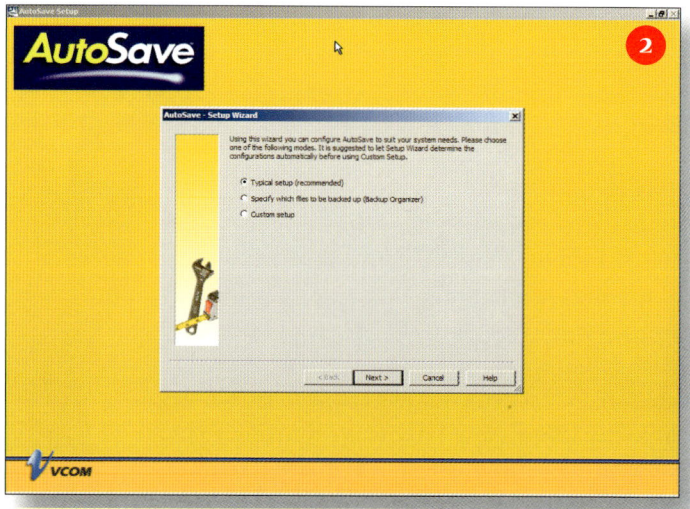

**AutoSave** follows standard practice in offering Typical and Custom installations. If a new program conflicts with an existing one, try a Custom installation and add extra features one at a time to see if this fixes the problem.

overwritten, but after reinstating the working system from a back-up you can try reinstalling the offending software with a different set of options (2). Even if you haven't got a back-up drive you can make a copy of crucial Windows registry and configuration files on a floppy disk and use these to restore a system to good health. This isn't as good as a full disk back-up, but it doesn't require any special kit and the software you need comes free with Windows (3).

## Hardware or hard luck?

Anyone unversed in the ways of Windows might think installing new hardware is foolproof – if a component doesn't work, take it out again. But it's not that simple. Every time you start Windows it identifies the components in the system, allocates resources to them and makes sure it has the correct drivers installed. This means that when you start up a PC after adding a new component, Windows might take resources from an existing device and give them to a new one. Removing the offending component doesn't restore an identical system. You need to restore your previous settings from the back-up.

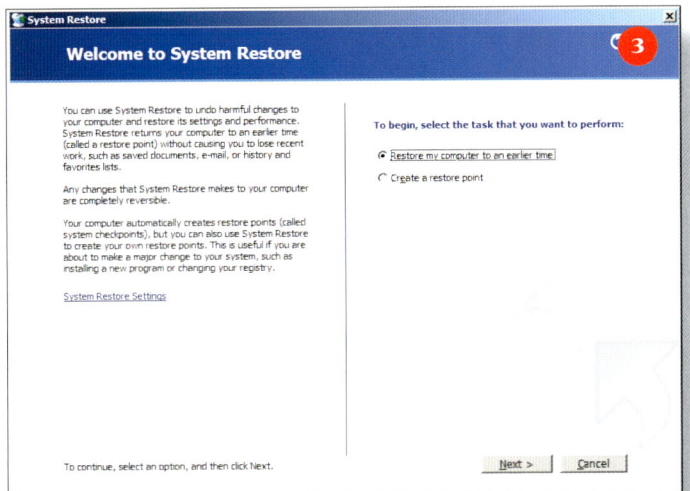

**You can back up your system configuration using Windows. Go to All Programs, then Accessories, then open the System Tools folder and select System Information. On the Tools menu choose System Restore (in Windows 98 choose System Configuration Utility). Use this to make a copy of your system settings. If you decide not to keep the new program, uninstall it and restore the original settings by selecting Restore My Computer to an Earlier Time.**

## Troubleshooting

When it works, plug and play is great, but when it doesn't, it's a pain. After installing a new component you should run your system thoroughly immediately afterwards to make sure that it's working properly, and you should check Device Manager (4) for conflicts. The effects of resource conflicts can be far reaching: installing a new soundcard might prevent a seemingly unrelated item such as a network card from working. This won't be evident if you're not currently logged onto a network, which is why checking Device Manager is so important.

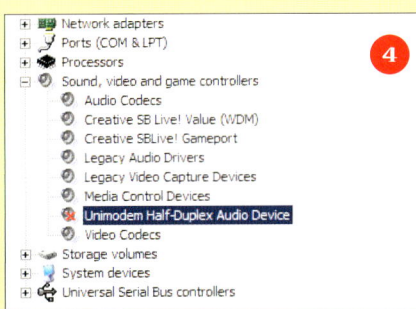

**In Device Manager a red cross next to a piece of kit means it has been disabled. A yellow exclamation mark means there's a problem with the device or its drivers.**

## Daily essentials

● Always close down Windows before switching off your PC. Don't cheat by hitting the power switch before the message appears telling you that it's safe to do so.

● Don't put any liquids near your PC. Assume that they're going to get knocked over and keep them far enough away so that if they *are* knocked over your equipment stays intact.

● Keep dust at bay. Inside your PC it clogs air vents and causes overheating. In CD-ROM and floppy disk drives it damages precision components and can lead to errors reading data.

● Spring clean your PC once a year. Vacuum the ventilation slots, make sure the external leads and cables are secure, and remove the lid of the system box to check that nothing has come loose.

# First aid

## Here's what to do if, despite the precautions you've taken, your computer lets you down.

The usual warnings of problems with Windows are that it tries to load but crashes before finishing, or it loads smoothly but then won't work properly. In these cases the fault is almost certainly a missing driver, corrupted file or invalid system setting.

The same is true even if there is no sound from Windows and the CD-ROM drive has apparently disappeared. Just because hardware won't work doesn't mean it's broken. The only time a problem is more likely to be a hardware defect than a software problem is when your PC won't even start.

### Define the problem
First ask yourself what has changed since your PC last worked. Have you installed new software? Have you installed new hardware? If the answer is yes, the chances are your problem stems from here and you can identify its source. Even if you haven't installed anything new, perhaps you've attached and subsequently removed a piece of equipment such as a borrowed printer. If your PC thinks the device is still there, it will try to use it.

It's not always possible to pin down the source of a problem, but it helps if you can find out what you have to do to make it happen. It's no good ringing a helpline with an intermittent problem. You'll spend hours on hold only to find that the problem won't manifest itself if somebody's listening.

### Check your disk
When looking for the cause of a glitch, start with your hard disk. It's a common source of problems and it's easy to check and fix. There are two conditions to look for: one is a shortage of disk space and the other is a corrupted filing system.

To check the free space on a disk, double-click on My Computer on the Desktop. Right-click on the drive you want to check and select Properties. The amount of disk space you need depends on the programs you use. Many won't run without enough space for their temporary files and anything less than 100MB is a serious cause for concern (**1**).

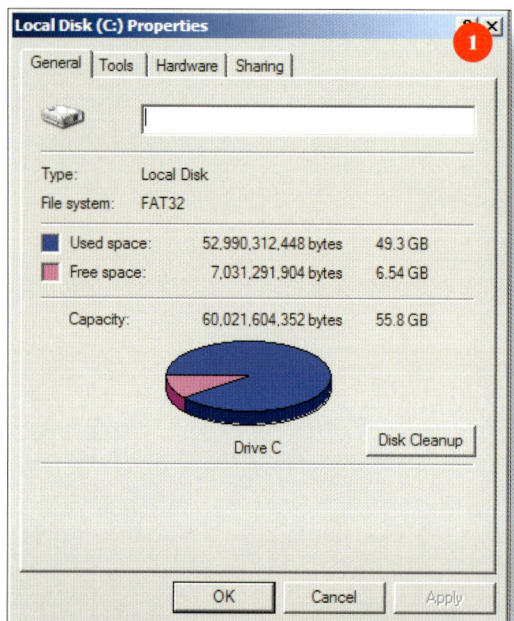

To check the amount of free space available on a hard disk, double-click on the My Computer icon on the Desktop; right-click on the drive you want to check and select **Properties**. You should regard 500MB of spare disk space as a minimum, but a better guide is to allow 10 per cent of the total disk space. Here, this 50 GB partition is fine because there's more than 6.5GB of free space.

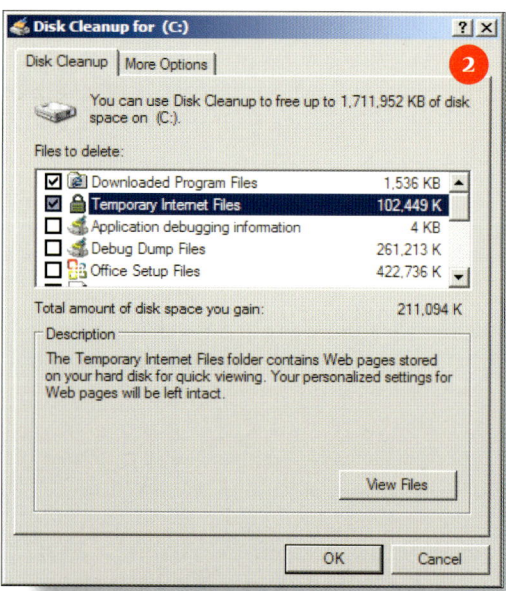

The **Disk Cleanup** utility calculates how much free space you can create by getting rid of temporary files – such as these Internet files that are taking up more than 100MB alone. Use Disk Cleanup regularly to improve your system's performance.

# TROUBLESHOOTING BASICS

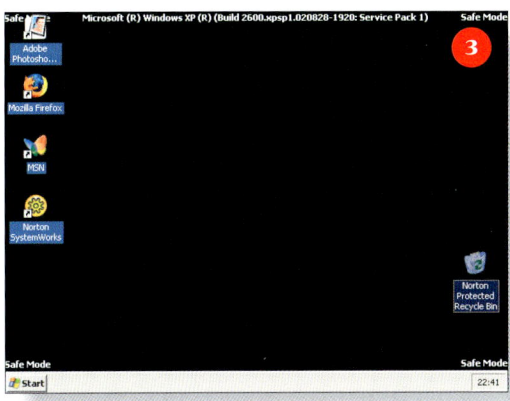

You can't forget you're in **Safe Mode** because there is a warning in each corner of the screen. Safe Mode can start a PC that has tangled drivers, but it can be a lengthy process, often involving trial and error, to discover the one causing the problem.

The disk filing system can become damaged if a PC is switched off without closing Windows first. The symptom is that a program crashes while reading data from or writing it to the hard disk. To repair a damaged filing system, check for free disk space as described opposite. To clear some space you can run Disk Cleanup. Go to the All Programs menu, choose Accessories and then System Tools (2).

## Resolve conflicts

If the hard disk is OK and you can't pin the blame for a problem on the installation of some new piece of hardware or software, suspect a conflict between existing programs or drivers. To check for driver conflicts, try starting your PC in Safe Mode (3). This is a diagnostic mode of Windows in which it starts without loading any inessential drivers.

Turn on your PC and when you see the message Starting Windows... press F8. This brings up a menu from which you should select Safe Mode. Because the usual display drivers are not loaded in Safe Mode, the screen will revert to a 640 x 480 simple VGA format. This is normal so don't worry.

If the problem goes away when you start in Safe Mode, you know there's a driver conflict. In this case use Device Manager to disable each driver in turn until you find the one causing the problem.

## Hardware faults

Only after performing all the checks described here should you start to suspect a hardware defect. To test hardware effectively you need special equipment and training, but a viable alternative (if you have access to spare components) is to swap them one at a time until you identify the culprit.

Most people don't have convenient boxes of spare kit in the corner of their living rooms or home office, but there is another option, which is to run a hardware diagnostic program, such as PCDiagnostics (4), available within VCOM's SystemSuite. This will run checks on your hardware such as the modem, the monitor and even your COM ports to see if any are faulty.

Windows 98 has its own hardware utility, the Hardware Info utility for Windows, that can be run by going to the Start menu and typing 'hwinfo/ui' in the Run... box.

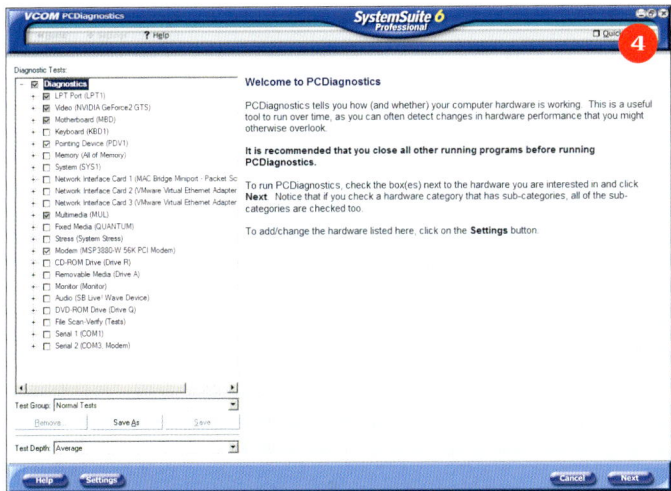

In **PCDiagnostics** you can select from the navigation pane on the left which parts of your computer hardware you want to test. It provides a lot of technical information that, even if it doesn't make sense to you, will help a support engineer.

# Software tools

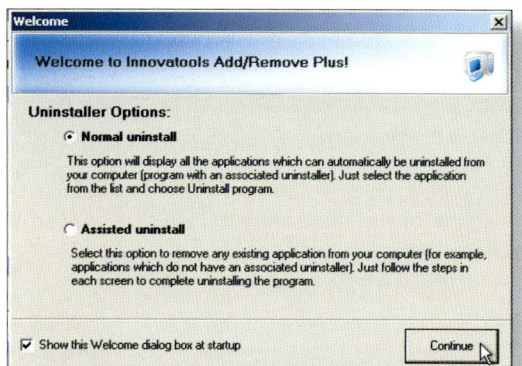

**Add/Remove Plus!** is a commercial uninstaller that extends the power of Windows' own Add/Remove programs tool enabling you to remove rogue files that can cause problems.

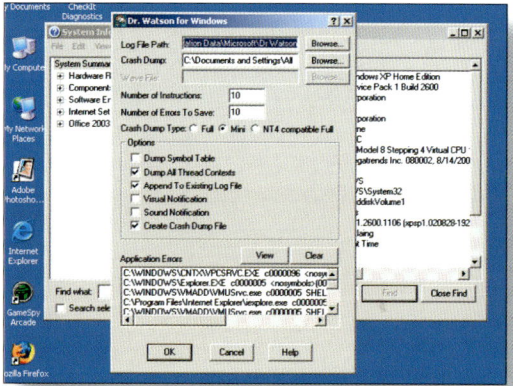

**Dr Watson for Windows** is a diagnostic tool for Windows. It will help you to discover the cause of any problems you may have.

## Watch out!

Don't install two utility products with the same function because they might interfere with each other and cause problems. Utilities that run permanently in the background such as virus checkers, crash detectors and Recycle Bin enhancers hook themselves into Windows in order to do their jobs, and if two programs try to hang on the same hook they might pull it out altogether.

**There's no shortage of software tools to help you keep your PC in order. Here's the pick of the bunch.**

When your computer's sick, it's time to call the doctor. There are various utility programs which will come to the aid of your ailing PC.

The first step is to make sure your machine can boot up, even if it is not well enough to run Windows. Some manufacturers supply an emergency boot disk with a new PC. If not, you should create one, when prompted, during the Windows installation process. There are also commercial programs available that provide emergency recovery utilities.

Windows itself comes with a useful diagnostic tool – Dr Watson for Windows. Access it by going to the All Programs menu, selecting Accessories and then System Tools. Click on System Information and then select Dr Watson for Windows from the Tools menu. Named after Sherlock Holmes' partner in detection, Dr Watson won't fix your problems but it will help track down the villain of the piece. If you have to call a helpline it will also provide answers to any awkward technical questions you may be asked about your system.

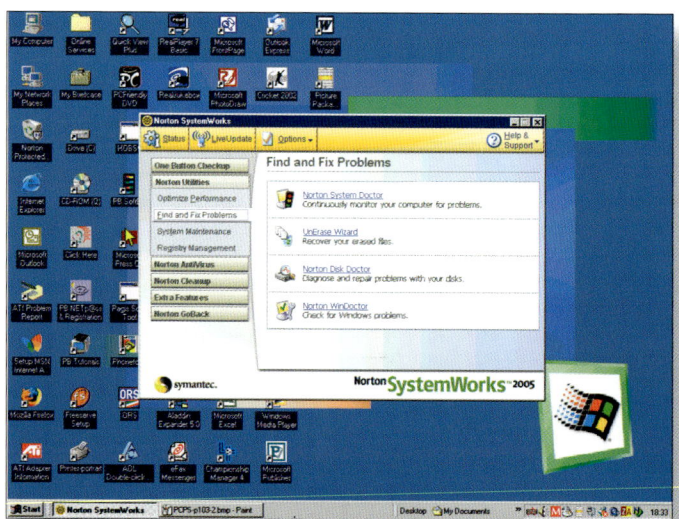

**Norton SystemWorks** from Symantec includes a number of tools designed specifically to find and fix problems – from WinDoctor for problems with Windows to Disk Doctor to check the health of your hard drive.

# TROUBLESHOOTING BASICS

**SystemSuite** from VCOM is one of the most comprehensive compilations of utility, recovery and diagnostic programs.

## Commercial programs

Hundreds of commercial utilities are available to help you fix ailing PCs, but it's no good dashing out to buy one after problems have manifested themselves. The utilities operate within Windows and they must be installed when Windows is intact, not when problems have started occurring.

Some utilities are designed to perform one task thoroughly, but the trend is to bundle products together. Uninstallers are popular single-task utilities. These tools remove all traces of a program you no longer require, instead of leaving stray files to jam up the works. CleanSweep, Ashampoo Uninstaller and Innovatools' Add/Remove Plus! are the most popular titles.

## All in one

Other types of program that are sold separately include back-up tools, anti-virus scanners and crash preventers, but these facilities are often provided in the all-in-one products, too. Programs like SystemSuite and SystemWorks incorporate more than 50 separate utilities to diagnose and repair PC problems. Many of these are preventative and if used judiciously will stop problems occurring. But you'll also find recovery and file management tools, along with diagnostic procedures.

### Internet tip

Several tools and utilities that are supplied with the Windows CD-ROM can also be downloaded for free from Microsoft's Web site.

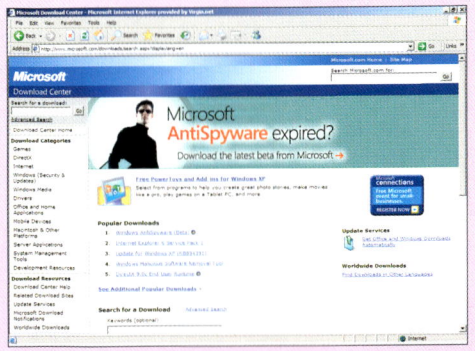

The Microsoft Windows **download site** is at www.microsoft.com/downloads/

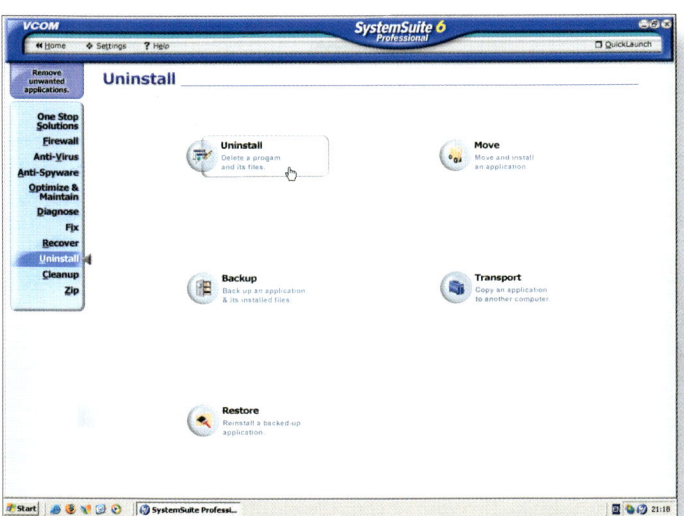

**Uninstall**, also part of Symantec's SystemSuite, is one of many programs designed to uninstall Windows programs cleanly and thoroughly. It works best when it's installed early in the life of a PC and is then used to monitor the installation of the other programs.

### Dead PCs

● If your PC is totally silent and there's not even a power light on the front, check the plugs and fuses and make sure the mains switch is turned on at the wall.

● Test the power cable by swapping it for another one. Most monitors use cables that are interchangeable with PCs, as do other items of household equipment including kettles.

● If the computer remains dead you h… defective power supply, whi…

● A PC that beeps when i… then locks up has a hardwa… loose chip, expansion card o… but it could also indicate a fa… Remedies include replacing int…

# Peripheral problems

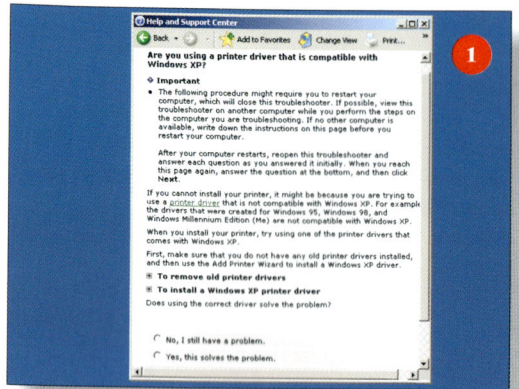

The Windows **Print Troubleshooter**, accessed via the Help and Support Center, leads you by the hand through the minefield of printer testing.

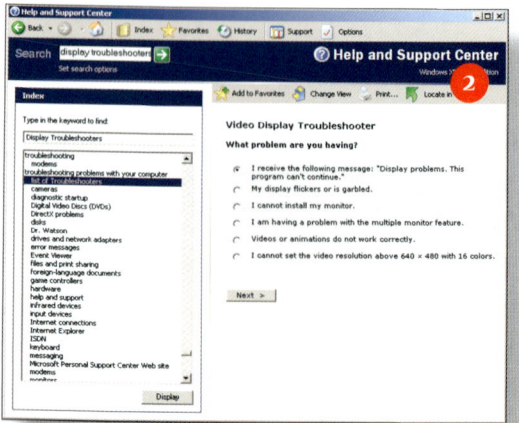

The **Display Troubleshooter** in Windows helps you to get to grips with any monitor and graphics card problems you may have.

**You should take the same care of the devices you plug into your PC as you do of those inside it.**

### Printer

Printers cause more problems than other peripheral devices. They are more likely to suffer a mechanical defect than the rest of the system because they have more moving parts, and they rely on a stable Windows installation and correct BIOS settings.

There are two printer troubleshooters built into Windows, but they don't tell you how to take care of your printer and the importance of checking the BIOS settings in your PC (1). Printers are designed for use by Windows and they have sophisticated printer drivers offering a number of output options. Advanced printer drivers rely on communication between the printer and the PC and can thus provide estimates of how much ink or toner is left in the printer and how long a print job will take.

If you are still using a printer that connects to the parallel port on your PC, you need to make sure the port is set to EPP (Enhanced Parallel Port) or to ECP (Enhanced Capabilities Port) in the BIOS. Refer to your printer manual for the settings

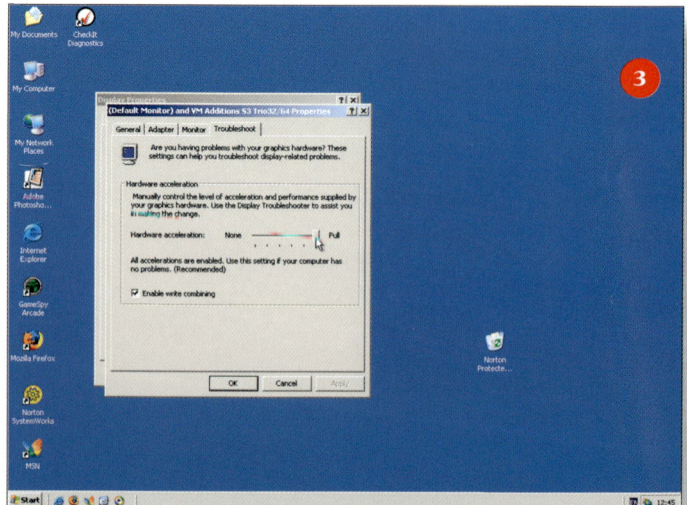

Right-click on the Desktop to view Display Properties. If the monitor and graphics card are correctly identified, adjust the **Hardware Acceleration**. Click on the Settings tab, then on the Advanced button then on the Troubleshoot tab. (In Windows Me and 98, the Performance tab.)

# TROUBLESHOOTING BASICS

for your printer and to your PC manual for advice on changing BIOS settings. The usual method is to hold down the Delete key during the boot sequence.

Printers also need some mechanical care. Dust from paper can clog up mechanisms. Every type of printer requires some kind of maintenance. Lasers have toner waste bottles to empty, fuser pads to change and corona wires to clean. Inkjets tend to sublimate vapourised ink, which must be removed. Even simple dot-matrix printers eventually require pulverised ribbon waste to be vacuumed away.

## Monitor

Problems with monitors almost always stem from inappropriate Windows settings and may be caused by a poorly configured graphics card. If your monitor is inert and you have checked the cables, switches and fuses, you probably have a hardware failure on your hands, but if you've got any sort of picture at all the chances are it can be improved by tweaking the settings in Windows (**2**).

Most graphics problems are caused by the wrong display adapter and monitor settings in Display Properties (**3**). If these are OK – the settings relate to the names on the box – the problem is almost certainly related to Microsoft DirectX. This is one of Microsoft's ongoing projects to turn Windows into a games platform. Use the DirectX Diagnostics Tool. Go to the Start menu, choose All Programs, then Accesories, System Tools, then click on System Information. On the Tools menu click on DirectX Diagnostic Tool and then on the DirectX Files tab. Any problems appear in the space at the bottom (**4**). If there is a problem, reinstall from the most recent copy of DirectX available. Look for the files on Windows games CDs, on magazine cover disks and at www.microsoft.com on the Internet.

## Practical Considerations

Keep mice and keyboards clean (see page 115). If you're having problems with sound, don't blame your speakers apart from checking that they're properly connected, but do make sure you've got them plugged into the Speaker output of your soundcard. If you have amplified speakers and the output is distorted, try plugging the speakers into the Line Out instead of the speaker jack.

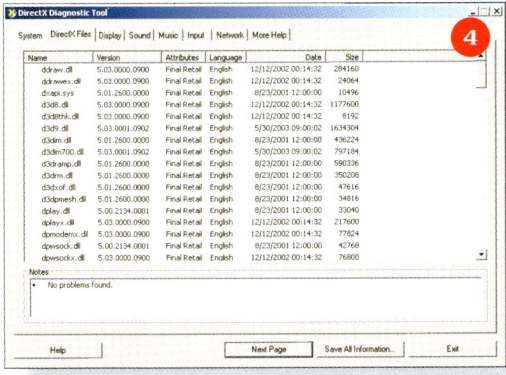

There are two simple rules to follow regarding **DirectX**. If it's working, do not under any circumstances change it. If it isn't, reinstall it from the latest version you can lay your hands on.

## Troubleshooting

Windows Help includes up to 17 troubleshooters. The exact number depends on how recent a version of Windows you have. The troubleshooters are in the main part of Windows Help and Support Center (accessible through the Start button). Enter troubleshooting as the keyword in the Search box and click on the green arrow to find them. Most people are more familiar with the Help systems built into their applications than the one in Windows, so the troubleshooters are often ignored. However, they're all good, and several of them are directly related to solving problems with peripherals – such as one for printing and another for modems. The troubleshooters use a practical question and answer approach that leads you to the cause of the problem.

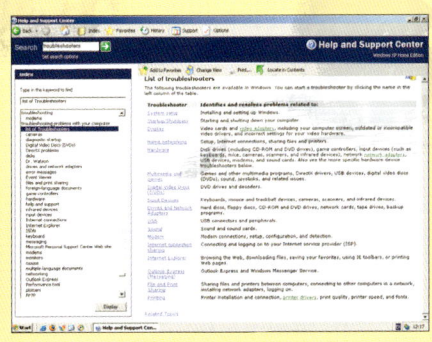

Whenever you have a problem with Windows, check the Help Center's **troubleshooters** first.

# Anti-virus tools

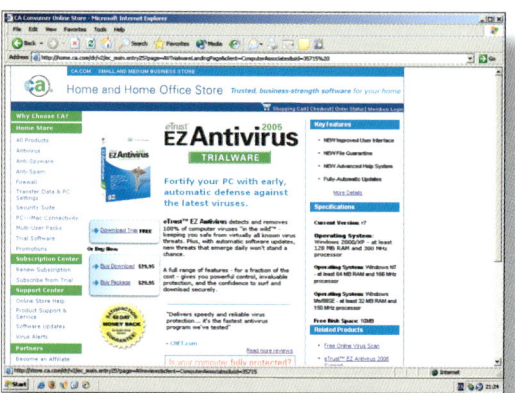

**EZ Antivirus** from Computer Associates is just one of the anti-virus programs available.

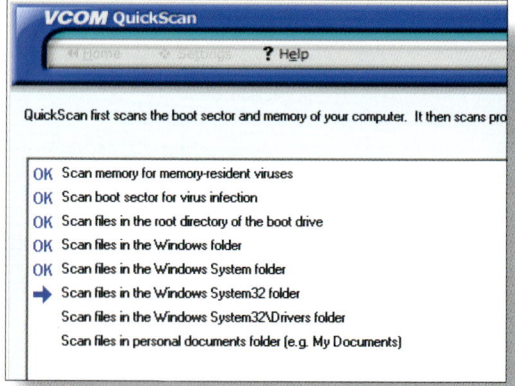

**SystemSuite's** anti-virus has several levels of scan from the quick system scan to a complete check of your computer.

## Viruses pose a genuine threat to PCs, but anti-virus programs can give you peace of mind.

Viruses may hit the headlines only occasionally, but they are an ever-present threat to PC users. For the novice, the only safe way of tackling them is with a commercial anti-virus program.

Early anti-virus programs found a virus on your hard disk only after you'd been attacked by one. Current products prevent contamination in the first place. Should a virus try to install itself on your system, the program will warn you and help you to deal with it. Even if you've been attacked by a virus it's not too late. Provided you follow the instructions of an anti-virus program scrupulously, most can detect an infestation and remove it.

### Dealing with a virus

If you have an anti-virus program installed and a virus tries to copy itself onto your PC's hard disk, the anti-virus program should detect the activity and prevent the virus from attacking. In the case of a pre-existing virus infestation, an anti-virus program might be able to remove the virus with no harm to the system, but there is a possibility that, in removing the virus, some program files will be altered. It's advisable to reinstall any software that does not work properly after a virus clean-up.

If you have a back-up that you know to be good, use it. Scan every removable disk you have and contact anybody with whom you exchange disks to get them to check theirs. For more information on viruses see pages 99–108.

### Minimise virus risks

- Most anti-virus programs can be updated free of charge for a period of up to 12 months. Make full use of the update service for maximum protection.

- An anti-virus program is not a substitute for regular back-ups.

- Don't use floppy disks from unknown or untrustworthy sources.

- Schedule a weekly or monthly virus scan to supplement your anti-virus program's background protection, which may not be as thorough as a comprehensive disk scan.

# Error messages

## Understanding error messages helps you to solve problems if Windows does not work properly.

When we make a mistake while using Windows, the system displays an error message. It may be that you've tried to carry out an impossible task — such as copying files to a CD-ROM drive without a disk in it, or there could be a fault with software or the PC itself.

### Fixing problems

Windows will tell you what has gone wrong and, in many cases, what action you need to take to correct the error. If there's a problem with the software, or a system error, the cause may be hard to find and the solution outside your control — for instance, you can't fix a bug in a program unless a software update for it is available. Fortunately, many errors are easy to put right and it's a good idea to familiarise yourself with some of the more common error messages and solutions to problems.

## Understanding error messages

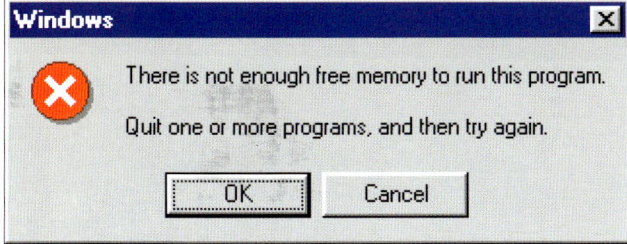

**There is not enough free memory to run this program. Quit one or more programs, and then try again.**

This message appears if there's not enough memory to run a program. Closing other programs often solves the problem. However, if the error occurs often, there may not be enough virtual memory available. Select System on the Control Panel, click on the Advanced tab, then on the Settings button in the Performance Options section. Select the Advanced tab and in the Virtual Memory section click on the Change button. (In Windows Me and 98 click on Performance in the System control panel, then Virtual Memory.) In Windows XP, make sure the Maximum size is well above the Recommended size. (In Windows Me and 98 virtual memory has no maximum size.) If no limit is specified, check the figure after Space Available – virtual memory will need at least 100MB to run well.

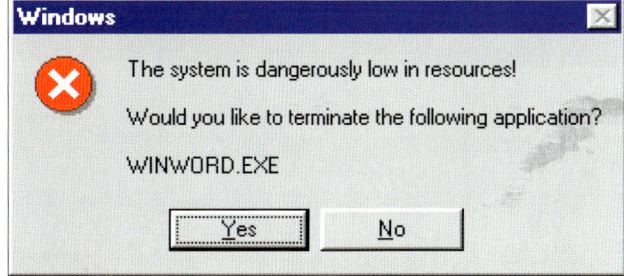

**The system is dangerously low in resources! Would you like to terminate the following application? <application name>.**

The cause of this error may be similar to the preceding one. Alternatively, it could be that other applications have used memory but not freed it up after use to make it available for other programs to use. This error usually occurs when you are using several programs at the same time — for example, writing something in a word processor while researching using a Web browser. Try to save your work, if necessary closing any applications as safely as you can to recover sufficient memory to do so.

Once you have saved your work, restart Windows before continuing. This will allow Windows to recover any memory that has been lost temporarily.

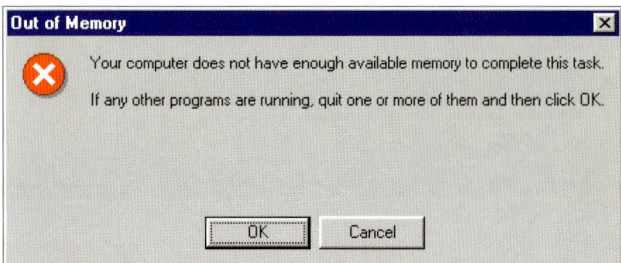

**Out of memory. Your computer does not have enough available memory to complete this task. If any other programs are running, quit one or more of them and then click OK.**

This message can be a little misleading. It usually means that Windows cannot find a suitably large block of memory in the place where the program needs it to be, rather than meaning that there is no free memory at all. Closing other programs may free enough memory to solve the problem. If that does not work, restart Windows and then repeat the operation that caused the error to see if the problem has been resolved.

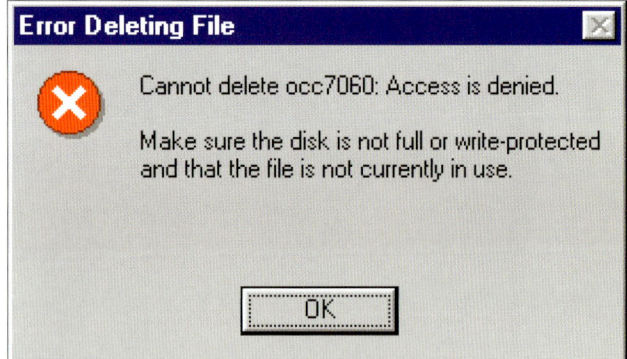

**Access is denied. Make sure the disk is not full or write-protected and that the file is not currently in use.**

This message usually occurs if you try to delete, move or rename a file that is in use. Close any applications that may be using the file and this should solve the problem. In rare cases, the error will persist because the application that was using a file crashed while the file was still open, causing Windows to think that the file is still open. In this case, you may have to restart Windows before you can rename or delete the file.

**The disk in the destination drive is full. Insert a new disk to continue.**

This message occurs if you are copying a group of files to a floppy disk and there is insufficient space on the disk for all the files. If you insert a new floppy disk and click on Retry, Windows will copy the remainder of the files to the new disk.

**The disk is write-protected. Remove the write-protection or use another disk.**

This message is fairly self-explanatory. You are copying files to a floppy disk and the write-protect tab is enabled. To enable you to write to the disk, remove it from the drive and slide the tab on the back until the write protection hole is covered. Then reinsert the disk and click on Retry.

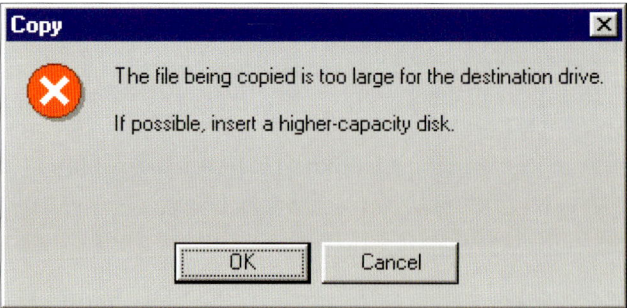

**The file being copied is too large for the destination drive. If possible, insert a higher-capacity disk.**

This means that the file you are trying to copy is larger than the target drive (around 700MB in the case of a CD-ROM). Windows cannot split the file across two or more disks, therefore the only solution to this problem is to use a third-party utility, for example a compression utility such as WinZip, to decrease the file size.

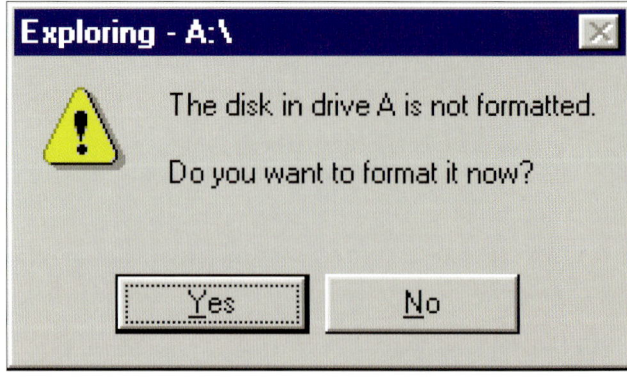

**The disk in drive <drive> is not formatted. Do you want to format it now?**

The drive referred to here is usually the floppy drive or a removable disk drive. The disk must be formatted before you can read or write to it. To format a floppy disk, right-click on the A: drive in Explorer and select Format from the menu. However, if you know that the disk already contains information, the error could be the result of a malfunction, such as a faulty floppy drive or the internal data cable coming loose. In this case, try the disk in a different computer before formatting it, because formatting a disk will destroy any information already on it.

# TROUBLESHOOTING BASICS     71

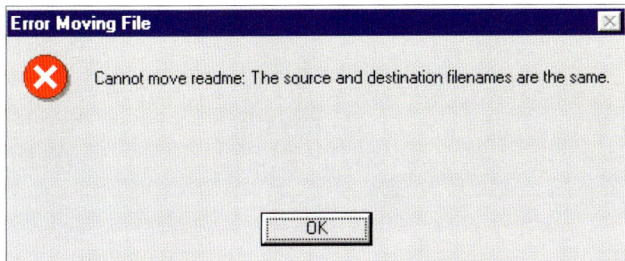

**Cannot move <filename>: The source and destination filenames are the same.**
**Cannot move <filename>: The destination folder is the same as the source folder.**

These messages appear if you try to copy or move a file or folder to itself. It is easy to make this mistake using drag and drop in Explorer. Just copy or move the file or folder to a different location.

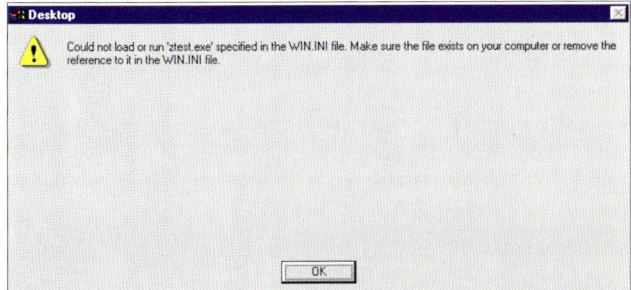

**Could not load or run <filename> specified in the WIN.INI file. Make sure the file exists on your computer or remove the reference to it in the WIN.INI file.**

This message will appear if a program has added its name to the load= or run= line in Win.ini, in order to be run automatically at startup, and the program has subsequently been moved or deleted. Either reinstall the program or open the Run box on the Start menu, type 'sysedit' and remove the reference in the Win.ini file.

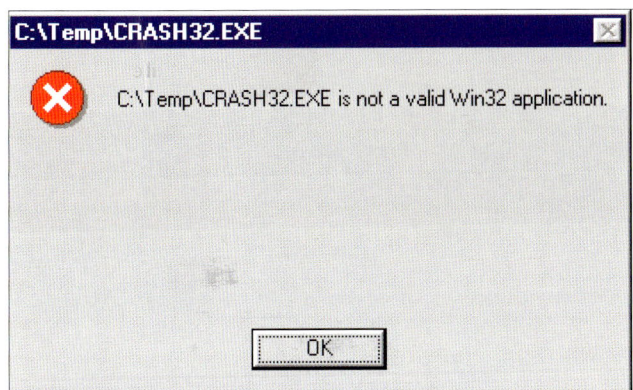

**<filename> is not a valid Win32 application.**

This error means that the program you are trying to run is corrupted. This could be as a result of a disk error – so check your disk for errors using the chkdsk command in the Command Prompt window. (See pages 89-90.) Alternatively, you might have copied or renamed a non-program file to a filename with an .exe (executable file) extension. Delete the file and, if it is a program that you need, restore it from a backup copy or reinstall it from the original Setup disk – this time without adding the .exe extension.

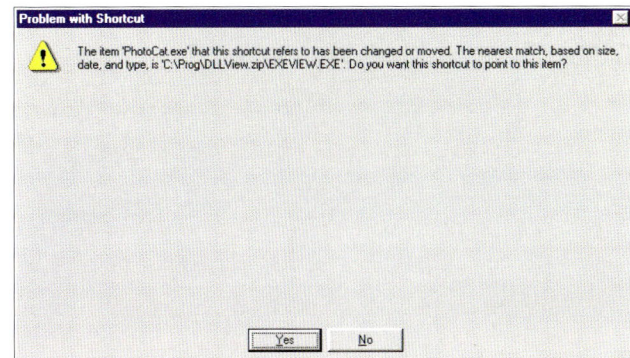

**The item <filename> that this shortcut refers to has been changed or moved. The nearest match, based on size, date and type, is <filename>. Do you want this shortcut to point to this item?**

This message usually appears after a program has been uninstalled or deleted but the shortcut used to run the program hasn't been removed. Windows attempts to locate the file that the shortcut should be pointing to, but cannot do so. You should either reinstall the missing application from its original disk, or delete the unwanted shortcut.

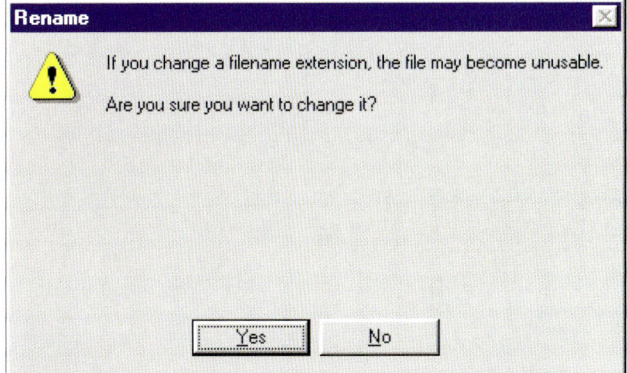

**If you change a filename extension, the file may become unusable. Are you sure you want to change it?**

If you try to rename a file using Explorer, Windows may display this message. The reason is usually that you are changing the file's extension – the three characters after the dot at the end of the filename that tell Windows what type of file it is. This is how Windows knows what application to use to open the file. If you change these three characters, Windows will either use a program that cannot read the file properly, or will not know what program to use. If you are not sure what effect your change will have, click on No so that Windows will ignore your change. You can still go back and change it later if necessary.

## Jargon buster

**Illegal operation** When a program performs an illegal operation, all it means is that the program has done something that the computer thinks it shouldn't have. Examples of illegal operations include protection faults, where a program tries to access a protected block of memory belonging to another program or Windows itself, and exceptions – errors made by the software as it runs the program. Stack faults can also occur when a program fills up the amount of space reserved for temporary data storage.

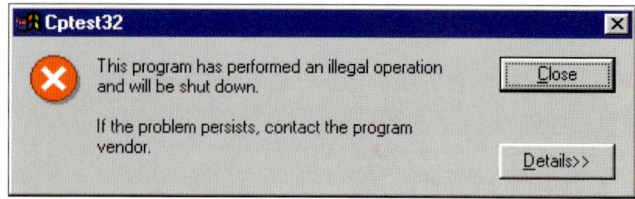

**Cannot find a device file that may be needed to run Windows or a Windows application.**
**The Windows registry or SYSTEM.INI file refers to this device file, but the device file no longer exists.**
**If you deleted this file on purpose, try uninstalling the associated application using its uninstall program or setup program.**
**If you still want to use the application associated with this device file, try reinstalling that application to replace the missing file.**
**<filename>**
**Press any key to continue**

If this message appears, it will be displayed in text mode during startup. When you press a key as instructed, Windows may continue loading, and run normally. However, having to do this every time Windows starts up is annoying.

This message occurs because a device driver that Windows is instructed to load in one of its configuration files has been deleted. Usually, this is because you have deleted some files manually using Explorer or an uninstaller utility, instead of using Add or Remove Programs in the Control Panel, and have accidentally deleted some vital files. If you know the identity of the program you deleted, reinstalling it should stop the error from appearing.

If Windows runs normally without this file, you can try removing the instruction to load it from the configuration files. Run Sysedit, select System.ini and search for the filename shown in the message. If it appears, delete the line containing it.

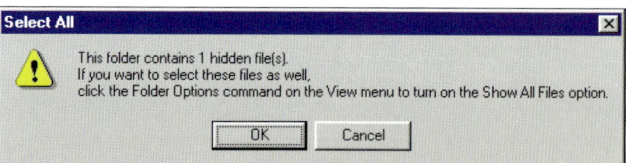

**This program has performed an illegal operation and will be shut down. If the problem persists, contact the program vendor.**

This error is one of the most common and is often the result of a program bug. If you can make the error occur by carrying out a specific sequence of actions, then it is definitely a bug and you should report it to the software vendor. If you are lucky, you may be able to get a software update that doesn't contain the bug.

If the error occurs frequently, seemingly at random, and if it affects a number of different programs, then it could be caused by faulty memory, an overheating processor or some other system malfunction, rather than a software bug.

Click on the Details button and you will see some diagnostic information that may help to determine the cause of the problem. To make a record of the information, highlight it with the mouse, copy it to the Clipboard, paste it into Notepad, then print it out. You can then try to solve the error.

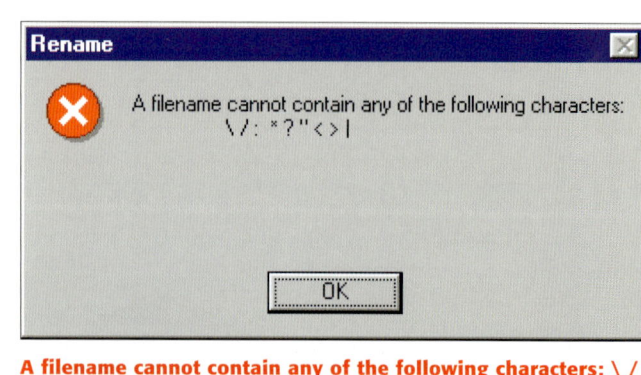

**This folder contains <n> hidden file(s). If you want to select these files as well, click the Folder Options command on the View menu to turn on the Show All Files option.**

This is another fairly self-explanatory message. Windows allows files to have a hidden attribute, which means that by default they are not shown in the file listings in Explorer. Files are usually hidden because they are for use by an application, not by the user, and hiding them helps to protect them from being tampered with.

If you use Edit, Select All to select all of the files in a folder, so as to move or copy them to another location or to delete them, and there are hidden files in the folder that Explorer is not showing, it will display this message. To delete, move or copy the hidden files, you must first go to Folder Options in Explorer's Tools menu and, on the View tab, choose to Show Hidden Files and Folders.

**A filename cannot contain any of the following characters: \ / : * ? " < > |**

This message is self-explanatory. You cannot use any of the characters shown when copying or renaming a file.

# DIY fixes

## Keeping your device drivers up to date will eliminate many of the problems you have with Windows.

Whenever you add a new piece of hardware to your computer, such as a graphics card or soundcard, Windows installs a driver program for it. The purpose of this software is to control the hardware device. It would be impossible for Windows to offer support for every device available, and using updatable drivers is a way of dealing with any problems that may arise.

### Download the latest version

Few device drivers are perfect and some cause problems for Windows. But the good news is that you can keep replacing problem drivers by paying regular visits to the hardware manufacturers' web sites, where you will find the latest versions of the relevant drivers. You can then download and install the new device drivers on to your system to try to fix any technical problems you may have encountered.

Windows Update will check if any new drivers are available. However, it will only check those that have been certified as Windows-compatible.

To keep your device drivers properly up to date you will have to do some of the work. A good place to start is with your graphics card, 3D accelerator and soundcard drivers.

## How to replace drivers

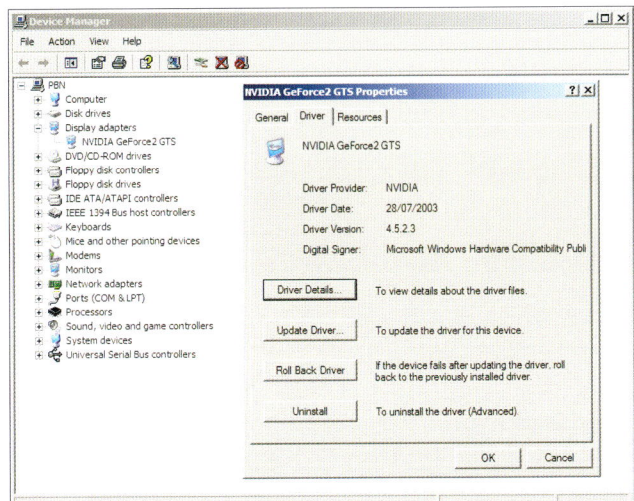

**1** The first thing to do is to find out the **version numbers** of the device drivers your PC is using at present. The quickest way to do this is through the Device Manager. Select it by right-clicking My Computer, choosing Properties and then clicking on the Hardware tab (this is the Device Manager tab in previous versions of Windows). Scroll down the hardware list and open a device by clicking on the + symbol. Select the device and click on Properties. Click on the Driver tab and then on the Driver Details button. This lists the Provider (manufacturer) and the File version. Here NVIDIA is the manufacturer, the graphics card is a GeForce2 GTS and the driver version is 4.5.2.3.

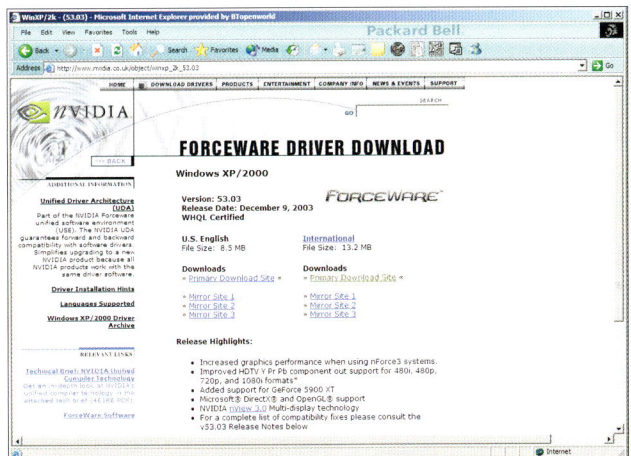

**2** It's a good idea to create a **Notepad document** listing the name, manufacturer and version number for each device on your system. This means you'll have all the current driver data in one place whenever you need to check it, and you'll be able to update the list easily when you install a new driver.

To locate a new driver, go to the manufacturer's web site and look for keywords such as support, drivers or downloads. (If you don't know the precise URL, use a search engine such as Yahoo.)

This is the NVIDIA web page that has the latest drivers for the GeForce card. By checking the version numbers, you can see that a later version of the driver is available. Create a Favorites sub-folder called Driver Updates and add the URL of the site to this to make it easier for you to return to the page to check for later versions.

# SOLVING PROBLEMS

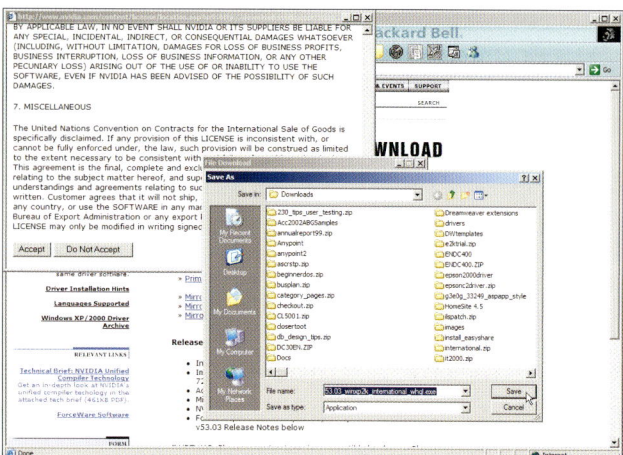

**3** To **download** the new driver, click on its file name. In the File Download dialogue box that appears, select the Save option and click on OK. Select a location for the file to be saved to and click on the Save button. Now select the Primary Download site for the International version of the driver and then click on Accept in the Licence Agreement window that appears.

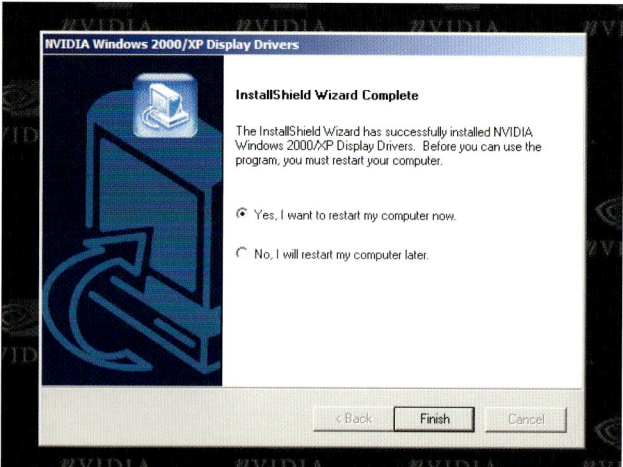

**4** To simplify downloading, the various driver files are archived in a single file. Double-click on the file to start the **Installation Wizard**. You will be asked to turn off any anti-virus software before starting and will have to restart the PC to complete the installation. Most drivers are supplied as self-unpacking executables, which means the archived driver files will be unpacked automatically during installation. Some drivers, however, may be supplied as compressed .zip files, which means you'll have to unzip – or expand – them using a utility program, such as PKZip or WinZip. Unzip the files to a temporary folder, such as c:\downloads.

## Unzip tip

There are several ways to unzip a file, but one of the quickest is to right-click on the downloaded zip file and choose from the options on the pop-up menu. For example, using WinZip you can select simply to unzip the files, or extract them to a default named folder, or even choose which folder you'd like the unzipped folders to be placed in.

**5** Now you're ready to update the drivers. Go to the Start menu and click on Control Panel. Then click on Performance and Maintenance and select System. Choose the Hardware tab and click on the Device Manager button. Now you need to find the device where the driver needs updating. Right-click on the name of the device from the list in the Explorer window. Click on Properties then on the Driver tab. Click on the **Update Driver** button to launch the Hardware Update Wizard (the Update Device Driver Wizard in earlier versions of Windows).

In Windows XP, select Install From a List or Specific Location and click on Next. Select Include This Location in the Search.

In Windows Me, select Specify the Location of the Driver.

In Windows 98, select No, Select Driver From List and click on Next. Select Display a List of Drivers, click on Next and then on the Have Disk button.

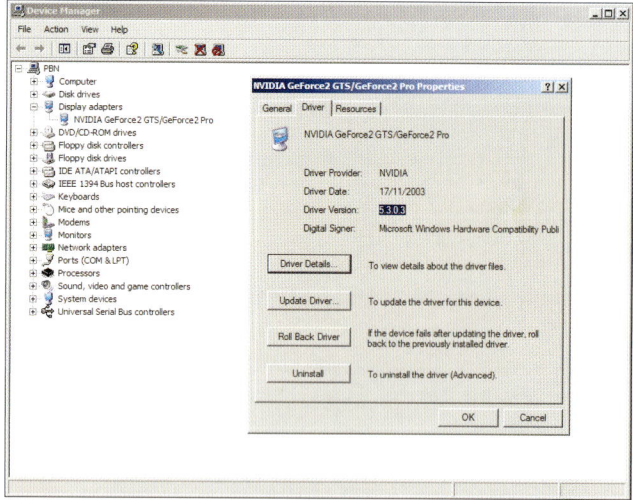

**6** Now you can specify where to **locate** the updated drivers or use the Browse button to find a location. In this case, type C:\downloads. Click on Next and the driver software will be installed. Click on the Finish button to close the Wizard. You'll need to restart your PC at this point. If the driver is older than the one currently installed, the Wizard will tell you and allow you to choose other drivers from the list previously displayed.

As you can see from the changed Driver Version number shown, the new driver has been successfully installed. If subsequent problems arise you can, with Windows XP, go back to the previous working version of the driver. Repeat the process described in step 5 to get back to the Properties window of the device. Then select the Roll Back Driver button from the Driver tab of the hardware device you're changing.

# Managing devices

**If your components refuse to work together, turn to the Device Manager for help.**

One of the strengths of a PC is its modular nature — you can install and remove different hardware components and software programs for any task you have in mind. Standardised features and connections mean that most devices will work together without problems, but occasionally components may conflict, or fail to detect each other. When they do this, Windows should recognise the problem and report the error, allowing you to correct it by adjusting a few system settings.

## Sorting out hardware conflicts

**1** When Windows detects a problem with a device, whether it is external or internal, the problem is flagged in the **Device Manager**. If a printer, soundcard or other device isn't working, and you've checked the connection to your PC and the power cable, look to see whether Windows has noticed a problem by opening Device Manager. The quickest way to access it is to right-click on My Computer, then select Properties and click on the Device Manager button on the Hardware tab (in earlier versions of Windows, simply select the Device Manager tab). You can also access the Device Manager via the Control Panel, as described on page 74. The Device Manager uses an Explorer-style method of showing you the different kinds of devices being used by your PC. Some of the items on the list are straightforward, but for others you will need to click on the + sign next to the icon in order to see a complete list of the different devices associated with that aspect of your computer's function. If there is a problem with a device, an exclamation mark in a circle appears next to its icon.

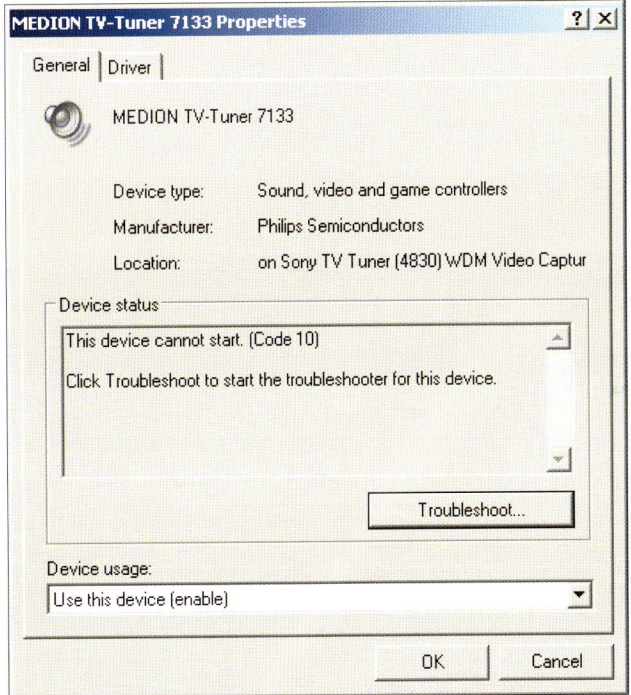

**2** Highlight the problem device and choose **Properties** from the Action menu (click on the Properties button in previous versions of Windows). The General tab of the Properties dialogue box includes a Device Status panel, with a brief description of the problem, an error code and a suggested solution. If your computer is running Windows XP, click on the Troubleshoot… button to launch the Windows Help and Support Centre. A full description of Device Manager error codes and suggested solutions is provided in the Fact File on the next page.

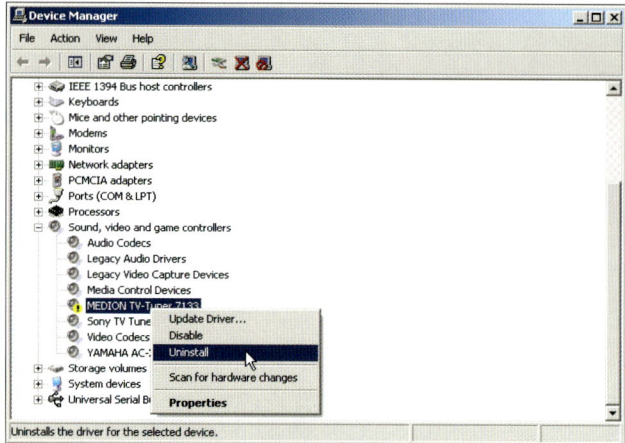

**3** For many errors reported in Device Manager, Microsoft recommends uninstalling and reinstalling the device drivers. In Windows XP, highlight the problem device, right-click on it and select **Uninstall**. In the Confirm Device Removal dialogue box that follows, click on OK. Close Device Manager and restart Windows. If the device uses plug and play (most do), Windows should detect it during restart, and install the correct drivers. If this doesn't happen, run the Add Hardware (Add New Hardware in previous versions of Windows) Wizard from the Control Panel.

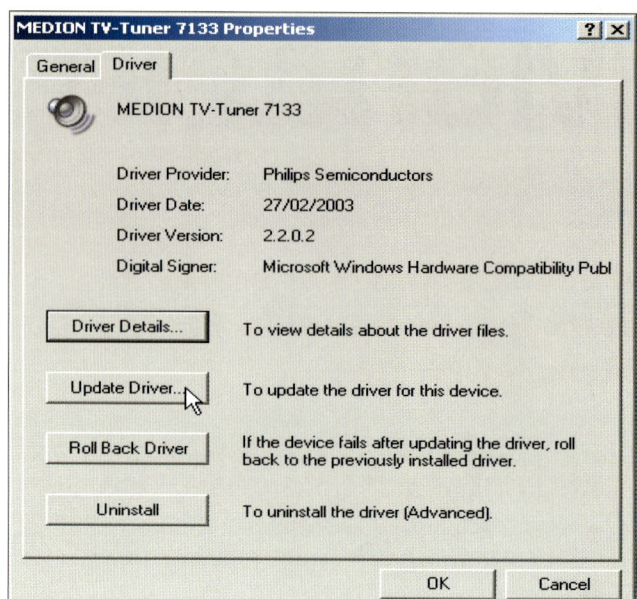

**4** If reinstalling the device driver doesn't help, there may be a problem in the driver software, or a hardware problem, such as incompatibility. You can get the latest version of the driver by clicking the **Update Driver** button on the Driver tab in Device Manager, but unfortunately, hardware problems cannot usually be overcome except by replacing the component.

## Fact file

The following is a list of the Device Manager error codes with suggestions of how to resolve them.

**Code 1** The system has not had a chance to configure the device.
**Code 2** The device loader failed to load a device.
**Code 3** The system has run out of memory.
**Code 4** The set-up information (.inf) file for this device is incorrect.
**Code 5** A device needs something that Windows does not know how to supply.
**Code 11** The device failed.
**Code 19** The registry returned an unknown result.
**Code 20** The loader for the device driver software returned an unknown result. This could be caused by a version mismatch between the device driver and the operating system.
**Code 23** The device loader delayed the start of a device and failed to inform Windows when it was ready to start the device.
● For these codes the recommended solution is to update the driver.

**Code 8** The loader for a device could not be found. The set-up information file for this device may refer to a missing or invalid file.
**Code 13** The device failed due to a problem in the device driver.
**Code 17** This is a multiple-function device and the set-up information file contains invalid instructions on how to split the resources between functions.
● For these codes, try removing the device and then reinstalling it using the Add Hardware Wizard. If that fails, contact the manufacturer of the device for an updated set-up information file.

**Code 6** There's a conflict between this device and another device.
**Code 12** The device requested a resource that was not available, perhaps because it is in use by another device or because the system is out of resources.
**Code 15** The device has a resource conflict with another device.
● For these codes, follow the advice in Windows Help under Troubleshooting Conflicting Hardware.

**Code 7** Windows cannot configure this device. (If it works correctly, you can ignore this error.)
**Code 18** An error occurred and the device must be reinstalled.
**Code 26** The device failed to load. There may be a problem with the device driver, such as the file being corrupted.
**Code 27** The part of the registry describing possible resources for a device is inconsistent.
**Code 28** The device was not installed completely.
● For these codes, try removing the device from Device Manager and reinstalling it. If this fails, obtain an updated driver.

**Code 10** The device failed to start. It may be missing or not working properly, or its drivers may be incorrectly installed.
**Code 24** The device was not found.
● If these codes are reported for an external device, check the connections and power to the device. If you can't see why it isn't working, try removing it from Device Manager and then reinstalling it using the Add Hardware Wizard.

**Code 14/Code 21** Both of these codes indicate that a problem was found that might be resolved by shutting down and then restarting your PC.
**Code 16** The device was not fully detected by Windows. Not all of its resources may be recorded. To resolve this problem, click the Resources tab of the Device Properties dialogue box and enter the resource settings manually.
**Code 22** The device is disabled in this configuration. You should enable it by unchecking the Disable in this Hardware Profile check box in the Device Usage panel on the Properties page.
**Code 29** This device has been disabled because it does not work properly with Windows. If you see this code, contact the device manufacturer for advice.

# Monitoring your PC

### Ensure your computer has sufficient resources in order to keep it running smoothly.

Although Windows XP is much better than earlier versions of Windows at making the most of its resources, all versions can be pushed to the limit. Running too many programs together or having inadequate memory for the task in hand can cause the PC to slow right down, or the mouse to start moving erratically. By this point it may be too late to take any corrective action and the computer may crash, causing you to lose your work.

Fortunately, Windows comes with its own built-in tools to monitor your PC's performance. These show you where there are problems so you can take preventative measures, whether it's turning off features in Windows that are eating up resources, or upgrading your computer with more memory or a faster processor.

### Fact file

Windows System Monitor displays information about the system as a graph, bar chart or as raw data. To access it in Windows XP, select Control Panel from the Start menu, then click on Performance under Administrative Tools. Windows Me and 98 have a slightly different version, run from the Accessories folder on the Programs menu. Here you will also find the System Resource Meter, which runs as an icon in the System Tray and gives details of various PC resources. The elements System Monitor covers include:

● **Dial-Up Adapter** This logs data about your Net connection. Choose the Bytes Received/Second item to monitor the speed of downloading items from the Web. The error monitors can be useful if you're having trouble with your Internet connection.

● **Disk Cache** A high number of hits shows the disk cache is working well. A high number of misses shows the cache is contributing little to performance. Increasing system memory increases the cache size.

● **File System** This provides information about the quantity of data written and read, and the number of read/write operations.

● **Kernel** Use this to view Processor Usage. If this is often close to 100 per cent, your processor is underpowered.

● **Memory Manager** This shows memory use. Unused Physical Memory shows how much RAM is free. If there's rarely any unused memory, your PC could benefit from more RAM. See how much memory you need by viewing Allocated Memory.

## Viewing system resources

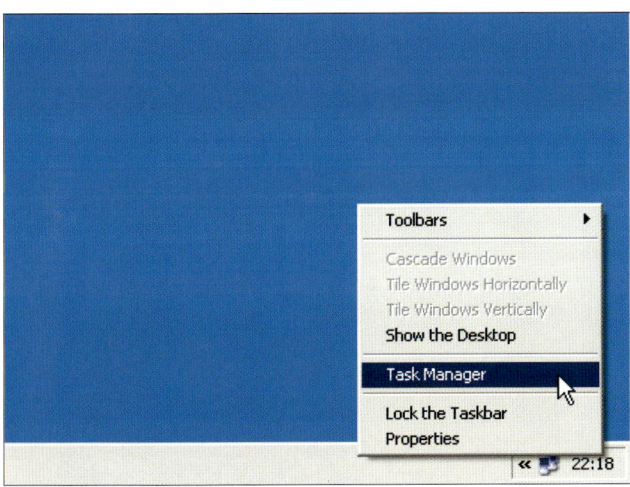

**1** Windows XP uses a utility called the **Task Manager** to monitor its own performance. It can show you how hard the main processor, or CPU, is working, which programs are in use and which processes are taking up your system resources. You'll be surprised how many there are. To open Task Manager simply press Ctrl+Alt+Del or right-click on the Taskbar and select Task Manager from the pop-up list.

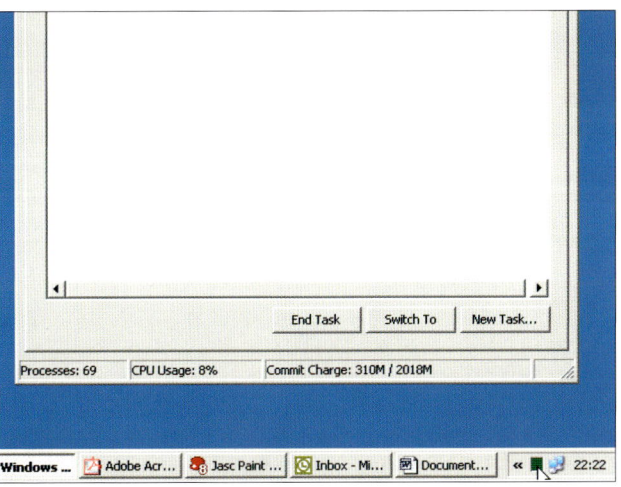

**2** A program window for the Windows Task Manager opens and a small icon with a green graph-style background appears in the **notification area** of the Taskbar. Light green bars on the icon indicate what percentage of the CPU is being used. To get the exact percentage, hover your pointer over the icon. The percentage is also shown in the status bar at the bottom of the Task Manager.

# SOLVING PROBLEMS

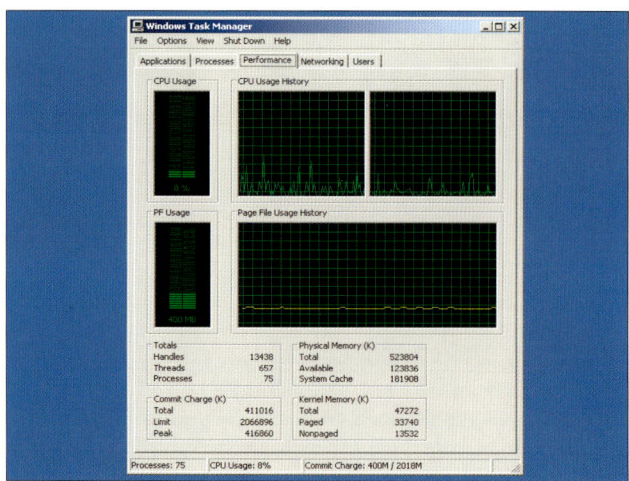

**3** Click on the **Performance** tab in the Windows Task Manager window and you'll see a chart plotting the highs and lows in CPU Usage. This can often highlight any problems with your PC. For instance, if the CPU reading is consistently high then you probably need to upgrade your memory. Although there will always be some movement in the graph, even when the computer is idle, if there is a particularly high reading and the mouse movement seems a bit slow, there is probably a problem with a particular program.

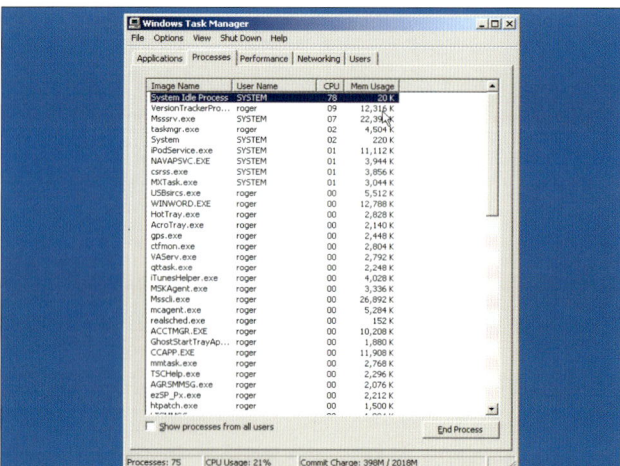

**4** Select the **Processes** tab. Click twice on the CPU heading so the processes that have the highest score – that is, those that are making greatest use of the processor – are shown at the top of the list. If the System Idle Process doesn't have a number from 0 to 99, then another process is interfering with it. (For example, programs that edit photographs or videos require a lot of processing power to carry out their tasks.) You need to close this process down. Look for a process with a high CPU score, and try closing it by highlighting it in the list and then clicking on the End Process button. If that doesn't work, you may need to restart the computer.

## Jargon buster

**System Idle Process** A measure used in the Windows Task Manager to calculate how much of the CPU is not in use at any given moment. The number appearing in the list on the Process tab represents the percentage of the CPU that is idle.

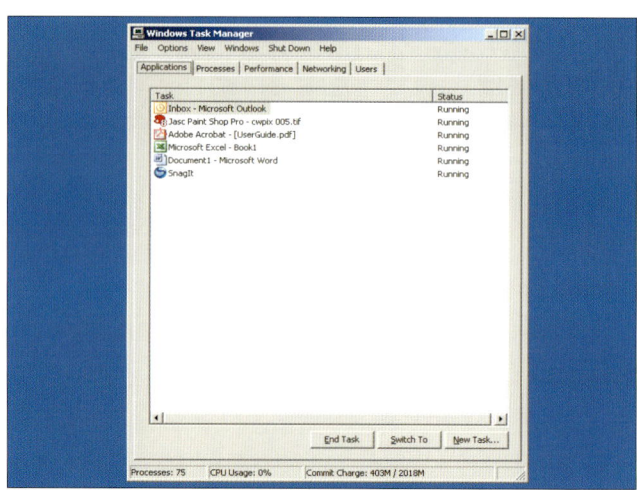

**5** The Task Manager can also help if **Windows freezes**, perhaps when you've tried to launch a program. In Windows XP each program works using its own bit of memory, so if it crashes it's not as likely to affect the other programs and crash the PC as in the older versions of Windows. As a result, if you close that one program you should be able to carry on working on the PC. To close the program, press Ctrl+Alt+Del and select the Applications tab. Windows lists the programs that are running. It will read Not Responding in the Status column next to the problem program. Select the program and click on End Task.

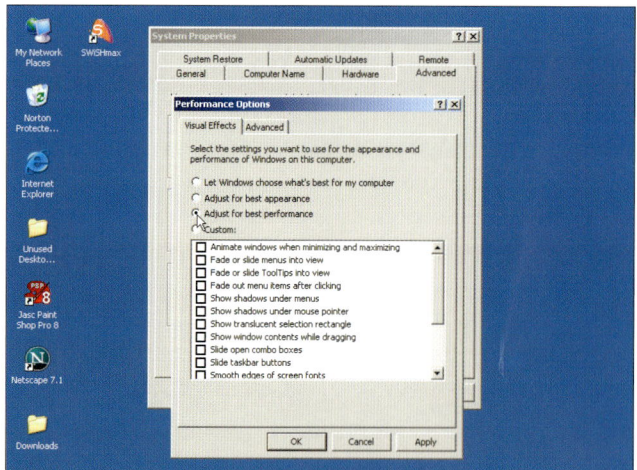

**6** The display effects in Windows, such as drop shadows or fade effects on the menus, all use up processing power and can affect the performance of slower machines. You can let Windows manage these settings itself to **maximise performance**. Access the Performance Options box by right-clicking My Computer, selecting Properties, then choosing the Advanced tab and clicking the Settings button in the Performance section. Select Let Windows Choose What's Best for My Computer from the list that appears on the Visual Effects tab, and Windows will adjust its effects to the available system resources. For older PCs you can achieve the best performance by turning the effects off. To do this, select Adjust for Best Performance.

# Safe Mode startup

## Use Windows' Startup menu to help you avoid startup problems.

Like any complex system, Windows can go wrong. Many computer startup problems are connected to one of the software drivers that Windows loads at startup. Software drivers perform specific tasks or control an item of hardware. Problems can occur when you install new hardware or a new program. In this case, sometimes simply removing the hardware drivers or uninstalling the program gets your computer working normally again. Otherwise, you may have to identify the cause of the problem using a process of elimination.

### Many options

Windows' Startup menu offers a choice of options, one of which should get you into Windows. The first option to try under Windows XP is Last Known Good Configuration. With this option, Windows will restart using the setup saved at the last shutdown – at a time when your settings were still working. The disadvantage is that any new information added since then – a new program, for example – will be lost.

If after resetting your computer to the last working configuration you are still having problems, the next option is to start in Safe Mode. In Safe Mode a very basic version of Windows is launched, with only the bare minimum of drivers needed to run the program. The items in the Startup folder will not be run, just in case it's one of these programs that is causing the problem.

If the computer manages to restart in Safe Mode then you know that the basic operating system itself is all right. From here, you can work with the settings that may be causing the startup problems. If, for example, your computer fails to boot properly after a new program, or driver for a new piece of hardware, is installed, you can restart in Safe Mode and remove the offending software.

### Safe Mode choices

In Windows there are three different Safe Mode options. The most basic setup, called simply Safe Mode, lets you run your mouse, keyboard and monitor and provides access to your hard drive. The second option, Safe Mode with Networking (not available in Windows 98), allows you to access another computer over a network — which is useful if the other computer holds troubleshooting software. The third option, Safe Mode with Command Prompt, should be used only if you are a very confident user and prefer the MS-DOS environment to Windows' more visual approach.

Also found in the Startup menu, Enable Boot Logging is a useful tool for discovering the cause of startup problems. As Windows boots up in any of the three Safe Modes, information about the loading of the drivers and services is logged into a text file. This file can be used to identify startup problems, though it is only really recommended for the expert.

### Restarting tip

If you enter the Startup menu by accident, choose Restart Windows Normally (Normal in Windows 98) to continue booting up Windows.

## Loading Windows in Safe Mode

**1** First, you need to enter the Startup menu. If you have Windows XP, access the menu by holding down the **F8** key while the computer starts up after you have turned it on. In Windows Me, you will need to hold down either the F8 key or the Ctrl key. In Windows 98, hold down the Ctrl key. When the Startup menu appears, release the key. Select Safe Mode and press Enter.

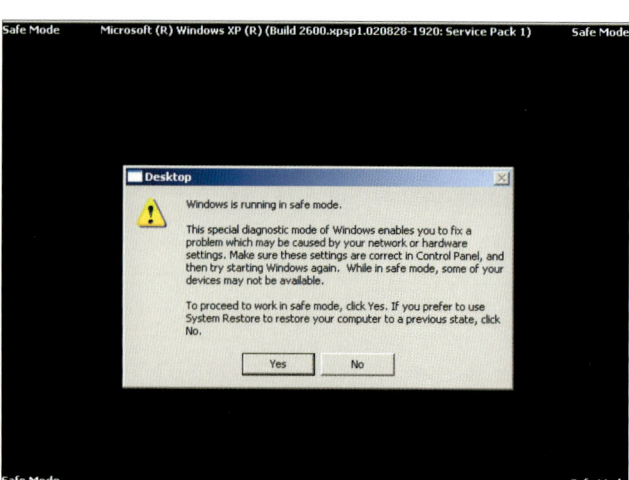

**3** When the list of drivers and files has finished loading, a dialogue box will appear telling you that Windows is running in **Safe Mode**, and asking if you want to continue in this mode. Click the Yes button. (If you'd rather use System Restore to return your computer to a previous state before a driver or piece of software was installed, click No. You can then return to the settings captured at any of the System Restore points you have created.)

**2** At the next screen, choose the operating system from which to boot, for example Microsoft Windows XP Home Edition, and press Enter – for most users there is, in fact, only one option. The drivers and files that are loaded are then shown as a **scrolling log**, or record, of the files as the computer reads them. The log is named ntbtlog.txt (or bootlog.txt in Windows Me and 98). If Windows freezes during this stage of the startup process, look at the last entry appearing in the log. This is likely to be the cause of the problems.

**4** You will now see a basic version of your desktop, although the desktop picture will have been replaced by a black background. A **reminder** is written in each corner of the screen telling you that you are in Safe Mode. You can now start to eliminate any startup problems. Under Safe Mode you can go to the Add or Remove Programs control panel and remove any newly installed program that could be the cause of the problems. You can also run any diagnostic software you have on your PC to help identify problem devices or launch a utilities program, such as Norton Utilities, to check for damaged files or Registry problems that could be preventing your PC from starting properly.

### Command prompt tip

Under MS-DOS the instructions – or commands – telling the operating system what to do have to be typed in. This 'command line' isn't needed with Windows' more graphical approach. However, it can still be accessed and used – for instance, to run old programs, or to run troubleshooter programs. To open the command prompt window in Windows XP click Start, All Programs, then select Accessories and click Command Prompt.

# Startup troubleshooter

**Learn what to do if Windows doesn't launch properly, or shows an error message during startup.**

However carefully you look after your PC, there may be times when it won't start properly. If the screen stays blank, or the PC refuses to start at all, this is most likely to be the result of a hardware fault that can be fixed by checking connections or replacing the problem part.

More commonly, Windows starts to load, but then freezes, or gives you an error message when you reach the desktop. These problems are linked to your software rather than your hardware. There may be a software bug, or a program may be unable to access something it needs, such as memory. Alternatively, the driver (the software that Windows uses to run hardware devices, such as printers) might have a fault. Sometimes conflicts arise with another program that's starting up, while delays in loading Windows may be due to too many services set to run automatically at startup. You can identify, analyse and fix the problems by carrying out a simple series of checks.

## Solve Windows launch problems

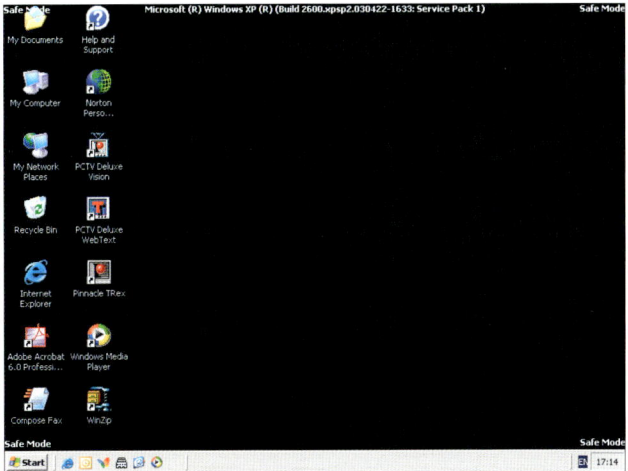

**1** If your **PC freezes** during startup, reboot it by pressing the power switch. Often, Windows will detect that there was a problem last time it started, and automatically launch itself in Safe Mode. If not, you can force Windows to run in Safe Mode by holding down the F8 key while the computer starts up (in Windows Me hold down either the F8 or Ctrl key, and in Windows 98 the Ctrl key). Safe Mode launches a basic version of Windows with a reduced set of drivers. Choose Last Known Good Configuration (your most recent settings that worked) to see if that clears the problem. Alternatively, if you believe you know what's causing the problem – for instance, you may have recently added some new hardware and suspect its driver is to blame – you can select Safe Mode and remove the driver, then restart to launch Windows normally.

### Watch out!

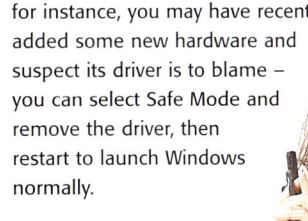

If you've recently installed a new program that you think may be the cause of the startup problem, you can try uninstalling the program to see if that will sort out the glitch. But you should never manually delete a program's files in Windows Explorer as this can do more harm than good – if you delete a program by simply removing its folder, you could delete a file that's needed elsewhere, or leave files in the Registry that cause problems later.

If the program's folder on the Start Menu also contains an Uninstall option, you should always use that to remove the program. Otherwise, use Windows' uninstaller under Add or Remove Programs on the Control Panel. If you have deleted a program folder by accident, try reinstalling the program and then use Windows' uninstaller to remove it properly for you.

# SOLVING PROBLEMS

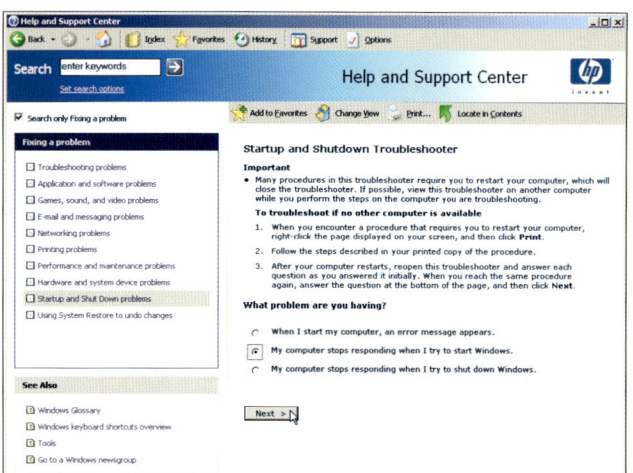

**2** Whether you're in Safe Mode or not, you can get help through the Help and Support Center (or Help in Windows Me and 98), accessed from the Start Menu. Click on Fixing a Problem in the list on the left and you'll be given a list of topics. Select **Startup and Shut Down Problems** (or search for Start & Shutdown Troubleshooter in Windows Me and 98). Click on the link to the Startup and Shutdown Troubleshooter, then select the problem that best describes the difficulties you're having. Follow the on-screen wizard to narrow down the possible solutions.

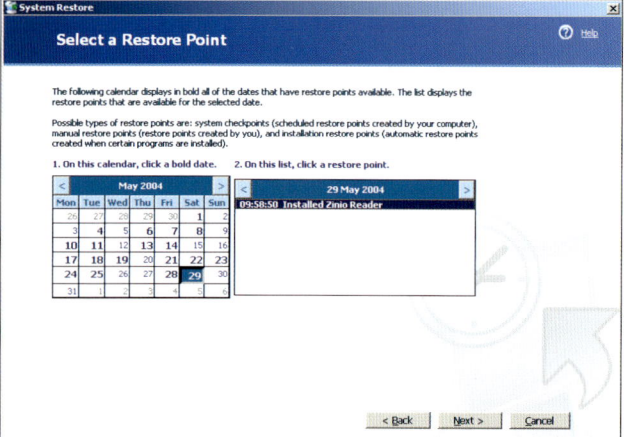

**3** If you changed any settings before the PC stopped working, in Windows XP and Me you can use System Restore to undo the changes. Go to the All Programs menu (Programs on Windows Me) and choose Accessories, System Tools. Follow the wizard to reset your computer to a time it was working properly. Select Restore My Computer to an Earlier Time, click on Next, then on the calendar choose a date in bold – which marks a date when a Restore Point was taken – closest to when you know your PC was working. Select a Restore Point – all changes made to your PC after this date will be reversed. Click on Next and on Next again.

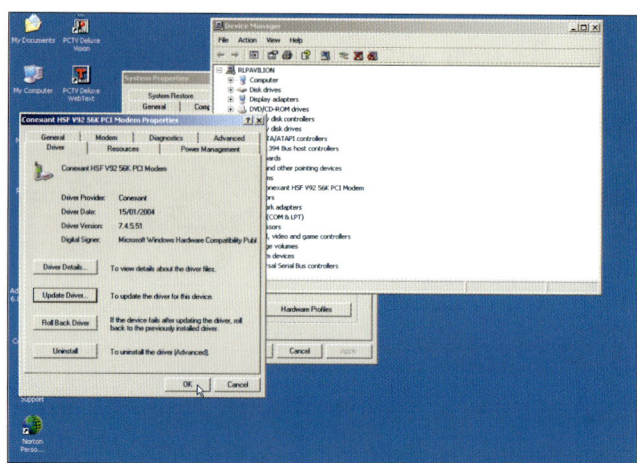

**4** If you suspect a driver for a new piece of hardware is causing the problem, you can check through Device Manager. Right-click on the My Computer icon, click on Properties, and then on the Device Manager button on the Hardware tab (just select the Device Manager tab in Windows Me and 98). Any items displaying a red cross aren't working properly. Right-click on the item to open its Properties panel, and click on the Troubleshoot button. Alternatively, select the Driver tab and click on Update Driver to get the latest version of the driver, if one is available. If it's an updated driver that's causing the problem, you can select Roll Back Driver to revert to an earlier working version.

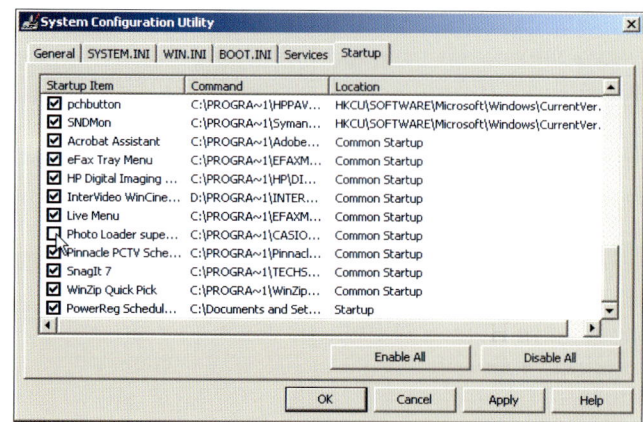

**5** Sometimes, an error message at startup includes the name of the program or file that is causing the problem. On the Start Menu, select Run and type 'msconfig.exe' into the dialogue box that appears. On the various tabs are the lists of drivers, programs, and services that Windows launches during the startup process. Click on the Startup tab and identify the program or file that appeared in the error message and you can then uncheck the box beside it to stop the program or file from running at startup.

## Fact file

Many Windows startup issues ultimately stem from a problem in the Registry – the huge database maintained by Windows that connects the operating system with the other programs loaded on your computer. Manually changing entries in the Registry is risky – doing so could cause Windows to stop working. However, there are several programs available that will automatically check the Registry and fix any problems they find. These include:
- **Registry Healer** at www.fixregistry.com
- **Registry Mechanic** at www.winguides.com
- **Registry FixUp** at www.wyvernworks.com

In addition, utility packages such as Norton Utilities (www.symantec.com) can also fix problems in the Registry.

# Shutdown troubleshooter

**Tackle shutdown problems to make sure Windows will close down properly.**

When the time has come to turn off your computer, it is frustrating if Windows takes ages to shut down, stops responding, or even restarts itself. The major culprits behind slow shutdowns are programs that aren't working as they should. When you click on Turn Off Computer on the Start menu, Windows tells all programs running in the background on your PC to save any information they need and shut down. Normally, this works flawlessly, but sometimes a program refuses to close and Windows has to display a dialogue box asking you to close it manually.

The same problems that cause difficulties during the startup process are often involved in things going wrong during shutdown, and the two topics share the same troubleshooter in the Windows Help and Support Center. Some of the remedies are the same, too — such as running System Restore, or using the System Configuration Utility to disable any troublesome programs from running automatically. Using these procedures, the problems are often easy to identify and resolve.

## Solve shutdown problems

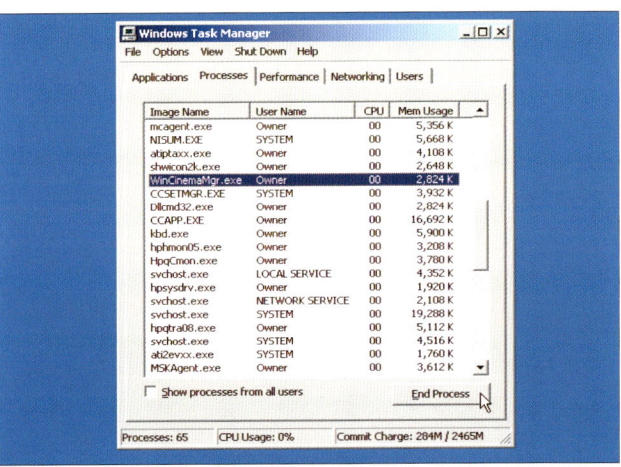

**1** When a program doesn't shut down after a 20-second time limit, Windows displays a **dialogue box** asking if you want to Wait Another 20 Seconds, End the Program Now, or Cancel the Shutdown. If clicking on the End Program Now button doesn't do the trick, you have to force the program to close. Press the Ctrl, Alt and Delete keys at the same time, to bring up Windows Task Manager. If the offending item isn't listed on the Applications tab (for instance, programs that display icons in the System Tray usually aren't), then it will probably be listed under Processes. Find the item and click on End Process and you should be able to shut down.

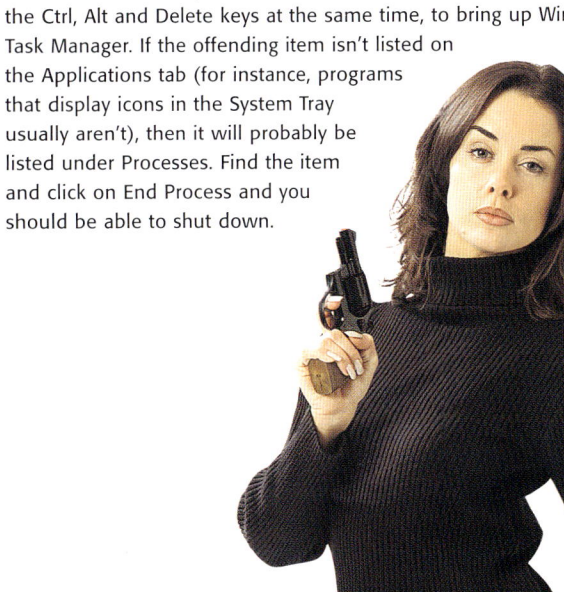

### Shutdown tip

Some programs are automatically scheduled to perform certain tasks when Windows shuts down, which can slow down the process and be very confusing if they don't tell you what they're doing. The most common culprits are anti-virus programs, which may be set to scan disks for viruses automatically on shut down. For example, if you have a floppy disk drive and you see the light on it flashing, your anti-virus program may be set to check the floppy drive on exit. If no disk is inserted, it can cause the system to freeze. Uncheck this option in the program's settings and check the scheduled tasks to disable any that might be causing problems.

# SOLVING PROBLEMS

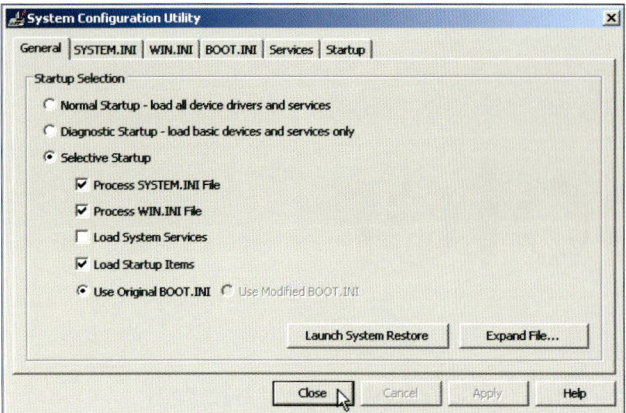

### Newsgroup tip

If you can trace your problem to one program but can't find an update or solution on the manufacturer's web site, try posting your problem on a newsgroup site devoted to that program. You may find that other users have had the same problem and found a solution.

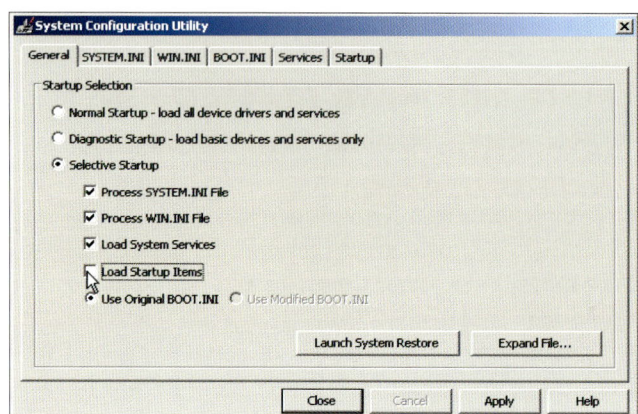

**2** Strangely, it may be a service or file in the Startup folder that is causing shutdown programs. Select Run on the Start menu, and type 'msconfig.exe' to launch the **System Configuration Utility**. Choose Selective Startup and then clear the Load System Services check box. Click on Apply and then on the Close button and restart your computer. If that resolves the issue then you know the problem is in that group of programs.

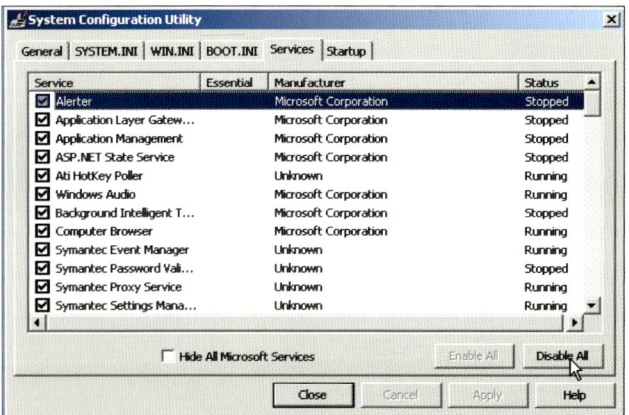

**4** Once the problem is located, click on the Enable All button then **uncheck the box** beside the faulty service as well as the others that you noted weren't running before. Click on OK and restart the PC. If it's not the services causing the problem, it could be the programs running at Startup, or the drivers for working with older programs, on the System.ini and Win.ini tabs. Go through the same process as before but uncheck Load Startup Items, Process SYSTEM.INI File and Process WIN.INI File in turn.

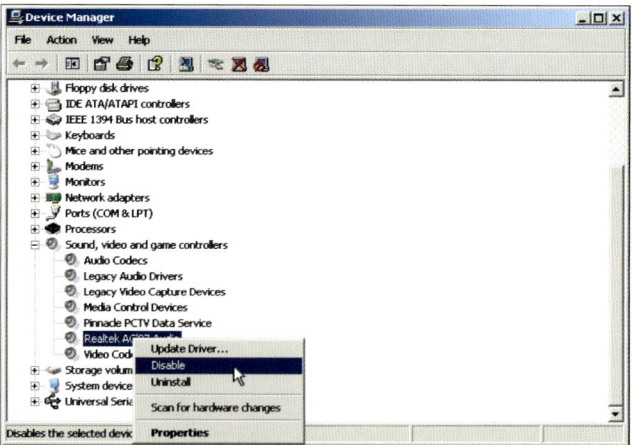

**3** Run msconfig.exe again and select Normal Startup – Load All Device Drivers and Services, then choose the **Services** tab. The problem file will be in that list. First, make a list of any services that aren't running – the box beside them will be unchecked. Click on Disable All, click on OK and then restart the PC. Run msconfig.exe and select the Services tab. Check the box beside a service to turn it on and then restart. Continue the process until the problem reoccurs and you can pinpoint the problem program.

### Sound file tip

If Windows is set to play a sound when it shuts down, a damaged sound file can sometimes cause the system to freeze. To see if this is the problem, click on Start and open Sounds and Audio Devices from the Control Panel menu (Sounds and Multimedia in Windows Me and Sounds in Windows 98). Select the Sounds tab that lists all your system sounds. Under Program Events (Sound Events in Windows Me and Sounds in Windows 98), highlight Exit Windows and select None from the dropdown Sounds (or Name) list. Click on OK, and retry shutting down your PC. If this solves the problem, you can then try locating and deleting the damaged sound file.

**5** Drivers for your PC's hardware can sometimes be the cause of shutdown trouble. The worst culprits are often **soundcard drivers**, but video and network cards can also cause problems. To see if this is the case, first you need to disable them. Say you suspect a sound device is at fault. Open Device Manager. Right-click on the My Computer icon, click on Properties and click on the Device Manager button on the Hardware tab (just select the Device Manager tab in Windows Me and 98). Double-click on Sound, Video and Game controllers. Then right-click on your sound device, click on Disable and then on Yes. Restart the PC and then try to shut down the computer to see if it has resolved the problem. If it has, visit the manufacturer's web site to see if a driver update is available for your sound device.

# Net doctor

**If you lose your link to the Internet, Windows' built-in troubleshooters can help.**

Connecting to the Internet should be as simple as clicking a button in your e-mail program or web browser. Windows deliberately conceals as much of the connection process as possible, and if everything works, there's no need to try to understand what is happening. But if your connection fails, you need to know where to fine-tune the various Net settings to help solve the problem.

## Solve dial-up errors

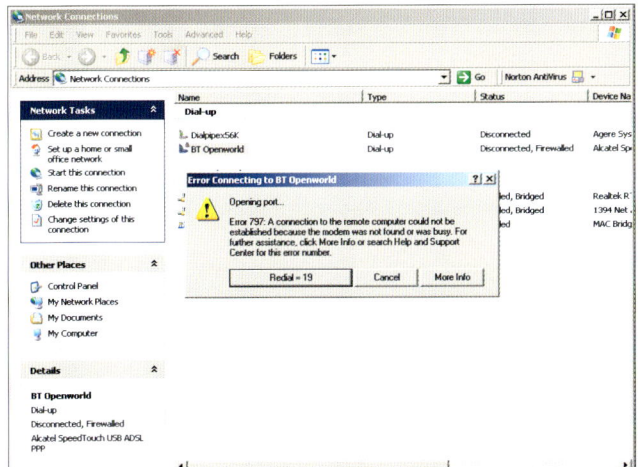

**1** An Internet connection operating through a **dial-up modem** relies on three elements. First, the modem must be properly connected or installed, along with an appropriate driver so that Windows can recognise it. Second, a communications system known as the TCP/IP protocol must be installed on your computer and configured for your Internet Service Provider. Third, the dial-up networking software (DUN) must be properly configured to call your ISP and establish communication between your computer and the Internet.

If your connection stops working, the most likely reason is that your modem or DUN software needs to be reset. The first step to take is to shut down the PC. If you have an external modem, switch it off, wait a moment and then turn it and your computer on and reconnect to the Internet.

The problem could also be a temporary fault at your ISP. Some ISPs have a phone number you can ring to check if there are problems. Call them if you can take advantage of this option. Otherwise, wait a couple of hours and try again before you decide that the problem is at your end.

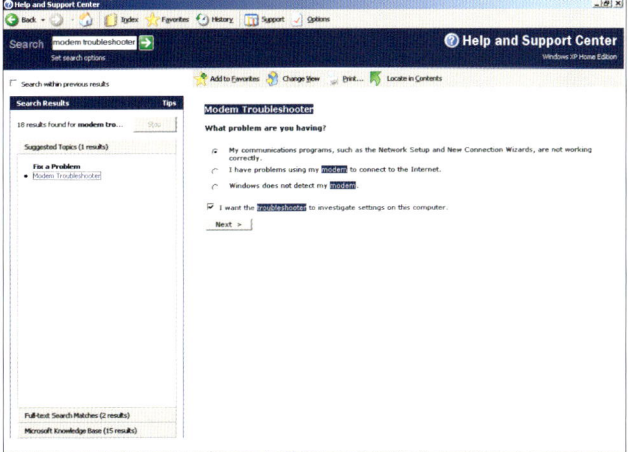

**2** If you still can't connect, seek help in the Windows Troubleshooters. Problems with your modem and DUN are covered by the **Modem Troubleshooter** – click on Start, then Help and Support, and type 'modem troubleshooter' into the Search field. The Modem Troubleshooter can help with faults such as failure to detect your modem, problems with dialling, and failure to establish a connection after your modem has dialled your ISP. To use it, select the description that matches your problem, then click on the Next button. Try the remedy suggested, then select one of the new options displayed to tell the Troubleshooter what the result was. Repeat this process as you work your way through the Troubleshooter.

### Jargon buster

**TCP/IP** This is the network protocol used to send information over the Internet. It describes how information must be packaged and addressed so that the information reaches the right destination and the computer can understand it.

# SOLVING PROBLEMS

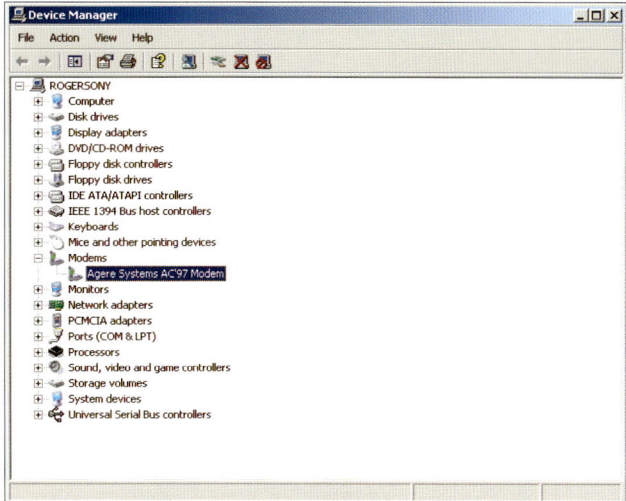

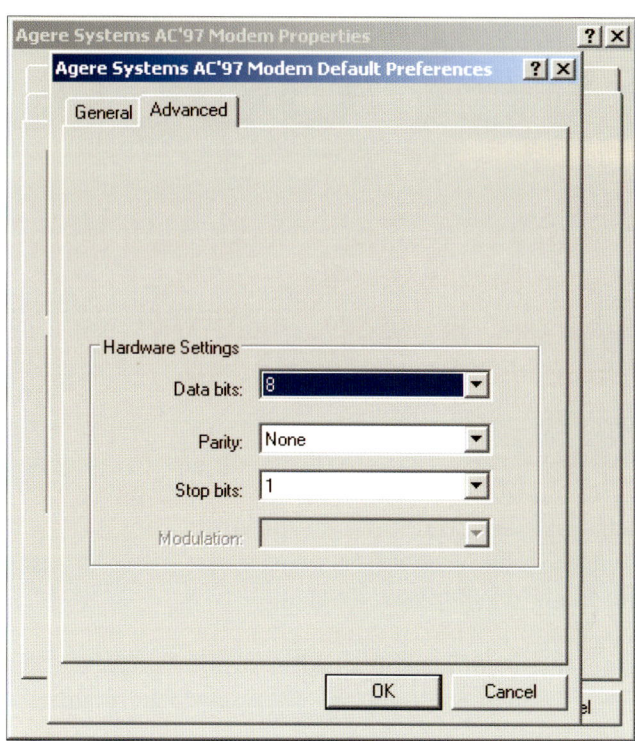

**3** If the Modem Troubleshooter doesn't solve your problem, you can investigate further with the **Device Manager**. To activate this, right-click on My Computer, click on Properties, then select the Hardware tab (the Device Manager tab in earlier versions of Windows). Expand the Modem entry to show the modem device – if the entry is marked with an exclamation icon, there is a problem with it. Click on Properties for more information. If there is a conflict, see if the Troubleshooters can help to resolve it.

If Device Manager displays the modem as a Standard Modem, then although your hardware may be working, you are probably not getting the best performance from it. You should install a driver provided by the modem manufacturer – consult the manual that came with the modem for instructions.

## Log tip

If you experience problems connecting to the Internet, the modem log (shown in Step 6) will often show what is going wrong.

## Jargon buster

**UART** Stands for Universal Asynchronous Receiver/Transmitter. This is a chip that receives high-speed information from the modem whenever it arrives and stores it ready for access by your computer's processor. It does the same thing for data going from the computer to the modem.

## Buffer tip

A buffer is an area in the memory used by UART chips for storing information temporarily. It's a good idea to check the buffer setting. If it is too low, performance suffers. If it is too high, information may be lost.

**4** Poor performance can also be caused by the wrong **port settings**. Check these in Modem Properties, accessed through the Phone and Modem control panel (the Modems Control Panel in Windows Me and 98). In Windows XP, select the Modems tab and highlight your model in the list. Click on the Properties box and then the Modem tab. Ensure that there is a tick in the check box beside Wait for Dial Tone Before Dialling. Click on the Advanced tab, then Change Default Preferences, and Advanced. The preferences should be set at Data bits '8', Parity 'None' and Stop Bits '1'.

In Windows Me and 98, all these settings can be accessed directly from the Connection tab. Click the Advanced Port Settings button (Port Settings in older Windows versions). Most PCs have a 16550 compatible UART chip, so the box at the top left of the dialogue box should be checked.

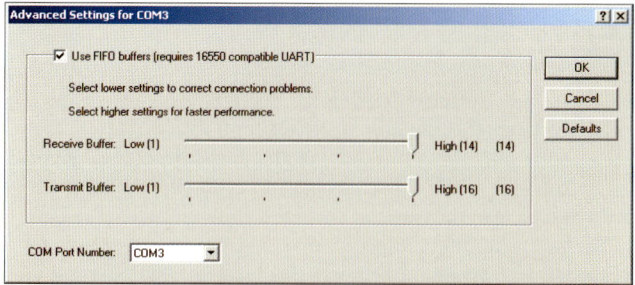

**5** A 16550 UART chip can store 16 characters of data in each direction in a buffer. This improves performance by avoiding the need for the PC to fetch one character at a time. The sliders in **Advanced Port Settings** determine how full each buffer can get before the PC moves the information out of it. Set them too low and performance suffers as the buffers are never fully used. Set them too high and characters are lost because the buffer may not be emptied fast enough to make room for the next. This is called an overrun. If the buffer overruns, lost data has to be re-sent. Check whether overrun errors are occurring by getting Windows to log the connection. If the log shows errors occur, reduce Receive Buffer with the slider. The Transmit Buffer can be left at maximum, but reduce it if you have problems uploading files.

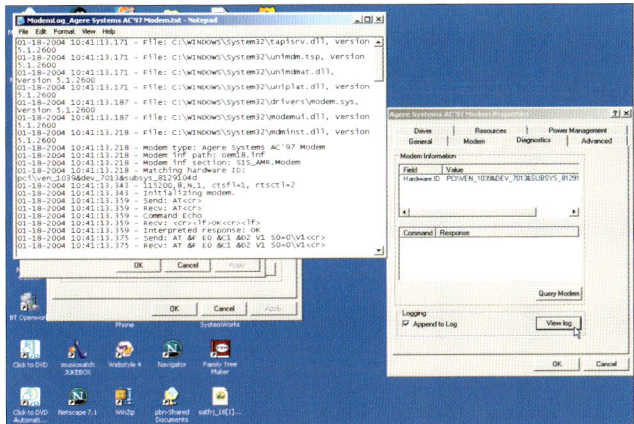

**6** Click on the **Diagnostics tab** in Modem Properties and check Append To Log to create a log in XP. (Click on the Advanced button in earlier versions of Windows.) Click on View Log to inspect the details – your most recent session, including error reports, is at the end. If everything is working, you can turn off the log. Check other settings by clicking on the Advanced tab and then on the Change Default Preferences button that will appear. Under Data Connection Preferences make sure Compression is set to Enabled and Flow Control is set to Hardware. If you can't get a connection to work with hardware flow control, there is probably a fault in your modem cable. In Windows 98, you can find these options by clicking on the Advanced button in the Modem Properties Control Panel.

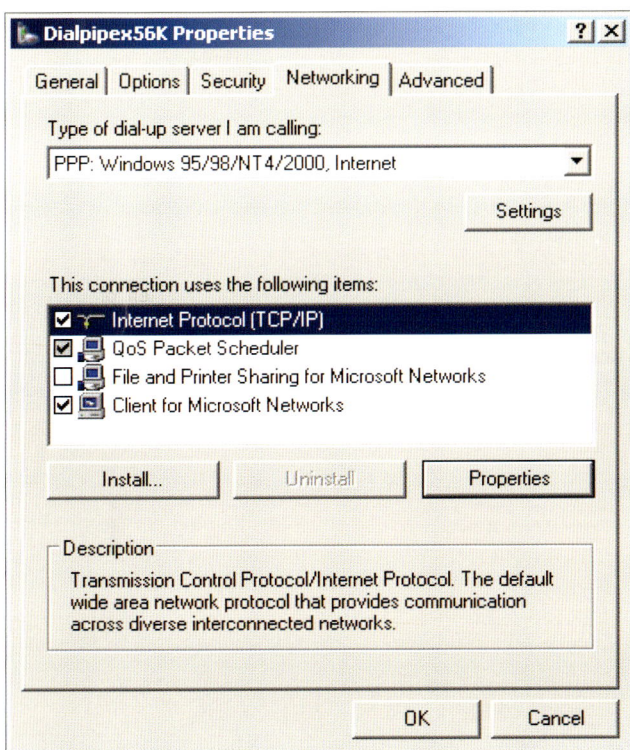

**7** If nothing happens after the modem connects, your **communications protocol** may be faulty. Open the Network Connections (previously Network) control panel. In XP, right-click on your dial-up connection, select Properties and click on the Networking tab. If your PC isn't networked, the only items in the components list should be a Dial-Up Adapter and TCP/IP. If you connect to the Internet with AOL, you will see an AOL Adapter instead. Select the Dial-Up Adapter and click Properties. The only protocol associated with the adapter should be TCP/IP.

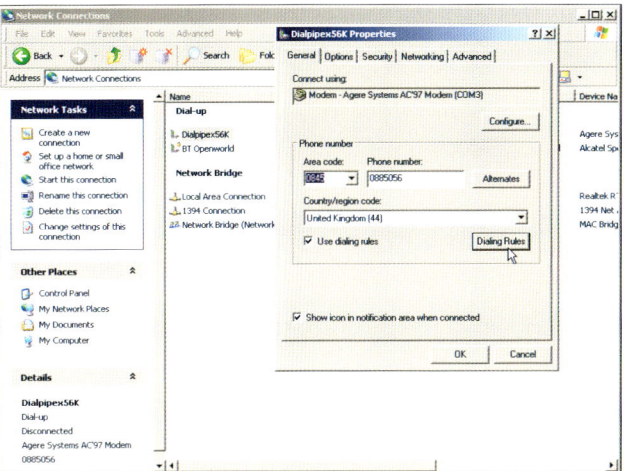

**8** You should also check that basic details – such as the phone number for your ISP connection – are correct. Click on the **General** tab (in earlier versions of Windows, select the Dial-Up Networking folder in My Computer, select the icon for your ISP, right-click and select Properties and then choose the General tab). Here you'll see the ISP's phone number. Put a tick in the Use Dialling Rules box (previously Area Code and Dialing Properties). This tells Windows to take account of Telephony settings – for example, you can disable Call Waiting signals that crash your Internet session.

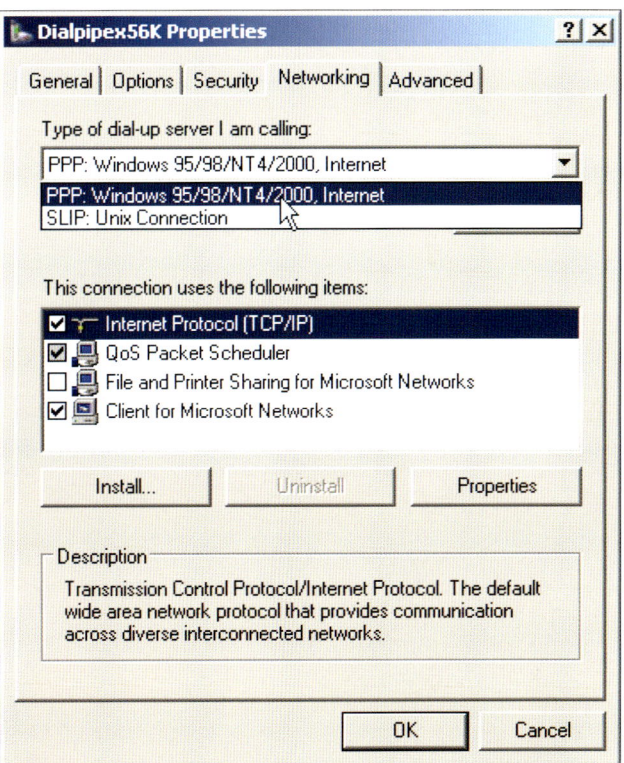

**9** On the **Networking** tab (Server Types in Windows 98), check that the Type of Dial-Up Server is set to PPP: Windows. If it isn't, you won't be connected. For Internet access you must also make sure that the box beside Internet Protocol (TCP/IP) is checked.

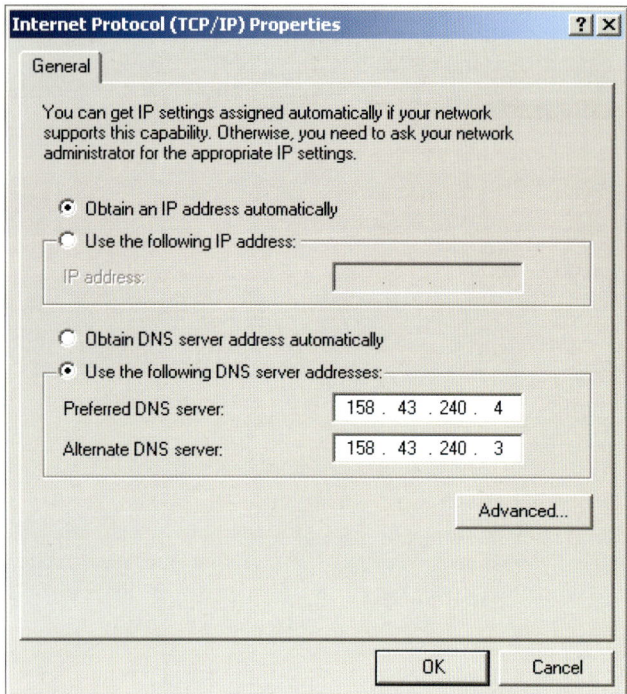

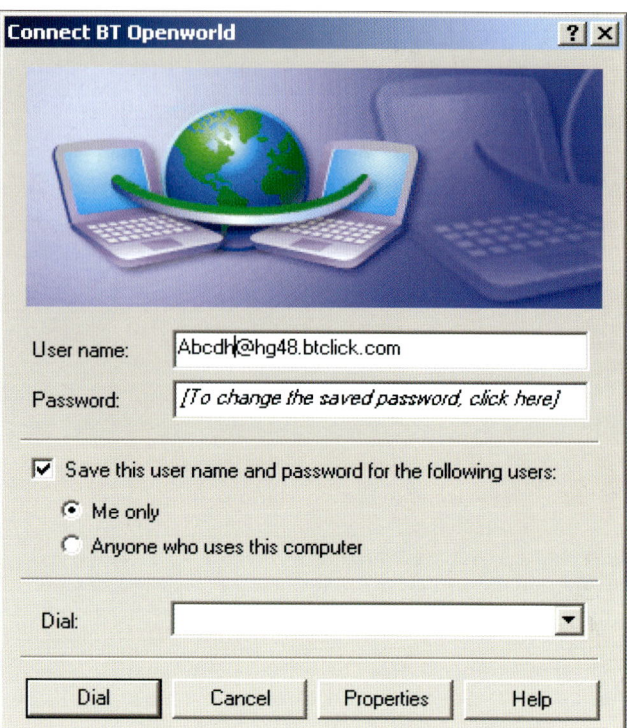

**10** Highlight the Protocol and select Properties (previously the TCP/IP Settings button) to **check the settings for your connection**. These will depend on your Internet Service Provider, but most ISPs now assign an IP address – the string of numbers that uniquely identifies your computer on the Internet – each time you log on, instead of allocating a fixed one. However, if you have been given an IP address, you should click on the button marked Use the Following IP Address, and type the number in the box below. The same applies to Domain Name Server (DNS) addresses. Click on the Advanced button to access further options in Windows XP.

IP header compression makes things work a little quicker, but if your ISP doesn't support it you won't get connected at all. If you can't connect, try disabling this option. Use Default Gateway should always be checked.

**11** Some ISPs ask you to give your user name and password after connecting, but Windows can do this for you. Go to the Network Connections control panel (in earlier versions of Windows, select Dial-Up Networking in My Computer) and double-click on the icon for your ISP. Fill in the **User Name and Password** – in Windows XP there is also a box to specify whether you want the details saved just for yourself, or for any user on your PC. If you want Windows to dial your ISP and log you in when it needs to, go to the Options tab in the connection's Properties box, and make sure the various Prompt options are unchecked. In Windows Me and 98, select the Connect Automatically box.

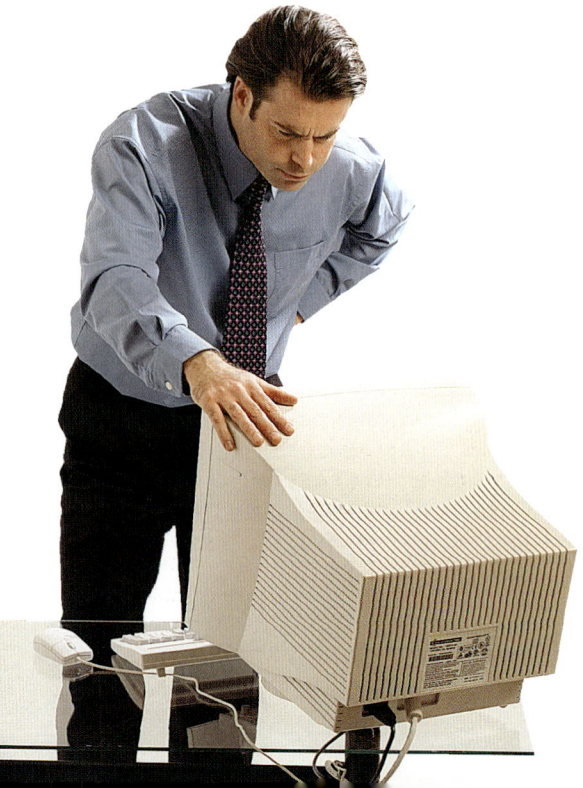

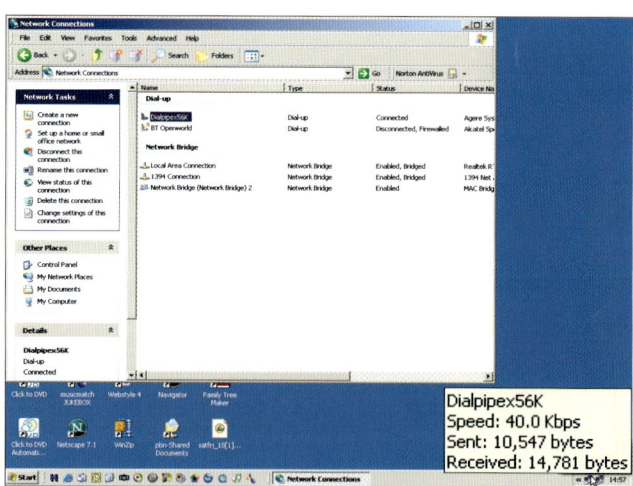

**12** For instant confirmation that you are online, use the **connection icon** in the taskbar's system tray. The icon shows two linked PCs, the screens of which flash during data transfer. Hovering your pointer over the icon to display the details Right-clicking gives you an option to Disconnect. To activate the icon in Windows XP, go to the General tab in the connection's Properties box, and put a tick the beside Show Icon in Notification Area When Connected. In Windows Me and 98, access the Dial-Up networking folder and click on Connections in the menu bar, then Settings. The equivalent box is on the General tab.

# Running MS-DOS

**With a few tweaks, Windows can be made to run most MS-DOS applications and games.**

Most software you buy today is written to run using Windows. However, you may still have older programs, particularly games, that were written to run using MS-DOS.

Before Windows became popular, most PC software was written for MS-DOS. Even now, games are often still written for MS-DOS, because they utilise the full screen and don't need resizable windows, a title bar, menus and so on. The games can also achieve better performance by controlling the PC hardware directly, instead of getting Windows to do it.

Most MS-DOS programs, particularly those with a text-based display, run well using Windows — but avoid any that don't claim to be Windows-compatible. If you do have problems with an MS-DOS program that won't run using Windows, you can often get it to work by changing some program property settings.

## Running DOS applications

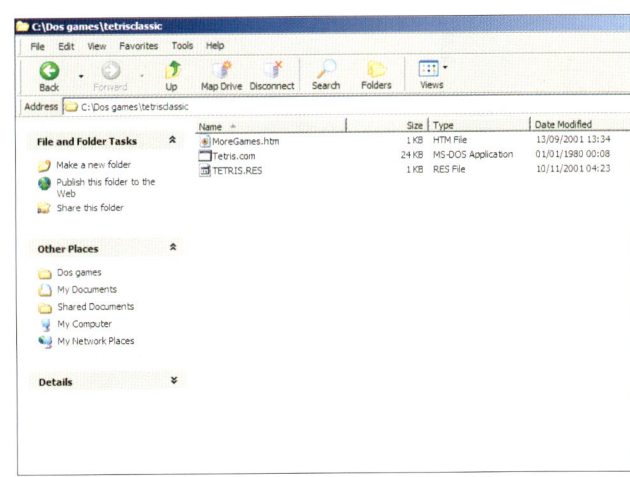

**1** **MS-DOS programs** are shown in Explorer by an icon that resembles an empty window frame. They can have a file type of .exe or .com. In an Explorer Details view, .exe files are shown as type Application. Windows programs are also Application files, so the presence of an icon is the only easy way to distinguish MS-DOS programs from Windows programs. You can run MS-DOS programs in the same way as Windows applications, by double-clicking on their icons. Windows-compatible MS-DOS programs may come with shortcut files. The shortcuts may have pictorial icons, and will contain special configuration information for Windows. If such shortcuts are present, you should use them to run the program from Windows.

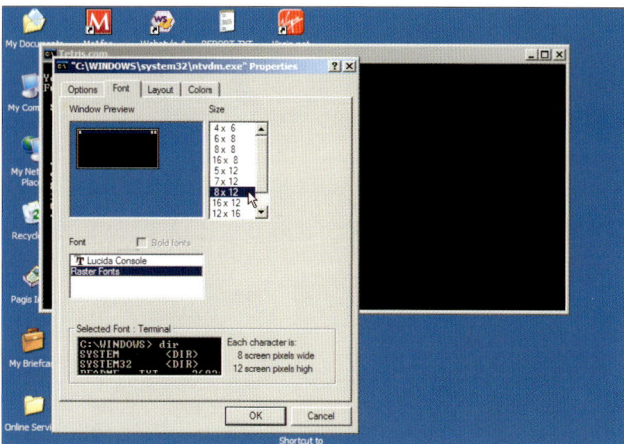

**2** MS-DOS programs were designed to use the whole screen. However, programs that have text-based or low resolution graphics output can be displayed using Windows in their own **window**. This allows you to switch between MS-DOS and Windows programs with ease, and even to copy and paste information from one to the other. If you right-click on the title bar of the Command Prompt window and select Properties, you can quickly change some of its settings. On the Options tab you can select the size of the cursor. Select the Font tab and you can adjust the character size (width x height) and see the result of the changes in the Preview box below. In earlier versions of DOS, you can select this from the dropdown menu on the toolbar.

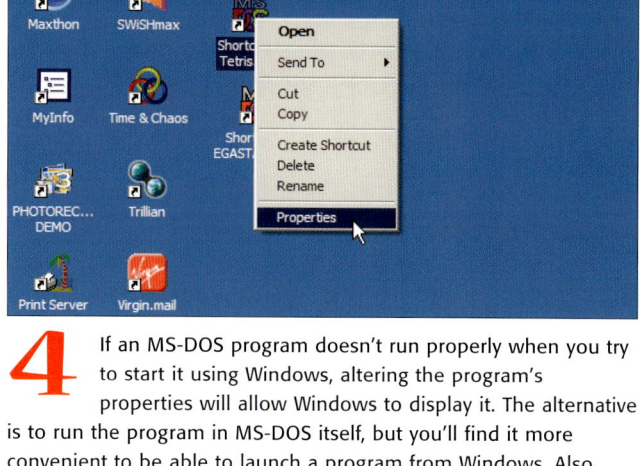

**4** If an MS-DOS program doesn't run properly when you try to start it using Windows, altering the program's properties will allow Windows to display it. The alternative is to run the program in MS-DOS itself, but you'll find it more convenient to be able to launch a program from Windows. Also, Windows provides some services, such as access to your CD-ROM drive, which are not normally provided in MS-DOS mode.

To access an MS-DOS program's properties, right-click on its icon and select **Properties** from the context menu. If a shortcut to the program already exists, open the shortcut's properties instead.

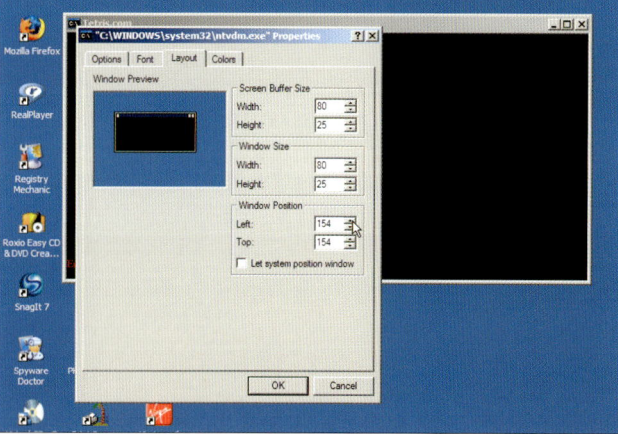

**3** In the Properties box, click on the Layout tab to adjust the size of the **DOS prompt window** itself. In the Window Size section, adjust the Width and Height using the arrows beside each box. You can see the effect by looking in the Window Preview pane. By default, Windows will position the window on screen. You can adjust this manually by unticking the box beside Let System Position Window, and then adjusting the number of pixels from the left and top, according to where you want the window to appear. Click on the Options tab and under Display Options you can select whether the DOS-based program opens within a window or in full screen mode. You can switch between the two more easily from the keyboard by pressing the Alt+Enter keys.

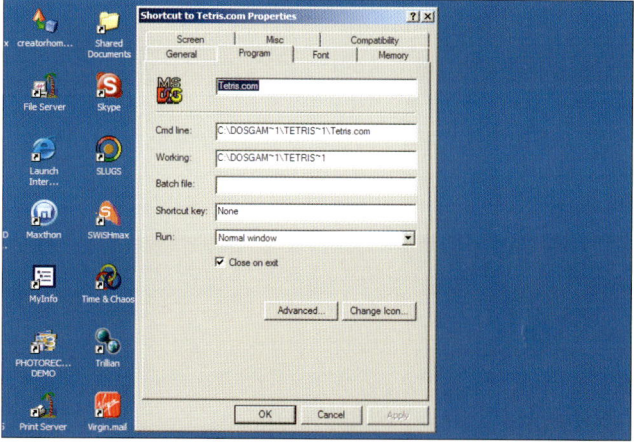

**5** The **Program tab** of an MS-DOS application's Properties box contains general information about the program. The information is shown in a set of fields. The first field contains a description that appears on the title bar of the MS-DOS window when the program is run. If you don't enter a description, the program filename is used.

The Cmd Line field contains the name of the program. If the program accepts command line parameters, you can edit this field to add them.

The Working field specifies the name of the working folder: the one the program starts up in. This is usually the folder that contains the program.

The Batch File field should normally be blank. In Shortcut Key you can choose a key combination (such as Ctrl or Alt plus another key) that can be used to bring this program's window to the front of the screen. Run offers you a choice from a drop-down menu. It should be left as Normal Window.

The Close on Exit tick box determines whether the MS-DOS window will close when the program terminates. Untick it if you want the window to stay open after the program finishes, to give you a chance to read any text it has displayed.

### Jargon buster

**Command line parameters** A short instruction in MS-DOS (such as 'admapidpwd') that defines what features of a program will be enabled or disabled.

# DIY FIXES

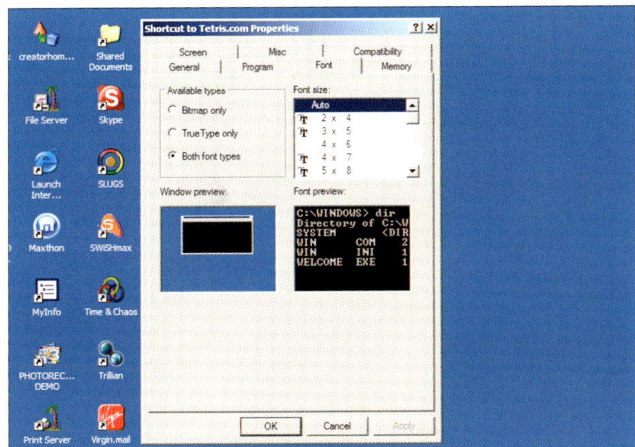

**6** The **Font tab** in the Properties dialogue box lets you choose the size of font used to display the text in an MS-DOS window. If you choose a specific size of font, the Window Preview panel shows the resulting window size in relation to your Desktop, while the Font Preview panel reveals an example of the font. If you choose Auto for the font size, you can resize the MS-DOS window using the mouse.

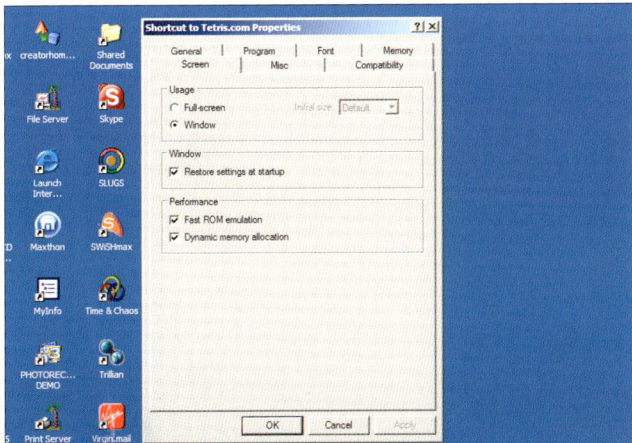

**7** If you select **Full-Screen** on the Screen tab of the Properties dialogue box, the MS-DOS program will start up full-screen, just as in MS-DOS mode. You will usually only need to select this option for programs that display graphics rather than text, such as some games. The Window tick box option lets you choose whether the font, size and position settings used should be saved and restored when you run the program. The Performance tick box options should both be left marked for optimum performance. Untick them if the MS-DOS program has problems when running under Windows.

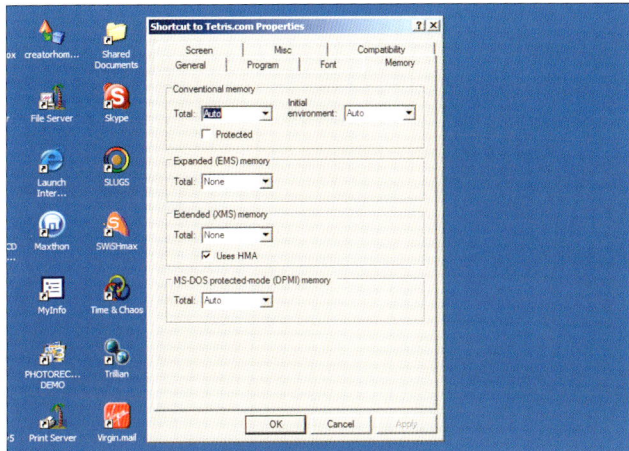

**8** The **Memory tab** in the Properties dialogue box lets you set up the memory that the MS-DOS program will see. Unlike Windows programs, MS-DOS programs can't automatically use all the memory available to the computer. The memory used by MS-DOS is divided into four categories: conventional, expanded, extended and protected mode. Windows does its best to work out how much memory an MS-DOS program requires, and will provide it if the memory is available, so the Memory properties are best left at the default settings. Change one of these settings only if a program reports that there is not enough of a certain type of memory.

Conventional memory is the type that usually causes problems with MS-DOS applications. The maximum amount of conventional memory that you can have is 640KB. However, MS-DOS itself needs some of this memory, and every driver loaded in your MS-DOS configuration files uses some more. If an MS-DOS program reports that there is not enough memory without saying what type, it usually means that the amount of free conventional memory is insufficient.

## Jargon buster

**Conventional memory** This is the memory in which MS-DOS applications run. The maximum amount of conventional memory is 640KB. Each device driver and memory resident utility – such as calendars and clocks – uses some conventional memory. MS-DOS applications have to make use of what's left over.

**Expanded, Extended and Protected Mode (DPMI) memory** These terms describe schemes for accessing the non-conventional memory in your computer. Your Windows software normally controls this. However, a memory manager is required when using MS-DOS. This manager allocates the amount and type of memory for your programs.

## MS-DOS tip

Instead of typing a program name to run it from an MS-DOS prompt, you can drag the program from Explorer and drop it on the MS-DOS window. Type the command line parameters, if required, then press Enter.

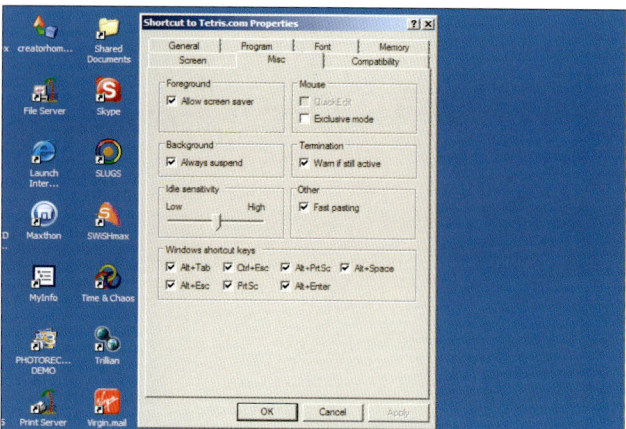

**9** The **Misc tab** of the Properties dialogue box contains a mixture of options. MS-DOS programs can waste processor time when they are idle in the background. Windows tries to detect when a program is idle. If performance slows when an MS-DOS program is running, change the position of the Idle Sensitivity slider. In the Background pane, tick Always Suspend to stop the program when it is in the background.

Windows Shortcut Keys controls which keystrokes should be used with the MS-DOS application. In the Termination pane, tick Warn if Still Active to display a warning if you try to close the MS-DOS window by clicking on the Close button. In the Other pane, Fast Pasting allows you to bypass the Edit menu when selecting the Paste command in Windows.

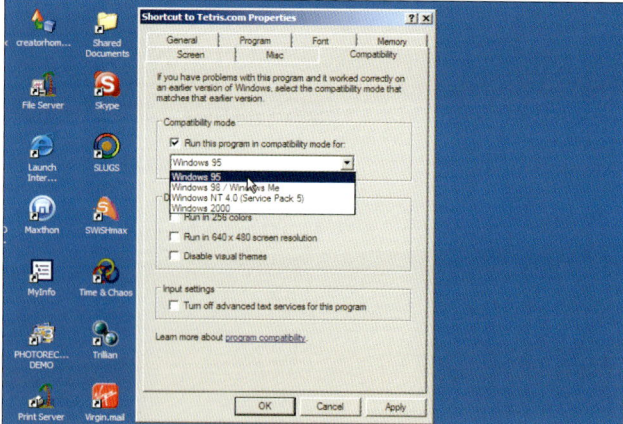

**10** Under Windows XP you can 'turn back' your version of Windows to an **earlier version** so that it will work with programs – such as games – that can only run correctly on previous versions of Windows. To do so, select the Compatibility tab. Under Compatibility Mode, tick the box beside Run This Program in Compatibility Mode For: and then select from the dropdown list the version of Windows that you know that the game will work with. As Display Settings can also interfere with the smooth running of the game, you can also select a lower screen resolution (640 x 480 pixels) and a reduced colour depth (256 colours) to see if that improves performance.

### Shortcut tip

Modify the MS-DOS configuration used when you restart in MS-DOS mode so your programs will run in that. Edit the properties for the Exit to DOS shortcut in the Windows folder. If the changes you make stop Windows restarting in MS-DOS mode, undo them by selecting Use Current MS-DOS Configuration.

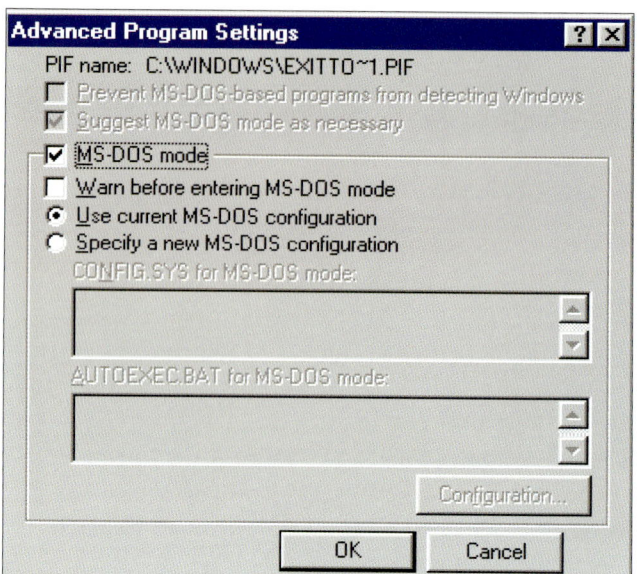

**11** In earlier versions of Windows the same compatibility effect can be achieved by running your computer in **MS-DOS mode**, in which Windows closes down and MS-DOS is the only program running. To configure a program to run in MS-DOS mode only, select the Program tab of the Properties dialogue box, then click on Advanced. Tick the MS-DOS Mode box. In MS-DOS mode, two files – Config.sys and Autoexec.bat – determine the configuration. If you choose Use Current MS-DOS Configuration, MS-DOS will not use new copies of these files. The settings will be the same as when you shut down Windows and choose Restart in MS-DOS Mode.

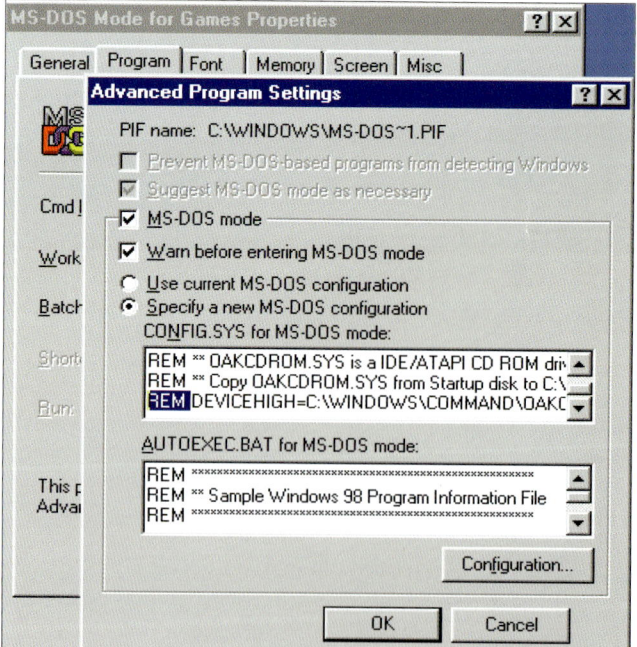

**12** If you have an MS-DOS program that won't run after you restart in MS-DOS mode, it's no good using the current **configuration**. You need to specify a new configuration. Click on the radio button labelled Specify a New MS-DOS Configuration in the MS-DOS mode pane of the Advanced Program Settings dialogue box, and use the edit boxes to enter the appropriate Config.sys and Autoexec.bat commands.

# Retrieving lost files

**A good filing system will help you keep track of your files, but if you lose them, Windows can help.**

Windows provides several ways to find information about your files. The Search tool in the Start menu or on the Explorer toolbar is probably the most flexible and with its help you can look for files based on their filename, folder name, location, creation date or keywords contained within them.

Other tools, such as the Properties page of a file, can also help you track down the file you want. If a file is on your hard disk, you will almost certainly find it, if you have given it a suitable name and entered any useful further information into the file's Properties box.

## Finding programs with Windows

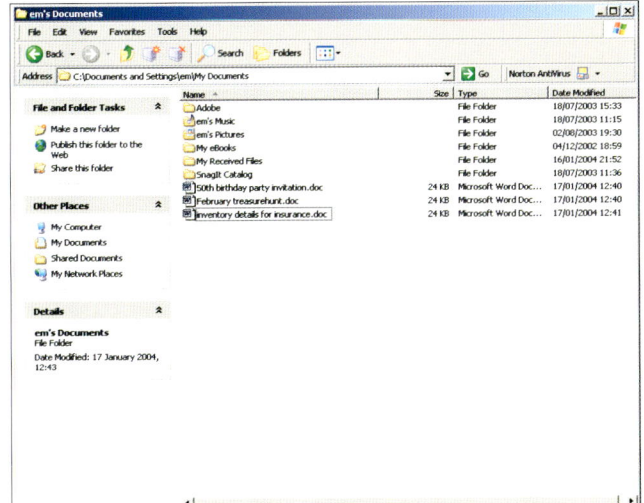

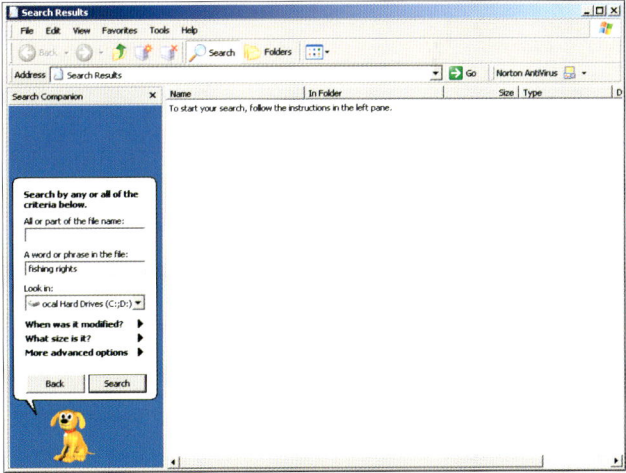

**1** The simplest way to make information easy to find is to file it well in the first place. Store files in folders with descriptive names, just as you would if they were documents in a filing cabinet. For example, if you have a folder of correspondence with your bank, call the folder LetterstoBank. If necessary, use **long filenames** to describe exactly what a file or folder is – that way, you won't have to open the file to see if it's the one you want. Filenames can contain up to 255 characters – and you can use most of the keyboard characters apart from colon (:), backslash(/), asterisk(*), question mark and a few others. If you use descriptive names you can get Explorer to sort all your files by name, so you can go straight to the one you want.

**2** If you use descriptive names, the Search tool (called Find in Windows 98) also becomes much more useful. It's far faster to search through file names than to search the contents of every file looking for a keyword. To locate a file just type a word or words that appear in the filename. When you click on **Search**, the Search tool will list all the files that contain one or more of those words. For a group of words to be treated as a phrase rather than as separate keywords, put quotes around them.

To locate files that contain specific strings of text within them, leave the Name: field blank and enter the search text into the A Word or Phrase in the File box (previously Containing Text: field) instead. In this case the text you enter will be treated as a key phrase, not as individual keywords. The complete phrase therefore has to appear in the document in order for it to be listed.

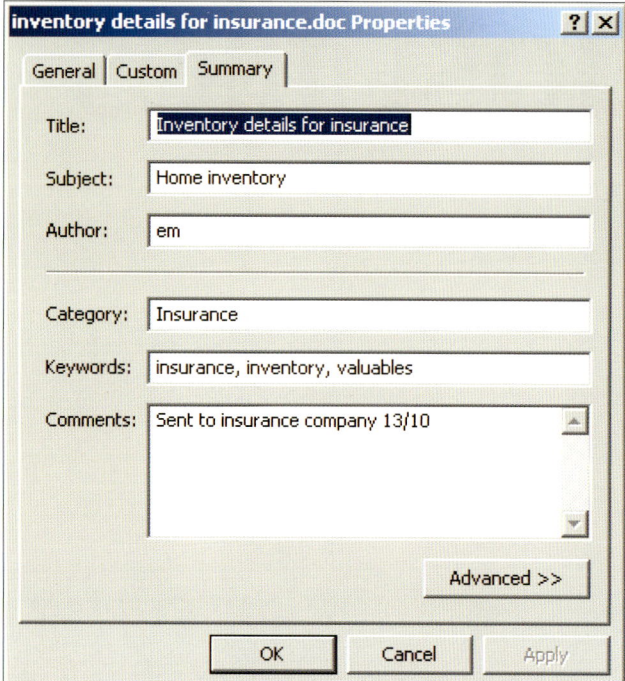

**3** You can make a file even easier to find by storing information about it in the relevant **Properties page**. You can't do this with all files – many file formats, for example .gif and .jpg, don't allow text-based information to be stored within them – however, if you use one of the popular Office application suites, or any Microsoft Office compatible application, this facility is available. Simply select Properties from the program's File menu, click on the Summary tab and type in the information.

To view the information you have entered, right-click on the file's icon in Explorer or in the list of files found by a search and select Properties from the pop-up menu. The details shown depend on the application used to create the file and on which fields have been filled in. Usually, though, they include details of who created the file and when, with a description and keywords. The Find tool will search the Properties pages of files when it performs a text search so, for example, you can locate files containing drawings but no searchable text.

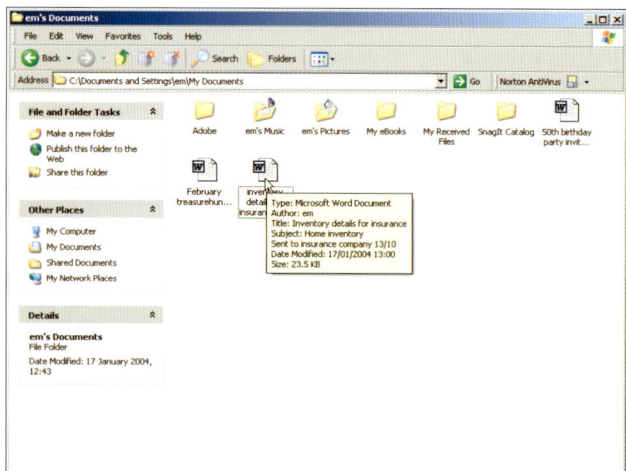

**4** If you place the pointer over a file's icon in Explorer, **property information** such as the file's author, subject and comments will be shown in a pop-up box. To view more detailed information, click on the file, and information will appear in the Details box on the left.

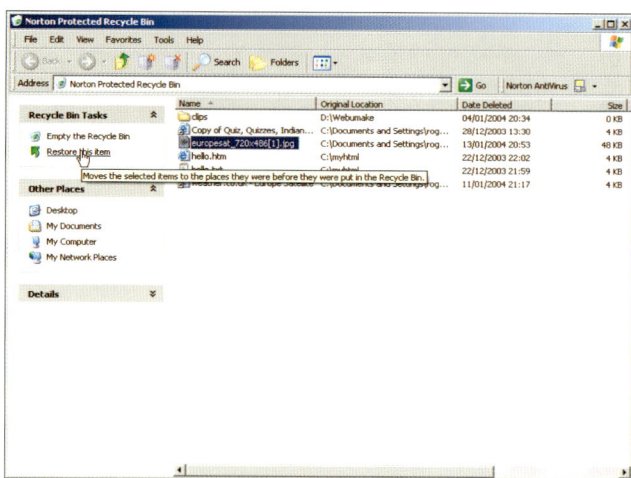

**5** If you can't find the file you are looking for by searching, check in your **Recycle Bin** – the Windows Search tool doesn't search the Recycle Bin, even if you tell it to search My Computer.

To see what files are in the Recycle Bin, right-click on it and choose Open or Explore. You will see a list of files, their names, where they came from and when they were deleted. You will be able to view the file's size and when it was created, but you can't open files to view them directly from the Recycle Bin, nor inspect their full properties. If you can't tell if a file is the one you want from its filename, restore it to its original folder by clicking on it and selecting Restore this Item from the Task Pane. You will then be able to view it as normal.

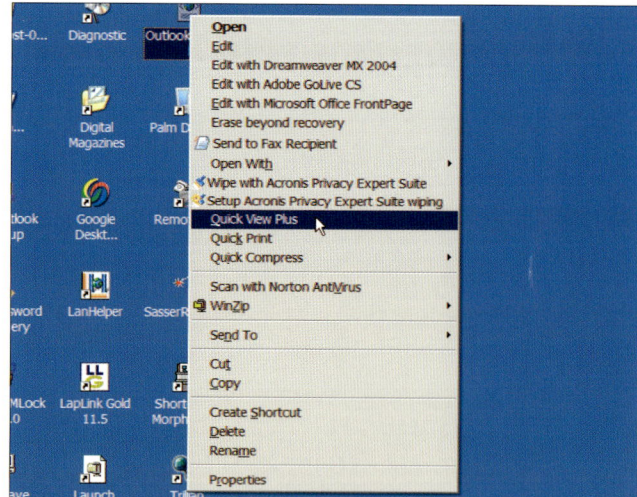

**6** If you use Windows XP or Me and want to be able to inspect details of files you cannot open (for instance, because you don't have the right application), you can buy Avantstar's Quick View Plus, available from www.avantstar.com. The program can integrate itself into several different applications and browsers – even Windows itself – so you can access it in several ways. For example, you can go to the Program menu, select Quick View Plus and then click on View a File. Or, right-click on the file you want to view on the desktop and click on Quick View Plus in the pop-up menu.

Windows 98 comes with its own **Quikview tool** free. Although it can only display information about certain file types, it is still quite useful for discovering information about application files and other system files. If Quikview isn't one of the options on the menu when you right-click on an Application file, you probably need to install it by going to Control Panel, then Add/Remove Programs.

# Fine-tune settings

## Some problems can be solved by a few simple adjustments to the settings of your PC.

Some problems you experience using your computer are caused by the settings in Windows XP itself. For example, if several people share the same machine, everyone can see what documents have been used recently under Windows' default settings. However, you can ensure everyone's privacy is respected. The TweakUI PowerToy (UI stands for 'user interface') offers options for customising your PC to fix this and other problems. It even allows you to set up your PC to log on to the network automatically at startup.

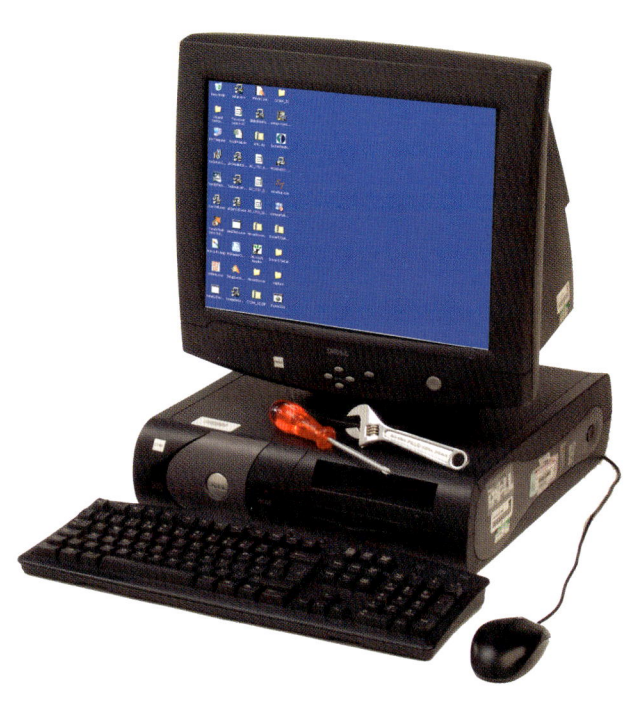

## Using TweakUI with Windows XP

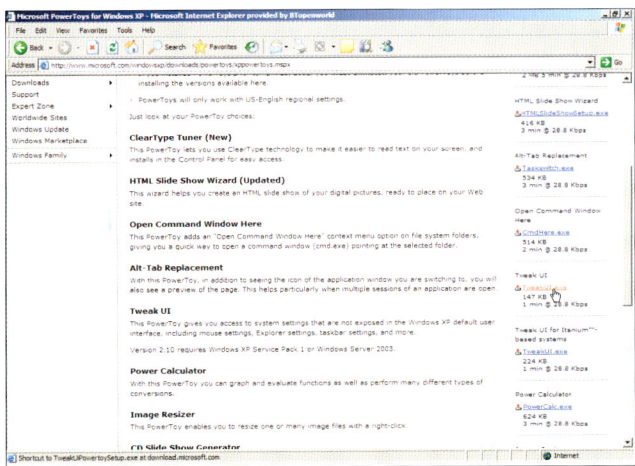

**1** First, download **TweakUI** by going to www.microsoft.com/windowsxp/downloads/powertoys/xppowertoys.mspx and clicking on the link to Tweak UI. Choose to save the file and browse to a folder on your PC in which to store it. When the download has finished, double-click on the downloaded tweakui.exe file to install it.

### Fact file

The version of TweakUI used in this project is for Windows XP. Go to www.annoyances.org/exec/show/tweakui to download an earlier version for Windows Me and 98. You will find that the interface is slightly different, using tabs along the top of the window in place of the navigation pane.

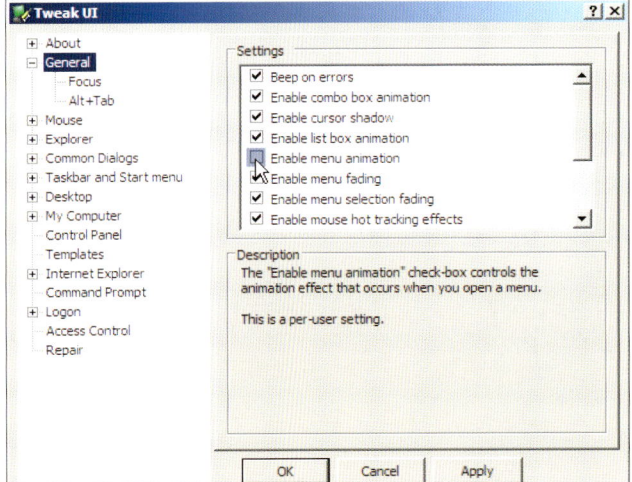

**2** Go to All Programs on the Start menu, select Powertoys for WindowsXP, then TweakUI. Select General in the left-hand pane and you are given a number of options. Click on any item in the **Settings pane** on the right and you'll see a description of what it does in the box below. To activate a feature, tick the box beside it. Or, if an option is slowing down your system or you simply find it annoying, uncheck the box to turn it off. You can choose to animate windows, menus, tooltips and dropdown lists, apply fade effects, select whether commonly used folders – such as My Pictures or My Documents – appear on the Start menu if you use the Windows Classic style, and more. You can also enable a couple of system-wide features. Beep on Errors gives you an audible warning when there's a problem, while Optimize Hard Disk When Idle will use periods when your PC is idle to reorganise ('defragment') files and improve your PC's efficiency.

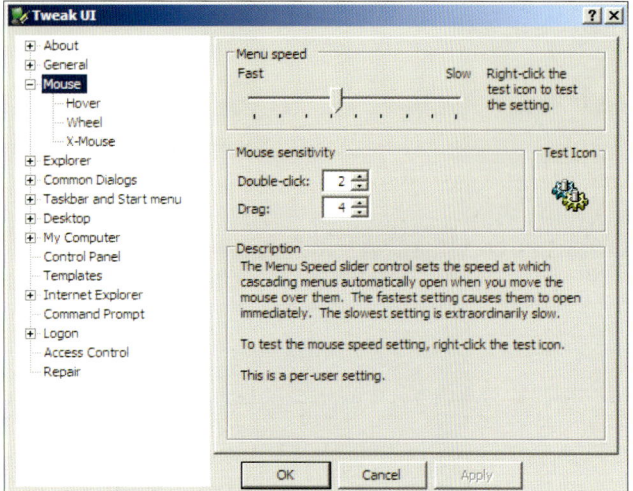

**3** Selecting **Mouse** enables you to alter the sensitivity of the mouse. Menu Speed controls how quickly sub-menus appear, Double-click Sensitivity determines how far the mouse may move between clicks and still register as a double-click, while Drag Sensitivity determines how far the mouse must move with a button held down to be treated as a move operation. You can use the Test Icon to try out any changes.

Click on the + sign beside Mouse and you're given further options. For instance, Wheel lets you customise how your mouse scrolls, if your mouse has a wheel. On the X-Mouse page, select Activation Follows Mouse and you will be able to make a window active — in other words, able to accept keyboard input — just by moving the pointer over it.

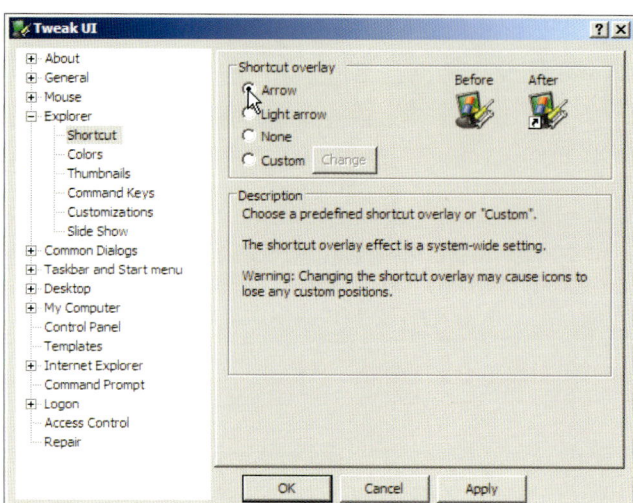

**5** Choose **Shortcut** from the Explorer sub-menu and you can customise the shortcut icons that appear on your desktop. In the Shortcut Overlay section you can specify whether you want an arrow on a white background, a subtle (light) arrow, or no arrow at all in the lower left corner of shortcut icons. Select the Custom option and click on the Change button to choose a different icon altogether. Click on Explorer in the navigation pane and in the Settings pane you can choose to have the words 'Shortcut To' to appear at the start of the names of new shortcuts.

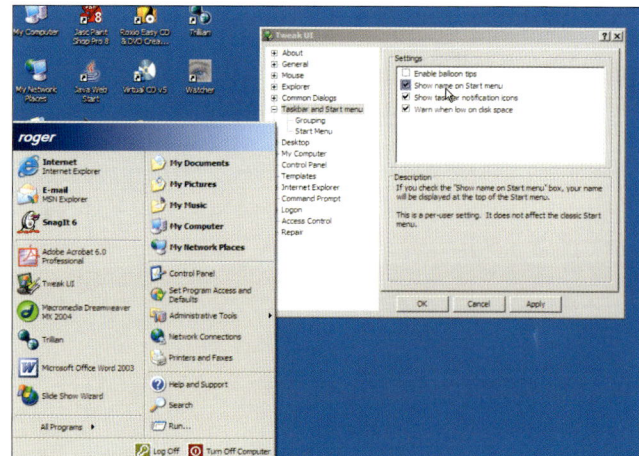

**6** Click on **Taskbar and Start Menu** in the navigation pane to alter your desktop settings. Show Name on Start Menu puts your username on the blue header above the Start menu. If you find that the lengthy balloon tips that appear when you hover over an item are getting in your way, you can turn them off here by unchecking the box beside Enable Balloon Tips.

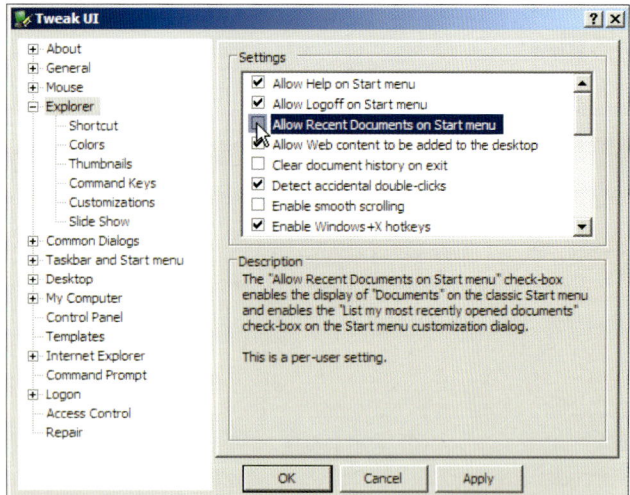

**4** If you are concerned about strangers accessing private information kept on your computer, select **Explorer** and tick the appropriate boxes in the list in the Settings pane. For instance, if you don't want it to be obvious which documents you've just been working on, disable Allow Recent Documents on Start Menu and select Clear Document History on Exit. (In Windows Me and 98, click on the Paranoia tab for similar settings.)

### Software tip

TweakUI works by altering settings in the Registry – the giant database that holds information about your PC and your preferences. If you want to alter even more settings, there are dozens of commercial – and freeware – programs that will help you. You will find some of these at www.soft411.com/software/tweak.html

# DIY FIXES

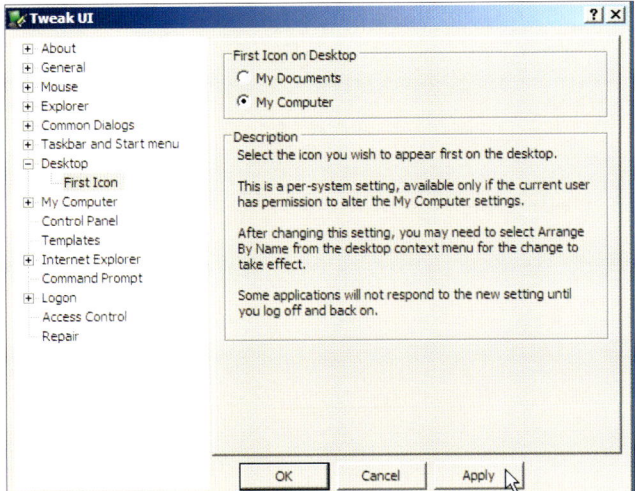

**7** Select **Desktop** and you can choose whether you want certain special icons, such as those for Internet Explorer, My Network Places or the Recycle Bin, to appear on your desktop. This is the only way to remove some of these icons – Windows itself won't let you delete them.

Click on First Icon in the Desktop sub-menu and you can choose whether My Documents or My Computer appears first on the desktop. Click on Apply. For the change to take effect you may need to right-click on the desktop and select Arrange by Name from the pop-up menu.

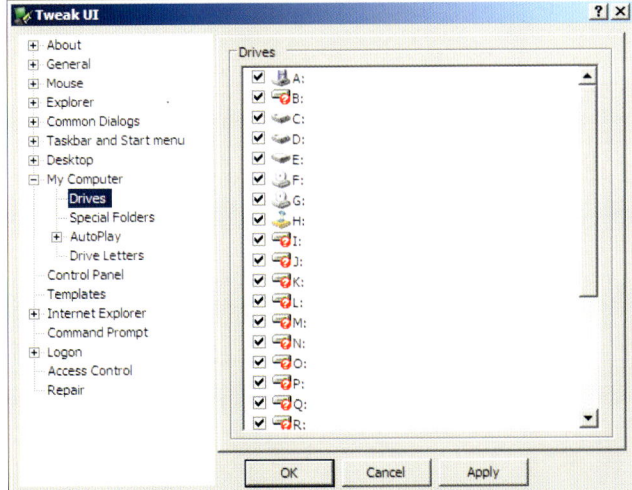

**8** Click on Drives in the **My Computer** sub-menu and you are given a scrollable list showing all the possible drive letters on your computer. If you uncheck the box against a drive letter, that drive will no longer appear listed in My Computer or Explorer. You could use this option to hide a drive from other users of the PC, for instance. However, this isn't a security feature and it wouldn't prevent someone from accessing the drive via MS-DOS. The drives with a red question mark over them are empty and won't show up even if ticked.

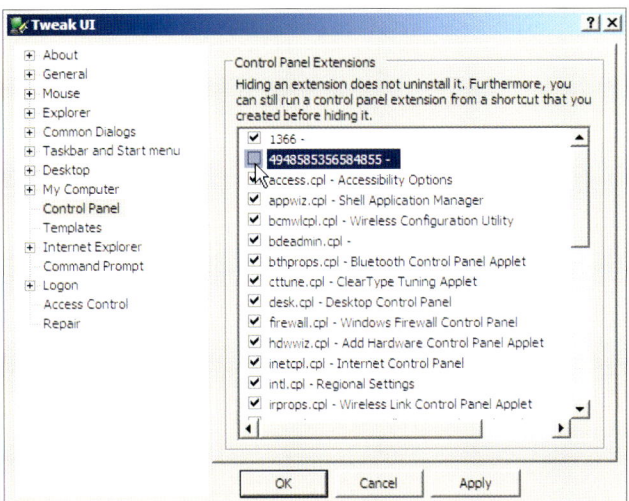

**9** The **Control Panel** page lets you choose the icons that appear in the Control Panel. It contains a scrollable list with the names of the programs that run each Control Panel item including, in most cases, a description. You can remove an icon you don't use by unchecking the box beside its name. This won't do any harm – the file isn't uninstalled so, if you decide you need it at a later date, you can easily reinstate it.

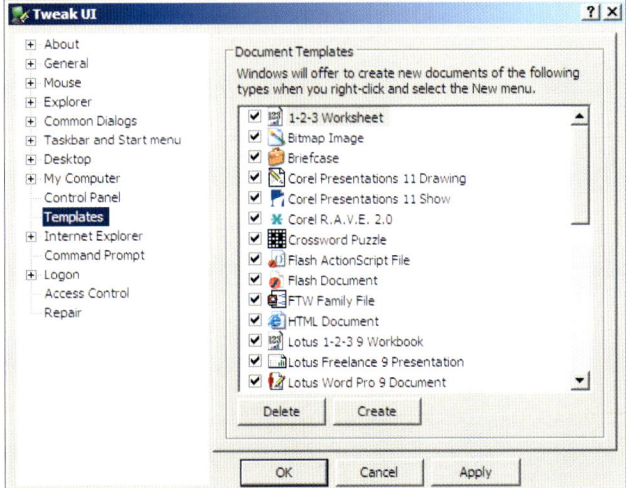

**10** By selecting **Templates** in the navigation pane, you can choose which items are listed in the menu that appears when you select File, then New, in Windows Explorer. This menu normally consists of a list of file types. Choosing one creates an empty file of that type, which you can rename and then open for editing in the appropriate application. Entries in this menu are added when you install applications. To remove entries you don't want, uncheck the box beside the file type in the list here.

## Help tip

Use the What's This? help tool for an explanation of any TweakUI option. Simply click on the question mark in the upper right-hand corner of the dialogue box, then click on the setting you want to learn more about.

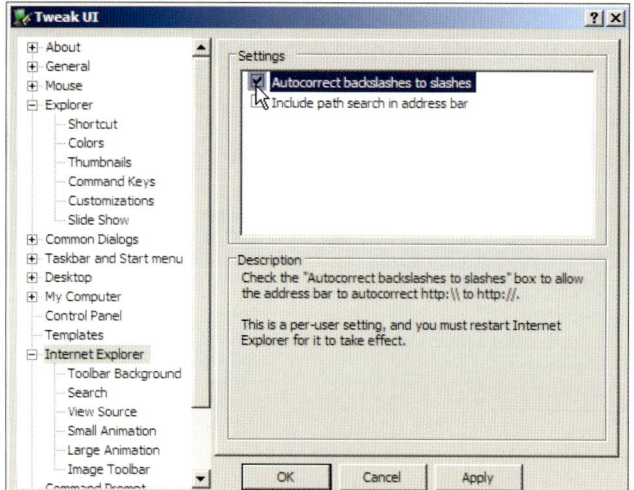

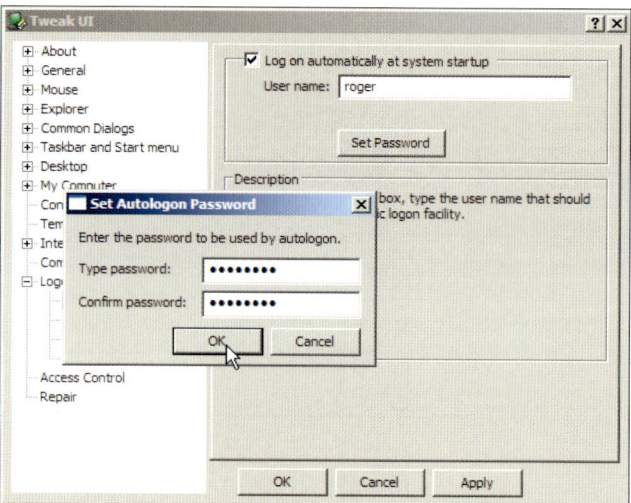

**11** Click on the + sign beside **Internet Explorer** to see the options for customising this Internet browser. However, one of the most useful options is accessed by clicking on the Internet Explorer option itself. In the Settings window, ensure there's a tick beside Autocorrect Backslashes to Slashes. This will reformat any backslashes that you input incorrectly when entering a web page URL.

**13** On the **Autologon** screen on the Logon sub-menu, you can enter the user name for any network you have set up, and set your password so that Windows logs on to your network automatically for you at startup. The password is encrypted for extra security. To enable this feature, click on the box beside Log On Automatically at System Startup and type your username in the box. Click on Set Password, enter the details, click on OK, then click on the Apply button.

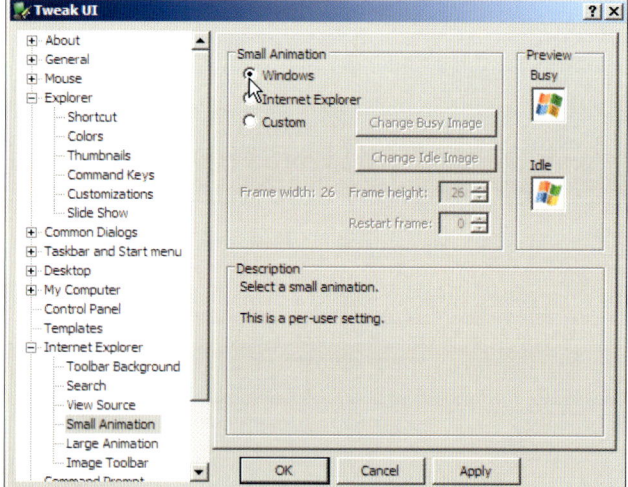

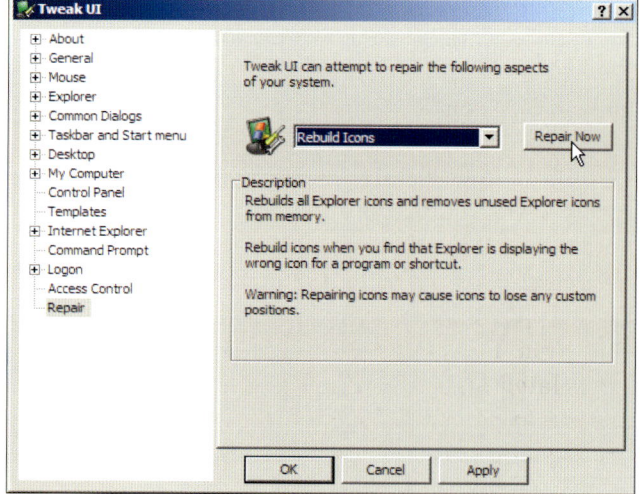

**12** One often overlooked feature is a **small animation** in the right-hand corner of Internet Explorer and Windows Explorer. The icon is static when nothing is happening, but ripples when busy, such as when a web page is loading. Select Small Animation in the Internet Explorer sub-menu, then select Windows if you want to display the Windows icon (the four coloured panes), or Internet Explorer if you prefer a circling globe. Or, click on Custom and you can create your own image to display when Explorer is busy or idle.

**14** The **Repair** page offers one of TweakUI's most useful features. Here you can fix a number of common Windows problems by resetting various items to the installed defaults. If some of the icons that are being displayed are wrong, for instance, select Rebuild Icons and click on Repair Now. Or, if the special icons for folders such as My Pictures or My Videos disappear, you can repair them by selecting them from the list and clicking on the Repair Now button. If you are having trouble with your fonts, this could be because Windows is treating the Fonts folder like a normal folder instead of a special one. You can restore its special status from here.

### Animation tip

If you want to make your own animation to go in the Windows or Internet Explorer toolbar, you need to create the 'busy' icon before you make the static one. Each image needs to be the same size – typically 26x26 pixels for the Small Animation and 38x38 pixels for the Large Animation. TweakUI lets you alter the frame size, but make sure the frame size of the Small Animation is less than that for the large one.

# Curing viruses

**PCs can catch viruses as easily as people, so it pays to have the right medicine for when they fall sick.**

PCs are only machines. They can go wrong, but surely they can't catch viruses? Unfortunately, they can. PCs get computer viruses – rogue programs that they can then pass on to other computers, and which may cause them to malfunction.

Computer viruses aren't usually fatal. Many of them are just an inconvenience. They can slow your computer down, and they might make it behave a bit crankily on occasions, but most don't actually do any lasting damage, unless of course files that you haven't backed up are destroyed.

## Fatal illnesses

A few viruses are more malicious. They can corrupt or delete files. Some attempt to wipe everything from your hard disk. Others just make it look as if all your data has gone. It is sensible to be aware that your PC could be at risk. Just as you can get inoculated against a human virus, so you can immunise your PC by taking a few simple precautions with the help of anti-virus software.

## PC medicine

The following pages describe the problem of computer viruses in some detail: what they are and how they spread, plus where they come from and who invented them. Symptoms of some of the common viruses are described. Anti-virus tools are summarised on page 68; here you'll find more detailed information on the steps you can take and the software you can buy to protect your PC.

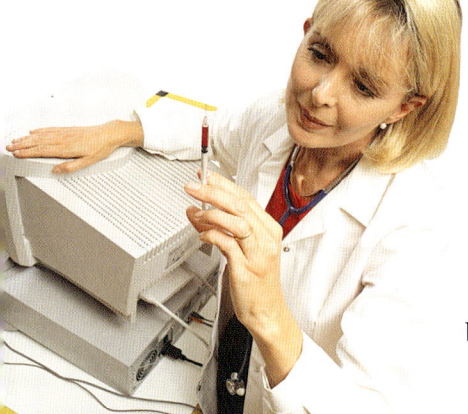

### Which software?

All anti-virus packages do the same basic job. The differences are in how good they are at detecting and removing viruses. The top products – **Norton's** and **McAfee's** – are the best at detecting viruses, although in practice almost any product you buy will detect all the viruses you are likely to encounter.

When destructive viruses like Melissa and IloveYou strike, it is best to be using a top vendor's product. Within hours of the bug first appearing, the vendor will have an update for their software available to download from their Web site.

When you do install the anti-virus products directly to your PC, the top programs will include highly effective background scanners. They detect all the viruses that standalone scanners can and they let you clean an infected file there and then, instead of making you run another program.

As viruses are often spread via the Internet, it is best to choose a scanning engine that will also check your e-mail attachments and screen any files you download. As files are often compressed to be sent over the Internet, select an anti-virus program that will check these files too.

If you are buying a package because your computer has a virus, choose a program such as Norton AntiVirus which includes a ready-to-use boot disk containing detection and disinfection software. Other anti-virus programs, such as McAfee's, include an Emergency Disk Wizard to guide you through the process of creating your own emergency boot disk, complete with virus scan information.

### You will need

**ESSENTIAL**
**Software** An up-to-date anti-virus package, a scheduler for regular sweeps of your hard disk and a write-protected bootable system disk to start the system from if the hard disk becomes infected — many packages include these.
**Hardware** A modem, as an Internet connection is useful so that you can download updates to the software.

# What is a virus?

## Jargon buster

**Boot sector virus** A virus that infects the part of your hard disk that the PC reads when it starts (boots up). This means the virus is activated whenever you turn on your PC. Boot sector viruses are often transmitted in the boot sectors of floppy disks. They copy themselves to the hard disk when you leave a floppy in the drive and accidentally boot from it.

## Jargon buster

**Macro virus** A virus written in the macro language of an application such as Microsoft Word. They are the easiest type of virus to write, and because people often send each other Word files, they can spread rapidly. You have a greater chance of encountering a macro virus in Word than in any other application.

## Computer viruses are destructive pieces of software written by pranksters or people with a grudge.

Viruses are software. Your PC runs them just like it runs other programs. The only difference is you don't tell your PC to run a virus. Your PC runs the virus because it has copied itself to a location in a file where it will be run without you realising it.

### Double trouble

Once a virus is active it reproduces by copying itself to other locations. This feature distinguishes a virus from other software. Most of the time, if a virus is active on your PC and infecting other disks or files, you won't even know about it. Unless you run a virus checker you'll only find out about it when the virus triggers its payload.

### Beware of infection

A virus can't do any harm until it is run. To be successful, a virus must infect things on your PC that have a high probability of being run, like the boot sector of the hard disk. This is a place on the disk that you never even see. It contains a program code that is run every time you start the PC. If a virus gets into the boot sector, it will run when you start the PC, so it will be active all the time.

The virus **Leprosy** displays this message while reformatting your hard disk.

# CURING VIRUSES

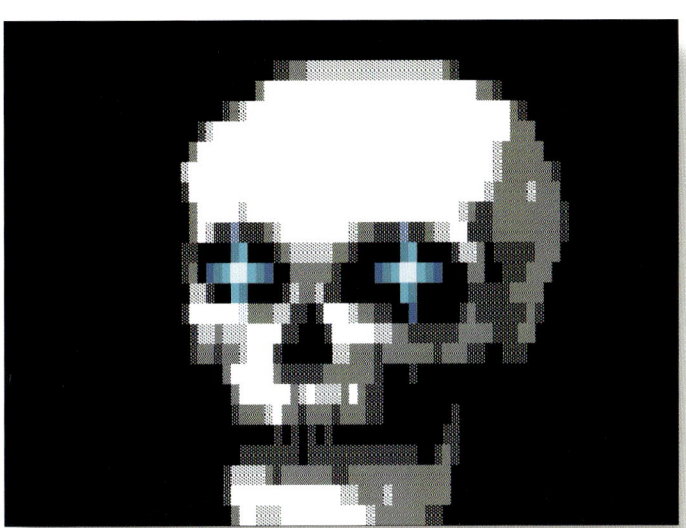

**The virus Phantom 1 displays this death's head and a message.**

Viruses that infect Microsoft Word documents are common. People often send Word files to each other instead of printed pages which makes Word documents ready vehicles for spreading viruses.

## Brainy stuff

The first intentional PC virus, called Brain, came to light in 1987 at the University of Delaware. This virus was unusual in that within its code was the address and phone number of its authors – two brothers in Lahore, Pakistan. The brothers claimed the virus had been written to punish people who made illegal copies of their software. It changed the volume label of a floppy disk to the message, '© Brain'. Brain was the name of the brothers' firm.

A month later, students at Lehigh University in the US found floppy disks were being corrupted. This turned out to be the work of a virus. The Lehigh virus, written by a student, counted the number of files it infected. When the count reached four, it overwrote the data on the disk.

## Catching on

By 1990 there were only a couple of dozen known viruses. Today, the number is around 60,000. But despite the large number of known viruses, few are a real threat. Most are never found outside the collections of virus writers and anti-virus software companies. Most viruses are not good enough at breeding to become a problem in the wider world.

### Jargon buster

**Parasitic virus** Viruses which infect program files. As the name suggests, they attach themselves like parasites to copies of ordinary programs such as your word processor or your spreadsheet, and are activated whenever these programs are run. Once active, they attach copies of the virus to other programs that you run. They can spread when you give copies of programs to other people.

### Virus myths

**Viruses harm hardware** Software can make your computer behave as if it has a hardware fault, but it cannot actually damage the hardware and cause a real fault. Removing all traces of a virus from your computer's hard disk will always result in a complete cure.

### Jargon buster

**Trojan Horses** A rogue program is not a virus unless it reproduces itself. Some malicious programs are designed to do harm when a particular event occurs, such as 'delete the database if my name is no longer on the payroll'. They are called logic bombs. A destructive program that masquerades as something useful is called a Trojan after the Trojan horse of Greek mythology.

In December 1989 a man calling himself Dr Popp mailed copies of an AIDS Information Disk to 20,000 European PC users. The program assessed your risk of contracting AIDS. Its method of spreading was to ask you to give copies of the program to friends and colleagues. Unbeknown to users, the disk also installed software that counted how many times you started your PC. When the count reached 90, the software scrambled the contents of your hard disk and invited you to send $189 to an address in Panama for an unscrambler program.

Since the AIDS disk didn't replicate itself, it was not strictly speaking a virus. It was a Trojan horse.

# PC doctor

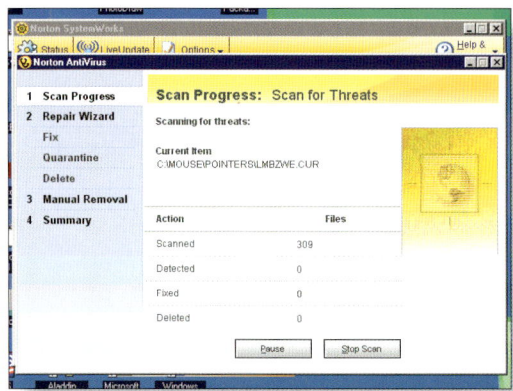

Once it has run its scan, Norton AntiVirus launches the **Repair Wizard** if a virus has been detected. This wizard guides you through the process of disinfecting the PC.

### Jargon buster

**Scanner** This is the name given to the most popular type of virus detector. It detects viruses by scanning computer files looking for the tell-tale signs of known viruses. A scanner has to know what to look for, and requires updating in order to detect the most recently discovered viruses.

**Auto-Protect** will ensure that any files downloaded or opened on your machine are scanned for viruses.

Internet **worm protection** is set on here.

**E-mail scanning** will check both your incoming and outgoing messages for viruses.

As yet a **full system scan** has not been run.

The red cross shows the **virus definitions list** is not up to date. To get the latest version click on the Run LiveUpdate button.

SystemWorks has an **activation system** to ensure a genuine copy of the program has been installed. After two weeks running as trialware, the software has to be activated or it will stop working.

## Regular use of good anti-virus software should ensure that your computer never falls seriously ill.

Viruses cause your PC to misbehave, destroy your files and make you unpopular with friends if you pass them on. You can avoid problems by installing anti-virus software, and using it regularly.

Most anti-virus packages protect your PC in two ways. They include a standalone virus scanner that you run whenever you want to check that your hard disk, a floppy disk or a file you just received is virus free. They also include a background scanner that loads into memory when you start your PC and checks each file as you access it.

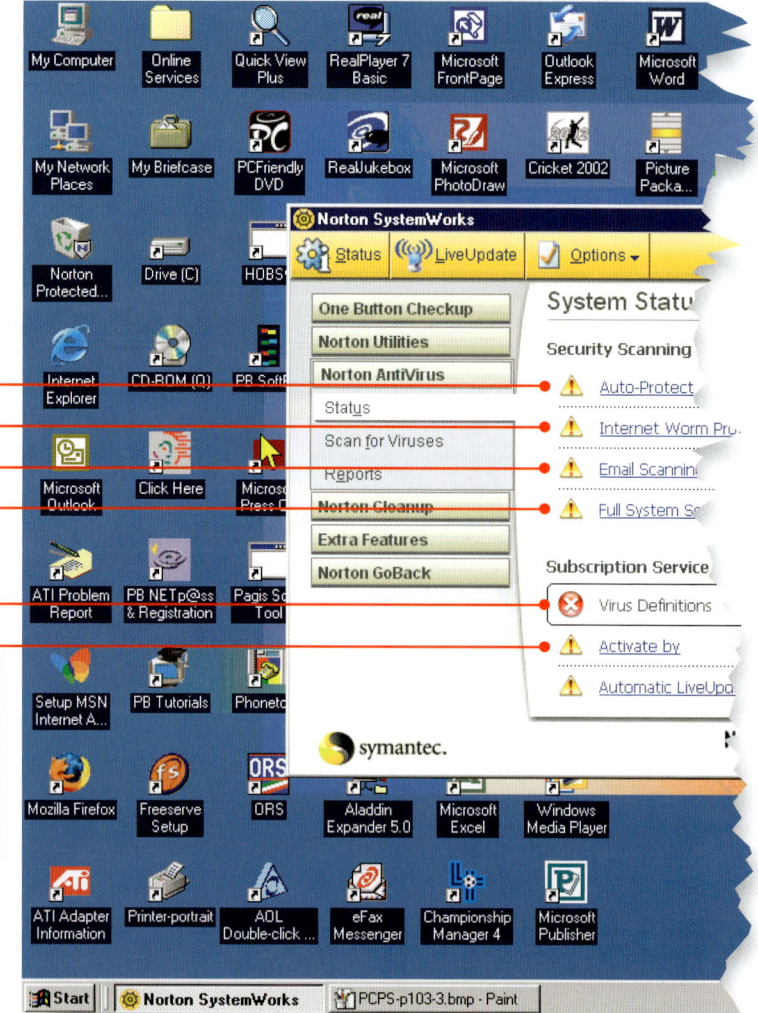

# CURING VIRUSES

A background scanner removes the risk of running an infected file and activating a virus because you forgot to check it. Some background scanners aren't as thorough as standalone scanners, so it's still worth checking your whole hard disk on a regular basis. Use a scheduler to run a full scan of your hard disk once a week. Many anti-virus packages have a scheduler; with Windows XP you can use its Scheduled Tasks control panel instead.

## Clean up

If your PC gets a virus, remove it. Some packages make this easier than others. Several include a boot disk or emergency disk that you can use to clean an infected PC. With others, you have to make a rescue disk after installing the software.

**With Norton AntiVirus you can download updates from the Internet to maintain the software's effectiveness at detecting new viruses. Just click the LiveUpdate button.**

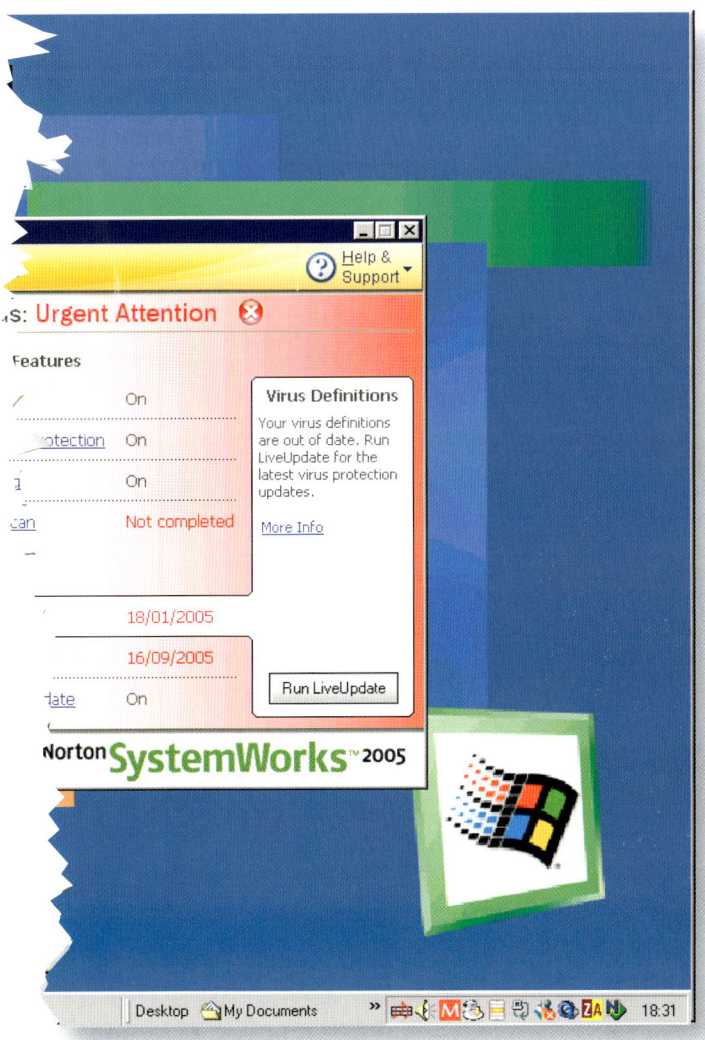

## Virus tips

**Sweeping up** With some products, the background scanner lets you remove a virus automatically as soon as it is detected. Others make you run the standalone scanner to sweep your whole hard disk and clean any infected files it finds. Viruses spread from file to file, so even if your background scanner disinfects the file it found, it's still a good idea to check your hard disk and floppies for any other infections. Some products have a Repair Wizard that guides you through the disinfection process.

**Updates** Anti-virus software must be updated regularly to maintain its effectiveness at identifying new viruses. If you are on the Internet, you can usually download updates free for a year or for the life of the product.

# Which type of virus?

## Jargon buster

**Heuristics** Sometimes called rule-based scanning, this is a method used by virus scanners to detect unknown viruses. Heuristics are not infallible, and they cannot say for certain that a file contains a virus. But they provide some protection from viruses that were discovered since your software was last updated.

## Watch out!

If you get a virus, don't just clean the infected file, check your entire hard disk and all your removable drives. It may have entered your PC from a disk you received and could have affected other disks. Viruses spread, and it will soon be back if you don't check all the places it could have spread to!

**The three most dangerous strains of virus to watch out for are boot sector, file and macro viruses.**

To spread widely a virus has to be active most of the time your PC is running and infect things that are passed around. Brain was a boot-sector virus. It was successful in its time, but it had a flaw. It only infected the now obsolete 5.25in floppy disks. It has become more or less extinct along with them.

Boot-sector viruses common today, like the Form virus, infect hard disks and floppies. They infect the hard disk so they can be active as soon as you turn on your PC, and they infect floppies in order to be passed around. The virus needs just a little help from you to get from floppy to hard disk.

## On the floppy

If you have ever switched on your PC with a floppy disk in the drive, you will have seen the message 'Not a system disk. Replace and press any key'. This is displayed by a program in the boot sector of the floppy disk. When you turn on a PC it checks whether there is a disk in drive A:. If there is, it runs the software in the boot sector of the floppy disk instead of that on the hard disk. If the floppy disk isn't a system disk, the message is displayed.

## Boot it out

Boot-sector viruses exploit this type of behaviour. When a boot-sector virus succeeds in infecting a floppy disk, it replaces the original contents of the boot sector with a program of its own. Usually it moves the original boot program somewhere else and runs that afterwards, so that when you boot your PC from the disk it will still start up – or display the 'Not a system disk' message – in the normal way. The difference is that the new boot sector program puts a copy of the virus on the hard disk, ensuring that the virus will always be active. Often this type of virus can prevent you from getting your computer to work at all.

## Creepy crawlies

File viruses infect ordinary files. When a file virus is active on your PC it adds virus code to other files you access, and modifies them so the virus code is run when the files are accessed in future. The longer the virus is active on your PC the greater the number of files it will infect.

File viruses only infect program files. Data files such as text files, image files or database files are only displayed or updated. They are never run and provide no way for a virus to become active. This means (with one exception) that data files cannot carry viruses. People tend not to pass program files around very often, so file viruses are rare.

## Malicious macros

The exception to the rule comes about because some data files contain macros. Macros are a way of building simple programs into a file like a word processor document or spreadsheet. Because macros are so powerful, they are dangerous in the hands of someone with a grudge.

Macro viruses are written in a macro language. The first example was written using the Microsoft Word macro language to show the concept of a macro virus – hence its name, Concept. Concept found its way into a document that was published on CD-ROM, and spread widely. Concept did no more than display a message box.

## Dotted about

Word macro viruses spread by adding macros to Normal.dot, the template that determines Word's startup default options. The macros are run when Word starts up. This means that after Normal.dot is infected, the virus will be active whenever you run Word, and any new documents you create will contain the virus. When these documents are opened by someone else they will transmit the virus to their own copy of Word.

Although macro viruses can be written for any application that has a macro facility, Microsoft Word and Excel are currently the only programs affected by viruses that are circulating in the wild. There are over 700 different Word macro viruses, of which about 60 have been discovered in the wild.

### Virus myths

**Viruses instantly destroy your data** Some viruses will result in the loss or damage of files, but no virus gives away its presence by doing something as destructive as that immediately after infecting a machine. A virus must remain invisible to you for a while to allow it to spread. If you catch the virus during that time, the likelihood is that no harm will have been done.

**Viruses can travel along the mains** Viruses are just software. They can only be transferred from PC to PC the same way ordinary programs and data files are transferred: on floppy disks, on CD-ROMs, over a network or from the Internet. Viruses cannot be transmitted down the mains cable, through the air or by mere physical contact with disks that contain viruses.

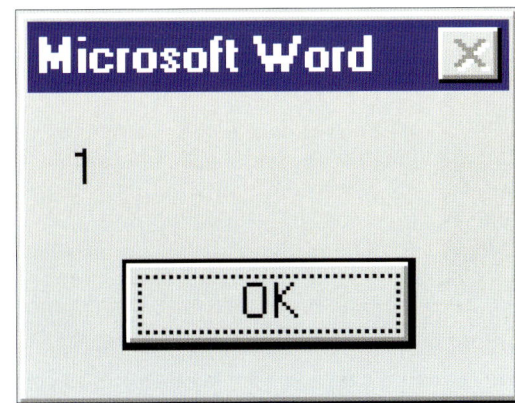

**The Concept macro virus simply displays this annoying little message box.**

# Don't panic

### Virus tip

Viruses have all sorts of effects, from strange messages to lost files and even inability to start your PC. If your PC develops an unexplained problem, a virus check is a quick way to identify or rule out one possible cause.

## Viruses are now an everyday part of computing life but it can be difficult to tell the threats from the hoaxes.

Thanks to the Internet, computer viruses and worms are more easily spread than they once were. For example, experts calculate that, when it first appeared in 2004, the MyDoom worm infected more than a quarter of a million computers in a single day. At the peak of this infection, one in 12 emails carried the virus. As the viruses are often spread by email, the only way to contain an attack may be by shutting down the email system temporarily. That's what happened with both the Melissa virus in 1999 and the LoveBug (also known as ILOVEYOU after the header shown in infected emails) virus in 2000.

Viruses can also be spread by file sharing networks or chat rooms. What makes worms like MyDoom particularly malicious is that they can open a 'back door' to computers. Beyond the initial disruption they cause, they can leave a piece of software on the computer's hard drive that can be activated by commands sent over the Internet.

### Harmless viruses

Any computer virus is a nuisance, but some have an amusing side. Cascade got its name because its effect is to cause the text on an MS-DOS screen to gradually slide down to make a heap of letters at

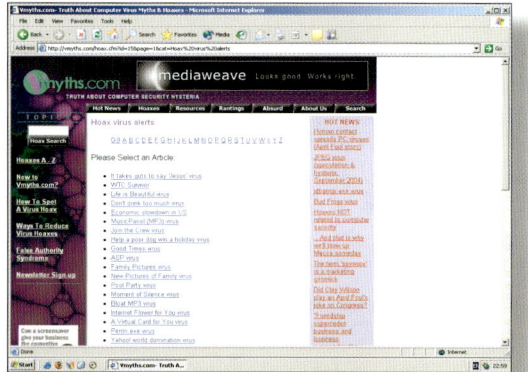

**True or false? Vmyths (www.vmyths.com) can help you discover if a security alert is genuine. It also has details of the Web's famous virus myths.**

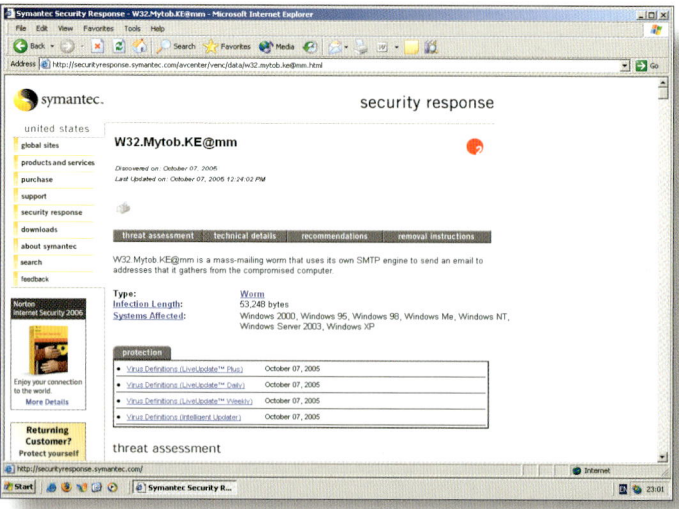

**The Symantec (www.symantec.com) site has detailed information about the latest alerts.**

the bottom. Ambulance causes an animated graphic of an ambulance to whizz along the bottom of the screen, while a siren plays on the speaker.

The Suicide virus displays a crude picture of a head in a noose and the message 'I will now kill myself. Press D to disinfect'. The Casino virus invites you to play a game of Jackpot. The prize? You get to keep the data on your hard disk.

## Spot a hoax virus

Difficult as it is to detect real viruses, there are also virus hoaxes. They may have come from a source you know – a friend or relative who has forwarded a warning about a new virus. That's how many hoax viruses spread. The email alert for the Family Pictures virus claims to come from Intel, the manufacturer of PC processors. In the email you are encouraged to send the warning to as many people as you know. In fact it is a hoax.

Genuine security alerts come from known experts or anti-virus software companies, and do not take the form of chain letters. What they will have are brief details of the virus with a link to the company's site. The link should take you directly to a page with more information about that particular virus – not just the site's home page.

If you're still not sure about an alert, there are sites on the Web – such as Symantec www.symantec.com/avcenter/hoax or Vmyths (www.vmyths.com) that list known hoaxes.

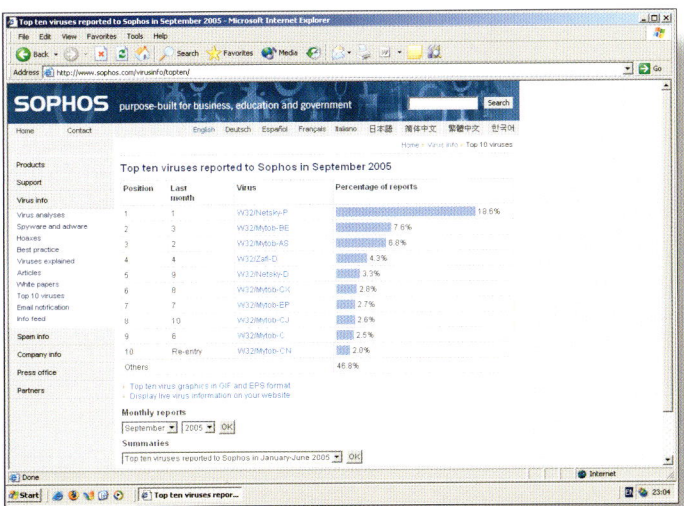

**Each month Sophos (www.sophos.com) runs a chart of the top 10 reported viruses.**

## Virus payloads

If you don't have any virus-detection software the first you'll probably know about a worm or a virus is when it starts tampering with your machine. Here are 10 of the most frequently reported ones. As well as the original virus, there may be several variants created, usually by different virus writers These variants are of similar design but may have a different effect.

● **Netsky-P** This worm collects email addresses from the PC and will try to mass mail them.

● **Mytob-BE** A worm that turns off anti-virus applications and allows others to access your computer over the Net.

● **Zafi-B** Email or peer-to-peer file-sharing networks spread this worm. It attempts to send itself as an email attachment to addresses gathered from the infected PC's files.

● **Sasser-B** Infected web sites deposit this worm on a computer where it then uses up the computer's memory and other resources so that programs can't run properly.

● **MyDoom-A** An email worm that arrives as an attachment that sends itself out to other email addresses when opened.

● **Bagel–AA** Part of a 'family' of worms that offers a fake message 'Can't find a viewer associated with the file' when it first runs. It will then try and shut down many of the system programs running.

● **Sobig** A worm that spreads itself as an email attachment to addresses gathered from the infected PC. It forges ('spoofs') the sender's email address making it more difficult to detect.

● **Blaster** A machine running Windows XP may repeatedly crash and reboot if this worm has infected it.

● **LoveBug (ILOVEYOU)** First this worm sends itself to addresses on the infected PC, then it starts overwriting specific types of files.

● **Melissa** Although this virus is designed to infect Word, the disruption it causes occurs when first launched. Then it sends itself to the first 50 names in an infected user's Outlook address book.

# Safety first

## Safety tips

● **Know your sources** If you use the Internet, only download software from reputable sources that check files for viruses before making them available. If you receive an e-mail from someone you don't know which contains an attachment, don't open it.

● **.rtf saves the day** When sending Word documents, save them in Rich Text Format (.rtf). Ask people to use the .rtf format when sending documents to you. These files preserve most formatting but won't include any macros.

● **Check it out** If you find a virus on your PC's hard disk, check every floppy disk and CD-ROM you can find, and remember to tell your friends. Anyone you may have given files or disks to should also check for viruses, otherwise you may find the virus returns.

## Virus myths

**My PC doesn't work, it must be a virus** Most PC malfunctions are caused by hardware or software failures, not viruses. Software failures are the most common cause of problems. They are the result of mistakes made by the software's programmers. These mistakes are called bugs. They are more widespread than viruses. If your PC plays up when you run a program, the problem is much more likely to be a bug than a virus.

**Only install shrink-wrapped software** This is a common myth. In fact, many PC viruses are widespread because they were distributed on mass-produced disks. The Form virus was found on thousands of pre-formatted blank disks. The Concept macro virus was first found in a Word document on a CD-ROM issued by Microsoft. Viruses have even been found on the driver disks of new PCs.

## The best way to avoid PC viruses is to keep your PC in good order and avoid taking risks.

Despite the fact that there are viruses around, you shouldn't be too alarmed; there are usually ways to keep your PC alive and kicking. For a virus-free PC, make sure that you take the right precautions for safe computing.

Always back up your system regularly. A back-up is the ultimate protection against data loss, whether through virus action or other disasters.

### Keep it clean

Make sure that the people you exchange disks and files with keep their computers virus-free and encourage them to use anti-virus software.

Always remove floppy disks from your disk drive after you've finished with them. And always write-protect the floppy disks supplied with a software package before you install them. This will prevent any virus from infecting the disks so you will know they are clean if you have to reinstall the software.

### Archive it

Don't run software that has been copied from someone's hard disk. If it's commercial software, it isn't legal in any case. If it's shareware, you should get hold of the original .zip file. A virus can't infect archived software.

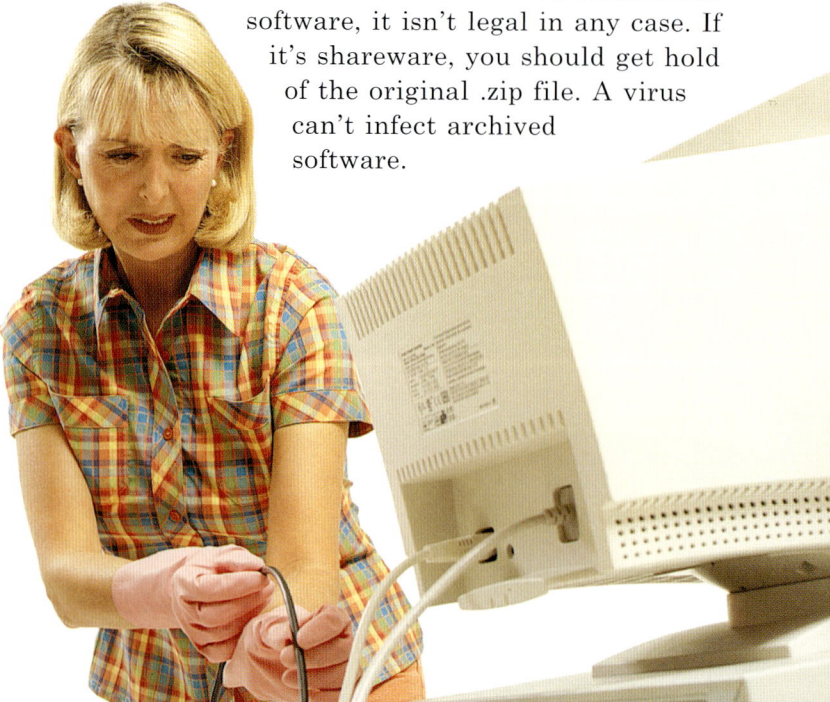

# 3

# Preventing Problems

## Housekeeping basics......111
Back it all up
Hardware care
Hard disk check-up
Tidying up
Keep it in shape

## Backing up......121
Storage facilities
Startup disks
Restore points

## Data protection basics....131
Physical security
Using passwords
When to back up
Multiple users
Copyright
Power problems

## Restricted access..........143
Encrypt it
Filtering Net content

# Housekeeping basics

**Dust off your hardware and chuck out all the old and useless software that's clogging up your computer.**

At least once a year you should spring clean your computer system, throwing away all the junk you've amassed over the previous year and cleaning what's left. Don't throw away any equipment, but get rid of unneeded files and programs.

## What you have to do
Cleaning is a two-level process: one involves removing dirt, dust and fluff from the hardware itself; the second involves scouring the hard disk to make more space and speed up the operation of Windows by relieving it of excess baggage. Your aim is to have a PC that looks good, works faster and is less likely to go wrong in the future.

## Preparation
Set aside a whole afternoon for the job. Assemble the various bits and pieces of cleaning equipment you'll need and if you're not absolutely certain which cable goes where in the back of your computer, have some masking tape handy so that when you start dismantling your PC you can label the cables by wrapping masking tape around them.

Before you do anything else, back up your hard disk. This process is described on the next two pages and is essential. If you don't have a back-up drive make copies of your data files on floppy disks. The chances of doing any real harm to your PC are remote but should not be ignored.

### You will need

**ESSENTIAL**
**Software** All the software you need to keep your PC in peak condition comes with the different versions of Windows XP.
**Hardware** You may have everything you need to clean the outside of your PC and its accessories already: a lint-free cloth, some non-abrasive, multi-surface cleaner, a kitchen roll, some cotton buds and a small clean paintbrush. The only specialist items you need are proprietary cleaning disks for the CD-ROM and floppy drives, and some disks for backing up.

**ALSO RECOMMENDED**
**Hardware** A vacuum cleaner with a tapered nozzle attachment is handy but not essential.

# Back it all up

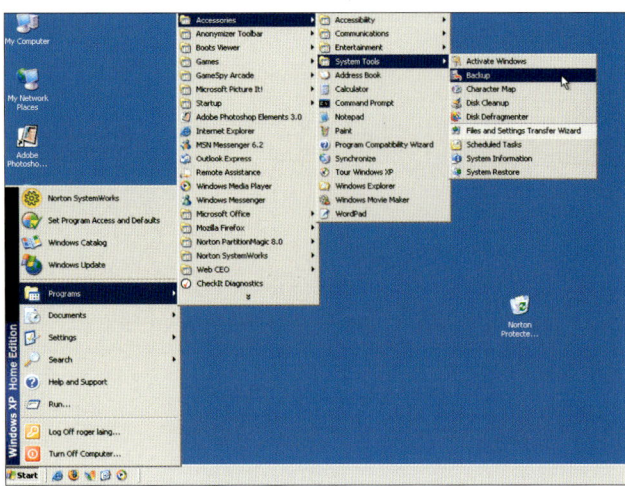

**1** To make a back-up in Windows XP, go to the Programs menu and select Accessories, then System Tools. Double-click on **Backup** to launch the wizard. In Windows Me and 98, double-click on the My Computer icon on the Windows Desktop. Right-click on drive C: and select Properties. Then select the Tools tab and click on the Backup Now button.

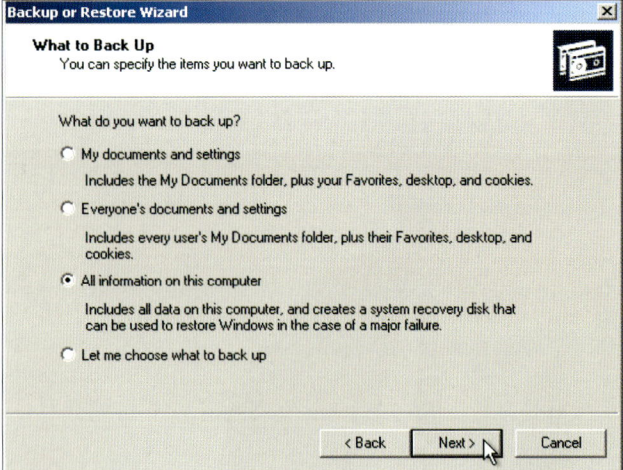

**2** This will launch the **Backup wizard**. Click on Next and select Back Up Files and Settings. Click on Next again. As you are doing a full back-up, when the next screen appears, choose to back up All Information on This Computer (All Selected Files in Windows Me and 98) rather than just those that have changed.

## Jargon buster

**System file** Any file on a PC that is essential for it to work properly. In Windows, the majority of system files are in the Windows folder and its subfolders but others are scattered about a hard disk in obscure locations. Some are hidden in an attempt to prevent their accidental deletion.

## It's essential to make a full back-up before attempting to tidy up the files on your computer.

Spring cleaning a PC involves removing files from its hard disk and because there's a chance that while doing this you might inadvertently delete crucial system files, you must make a back-up first. That way, if anything goes wrong you can restore the files from your back-up and get your system up and running again. Once you've tidied up your system and it is working at maximum efficiency you should remember to make regular back-ups. (See pages 18–19 and 121–30 for more information on backing up.)

## Ways and means

The sort of back-up to make is a full system back-up that includes everything on your hard disk: Windows, programs and data. Use the Backup program that comes with Windows or a more flexible product from a commercial vendor.

The back-up has to be stored somewhere and there are several alternatives. If you have two hard disks you can back up the primary hard disk onto the secondary one. The same applies if

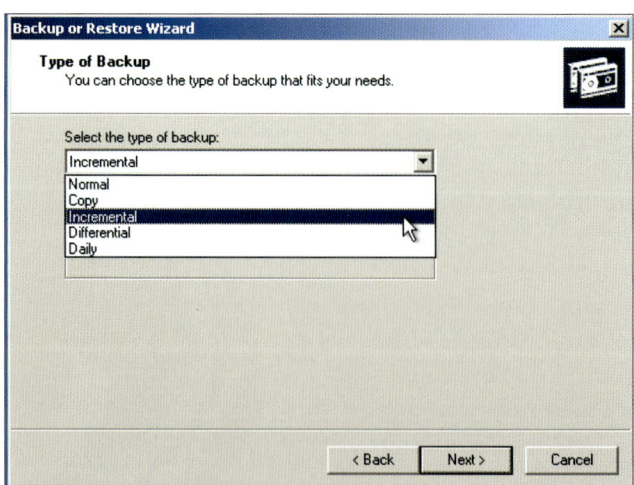

**3** Click on the Next button and select where you want to **store** the back-up. If, instead of a full back-up you selected Let Me Choose What to Back Up, you can select files. Check Advanced and then select Incremental for just those files that have changed since the last back-up.

## Installation tip

Backup is not installed during a typical Windows installation. In Windows XP Home edition, you'll need to insert your Windows XP CD. When the Welcome to Microsoft Windows XP screen appears, click on Perform Additional Tasks. Click Browse This CD. Go to the Value Add folder, then Msft, and then Ntbackup. Double-click on Ntbackup.msi to install the software.

## Jargon buster

**Partitioning** A way of dividing the space on a hard disk so that its host computer sees it as two or more disks. Partitions may be further subdivided into logical disks, each of which can be formatted without affecting the others.

you have a single hard disk that has been partitioned into two or more logical drives.

Of course, if you're lucky enough to have a back-up tape drive you can use that, but any form of removable storage will do. Zip disks that store 250MB or 750MB disks are fine, although none of these are likely to be big enough for a complete back-up, so make sure you've got plenty of blank disks. High-capacity removable hard disks such as the Iomega REV drive which can store up to 35GB (more if the data is compressed) are a better bet.

### More cash, more dash

If you're in the market for a back-up program, Drive Image from PowerQuest offers a unique solution. Instead of backing up each file on a disk, it makes an image of the entire disk and stores it on virtually any type of media – tape, removable disks or another hard disk. It's much faster than conventional back-ups – as little as five minutes per gigabyte – and the clever part is that you can restore a damaged system from the DOS prompt by booting from a floppy disk. The drawback is that you can back up and restore complete disks only, not individual files.

### Zip it up

If you haven't got a drive suitable for storing back-ups, buy one as part of your housekeeping regime. Remember that removable disks such as Zip disks or CD-ROMs/DVDs are best for partial back-ups or saving selected files – a full back-up would mean buying a lot of disks, which would be expensive.

## Back-up tip

The days of being able to back up a system onto floppy disks are long gone. It's technically possible, but you need so many disks and it takes so long that few people have the time or the patience.

If floppy disks are all you have, the best you can do is make copies of your data files using Windows Explorer and then create an emergency boot disk.

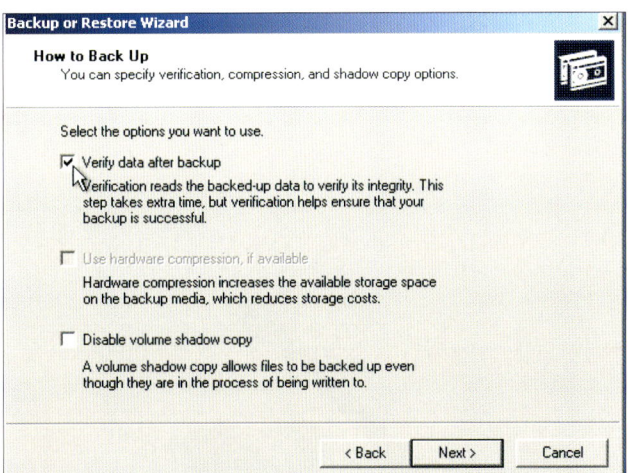

**4** Before the back-up starts, further **options** appear. Select Verify Data After Backup (in Windows Me and 98 this option is called Compare Original and Backup Files to Verify Data was Successfully Backed Up). The copied files will be checked against the originals to make sure they are correct. This will double the time the back-up takes. Click on Next and you can schedule a time for the back-up.

**5** With the full back-up ready, click on **Finish** and the program goes to work.

# Hardware care

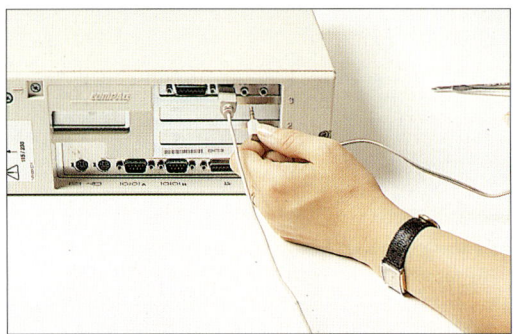

When reassembling your computer after cleaning it, insert and remove the audio cables several times to clean their contacts.

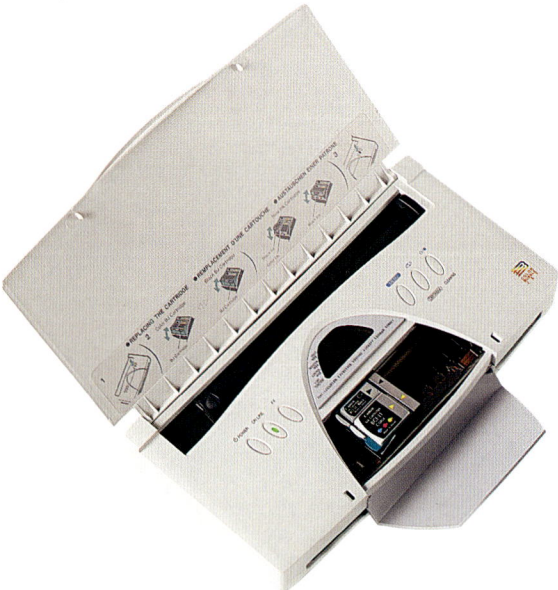

Remove dust and paper particles from the inside of an inkjet printer but don't remove an ink cartridge to clean its nozzles. There will be a button on the outside of the printer or a utility in its Windows controller for this purpose.

**Keep your computer and peripherals as clean as you can to extend their lives and stop them breaking down.**

Keeping the outside of your PC and its accessories clean isn't just a matter of pride, although it's undeniably satisfying to see a PC looking as clean as the day you first took it out of its box. The main reason for keeping kit clean is to prevent dust and dirt finding its way into floppy and CD-ROM drives, ventilation slots and even into the PC itself, where it can clog up cooling fans and cause overheating.

## Cleaning your PC

Disconnect the cables from the back of your PC and move the system unit somewhere you can turn it around and get at it easily. Remove all the thick dust using a damp cloth or a piece of kitchen roll. Use a vacuum cleaner fitted with a tapered nozzle to suck dirt out of the ventilation slots, the fan grille on the back and the gaps around disk drives.

You can buy tiny PC vacuum cleaners for this purpose but a domestic machine works just as well provided you're careful with it. Use a clean, dry paintbrush if you have nothing else. Ingrained marks can be removed with an all-surface cleaner, but make sure it's non-abrasive and choose one that doesn't have to be cleaned off with water.

## Internal checks

Remove the case from the system unit and earth yourself by touching the metal frame of the PC and briefly holding a nearby radiator or pipe. Examine the inside of the PC for dust and carefully remove

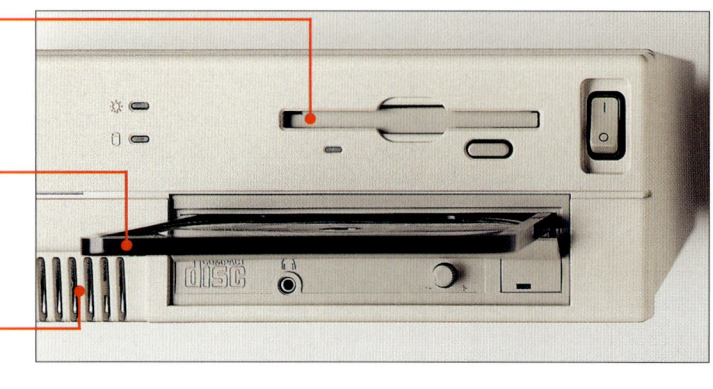

Push in the flap of the floppy disk drive and remove any obvious dirt and fluff with a brush or cotton bud. To clean the heads inside you need a special cleaning disk.

Blow away any dust and wipe the tray of a CD-ROM drive with a damp cloth. Clean the inside using the same sort of cleaning disc that's available for audio CD players.

Remove dust and fluff from ventilation slots using a soft brush or a vacuum cleaner.

# HOUSEKEEPING BASICS

any build-up around fans and ventilation slots using a dry paintbrush or cotton buds. Most of the chips in a PC are soldered to the circuit board, but some are mounted in chip carriers. Over time, expansion and contraction caused by heating and cooling causes these to rise out of their sockets. Push each one into place without using undue force and without flexing the main circuit board.

Check that all cables, connectors and expansion cards are firmly in their sockets and tighten the screws retaining any cards that have worked loose.

## Accessories

Mice, keyboards, printers, monitors and scanners all attract dirt, yet they're easy to clean and work much better when they are. Clean the outside of your mouse with a damp cloth and remove its ball. Wash the ball in soapy water or washing-up liquid, rinse it and leave it to dry. Clean the exposed rollers (there are usually three of them) with a tissue. Stubborn contamination can be loosened with a cotton bud soaked in isopropyl alcohol, which is what's in the cleaning fluids sold for cassette and video tape heads.

## Keyboard clean

Clean your keyboard by turning it upside down and shaking it gently. You'll be surprised at what comes out, especially if you smoke or eat at your PC. Clean the keys with a small brush. Stubborn dirt can be blown out using a can of compressed air or sucked out with a vacuum cleaner.

When you're putting everything back together it's a good idea to insert and remove the audio cables several times to clean their contacts. Once you've powered up the PC you're ready for the final stage, which is to clean the CD-ROM and floppy drives.

## Final touches

Eject the CD-ROM tray, blow away any dust and wipe it clean. The working parts of CD-ROM and floppy drives can only be cleaned using special cleaning disks. If your floppy drive isn't giving you problems you can probably ignore it, but CD-ROM drives need regular attention. Don't waste money buying a CD cleaner if you already have one for your audio CD player. They work in the same way.

### Cleaning tips

Treat the cases of your monitor, printer and scanner in the same way as the PC's system unit. The monitor's screen and the glass plate of a flatbed scanner should be cleaned with a proprietary non-abrasive glass cleaner. Don't open your scanner to clean inside unless its performance has deteriorated, in which case follow the manufacturer's recommendations.

Inkjet printers don't need much attention. The main cause for concern is tiny particles of paper dust that can cause the paper to slip as it feeds through. Prevention is better than cure, so open the cover of the printer and brush away any dust and paper particles. Treat laser printers in the same way and carefully remove any particles of stray toner with a damp cloth. Wear gloves and avoid breathing in the carcinogenic toner.

**The mouse ball picks up dirt and this sticks to the rollers. Clean the rollers with a cotton bud soaked in an alcohol-based cleaning fluid.**

# Hard disk check-up

**Maintain your hard disk and your computer will stay as fast and reliable as the day you bought it.**

One important way to ensure your computer runs smoothly and efficiently is to check the data on the hard disk. If you don't do this regularly, you may only find out that something is wrong when you try to access a file.

## Checking in XP

Windows XP comes with its own program, Check Disk (called ScanDisk in previous versions of Windows). It checks the physical surface of disks — hard drives, floppies or other types of disk — to look for faulty areas that could lead to data being lost. It also fixes mistakes in the file directory.

## Maintaining your hard disk

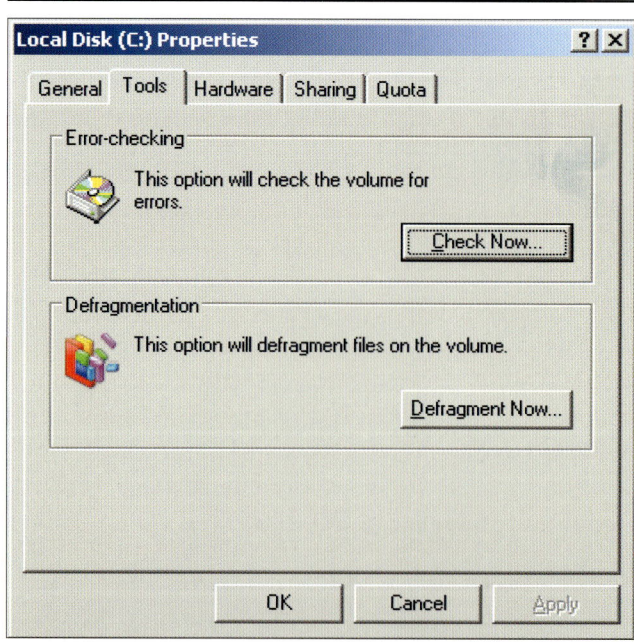

### Fact file

Your computer stores data in electromagnetic form at two main levels, so the computer processor can access it. Primary storage refers to the random access memory and other built-in devices, where data is kept on a short-term basis for fast access. Secondary storage facilities (on hard disks and other external devices, such as CD-ROM and Zip drives) keep and retrieve data on a long-term basis, and can hold much more data than primary storage.

**1** **Check Disk** attempts to detect and fix any errors. Repairs can't be carried out while files are open and Windows is running, so although you can set Check Disk to run, it won't start until you reboot your computer. To schedule it to run, double-click on the My Computer icon on the desktop and then right-click on the drive you want to check (here it's Drive C:). Select Properties and in the dialogue box that opens, click on the Tools tab. In the Error-checking section click on Check Now…

# HOUSEKEEPING BASICS

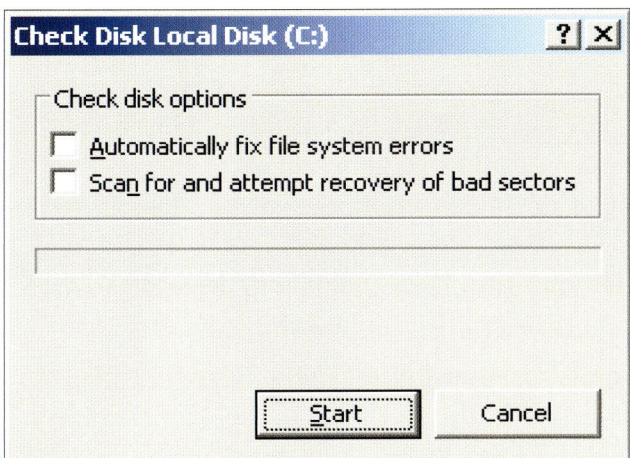

**2** The Check Disk box opens and offers **two options**. Selecting the first means Check Disk will automatically try and fix any errors detected. The second option carries out a full check of the disk's surface and will attempt to fix any problem areas where data could be lost. Make your choice and click on Start.

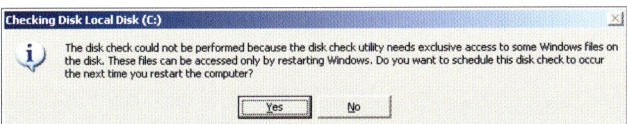

**3** A message tells you that Check Disk cannot run while Windows is still open, and offers to run the check when you next **restart the Computer**. Click on Yes to accept. If you choose No, the error check will be cancelled.

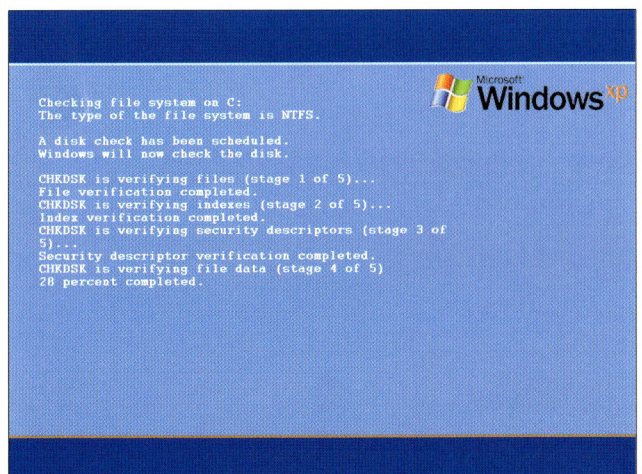

**4** The next time you restart the computer you will get a message that **a disk check is scheduled** and the program starts automatically. The blue screen shows a progress report of how much of the disk has been scanned, and any errors that have been detected and fixed. A full check can take 30 minutes or more to run, depending on the size of the disk you have. Once the check is finished, Windows loads normally.

You'll also see that Check Disk (or ScanDisk in earlier versions of Windows) runs automatically when your computer restarts after a crash, or if the computer hasn't been shut down properly. It is still good practice to run the program yourself every month or so.

**5** In contrast, **ScanDisk**, the hard disk maintenance program that comes with Windows Me and 98, can run alongside other programs. It does, however, take longer to carry out its checks because it's affected by other applications, particularly anti-virus software. To access the program, right-click on the drive you want to check, select Properties and the Tools tab. Under Error-checking status, you'll see how long it was since the drive was last checked. Click on Check Now…

### Check Disk tip

An alternative way to run Check Disk is from the DOS command prompt (accessed from Start, All Programs, Accessories). At the prompt, type chkdsk and press enter. If you want any errors to be fixed automatically type chkdsk /f. You will see a message saying it can't run until the system restarts. Press Y to go ahead or N to cancel.

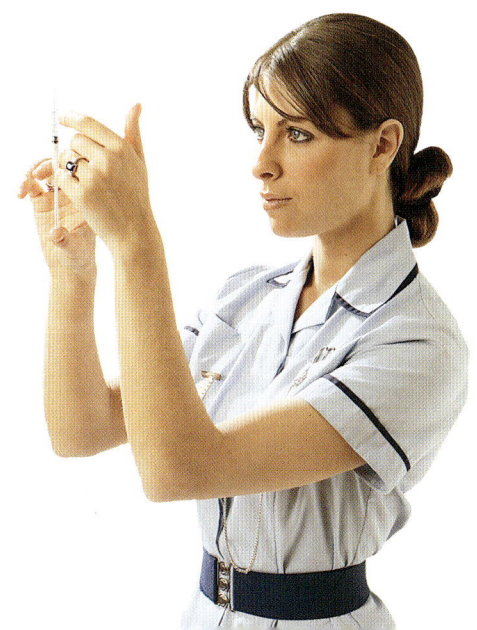

# Tidying up

## Defragging your hard disk

**Arrange your files efficiently and speed up your computer by defragmenting your hard disk.**

When you're working it helps to have your papers arranged neatly on your desk and folders filed in appropriate places. This is just as true for your PC. A computer must read programs and files, and if it wastes time hunting for them it won't run efficiently. At first your hard disk is filled with files in the order they were written. New files are added to the empty space. But, after a time, as you delete files or programs and install new ones, fragmentation occurs. Windows just looks for areas of free space on the disk, and if a block of free space isn't big enough for an entire file, it writes only part of the file to that space and puts the rest elsewhere, spreading it around the disk.

Defragmenting, or defragging, organises data on disk, so files are stored efficiently. It can take several hours, depending on the disk's size, so you won't want to do it every week.

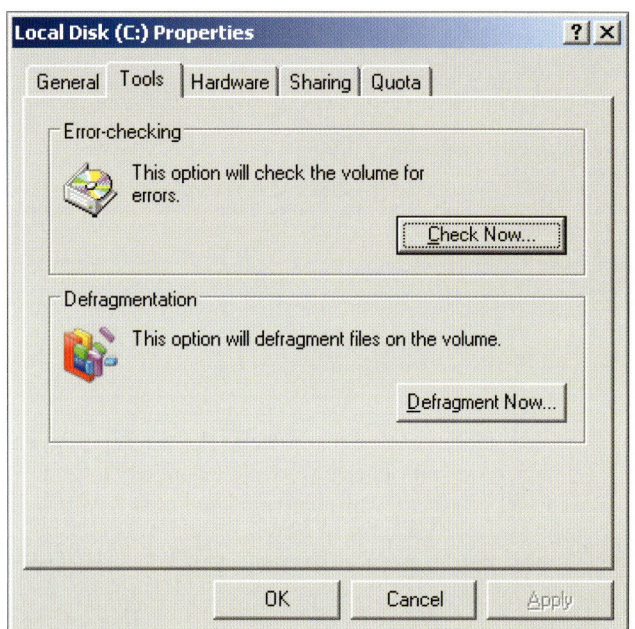

**1** The **Disk Defragmenter** in Windows XP has been upgraded. Now, instead of leaving you to guess when your hard drive needs attention, it analyses the drive for you and tells you if it needs defragmenting. In all versions of Windows, access Disk Defragmenter by double-clicking on the My Computer icon, right-clicking on the drive for checking, selecting Properties and clicking on Defragment Now…on the Tools tab. Alternatively, choose Start, All Programs, then Accessories, System Tools, and Disk Defragmenter.

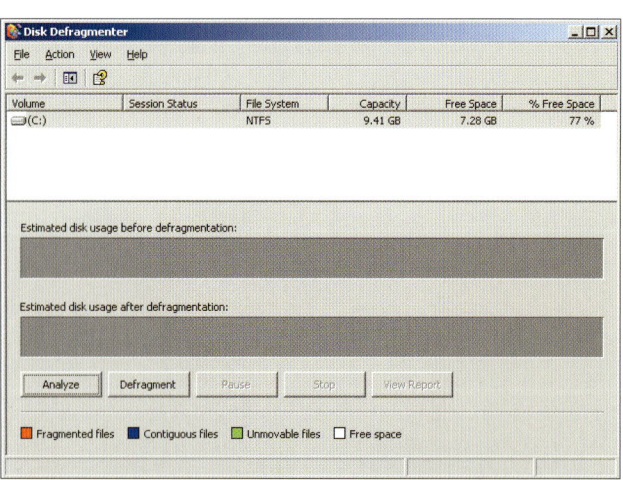

**2** In the Disk Defragmenter for Windows XP, the top panel shows **a list of the drives** that you can check. For each drive, it shows not only the type of file system, but also the percentage of free (unused) space available. Even if there is plenty of space left, the drive's performance might still benefit from defragmentation. To check if this is the case, you simply click on the Analyze button.

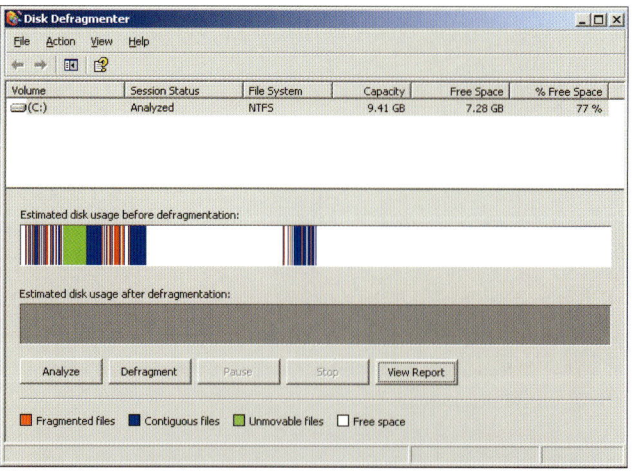

**3** Disk Defragmenter gets to work. You can keep an eye on its progress in the **Status bar**. You will also see several coloured bars – like a stretched out bar code – appearing in the box named Estimated Disk Usage before Defragmentation. The meaning of the different colours is explained below, but a lot of red bars shows heavily fragmented files. Once complete, a message box pops up recommending whether to defragment the drive or not.

## HOUSEKEEPING BASICS

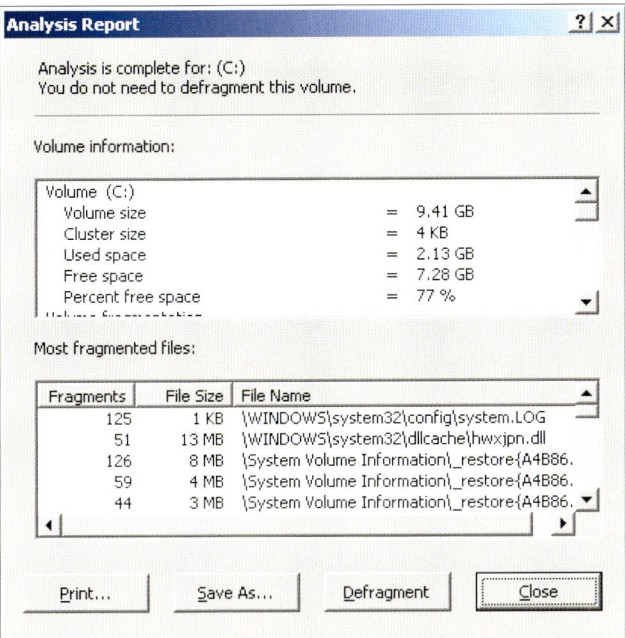

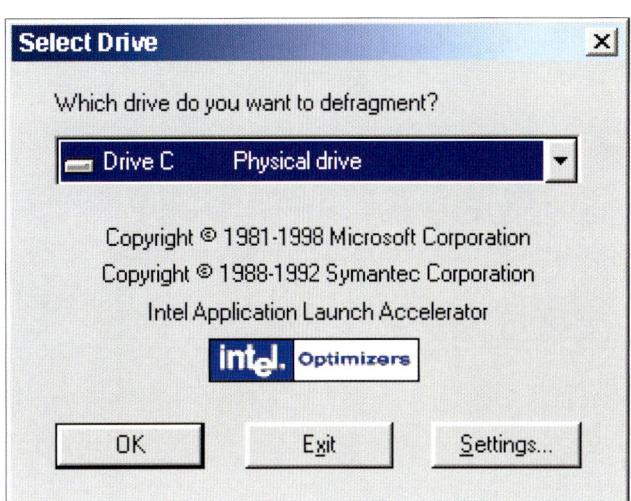

## Defragging in Windows Me and 98

**1** In **Windows Me and 98**, select the drive from a dropdown list. Click on the Settings button and select the two options to check the drive for errors and to rearrange the files so programs start faster. Click on OK and go to Step 7.

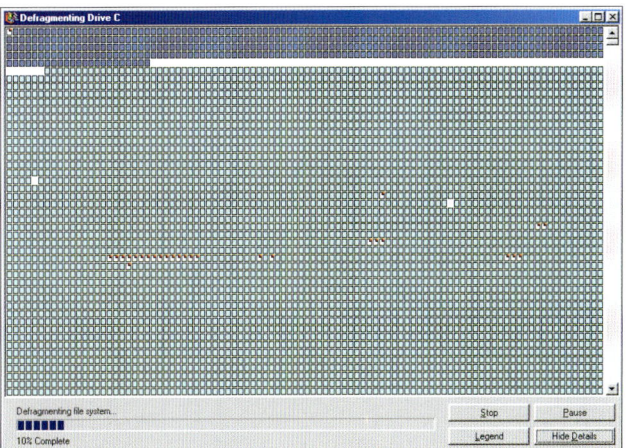

**4** If you click on **View Report**, you get more detailed statistical information about the drive, including the total number of fragmented files or programs, together with a list of the most heavily fragmented files. To start the file reorganisation, simply click on the Defragment button. To return to the main Disk Defragmenter screen, select Close.

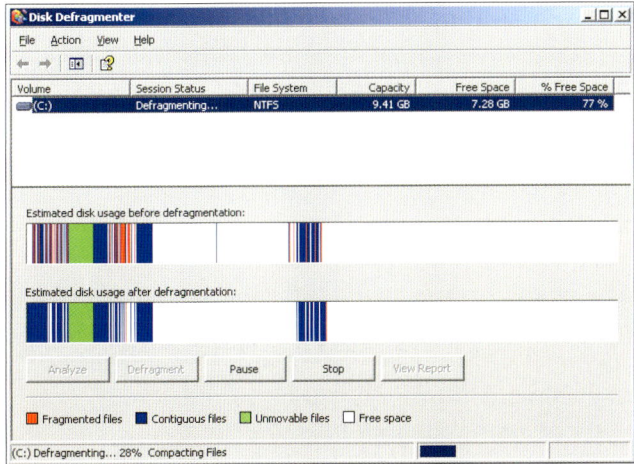

**5** While Disk Defragmenter is working, you'll see a series of changing coloured bars in the two boxes at the bottom of the screen. The first, as we saw earlier, is the state of your files now, the lower box is an estimate of what it will look like after defragmentation. Disk Defragmenter needs a certain amount of **usable free space** to work with – typically 15 per cent. If there's less than that, you'll receive a message asking if you want to continue, but suggesting you delete some files to free some space.

**2** The options for Disk Defragmenter under Windows Me and 98 are more straightforward. Having selected the Drive and chosen the Settings (see Step 2), Defragmentation is started by clicking on OK. If you want to see a more graphic illustration of how your data is being sorted into the best possible order, just click on **Show Details**. In order to see what the coloured blocks symbolise, click on Legend.

### Defragmenting tip

Whichever version of the program you run, it can take several hours to defragment a large hard drive. The process can take even longer if the drive contents change, because Disk Defragmenter has to start again. Background programs such as screensavers, schedulers, system monitors and anti-virus programs can cause disk activity even if you don't touch the computer. To prevent this, disable the screensaver and close down all applications.

# Keep it in shape

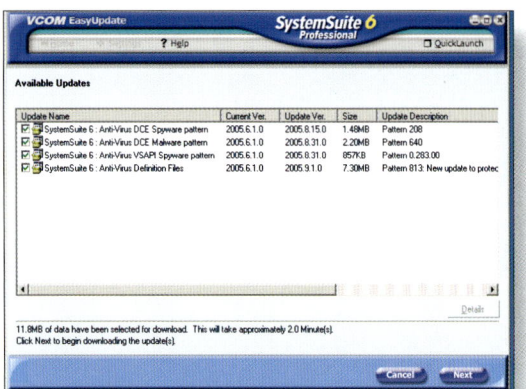

An integral part of keeping your PC in shape, of course, is to run anti-virus software. **System Suite's Anti-Virus** can be kept up to date by downloading new virus definitions direct from VCOM over the Internet.

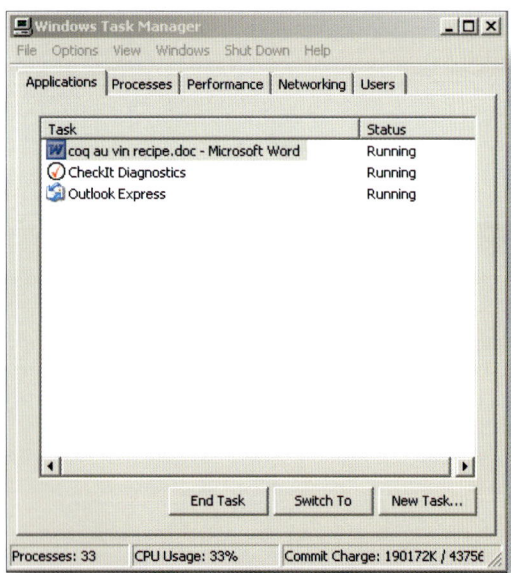

**Ctrl-Alt-Del** will soon show you whether you have any programs open but remember to press this once only otherwise your PC will restart.

**Before you run any disk cleaning software, it's a good idea to disable other programs that may be in use.**

Before running system utilities such as Disk Defragmenter on your hard drive – or restoring backed up data – it is advisable to disable other programs running under Windows that may slow them down or cause your PC to crash. Although you might think you've got nothing open, press Ctrl-Alt-Del and the dialogue box will prove you wrong. It shows a list of all the programs currently running. Programs to look out for include:

● Microsoft Office Fast Searching (Find Fast in Windows Me and 98), which regularly indexes your folders to speed up searches for Office documents. This can be disabled through the Task Pane that opens when you run a search from the File menu.

● Uninstaller programs that sit in the system tray ready to monitor the installation of any new programs. These can usually be disabled by right-clicking and selecting the appropriate option.

Similarly with anti-virus software which will stay 'on' monitoring your system and be confused by the changes made by the disk utilities into thinking your PC is under attack.

● Any scheduled program, such as one set up under Task Scheduler, suddenly bursting into action could upset the disk maintenance program. These can be disabled through the Scheduled Tasks folder.

● Any communication software – such as answering machines or fax receiving software which are set to open automatically. Again these can usually be disabled by right-clicking on the icon in the system tray and selecting the appropriate option.

# Backing up

**Feel confident and secure while you work, by regularly backing up and saving files.**

A back-up is a copy of the files on your computer, made in case your hard disk fails or your computer simply won't boot up. There are several kinds of back-up. You can keep a copy of the entire contents of your hard disk, or only back up the file or files from a single, important project. You can back up system files to restore Windows to a working system if something goes wrong. You can also back up files that you no longer use regularly, but wish to keep. (See pages 112–113.) Main back-ups are usually just of data files. Keep the original disks or CD-ROMs for the software applications you use somewhere safe.

## Options

Floppy disks are a good option for backing up a few small text files. They are cheap, easy to use and readily available, but they do not hold enough data to be suitable for regular back-ups. More convenient is a Zip drive, which uses 100MB or 250MB Zip disks developed by the Iomega Corporation. A Zip drive comes with special software to speed things up by backing up only the files you changed since the last back-up. If you have a CD-R or CD-RW drive, you can also back up on to CD-ROMs.

Whichever you choose, if the worst happens and you have to replace your hard disk, you can transfer your latest back-up copy of your files to the new hard disk. Back-ups of vital data, should be stored off-site in a fire-proof safe. Even a dry place in a garage is safer than next to the PC.

## When to back up

Hard disks have become more reliable in recent years, and there is a strong temptation to trust them. Nevertheless, backing up important data is crucial to avoid disaster. The best way is to develop a routine, rotating your back-ups between at least two different sets of disks or CD-ROMs. Zip disks or CD-ROMs are particularly useful for storing the larger files produced by sound, video or multimedia software programs.

## Making back-ups of documents

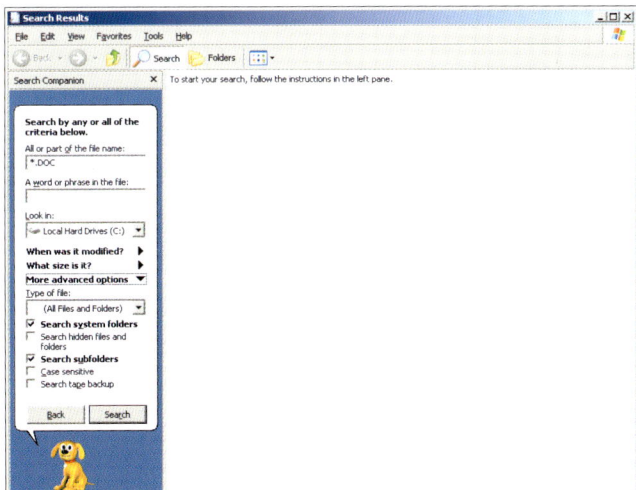

**1** Back up files quickly using **Search and Copy**. Go to Start, Search, followed by All Files and Folders in XP. In Windows Me, it is named For Files or Folders. In Windows 98, go to Start, Find, Files or Folders. You can use wild cards to select all word-processor files. If you're using Word, the default file extension is .DOC, so type *.DOC in the All or Part of the File Name box. (In Windows Me it is the Search for Files or Folders Named box, and in 98 it is the Named box.) Next, enter the location in the Look In box, though the default Hard Drive (C:) will usually be correct. Check that the Search Subfolders box under More Advanced Options is ticked. In Windows Me, this is the Advanced dialogue box under Search Options. In Windows 98, simply tick the Include Subfolders box.

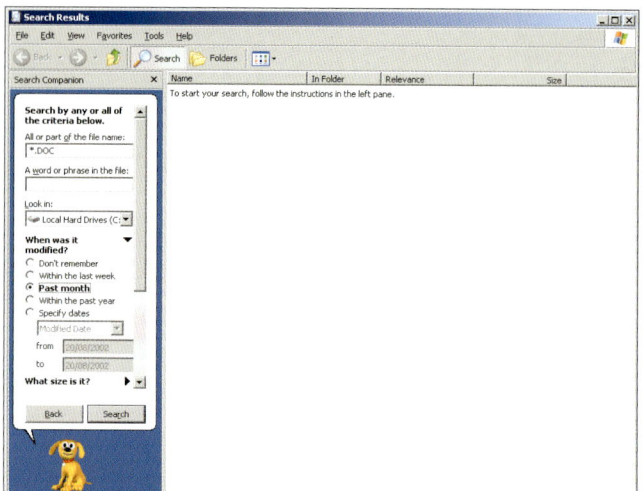

**2** In Windows XP, click on the arrow by When Was it Modified? Select **Past Month**. In Windows Me, choose the Date option and ensure Files Modified is selected in the dropdown list, then select In the Last One Month. In Windows 98 use the Date tab and select Previous Month. As shown above, you can also specify within the last week or year, or particular dates between which you want to find all modified files. With the time span set to one month, click on the Search button (or the Search New button in Windows Me).

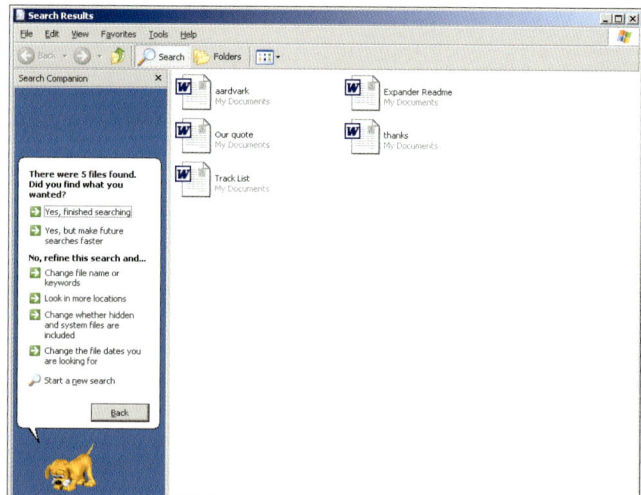

**3** Your hard disk will whirr for a while during the search. Then, in an area to the right of your search box, a **file list** will be built. If necessary, drag the bottom edge of the window to increase its size, so you can see all of the list. If the list is very long, you'll have to resort to the scroll bars to move down. Just as you requested, all the word-processor files that were modified within the past month are shown, regardless of their location on the hard disk.

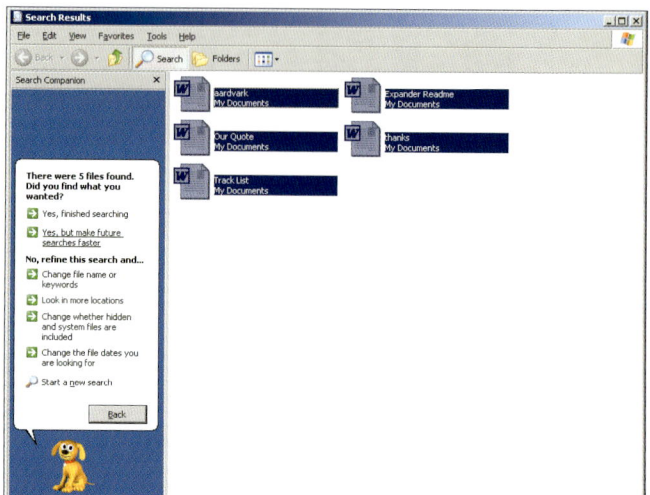

**4** On screen you need to be able to see the files and the desktop shortcut icon to the **back-up drive**, whether the floppy, Zip, or CD-R/CD-RW drive. Put in a new disk and highlight all files by clicking on the first and last ones. Click within the highlighted block and drag it to the shortcut. An outline of the files moves with the cursor, and a plus sign appears as you get near the icon. Once the icon is highlighted, release the mouse button.

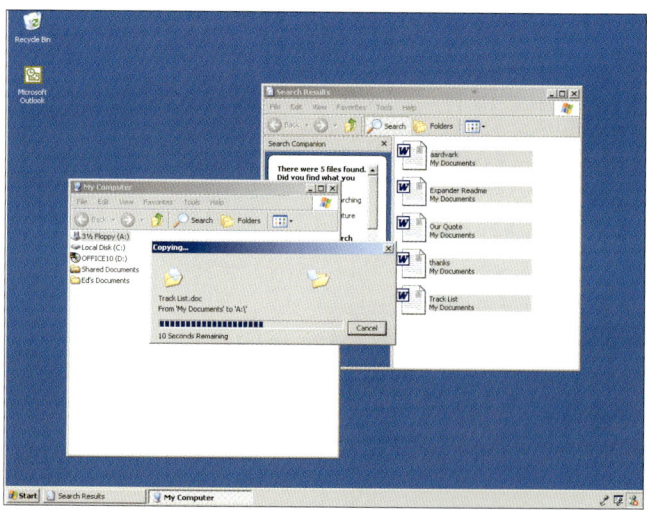

**5** The **Copying** dialogue box opens. Copies of your documents move across the screen from one folder to the other. When this is finished, copies of all the document files will have been placed safely on the disk. Put the disk in a safe place.

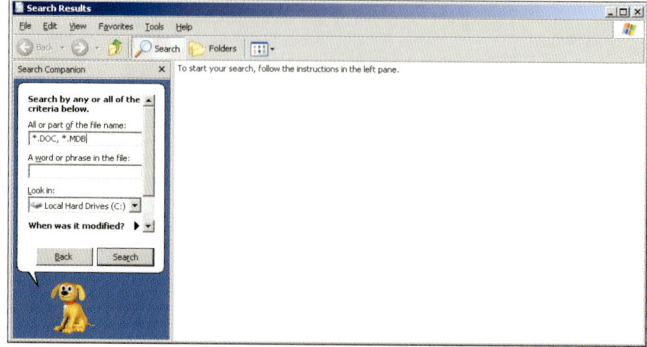

**6** If you've been working on database files in MS Access as well, for example, you can search for **both types of files** at once. In the Search section where you asked for all *.DOC files, simply add a comma and type in *.MDB (the Access file extension). Both types of files will now appear.

# Storage facilities

**Increase your system's storage capacity and keep your valuable computer data safe.**

There's a difference between storage drives and back-up drives. Whereas a storage drive can be pressed into service to make back-ups, the reverse is seldom true because traditionally most back-up drives have used tapes instead of disks. (See pages 18–19.)

The tape resembles an audio cassette, but the tape itself is wider and the cartridges are more sophisticated. Data is recorded magnetically and arranged sequentially on the tape, with one file following another, just as one track follows another on a pre-recorded audio cassette. The data is usually compressed to squeeze more on a tape. Restoring a single file from a back-up involves waiting while the tape spools to the correct location and the file is decompressed.

## Disks or tapes?

Removable disk drives are much faster in operation and easier to use than tape back-up drives. As with the hard disks built into computers, files can be randomly accessed at high speed because the read head inside a drive can jump straight to any file on a disk regardless of its position.

### Fact file

**AIT** Advanced intelligent tape drives and DLT (digital linear tape) drives push tape back-up capacities to over 80GB, but are prohibitively expensive for home users.

**Gigabyte (GB)** A measure of how much data a disk can store. A gigabyte is 1,000MB.

**IDE** Refers to the disk controller fitted to most PCs. The most common type is EIDE (enhanced IDE) which permits the attachment of a hard disk, CD-ROM drive and two other storage devices.

**SCSI** An interface that is seldom fitted to a PC as standard equipment but may be added by slotting a controller card into an internal expansion slot. SCSI may be used for hard disks, tape drives and diskless devices such as scanners.

**Streamer** Another name for a tape back-up drive, so called because it stores data as a continuous stream of information and not as separately accessible files.

**Travan** There are five variants of this tape back-up system (with compressed storage capacities from 800MB to 40GB) plus a special high-capacity, high-speed version for network servers.

### Buying tips

● Hard disks are very rarely fully packed with data, and program files don't need backing up if you've got them on CD-ROM, which makes it possible to back up a 3GB or 4GB hard disk onto a much smaller removable disk of 1GB.

● Choosing between SCSI, IDE, USB or Firewire drives is not difficult. Buy internal IDE drives for ease of installation or SCSI for slightly faster access. USB ports are more common than Firewire, so USB external drives are best if you are likely to be using them with different PCs. However, Firewire does offer the advantage of greater speed in data transfer.

### Watch out!

The capacity of a tape drive is often quoted as the amount it can store after compression. The true capacity is half the compressed figure. This is misleading because some files compress very well and others, such as program files and compacted JPG graphics, barely compress at all. There is no guarantee that compression will always double the actual storage capacity.

### Top five brands

● **Hewlett Packard**
www.hewlettpackard.com
● **Iomega** www.iomega.com
● **Seagate** www.seagate.com
● **Sony** www.sony.com
● **Imation** www.imation.com

The original advantage of tapes over disks was that they store more data. However, removable hard drives now rival tapes in capacity. The most popular tape format, simply because it has been around the longest, is Travan. This can store up to 40GB of compressed data on a single cartridge whereas Iomega's removable hard drive stores 35GB (up to 90GB using compression). Another tape format called DAT (digital audio tape) can store 80GB, but the drives are expensive.

### Use the same make

If you choose a removable hard-disk system rather than a tape drive, you should be aware that not all disk systems are compatible. For instance, you can't use the different capacity Zip cartridges in different drives. So if you want to share disks with others, make sure you all have compatible drives.

When the function of a drive is to store large data files or back up portions of a hard disk instead of its full contents, a Zip drive should be considered. The disks, based on floppy disk technology, are available in 250MB or 750MB sizes, but they are quite expensive if you have a lot of data and need to buy a large quantity.

You can also use a CD-ROM or DVD to store your information. CD-ROMs are about the size of a large Zip disk. DVDs can hold more data, but you would still need several to hold the contents of the average hard drive. While you can re-write data to CD or DVD re-writable disks, these may not be as durable as tape.

You should also consider how you want to connect the new drive to your PC. Most tape drives require a SCSI interface, which means buying an adapter card for your PC, whereas removable disk drives can be plugged into USB or Firewire port connectors. Drives are made for a single interface so you need to decide which one is best for you before you buy.

# Startup disks

## Create backup disks and configure XP to boot from a CD in case Windows refuses to load.

When you first switch on your PC it starts up, or boots, by loading the operating system from the hard drive. However, if Windows refuses to load, even in Safe Mode, you need a method of reinstalling the operating system.

In earlier versions of Windows, using a floppy disk containing the basic startup files and some troubleshooting software was often the only way to restart. Having such a disk to hand is useful even now, because it lets you access your files in order to correct startup problems.

Most programs are now installed from a CD. While you can create a floppy disk for booting in Windows XP, it's better to reset the PC to boot from the Windows XP CD. You can then access a special program called the Recovery Console to handle troubleshooting tasks, or even get Windows to repair itself.

## Creating a boot disk

**1** Put the Windows XP CD in the drive and restart your PC. On restarting, a dialogue box appears prompting you to press any key to **boot from the CD**. Do so and there's a message that Setup is inspecting your system's configuration before it starts loading files. If this message doesn't appear and Windows tries to load normally, it is because the PC is set to boot from the hard drive, not the CD-ROM drive. To change this, restart the PC and as it boots up press the key to enter your BIOS (basic input/output system). The method varies according to manufacturer, but you normally press the Delete key or a function key such as F1 or F2.

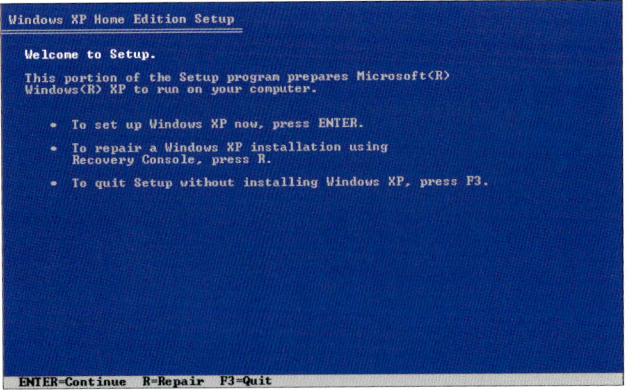

**2** The exact layout of the **BIOS** on your computer also varies according to manufacturer, but go to the Boot section that lists the order in which the drives are searched for the information needed to boot up. Move CD-ROM to the top of the list. Now the CD-ROM drive will be accessed first when the computer starts up next time. On the Exit tab click Save the Changes, click on Yes in the dialogue box to confirm, and then exit. The PC restarts and goes through the loading process for Setup as in Step 1. The blue Welcome Screen will appear with a list of the options available to you.

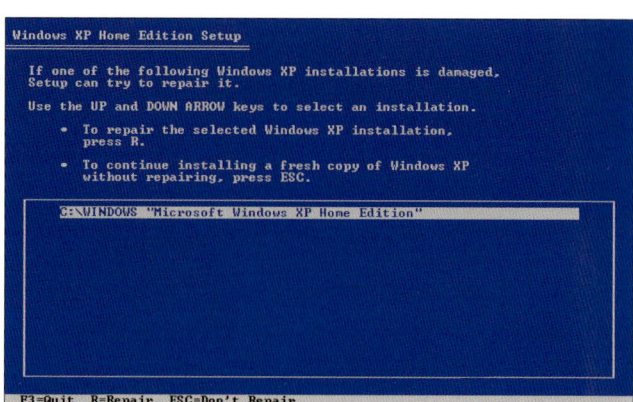

**3** You are prompted to press the R key to repair a Windows XP installation using **Recovery Console**. Do so. You'll then be asked which installation of Windows (that is, XP, Me or 98) you want to access. Unless you are running more than one operating system there will only be one option, so press 1 followed by Enter. At the next screen you'll be asked to enter the Administrator's Password. Type it in and press Enter, or if there is no password, simply press Enter and you'll have access to the console.

**5** Having made sure there is no problem with the drive, you can use the Windows XP CD to try and **repair Windows**. As in Step 2, restart your PC and when you get to the blue Welcome screen select the first option (To Set Up Windows XP Now, Press ENTER). At the next screen select F8 to agree to the licence terms, and then press R at the third screen to select the option to repair your Windows installation. Setup will copy over the files and reinstall Windows. Once finished, it automatically restarts.

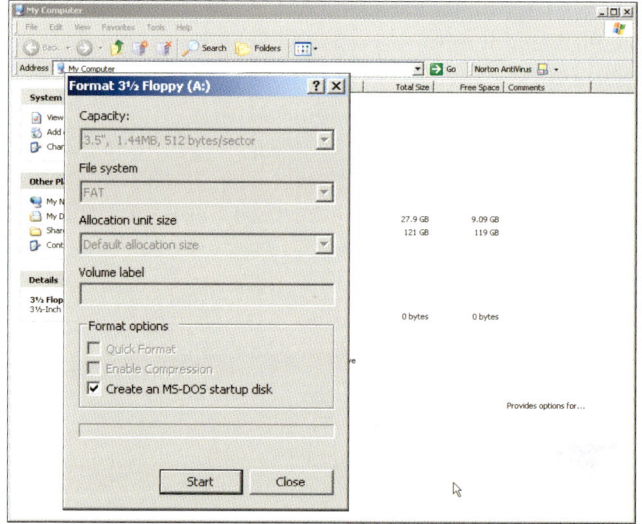

**4** You are now in the **MS-DOS command prompt**. There are 22 commands that can be typed in. To find out what they are and how to use them, type 'help' and press the Enter key. For further information, type 'help' followed by the command name and press Enter. Although many of the troubleshooters are for experts, you should at the very least run a test to check the hard drive. Type 'chkdsk c: /r' (or replace c: with the letter of the drive you want checked) and press Enter. The /r means that if chkdsk finds a fault it will mark off that area as bad and try to recover the data.

**6** You can create a standard **floppy disk** for rebooting in Windows XP by inserting a floppy disk into Drive A:, double-clicking on the My Computer folder, right-clicking the drive icon and selecting Format. Go to Format Options in the dialogue box and select Create an MS-DOS Startup Disk. In Me and Windows 98, open the Control Panel, open Add/Remove Programs and select Startup Disk. Click the Create Disk button. When prompted, insert a floppy disk, click OK and the files will be copied over. After the disk has been created, write-protect it to prevent it being infected by a virus. The Windows XP Startup disk will just take you to the MS-DOS prompt and has no recovery programs itself.

### Fact file

Most new PCs come with Windows XP preinstalled. You can make your own CD for rebooting by copying over an image of the rebooting floppy disk mentioned in Step 6, plus the Windows system files you need. However, it's best to check if a recovery CD, including the operating system files, is available for your computer. It may have come with the PC or be available on request from the manufacturer. Check the company web site for information.

# Restore points

### In order to protect your computer system, make a back-up of its configuration files.

Computers are complex pieces of technology. They are controlled by an operating system, which must be set up for the hardware that is installed and can be customised to your preferences. Settings are stored in the Registry, or other data files, and collectively these are called configuration files.

If configuration files are lost or damaged, your computer may not work correctly. To adjust your computer's settings in both Windows XP and Me, you can use System Restore. This enables you to restart your machine and go back to an earlier time, or restore point, so you won't lose any work you've saved. Windows XP and Me take this further, allowing you to create your own restore points. In addition, you can save several of them, depending on the space you allow.

## Backing up your configuration

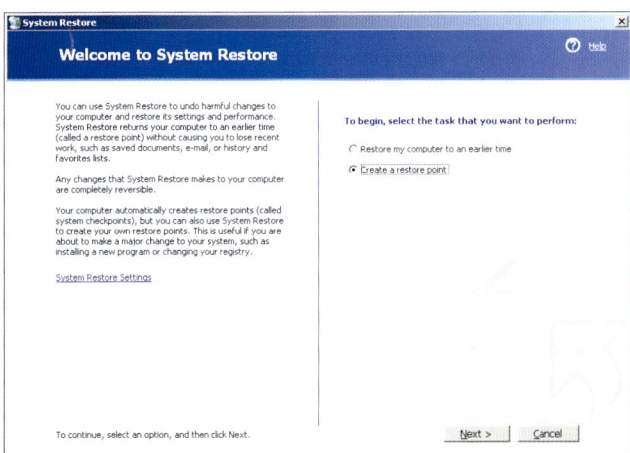

**1** If you are about to make changes to your computer – such as installing a new program or changing the Registry – it is wise to create a **restore point**. Start the System Restore Wizard. There are two main ways to access it. In XP, click on Start, then on All Programs (or Programs in Windows Me). Under Accessories, choose System Tools and then select System Restore. Alternatively, go to Help and Support on the Start menu and click on Undo Changes to Your Computer with System Restore. In Windows Me select Help, then click on Use System Restore under Fix a Problem. At the Welcome screen, select Create a Restore Point and click on Next.

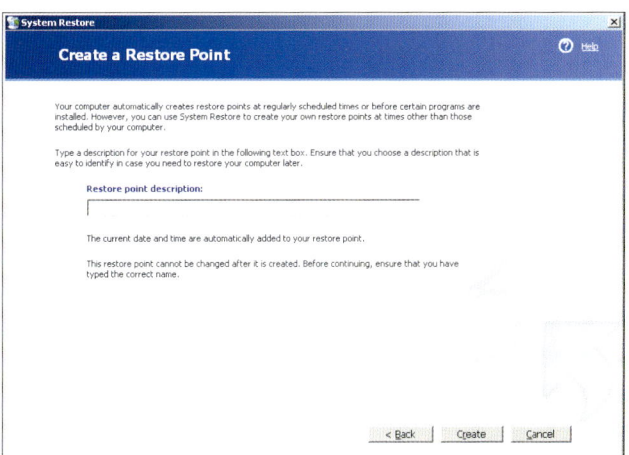

**2** Although the computer has its own **schedule** of restore points, this restore point is one controlled by you. You know that your PC is working correctly, and that the hardware is functioning. As this is the case, you want to be able to easily identify the ones you have created from the list of Restore points kept by your computer. Type a distinctive name in the field under Restore Point Description and click on Create (or Next in Windows Me). If you decide not to go ahead, simply click on the Cancel button. After choosing Create, Windows starts collecting the information needed to make a restore point.

# PREVENTING PROBLEMS

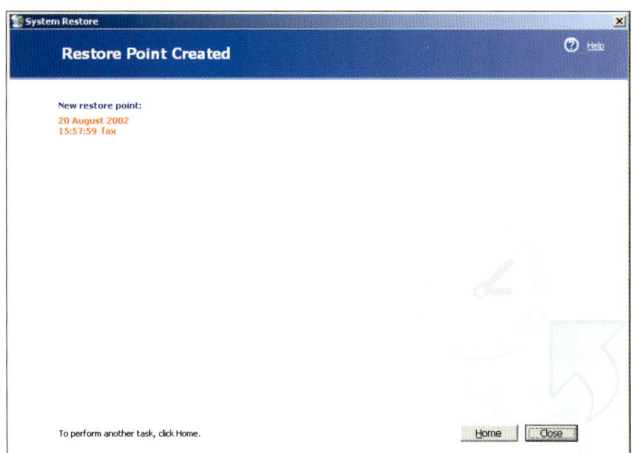

**3** The confirmation screen shows that every restore point is automatically **timed and dated**. A memorable name will help when you have to choose which restore point to use. In this example, the restore point was called Fax because it was created before installing new modem and fax software. To finish, click on Close (OK in Windows Me). Selecting Home will take you back to the beginning of the Screen Restore Wizard.

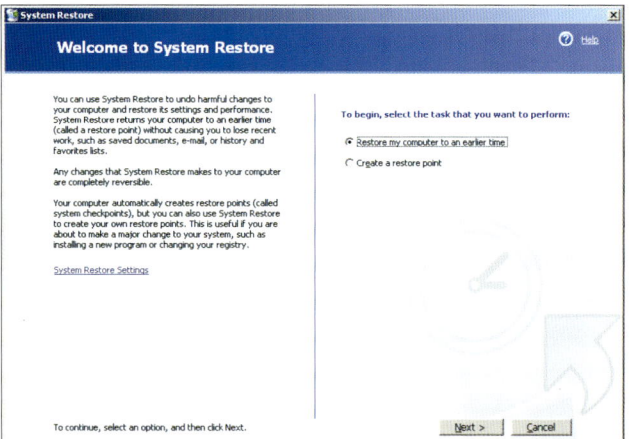

**4** If after making changes, such as installing new software, the computer isn't performing well, you need to restore its settings to a time when they did work smoothly. To do this, start the Wizard as before (shown in Step 1) and click on **Restore my Computer to an Earlier Time**. Then click on Next.

## Back-up tips

● Back up your configuration data regularly and frequently. If you don't, and you need to restore from a back-up that is out of date, important configuration changes made since the back-up was taken will be lost.
● System Restore needs a large amount of space to operate – at least 200MB on your hard drive. If that's not available, monitoring of the drives is automatically suspended and the System Restore Wizard won't run. To make more space, use Disk Cleanup to remove old files, or use the Add or Remove Programs control panel to uninstall programs or Windows components you don't use. When sufficient space is available, System Restore automatically resumes the monitoring of drives.

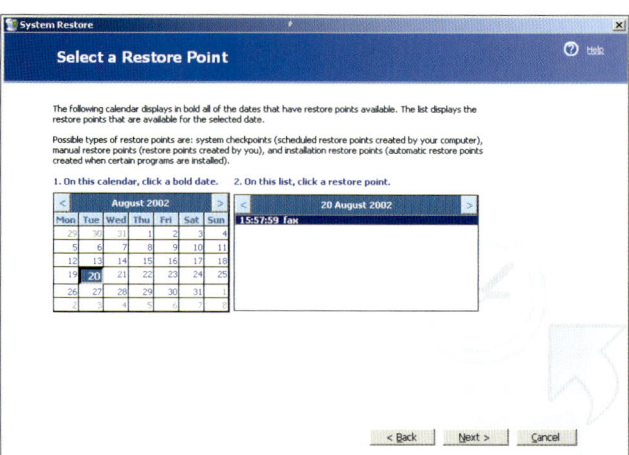

**5** The new screen shows a **Calendar** with the current date highlighted. On the right are the restore points recorded that day and the time they were taken. The dates in bold show when restore points were taken.

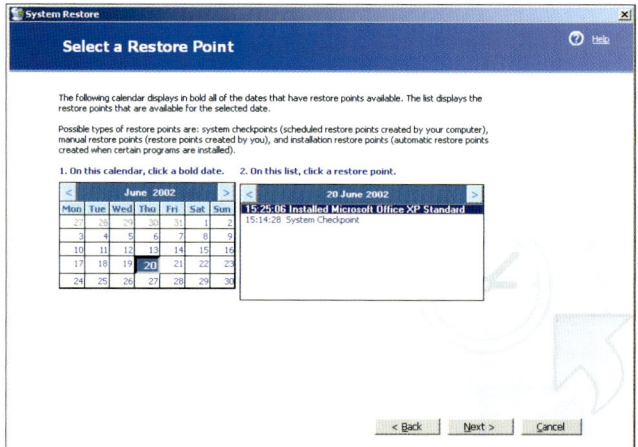

**6** There are **three different kinds of restore point**: the System Checkpoint, made regularly and automatically by the computer; an installation restore point, made automatically when drivers for new hardware are added; and a manual restore point of the sort created in Steps 1–3. Here, you need to go back to the current date (20 August in Step 5) and select the manual restore point – Fax. Then, click on Next.

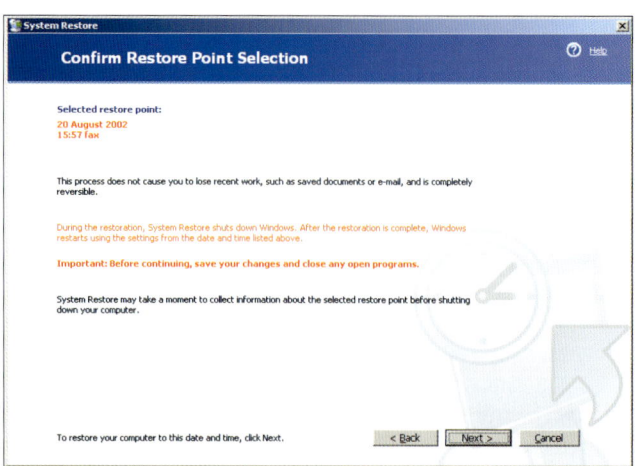

**7** Before you confirm your selection, this screen warns you to **save** your current work and close any open programs, because Windows will shut down to restore your chosen settings. Click on Next.

# BACKING UP

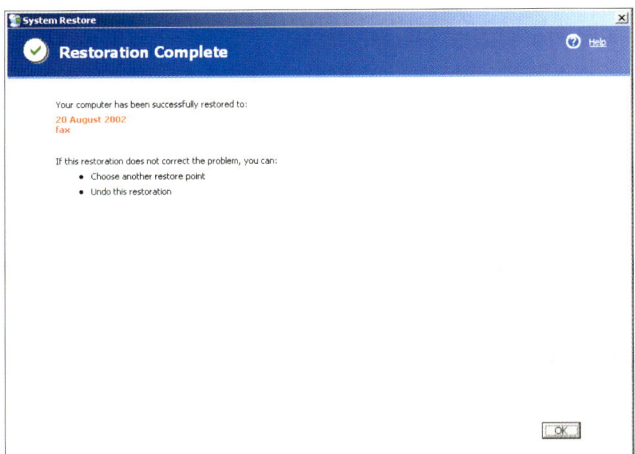

**8** The process may take a few minutes because Windows has to **gather the information** about your current settings before restoring the previous one. It will then log off and you'll see the System Restore dialogue box with a blue bar marking its progress. Then, Windows restarts and a Restoration Complete message pops up. Click on OK.

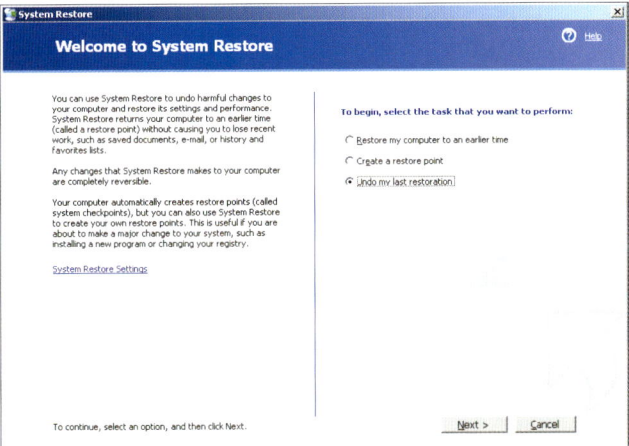

**9** If you realise that you chose the wrong restore point, there's no need to worry. All the changes made by the restore point are reversible. You can either go through the whole process again and choose a different restore point, or **undo** the one that you've just run. If you go back to the System Restore Wizard, you'll see a third option on the Welcome screen, which is called Undo my Last Restoration.

### Watch out!

When you set your computer back to an earlier restore point, using System Restore, you will lose any programs you have installed after this point. However, any data files created by these programs won't be removed. To open them again you will need to reinstall the program that was used to create them.

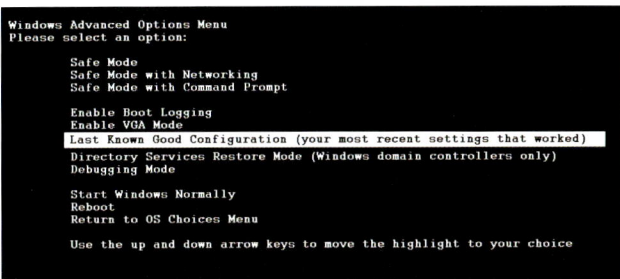

**10** In some cases, changes made to the computer's configuration are so severe that Windows won't start, and you can't access the System Restore Wizard. If this is the case, you can still restore **a backed-up copy** of the Registry to get your system running again. Simply start your computer and press the F8 key. This will access the Windows Advanced options menu. Use the arrow keys to highlight Last Known Good Configuration (Your Most Recent Settings that Worked) and press Enter.

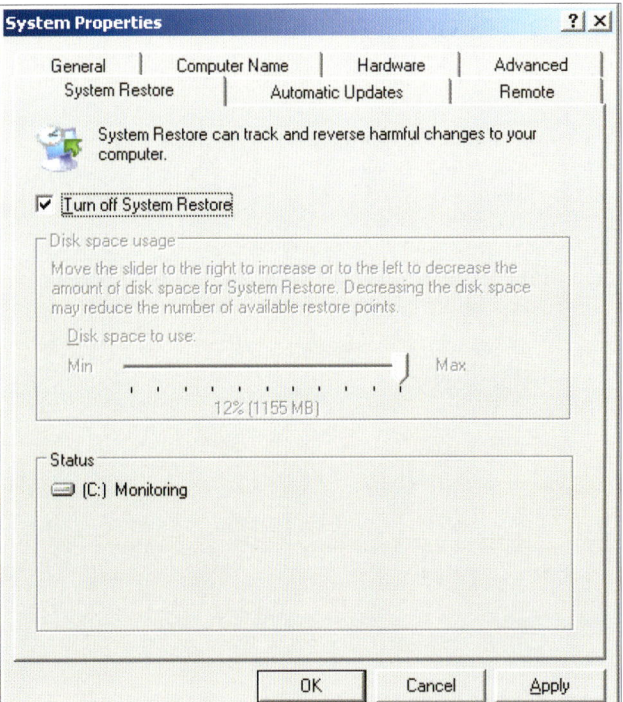

**11** It is possible, though obviously risky, to turn System Restore off in Windows XP. This has the advantage of **saving memory**. Each restore point is, in effect, a full back-up of the Registry. They are compressed files, but obviously the more restore points you have the more space they take up. To turn off System Restore, right-click on the My Computer icon on your desktop, select Properties and then the System Restore tab. Tick the box that says Turn Off System Restore. If you have several drives, it will say Turn Off System Restore On All Drives.

Alternatively, in the same tab, you can alter the amount of space allotted to System Restore (in Windows XP only). If you have several drives, the System Restore tab will look slightly different, with a Drive Settings panel showing all the drives that are being monitored. Highlight the main drive (normally C:) and click on the Settings… button.

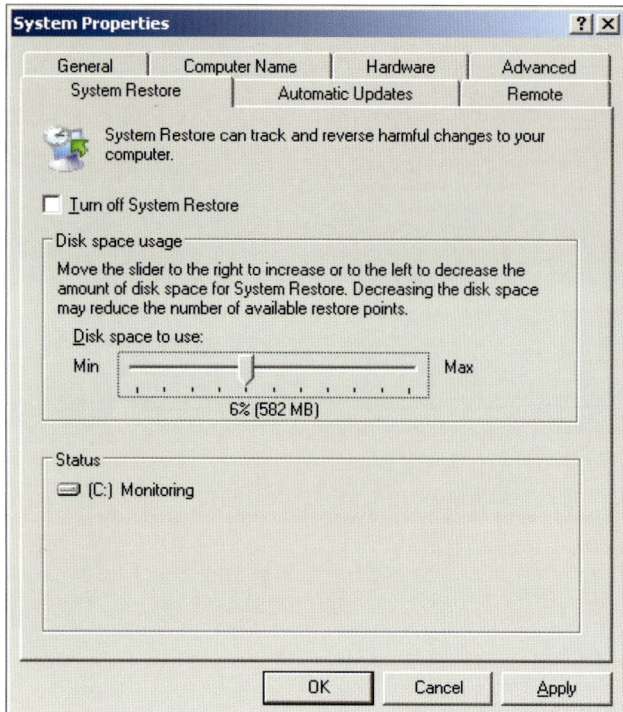

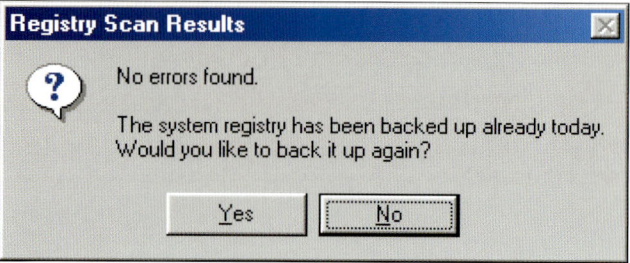

**14** The other disadvantage of the Registry Checker is that it will only keep one **back-up copy**. This is usually from when you last started Windows successfully, but you can make your own by starting Registry Checker. In the Start menu, go to Programs, select Accessories, then System Tools, choose System Information and on the Tools menu click on Registry Checker. A message appears saying that the Registry has already been backed up and asking if you want to replace it. To make your own system back-up, click on Yes.

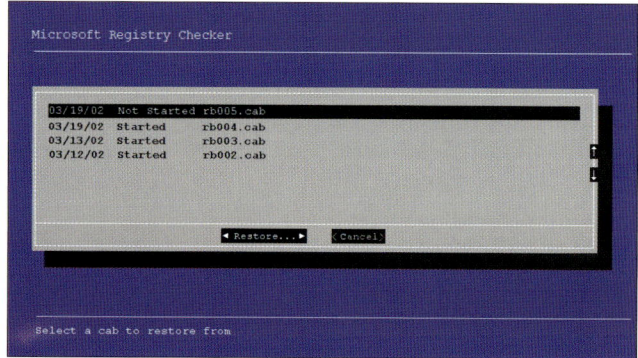

**12** In the **Disk Space** usage panel, you can move the slider to the right in order to maximise the number of restore points possible. In this example, it allows six per cent of the available disk space to be used for storing restore points. To restrict the space used – and lower the number of restore points that can be stored – move the slider to the left.

**15** The Registry Checker has a complementary tool that you can run from a command prompt if you are having Registry problems and you can't start Windows. You simply boot up, and when the computer reaches a command prompt on screen, type **Scanreg** and hit Enter. The text-based interface lets you check the Registry, make a back-up, or View and Restore from previous back-ups. Registry back-ups are stored as .cab files (a compressed format) and Registry Checker shows you the date the back-ups were made, so you can pick one that pre-dates the problem. For an even easier way to solve Registry problems, from the command prompt, type Scanreg/restore – which will restore from the previous day's back-up – or Scanreg/fix – which attempts to fix any problems in the current Registry.

**13** Although it's not possible to create your own restore points with Windows 98, it comes with a similar feature called **Registry Checker**. This program automatically keeps a back-up of your Registry files, including all your user preferences, program settings, and so on. Each time you start up, Registry Checker will scan the registry. If it detects a problem, it attempts to fix it by restoring the back-up copy, which was taken the last time Windows successfully launched. This is not as comprehensive a program as System Restore, and won't correct any drivers (.vxd files) that have been deleted. This means you may still get annoying messages about missing files.

### Fact file

In summary, the possible types of restore points for your system's configuration are:
- **System checkpoints** which are scheduled restore points that your computer creates;
- **Manual restore points** which you create yourself;
- **Installation restore points** which are automatically created when you install certain programs.

# Data protection basics

**Protecting your PC from physical damage or theft is important, but protecting data is absolutely vital.**

### You will need

**ESSENTIAL**
**Software** Security software like anti-virus, encryption and recovery programs can be bought separately or in suites such as VCOM's SystemSuite and Symantec's Norton Utilities.
**Hardware** A PC system running Windows can be made reasonably secure but additional hardware such as a removable tape or disk back-up drive is highly recommended.

Your PC is valuable but the data and programs it contains are worth even more. If your computer is stolen or irreparably damaged in an accident you might be insured for its full replacement value, but however generous the compensation, it won't begin to cover the real cost of your lost data.

### Time machine
What can never be replaced is the time you put into getting your PC to work properly and into creating, collating and entering data. Even on a domestic computer system there'll be letters, household accounts, homework projects and all manner of documents that could take ages to retype – and then only if you're lucky enough to have printed copies to work from.

Reconstituting the data on a business system for which there's no back-up might be impossible, unless scrupulous paper records have been kept. At best it's an expensive and time-consuming process.

### Configure it out
Entering data is a tedious enough affair, but you might also have to spend days or weeks reinstalling programs, customising them and creating templates and report layouts for your word processor, spreadsheet and other software. So while protecting your PC against total loss or theft is important, preserving your system configuration and data is vital.

### Plan ahead
Fortunately, there are many precautions that you can take without spending anything at all, and some of them are described on the following pages. If you're also prepared to make a few relatively minor investments in security hardware and software, you should be able to sleep peacefully.

# Physical security

## There is plenty of equipment you can buy to protect your hardware and software from damage or theft.

If your home is broken into and you lose your TV, hi-fi or camera, the cost of replacement should be covered by the sort of all-risks policy provided by reputable insurance companies.

There are also insurance policies which will cover against the cost of restoring stolen or fire-damaged computers, programs and data. But it's small compensation for the immense effort needed to get the new systems up and running smoothly.

There are firms that offer back-ups or storage of critical data over the Web, so it can easily be retrieved in an emergency. Some also provide a disaster recovery service where replacement computers can be delivered within hours.

### Anti-theft devices

The main risks to PCs are theft, fire and accidental damage. In business, you take the same measures to protect against opportunistic theft by employees as you would to safeguard other items of business equipment. These include asset tagging and security marking, securing rooms and kit when not in use, and implementing access control to keep staff or visitors straying from public areas into offices.

**Lockable cables** are a cheap form of security that's not too expensive for home use. Several pieces of equipment can be protected by a single cable, yet still be easily moved when required.

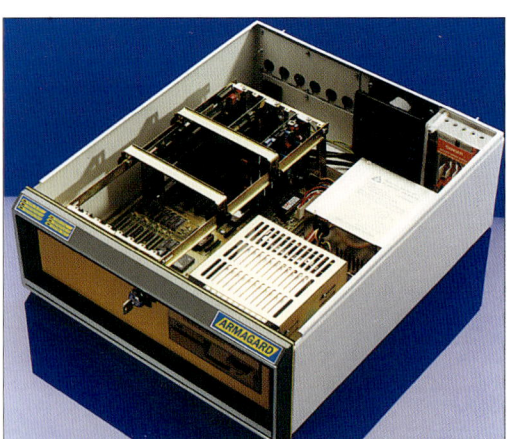

**Disk drive locking devices** prevent the use of unauthorised software and protect against intrusive fingers and objects.

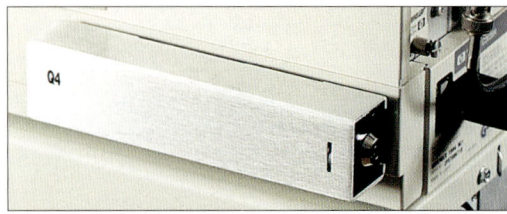

**Motion-sensitive alarms** are great if somebody hears them, but there's always the danger thieves will trash equipment to silence the alarm.

### Insurance tip

In the UK, the Association of British Insurers advises those who think that their computer equipment is covered by a household policy to check the terms of the policy regarding high-value items. Typically, cover is limited to around £1,500 per item, but many insurers regard a computer system as a single item and the value of a PC, printer, scanner and other peripherals taken together is almost certain to exceed the single item limit on many insurance policies.

Disclosing your possession of a high-value computer system to your insurance company does not necessarily result in increased premiums unless you specifically want to cover the uninsured risk, which costs much the same as additional cover for jewellery, pictures and other high-value items.

Professional theft is the most difficult to prevent. Keeping thieves out of your premises is the highest priority but, assuming that a determined thief will gain entry, individual items of equipment can be protected. Most systems involve fixing the computer to something that's immovable or difficult to move, such as a desk or workstation. This can be done using a cabling system that connects several pieces of equipment to a single locking point.

## Cage it

Another approach is to lock equipment directly to work surfaces using bolts or industrial adhesives. This is an effective but drastic step that makes PCs hard to service and may invalidate manufacturers' warranties. It's more common to bolt steel security cages around equipment. Cages are available that allow PCs to be used even with the cage in place. Motion-sensitive alarms can be attached internally or externally to key items of kit, but these are of little benefit if there's nobody around to hear them.

In the home, cable systems or alarms are the practical choices. When fitting a cable security device, it's important that it should also prevent the removal of the case because thieves are just as likely to take valuable processors, memory and hard disks as they are to remove a complete system.

## Fire precautions

There are no specific fire risks attached to PC equipment, which is protected by whatever standard fire prevention measures apply to the rest of a building. What is important is to protect the data that's stored on PCs. The key concern in the event of a fire is to protect back-up tapes or disks so they are not destroyed along with the PC itself.

In business, this means a fireproof safe, which also protects against the loss of back-ups through theft. A specialist fireproof safe need not be too expensive because tapes and disks are not bulky. Fireproof safes do not cost a huge amount of money and can be accommodated almost anywhere.

In the home, where a fireproof safe may not be necessary, store back-up media in a room as far away as possible from the PC itself. The total destruction of buildings through fire is not common so this may be enough to preserve your back-ups.

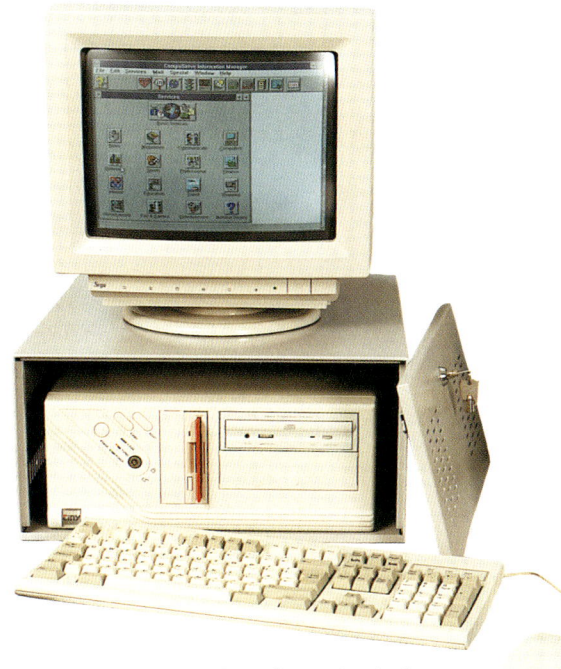

**Though not the prettiest of security devices, an equipment cage is highly effective and it's the form of security preferred by insurance companies.**

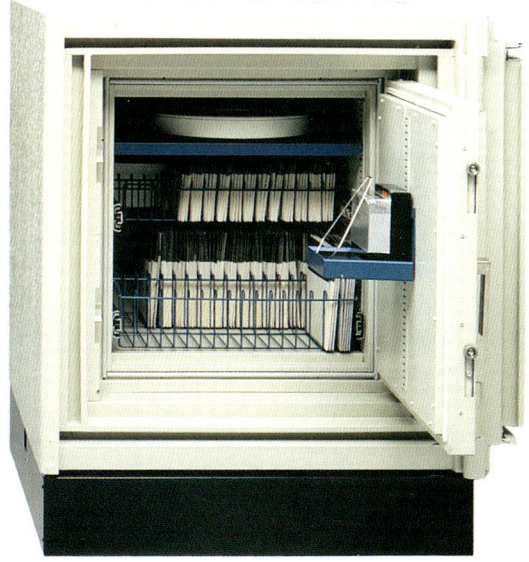

**A fire safe makes sure that your back-ups don't get fried along with your computer.**

## Virus tip

Accidents can happen in the home where dogs chew cables and small children poke unsuitable objects into disk drives. But the worst type of accident, because it's the hardest to correct, is introducing a computer virus by installing software from dubious sources. You should protect your PC with anti-virus software, which will also guard against viruses downloaded from the Internet or transferred via CD-ROM or floppy disks.

# Using passwords

## Keep your files safe from prying eyes with password protection and encryption technology.

Preventing others from seeing what is on your PC is not a sign of paranoia, nor does it mean you have got something to hide. Computers are often used to store sensitive documents — private letters, passwords, financial details, and so on. A typical family computer may be used by several people, all of whom may be able to view each others' files.

On a home computer there may be information you'd rather young children didn't read. If you run a home business or are a club secretary, there may be commercially sensitive information that you don't want other people to know about. There may also be legal obligations to maintain confidential records.

### Logging on

Windows can easily be set up so that each person using the computer needs to log on with a password, and a password-protected screensaver appears to stop people reading your files. This won't prevent dedicated spies re-starting your computer from a floppy disk, but it should deter the merely curious.

You can also password-protect your files, usually from the Save dialogue boxes of individual programs. Password options vary, but there is always a facility to stop people loading a file without the password. It may also be possible to set levels of restricted access, for example, allowing a file to be read but not changed.

In addition, when you set a password, it often scrambles the structure of a file so that even if someone opens it in another program, the contents will be unreadable and meaningless.

### Coded documents

If you need to encrypt (translate into a special secure code) a file from a program without its own password facility, you'll need an encryption utility. These are available in utility suites and compression programs such as ZipMagic. You can password protect the zip files or convert them into self-extracting archives that can be opened by simply double-clicking and entering your password. Since these files are compressed, they are ideal for sending confidential material by e-mail, but be sure to send the password in a separate e-mail. Otherwise, you might defeat the object of encrypting the file in the first place!

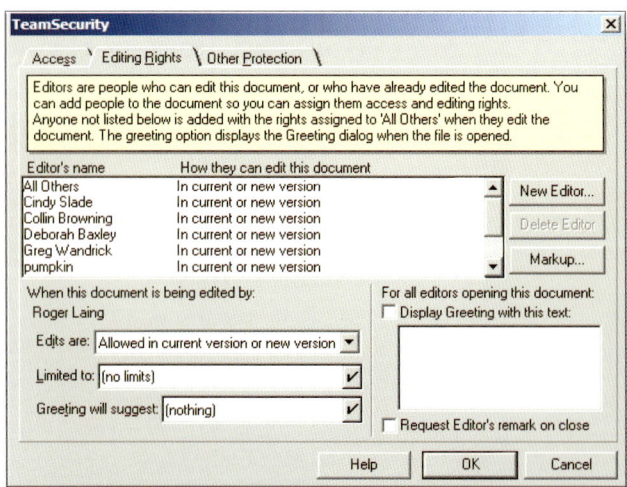

Password options such as these in Lotus WordPro can be used to allow different users various access rights.

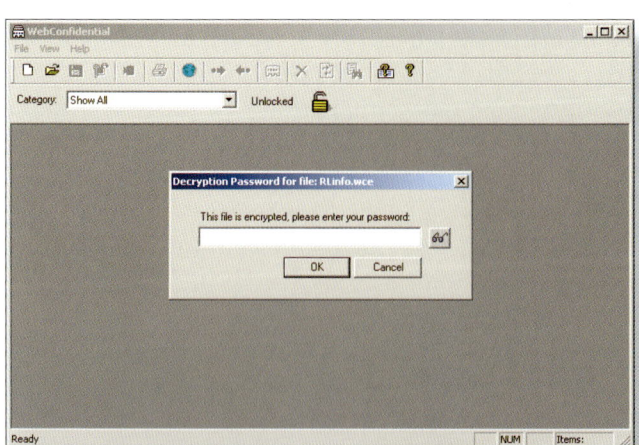

As you make your system more secure you will have more passwords to remember. The easiest way to store them is in a password manager program – such as Web Confidential. The program itself needs a password to open, but at least it's the only one you have to remember.

## DATA PROTECTION BASICS

## Adding password protection

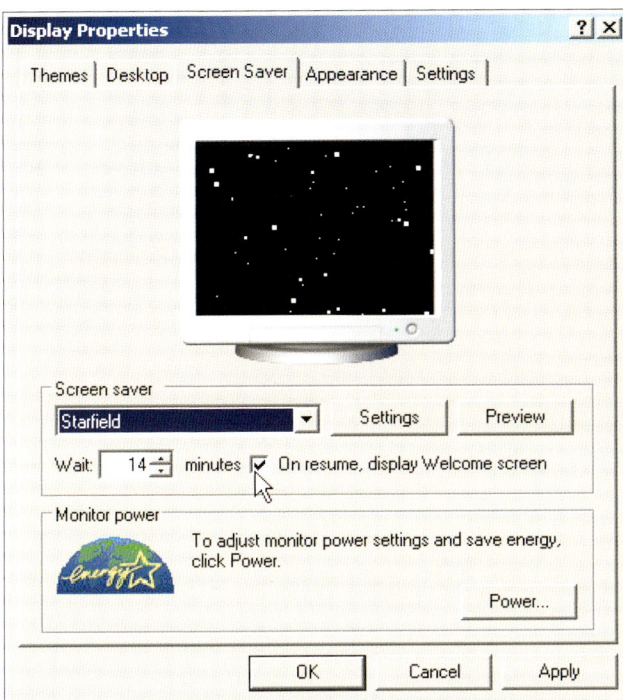

**1** To install a password-protected screensaver, right-click the desktop to bring up Display Properties. Click the Screen Saver tab, and choose a saver from the list. Click the On Resume, **Password Protect** check box (or On Resume, Display Welcome Screen, if you have Fast User Switching).

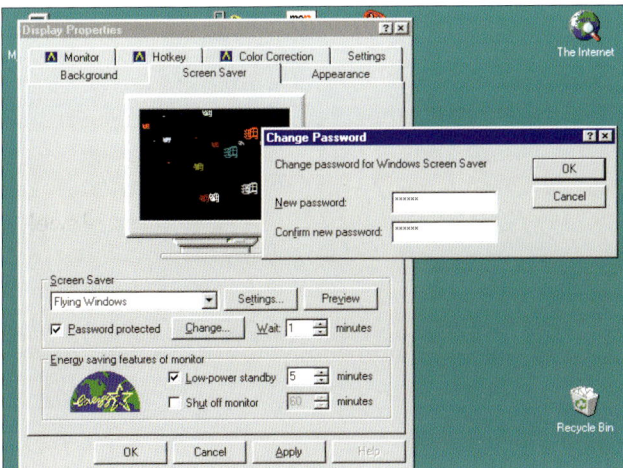

**2** In earlier versions of Windows, you may find a Password Protected **check box**. Check this, then click on the Change button. Enter a password in the dialogue box and confirm it in the box below (to ensure it isn't misspelt), then click on OK.

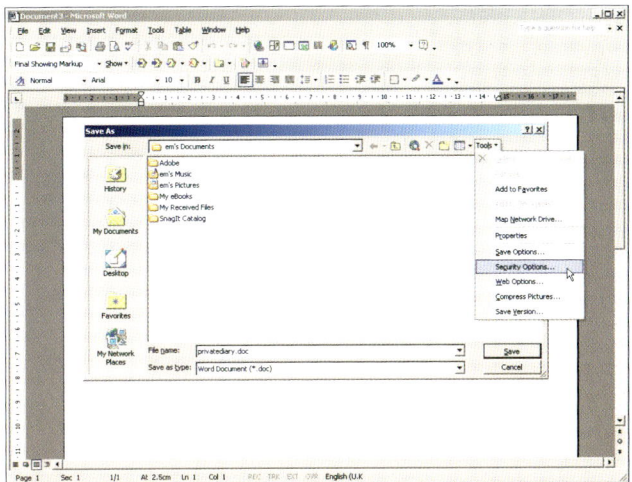

**3** To assign a password to a file in **Microsoft Word** choose Save or Save As... from the File menu. Type a file name, then click the Tools button and choose Security Options.

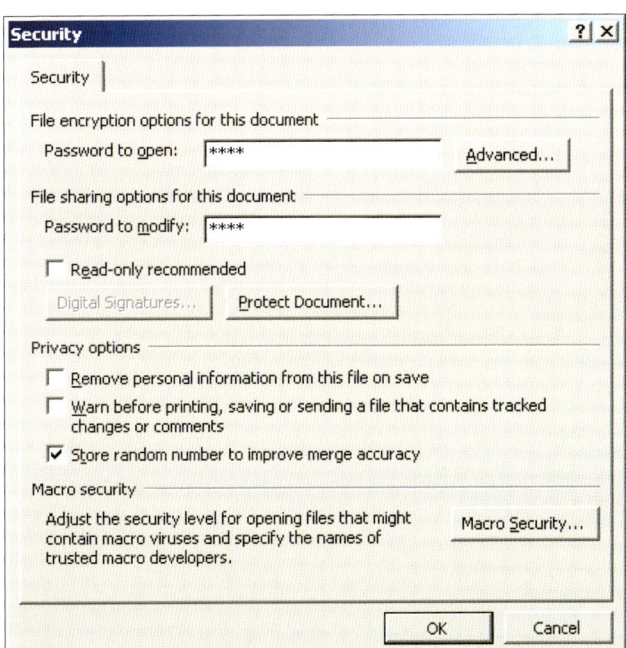

**4** Fill in the Password to Open box to **restrict access**, or Password to Modify to let people open but not edit the file. Click OK and confirm the password.

### Watch out!

For ultimate security, store work on removable disks and lock them away. But if you work from a hard disk there are other solutions. If you simply copy the finished file to a removable disk and delete the original, you leave behind an invisible image that a data thief could use to reconstruct the file. When you delete a file, you're just removing its name from the hard disk's index. The pattern of letters and words it contained is still on the disk and can be recovered. Symantec's Norton Utilities includes a utility to 'unerase' files.

The solution is not just to delete your files, but shred them too. File shredding programs such as Shred-it overwrite the data on disk to make it unrecoverable.

# When to back up

## Saving your settings

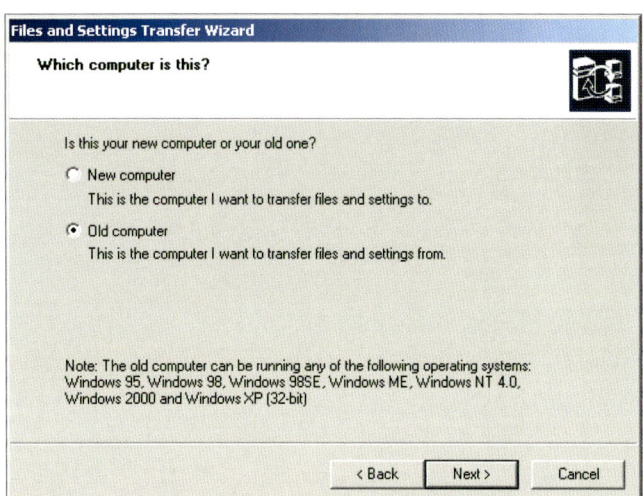

**1** The **Files and Settings Transfer Wizard** is found under System Tools in the Accessories folder of the All Programs menu. On launching, you must first tell Windows if you are backing up your files (in which case select Old Computer) or restoring them (choose New Computer). Click on Next.

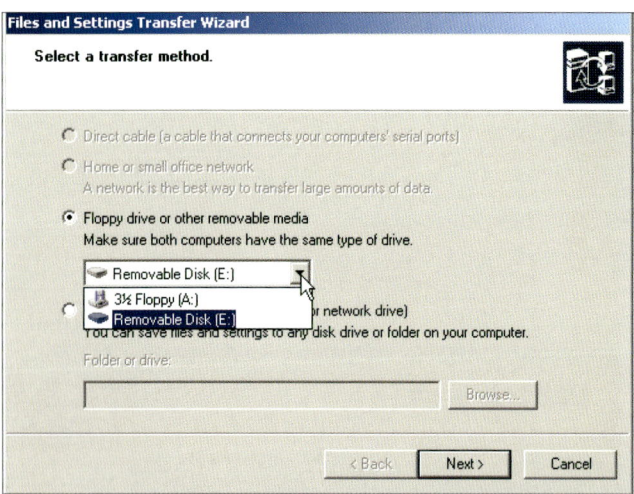

**2** Then select **where** to save the files. This can either be on a removable disk, a folder on your computer, another computer on your network (if you have one) or an external drive. Make your selection and click Next.

## In Windows XP you can not only back up your files, but also the program settings.

Back-ups are the first line of defence against the total loss of your programs and data. Should there be a disaster – your computer is destroyed or stolen, for instance – you can duplicate your previous system within a few hours of getting a new machine. This involves having a regular back-up schedule. The professionals recommend a weekly back-up cycle of the material you want to have safe. During the rest of the week you should do incremental back-ups – that is, save the files which have changed.

These incremental back-up files are appended to the full back-up. The following week follow the same procedure but use a different set of back-up tapes. The system can be damaged without you noticing and you could end up copying bad files over good.

## Extra precautions

It's also important to decide what to back up. Many people back up their data, but not their programs on the basis that if anything happens these can be reinstalled from the original program

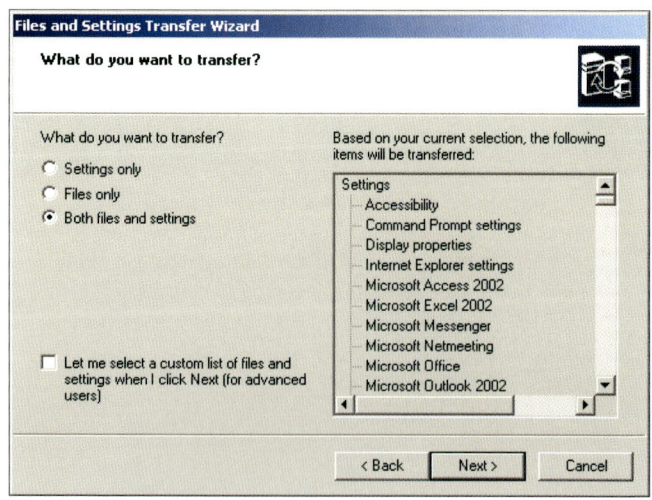

**3** Select whether to backup your files, your program settings, or both. A **panel** shows the programs and settings to be saved – you can customise it by clicking the check box at the bottom left. Click Next twice to begin the back-up.

# DATA PROTECTION BASICS

disks or CD-ROMs. But these can be destroyed or stolen too. Even if they aren't it is a huge undertaking to install a full set of programs. Setting up Internet accounts, installing upgrades and utilities and re-establishing program settings and preferences can take days. It is worth doing a program back-up once a month.

Although you can back up the Windows registry separately, it is as well to include it in any back-up if the software allows. In Backup, for example, you can choose to back up all information on the computer and the program will also prompt you to create a system disk for starting Windows in the event of any problems.

A tape drive is an inexpensive, reliable back-up medium but high-capacity, removable hard drives such as the Iomega REV are more versatile (see pages 18–19 and 112–13).

If you are worried that others could access files if the back-up tape falls into the wrong hands, you can password-protect access.

In the hurry of the working day it can be difficult to remember to run a back-up, but Windows can help. Regular tasks can be scheduled so that the program will run automatically at a set time.

To schedule a task go to Start, Programs, Accessories, System Tools and Scheduled Tasks. Click on Add Scheduled Task and it launches a wizard which takes you step by step through the process of setting up a new task.

**Iomega REV** disks can be used to run programs and store data as well as to make back-ups.

## Back-up tips

- **Back-up sets** A common mistake is to have only one set of back-up tapes. If your system develops a problem and you don't notice it, there's a possibility when using a single back-up set that you'll copy a damaged system over a good back-up. Keep at least two sets of tapes or disks and use them in rotation.

- **Disk organisation** To make backing up easier, keep your data separate from your programs. Keep all your data in a single folder such as My Documents, or, better still, when you're setting up a PC, split the hard disk into two partitions and keep programs on one and data on the other. You can then back up complete partitions or folders without having to select individual files.

- **Incremental back-ups** Save time by using incremental back-ups. The first back-up you make should be a full one that includes everything on a disk. For subsequent back-ups, copy just the files that have changed or been added to.

# Multiple users

### Watch out!

Under Windows Me and 98, the multi-user settings aren't secure. The log-in screen can be bypassed by pressing the Escape key — which is useful if you forget a password, but also means other people can read your files, because each user's personal folders can be accessed by looking in the Windows folder. If you want a safe and secure multi-user system for your computer, you'll need to buy extra software.

### Fact file

Don't get carried away when customising the look of your individual desktop. Large picture files used as screensavers will slow down your system, and a stunning image of an exotic beach won't be relaxing for long if you have to wait minutes to perform simple functions. Bitmaps are massive files, so stick to a .jpeg format when downloading image files.

## Everyone in your family can have their own Windows desktop with individualised profiles.

A computer is a great resource for any family, but sharing one can cause problems. Tastes in desktop colour schemes differ and everyone has their own files that they don't necessarily want other people to access.

Windows lets you set up separate profiles for each user. This allows for individualised desktops, My Documents folders and so on. Application preferences are stored separately for each user, so that when they run a program and click on the File menu, for example, the list of most recently accessed files shows only the ones they have opened.

Windows user profiles don't control access. Although each user can have their own password, this only makes it harder for other users to interfere with their settings. Depending on your file system, all users' files are accessible with Explorer if you know where to look. But, with Windows user accounts, each member of the family can be set up to have their own computer.

## Setting up for multiple users

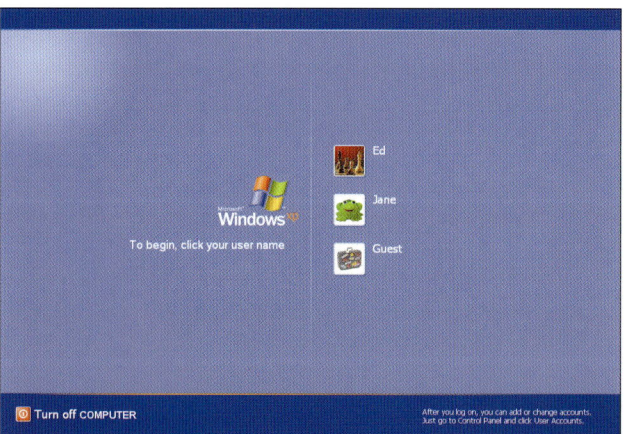

**1** Windows XP sets up user profiles (known as **accounts**) differently. By default, two new accounts are created — one for the owner (or administrator) and one for a guest. If you tell the Setup Wizard the names of the other users, new accounts with administrator privileges are set up for them. Windows Me and 98, however, are set up by default for a single user. Support for multiple users has to be activated through the Users control panel.

**2** When you first log on to Windows XP, you'll see the new welcome screen contains a **list of icons** with user names beside them. To either change details of your user account, or, if you are an owner, to add new users, you first need to log in. Do so by clicking on your user name and entering your password (if you have one). Your personal settings are loaded. From the Start menu, select Control Panel and click on User Accounts.

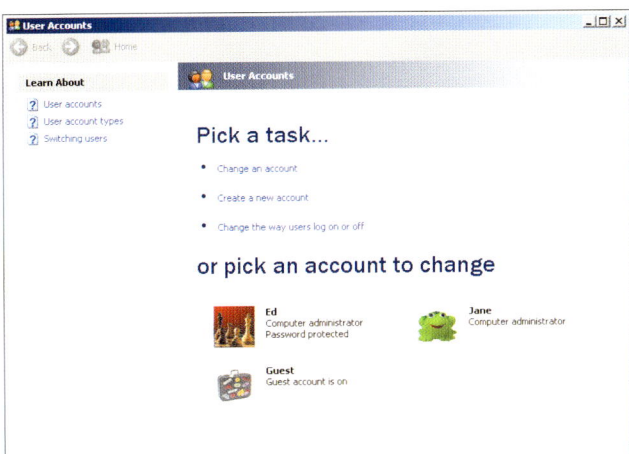

**3** You have a choice to either pick a task from the list, or to click on the particular account you want to change. The example above will show how to create a new user account. Select this option from the **Pick a Task**… list. The first step is to choose a user name, which will be what appears on the Welcome Screen and at the top of the Start menu on your personalised desktop.

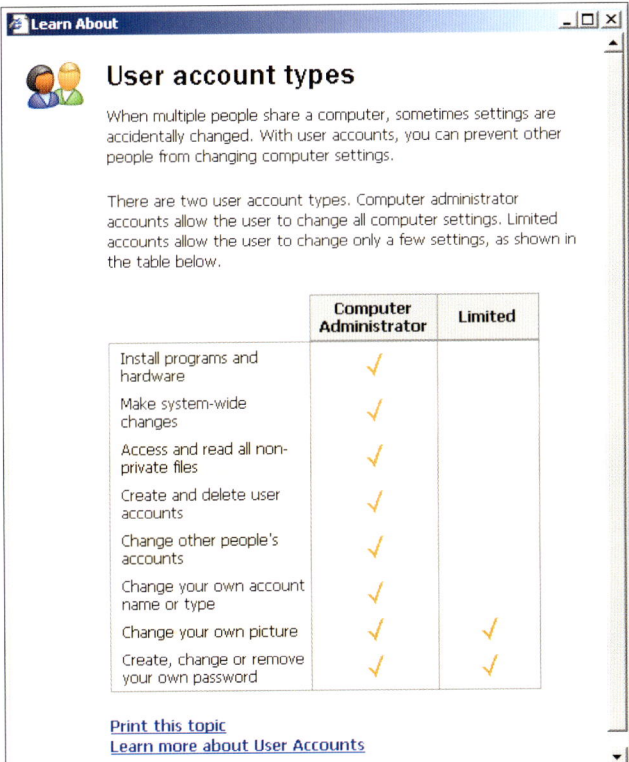

**4** The next choice is the **type of account** you want. An administrator account enables the user to make changes across different accounts, change the type of accounts and rename them, install programs and access all files. A limited account restricts the changes the user can make to their own settings. (The guest account set-up initially lets anyone without an account log on and use the computer, although they can't access password-protected files or change any settings. If you are worried about security, anyone with administrator privileges can disable this kind of account.)

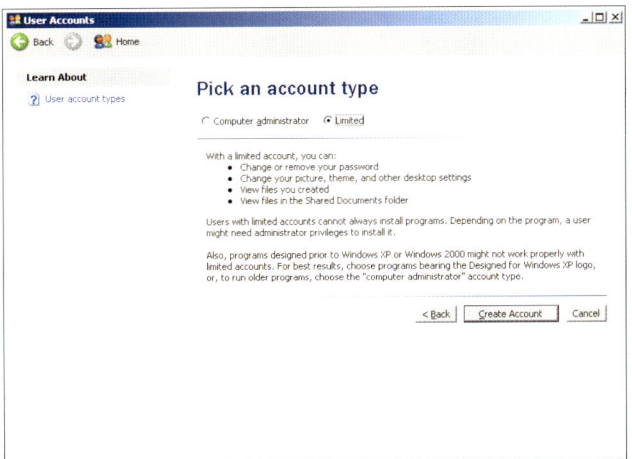

**5** The above example deals with setting up a **limited account**. Once created, the new account icon will appear among the list of accounts at the bottom. To personalise it further click on Restart and log on as the new user. From the Start menu, go to Control Panel and User Accounts. As this is a limited account, you'll see the tasks you can pick are fewer than before and there is only one account you can change – your own.

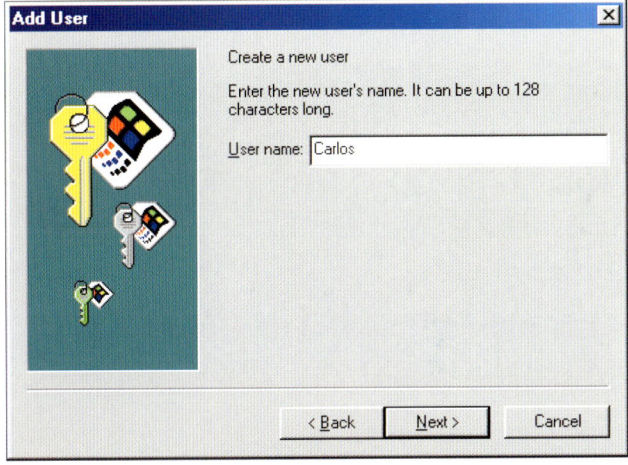

**6** To set up **multiple user profiles** in earlier versions of Windows involves double-clicking on the Users icon in the Control Panel to start the Add User Wizard. The screenshots here are from Windows Me but earlier versions are much the same. The first step is to enter a User name, click on Next and enter and confirm a password (or leave it blank if you don't want one). At the next step you must decide which aspects of Windows you want each user to be able to personalise. For simplicity, tick all of the boxes and select the Create New Items to Save Disk Space option. Each user can then have a personalised desktop and Start menu, together with his or her own folders for documents, Internet favourites and downloaded web pages. Click on Next, then on Finish, and all that remains is for you to restart.

# Copyright

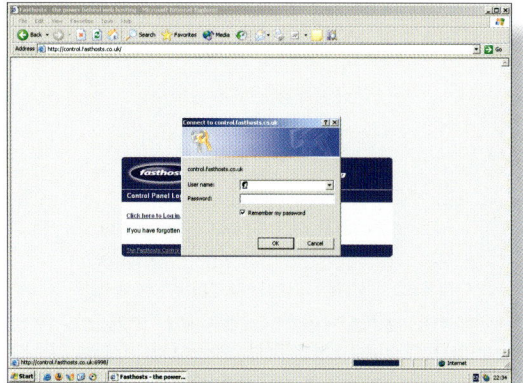

Passwords are fairly common on commercial web sites, especially ones where you have to sign up and pay a fee, but you can use them to preserve the confidentiality of your site.

Prevention can be better than cure when it comes to enforcing copyright. Online music stores allow you to sample part of a track, but you have to pay to hear all of it.

## Protect the information on your web site by claiming copyright or issuing passwords to people you trust.

If you want to protect information on a web site from indiscriminate use by others, you should claim copyright. Under the Universal Copyright and Berne Conventions this is straightforward. All you do is display, in a prominent position, the word copyright and a © symbol, along with the name of the copyright owner and the year of publication. The first page of a web site is prominent enough for a copyright notice or, if you wish, add the copyright declaration to every page on the site.

### Keep out

Copyright applies to pictures, sounds and music as well as the written word, but you can't copyright your thoughts. So if someone expresses ideas from your web page in different words you can't do anything about it.

In practice, it's so easy to cut and copy data from a Web page that whatever rights you claim, it's very difficult to assert them. If you really want to prevent people from using your material, as you would on a Web site intended for a closed group of users, the safest way is to require visitors to enter a password on the first page of a site and issue passwords only to those who are part of the group. You can then change the password as membership of the group changes, and circulate the new one to those who need it. If you only want some people to access chosen pages then create a system of hierarchical passwords. These site passwords are specialised input forms, which can be created with Web design programs such as Microsoft Front Page.

### Jargon buster

**Hierarchical passwords** A system of multiple passwords in which the PC system is treated as a layered structure. Each layer has a password so you can control how deeply other uses can delve into the system or a web site by restricting their passwords to specific layers.

# Power problems

**Protect your PC and computer equipment from unexpected surges or cuts in the electricity supply.**

If you're lucky, you've probably never known the sense of despair that comes from spending hours working on your computer, only to have it crash just when you go to hit the Save button. While there are lots of things that can cause a crash, one of the most annoying is a power problem.

## Lightning strikes

A nearby lightning strike, a momentary flicker of the lights or a complete power cut can affect your computer. The result could be a disastrous crash at a crucial moment. You stand to lose whatever information you're working on, and potentially much more. Not shutting your system down properly can damage your hard disk resulting in the loss of other data you have saved. There are other risks. Your modem can be damaged by lightning striking the phone line, which could potentially damage other parts of your computer too, if it's not properly protected.

Are you at the mercy of the phone and electricity companies? Fortunately not. There are many ways of protecting your PC and other equipment, which come in the shape of surge suppressors and uninterruptible power supplies (UPSs).

## Spiky stuff

Surge suppressors do more or less what you'd expect them to. They contain special components that prevent serious spikes in the electrical supply from reaching your PC. They're also available in versions designed to plug into your phone line, protecting modems and fax machines.

The smallest suppressors are slightly larger than an ordinary plug. You fit them on the cable of your computer instead of a plug, and it's instantly protected. There are larger suppressors that the existing cable can plug into, and even multi-way connectors with up to six sockets, so you can connect all your computer equipment, such as printers, scanners and monitors.

### Power protection

These gadgets shield your computer against problems caused by electrical malfunctions in the home.

● **APC Back-UPS ES** Aimed specifically at home computer users, the Back-UPS ES is specifically designed to offer battery back-up and surge protection. In particular, it has built-in protection for your phone, fax and modem (including an always-on broadband ADSL connection). www.apc.com

● **Belkin SurgeMaster** This is a low cost six-way connector block that will protect all your computer equipment from surges. It also has a socket for protecting your phone line, so you can make sure the modem is safe. www.belkin.com

● **OPTI-UPS** These offer uninterruptible power for PCs, covering blackouts, surges, and other power blips. They also have power management software, OPTI-SAFE+, which saves data in the event of power failure. www.opti-ups.com

● **Liebert PowerSure** This is a compact offline UPS designed for single computers, in a range of sizes, with upgrade options and replaceable batteries. www.liebert.com

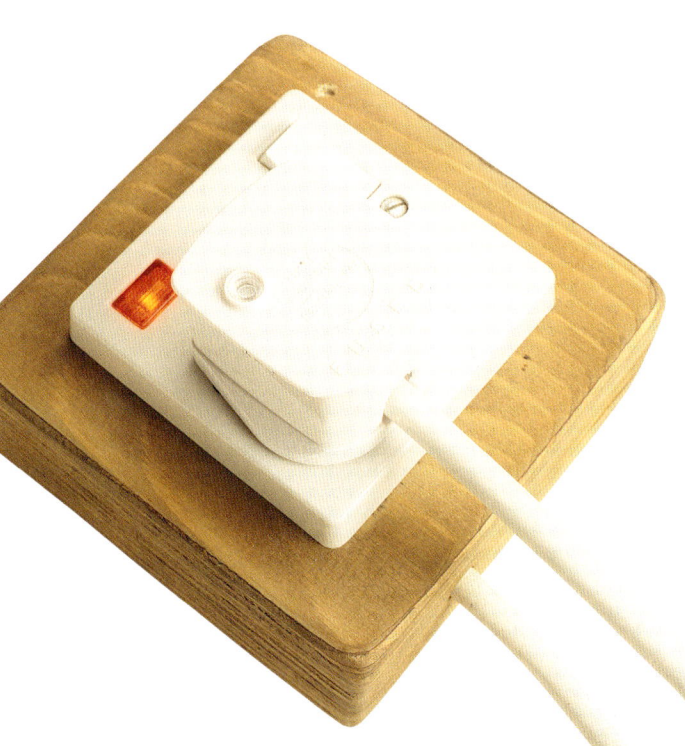

## Buying tips

● Check the ratings of your equipment and of the UPS. UPS ratings are usually quoted in VA, which is roughly the same as the rating in W on the back of your PC.

● Find out how long the UPS will run. Is it long enough to shut down your PC easily and safely?

● Is software supplied to run on your computer that will let the UPS tell it to shut down when the power fails, so everything is safe, even if you're away from your desk?

● How long do the batteries in the UPS last, and can you replace them easily, or will you have to buy a whole new unit?

● Does the UPS or surge protector have a connector for protecting a phone line, to look after your modem or fax machine?

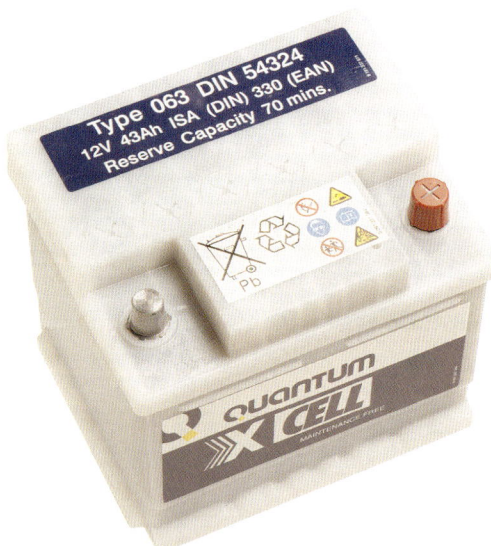

## Fact file

● **Line interactive** A type of UPS that continuously monitors the power supply to even out surges and dips.

● **Online** A type of UPS that creates clean power continuously.

● **Run time** The number of minutes for which a UPS will supply power at a stated number of VA.

● **Standby** A type of UPS that switches to battery power when the mains supply fails.

● **VA (Volt Amps)** A rating of how much power a UPS can supply. Similar to Watts (W).

● **W (Watts)** The amount of power consumed by a piece of computer equipment. You'll usually find this on a label near the power connector.

## Constant power

UPSs are much more complicated. As the name implies, they promise to provide constant power to your computer. They have a battery inside them which takes over in the event of the mains power supply failing. They contain circuitry to boost the battery power to the required level, and to monitor how much battery life is left.

There's more than one type of UPS. Your choice depends on what you want to use them for. Offline or standby UPSs simply pass mains power to your computer, switching to battery when the mains fails. These are the simplest and cheapest sort, but they don't usually incorporate surge suppression.

If you use an online UPS, the power that your computer receives is created by the UPS all the time, either from the mains supply, or from the battery. This means you always have a perfectly clean power supply, with no surges, no dips and no interruptions. Online UPSs are more expensive.

The most common UPSs in use are inline or line-interactive. These are a cross between standby and online UPSs, which constantly monitor the power supply to your PC, evening out surges and dips. Most of the power comes directly from the mains, unless there's a power cut.

## Shut down safely

How you choose to protect your computer depends on what you are doing with it. If you simply play games, you will probably feel that all you need is a surge suppressor to protect your system from damage. If you work at home, a cheap offline UPS that can run your system for long enough for you to shut it down safely when the power fails should do the trick. But if you want to protect a server that's providing files to other computers, then it's worth looking for a unit that's better protected, like a line-interactive UPS.

Check to see what sort of battery life is being offered. You need to match the size of the UPS you choose to the equipment you're hoping to protect. Just as there's little point putting the battery from a Ford Fiesta into a large truck, so there is little point having a small UPS to protect two computers, a printer, a scanner and a modem. The battery will go flat in no time.

Before choosing a power supply, check the power ratings on the back of your equipment to see how much electricity they consume and bear in mind that this is usually a worst-case figure. If you have a computer you simply have to have on all the time, buy the biggest UPS you can afford, to try to outlast all but the longest power cuts.

# Restricted access

## When several people are using the same PC, each will need to have enough hard disk room.

If two or more people are using the same computer, each individual can have their own personalised set-up on the system, with their own choice of settings such as screensavers and shortcuts. All their folders and documents can also be kept private from anyone else using the same machine. But it's important to ensure that each person is given enough hard disk space.

### Setting limits
By introducing disk quotas you can ensure that no one person can monopolise all the available free disk space. If they do so, that person can be blocked from saving any files until they've freed up enough space on their share of the disk — or else they can just be alerted to the fact that this problem exists, so that they can do something about it.

## Allocating disk quotas

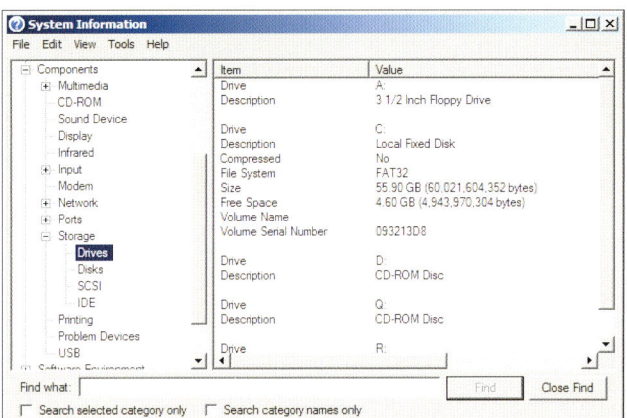

**1** You are only able to **set disk quotas** if you are using the NTFS file system. To check which system you are using, go to the Start menu, select All Programs, then Accessories, then System Tools and then System Information. In the System Information window, choose components from the System Summary pane. Select Storage and then Drives. You'll see the File System listed on the right – here it's FAT32.

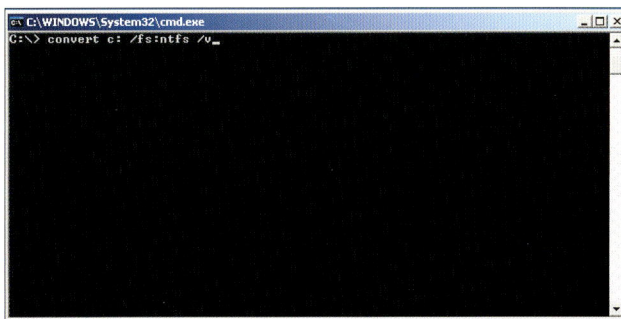

**2** If the system is FAT or FAT32, it is simple to **convert** to the NTFS system, which is more space efficient. You can do so from the Command Prompt window. Go to All Programs, select Accessories, and the Command Prompt. Simply type in C:> convert c: /fs:ntfs /v where c: is the letter of the drive you want to format. The conversion will only start once you reboot your PC.

### Switching tip

Fast user switching makes it easier for several people to use the same computer. It means you won't have to log off or shut down just to let someone else check their email. Go to the Start menu, click Log off and then Switch User. The welcome screen reappears and the user can then select their account icon and access their data on the PC.

# 144 PREVENTING PROBLEMS

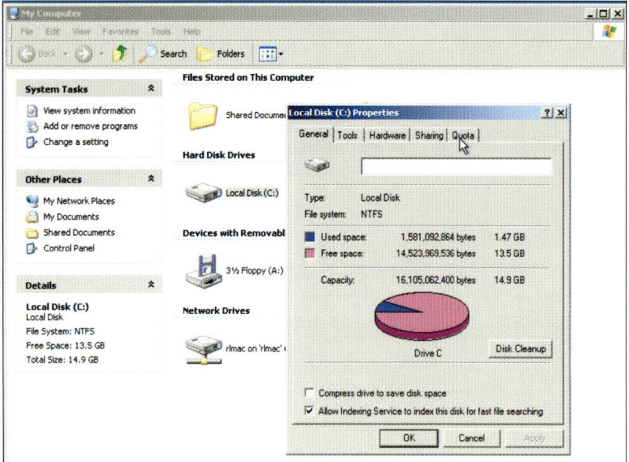

**3** To **set the quota** for each user, double-click on the My Computer icon on the desktop, then right-click on your C: drive. From the pop-up menu select Properties, and select the Quota tab from the Local Disk (C:) Properties box that opens.

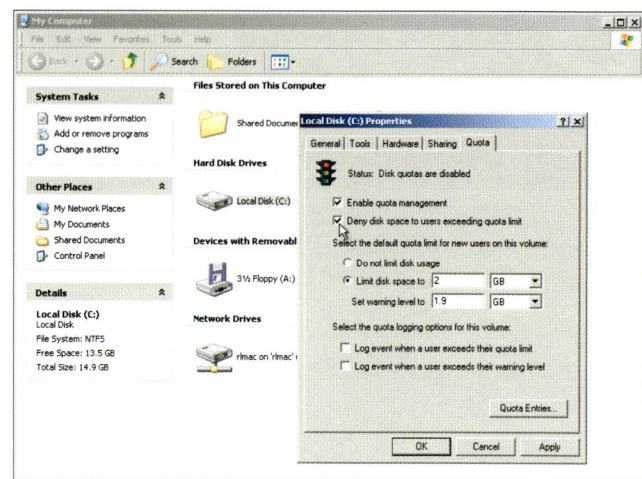

**5** You can further **limit people** by putting a tick beside Deny Disk Space to Users Exceeding Quota Limit. If someone tries to save a file when they are over their limit, they will receive an 'insufficient disk space' error message. They won't be able to save any files to the PC until they have first deleted some of the existing material. (They still can save their work by copying it to a removable disk, or burning it to a CD.) Click on Apply and on OK.

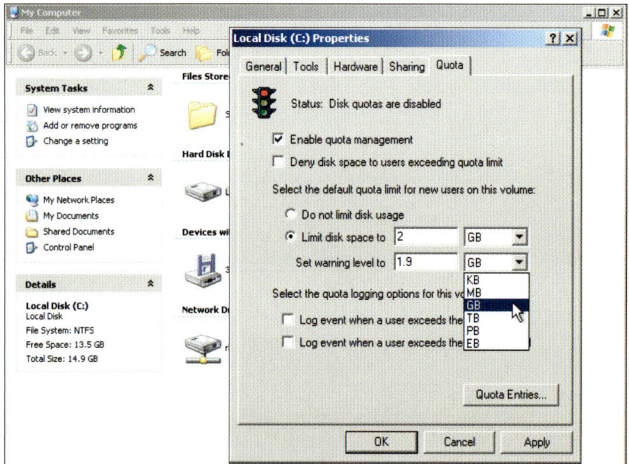

**4** Put a tick mark beside **Enable Quota Management**. Select Limit Desk Space To, and in the box beside it set the quota for each user. Select the unit of measurement from the dropdown list – here it's 2GB per user. If you want to warn people before they exceed the quota, select Set Warning Level To and type in a slightly lower figure (here it's 1.9GB).

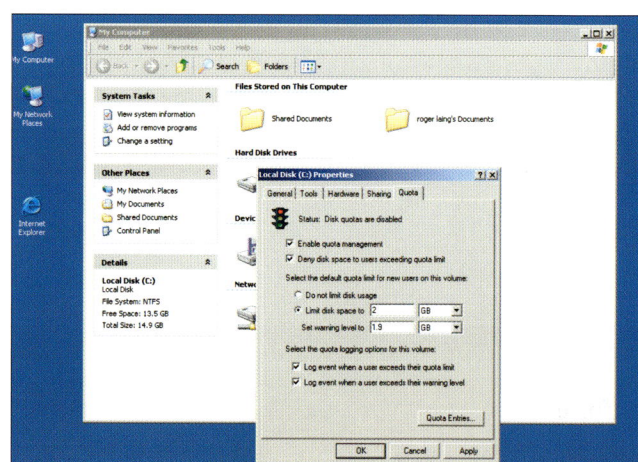

**6** Under Select the Quota Logging Options for This Volume you can choose to record whenever anyone **exceeds** their quota or is over their warning limit. That way you can find out who is taking up all the space!

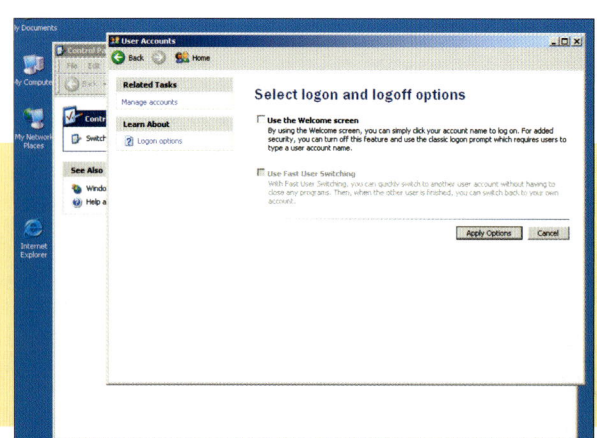

## Log-in tip

Instead of the Welcome screen, you can substitute a more secure log-on screen where each person must enter a user name and a password. To create this, go to the Start menu, select Control Panel and then User Accounts. Click on Change the Way Users Log On or Off, and then untick the box beside Use the Welcome Screen.

# Encrypt it

**You can keep all your private files safe from prying eyes with encryption software.**

'Innocent people have nothing to hide' is a popular saying, but anyone who's ever kept a diary, or thought about looking for a new job before leaving the one they are in knows that's not strictly true. There are lots of times when you might not want other people to know all about what you're doing.

## Keep it private

Now that so many people use computers for just about everything, it's not always simple to keep things as private as you might like. While you can lock a diary in your desk drawer or tuck it under the mattress, or keep a love letter with you all the time, what do you do with the job application you're writing on the PC, or the invitations to the surprise party for your partner's birthday? Or maybe you want to send information over the Internet, and don't want to risk it being read by prying eyes along the way.

Whatever your reasons, there is a way to keep information private when it's stored on a computer. It's called encryption, and it can be a very useful tool, whatever the reason you have for wanting to keep your information private – although see the box called *Encryption Issues* on page 146 to check the legal situation.

## Cracking the code

Encryption is the use of cryptography, the science of making and breaking codes. When you encrypt something, what you're doing is turning it from one format into another. For example, the simplest form might be just moving every letter one space to the left in the alphabet, turning 'apple' into 'zookd'.

Of course, that sort of encryption would be very easy to turn back into the original text, so there are much more sophisticated techniques available. Most of these work using a system called Public Key Cryptography. That's where you have two keys which can be used on

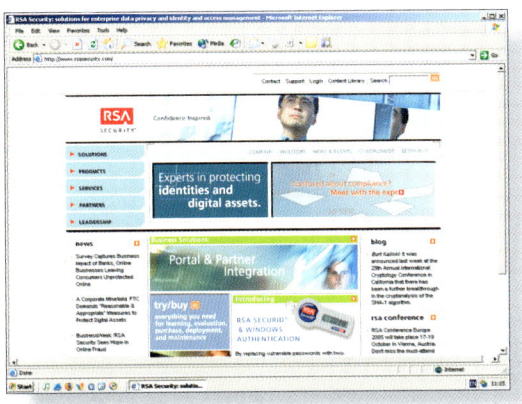

**The RSA system is used by Web browsers, office e-mail systems and many other programs.**

**Data Vault can divide your hard drive into a number of 'safes', all of which can be encrypted and password protected. If you need to leave your PC for a while, any open 'safes' can be locked to keep your information secure until you return.**

## Encryption issues

Encryption can certainly be useful, but there are times when people would rather that the information they want to see was freely available. Law enforcement agencies, for example, may want to check the e-mail messages being sent between different people as part of an investigation into something illegal.

Obviously, if a message is encrypted, that's much more difficult, and in some cases, either impossible or so time-consuming as to mean that there's no point trying.

Working on the principle that innocent people have nothing to hide, some countries have strict laws that regulate the use of encryption. In some cases, that means that you can access only what are called weak systems, which the authorities will be able to crack easily.

Other countries rely on a system called key escrow, which means they can use encryption, but you have to give a trusted agency, possibly part of the government, the key that can be used to decode your messages if a court orders it. Some countries outlaw encryption completely, so if you decide to download and use an encryption program, you could run the risk of prosecution.

In the UK there are no restrictions on using encryption programs at the time of writing, but the issue is under review and may change.

your messages, a public one and a private one. If you want to send information to someone, you look up their public key, and use that to turn the information into a code. It can only be decoded by using the private key. You can also use your private key to sign a message; by checking it against your public key, people will know that something is really from you.

## The key is the key

If that sounds complicated, imagine it like this: you have a message in English, and want it to be hard for people to read. Your public key is an English to German dictionary, so anyone can turn a message into German and send it to you. If you're the only person with a German to English dictionary, it'll be very hard, but not impossible, for anyone who sees the encoded message to work out what it means.

Encryption can be broken. For example, the encryption used by the majority of web browsers outside the US can be broken in just 22 hours using powerful computers. The strength of encryption is measured in bits. The more bits the encryption software uses, the harder it is to break the code, so when you're looking at software to keep things private, check how many bits it uses. Originally web browsers typically used 56 bits, but 128 is much more common – and secure.

## Web encryption

One of the most well-known encryption companies is called RSA, which licenses its encryption to many firms. It's the RSA system that's used in web browser, office e-mail systems and lots of other programs. The company also provides a good web site where you can find out more about encryption.

What other software is available for encryption? One of the most popular programs is called Pretty Good Privacy, and you can find information about it at www.pgpi.com. It's a simple program that can be used to turn a file into an encrypted form which you can then send via e-mail. There are other similar programs, some free, some commercial.

That's not the only type of encryption available for a PC, however. There are programs available that will encrypt your whole disk automatically. For example, Data Vault is a program that runs on your computer and makes it look like you have an extra disk drive. Each of the extra drives can have a password of its own, and anything you save to that drive is automatically encrypted, so you don't need to remember to run a separate program like PGP – you'll know instead that everything you save is safe from prying eyes.

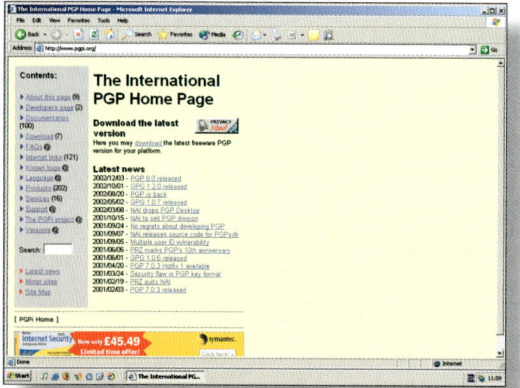

**Pretty Good Privacy** offers a simple encryption system that is suitable for e-mail.

## Where to go

To obtain encryption software try:
- **RSA** www.rsa.com
- **Data Vault** www.reflex-magnetics.co.uk
- **PGP** www.pgpi.com

# Filtering Net content

**With a little browser knowhow you can avoid sites containing indecent or offensive material.**

Adult sites containing bad language, violent imagery or pornography are, unfortunately, plentiful on the Internet. For most people they present an unwelcome experience. The risk of children finding these by accident is one that all home computer users need to take into account. Fortunately, there are ways to protect those using your computer from accessing them.

The first line of defence is to configure your browser to filter out offensive content. Internet Explorer has a Content Advisor that uses a ratings system to classify sites. You enter acceptable levels of violence or sexual content and if someone tries to connect to a site that exceeds these levels, access is denied.

### Third-party options
There are dozens of programs that act as filters, and work with Internet Explorer and other browsers. These either respond to keywords (sexual terms and offensive language), or compare a site address to a list of disallowed sites stored on-line. There are plenty of options for anyone concerned about what might be found while browsing the Net.

### You will need
- **Software** Microsoft Internet Explorer 4 or later. Version 6 is shown here.
- **Hardware** A modem or other means of connecting to the Internet and an account with an Internet service provider.

## Censoring the Internet

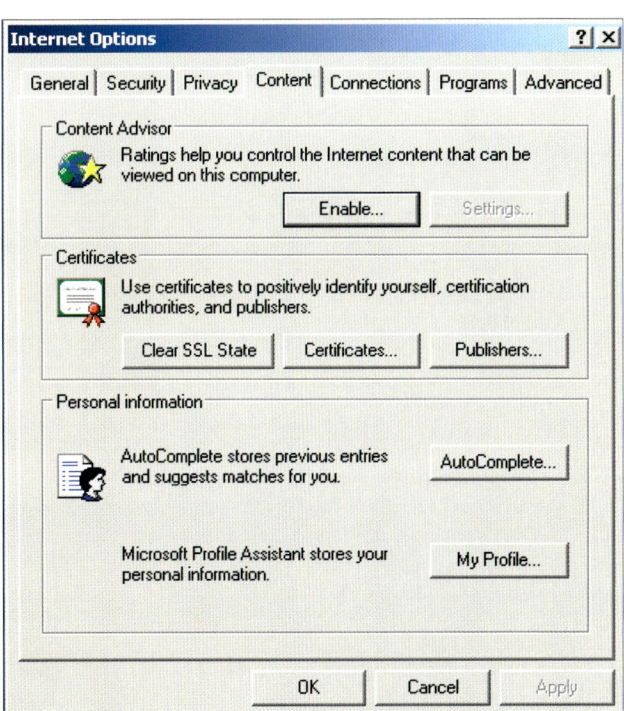

**1** Launch Internet Explorer from the Start menu, go to the Tools menu and select **Internet Options**. The Internet Options dialogue box appears. Click on the Content tab to see the Content Advisor options. At the top of the Content section is the Content Advisor. Click on the button marked Enable.

### You will learn
- How to use the filtering software built in to Internet Explorer.
- How to block out bad language and violence as well as nudity and sex on-line.
- How to configure Internet Explorer correctly so that educational sites that may contain nudity or sexual reference are still available.

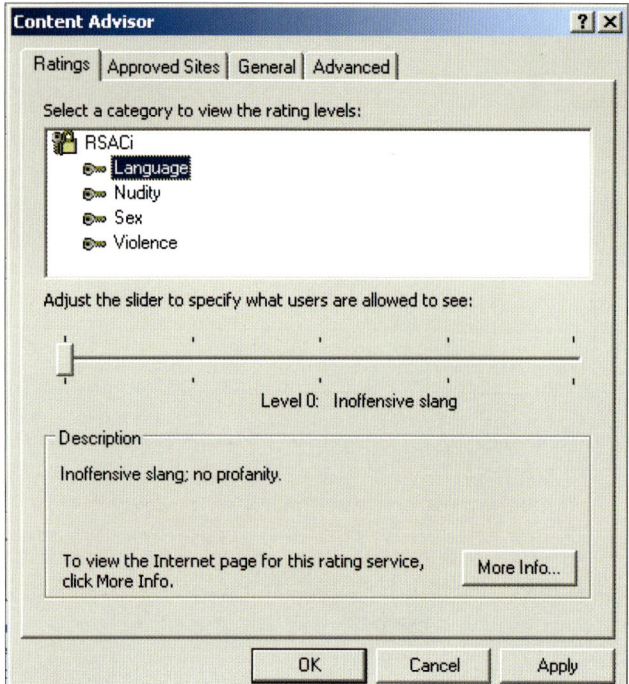

**2** A dialogue box opens, with more index tabs across the top and a slider bar in the centre. Selecting any of the categories in the RSACi pane and dragging the slider bar alters the level of censorship. You can filter out language varying from inoffensive slang (level 1) up to explicit or crude (level 4) with others in between. The same applies to sex (from none to explicit sexual activity), violence (none to wanton and gratuitous) and nudity (none to provocative frontal nudity).

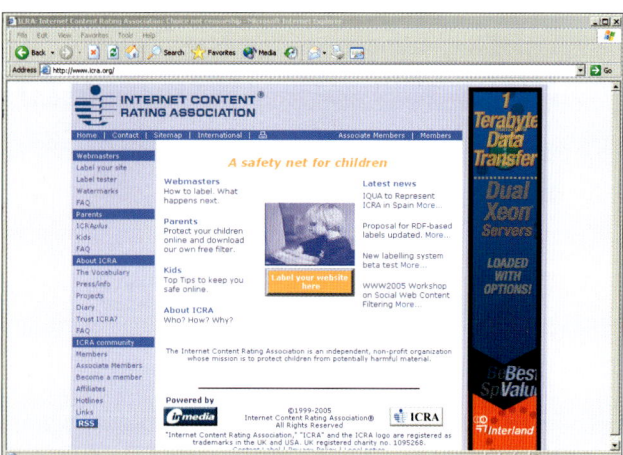

**3** Click on the **More Info** button and you are taken to the Recreational Software Advisory Council web site. The ratings system originally devised by them is now part of the Internet Content Rating Association (ICRA). Details about ICRA are on their site at www.icra.org.

### Jargon buster

**ICRA** The acronym of the Internet Content Rating Association, a ratings scheme for Internet content that replaced the RSACi in 1999.

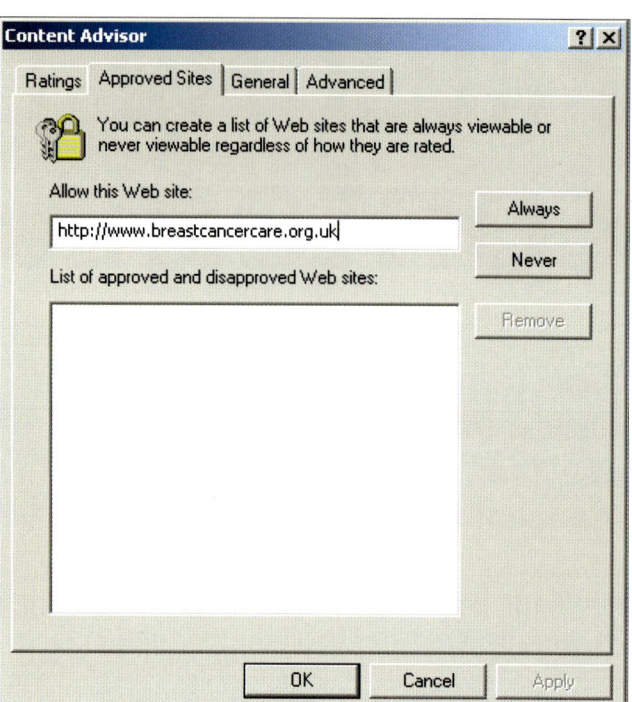

**4** The second tab at the top of the Content Advisor window is **Approved Sites**. Click on this and you can add web sites that break the rating settings, but give useful information. Examples could be sites covering AIDS or breast cancer. You can also enter sites you want to ban permanently.

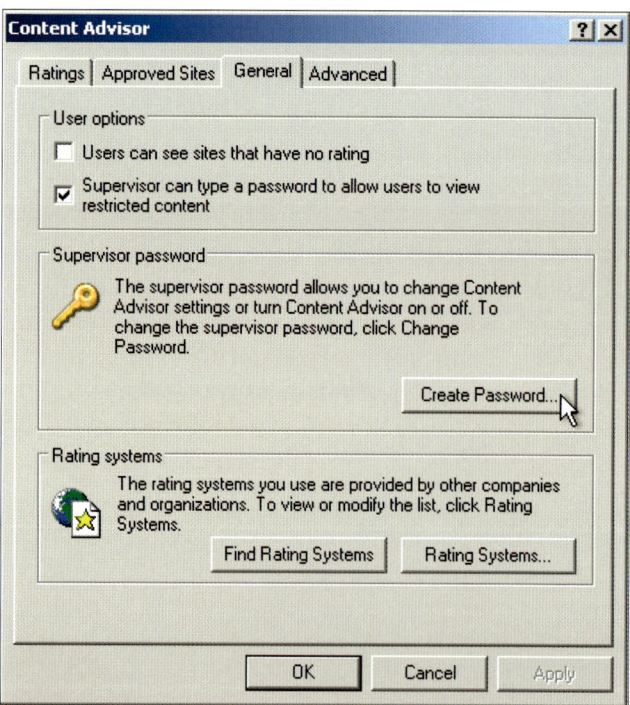

**5** Next, move to the **General** tab, which opens a window containing several options. The first lets you decide if users can see sites that have no ratings. If you leave this unticked, you will limit the usefulness of the Web, since many innocent sites are not rated. The supervisor password option allows you to type a password that will enable access to a banned site. This feature enables you to restrict access to questionable sites until you've had an opportunity to review and (if they are appropriate) to add them to your list of approved sites. To use it you need to set a password. Click on Create Password.

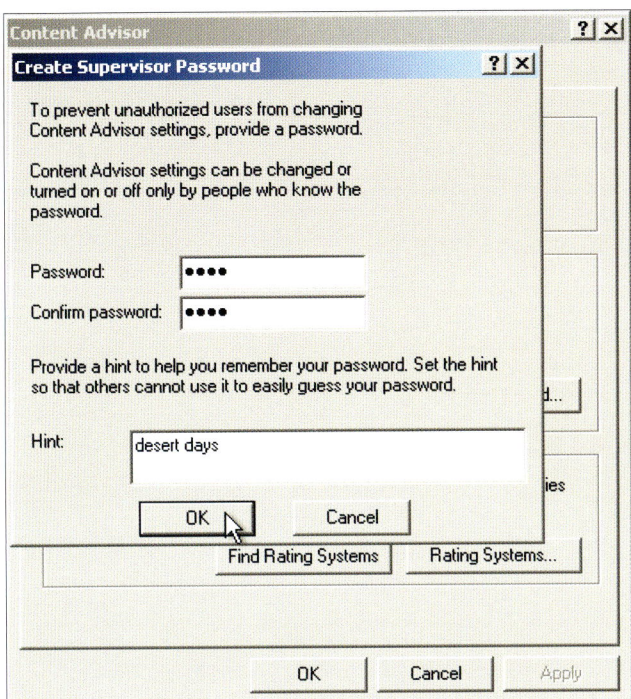

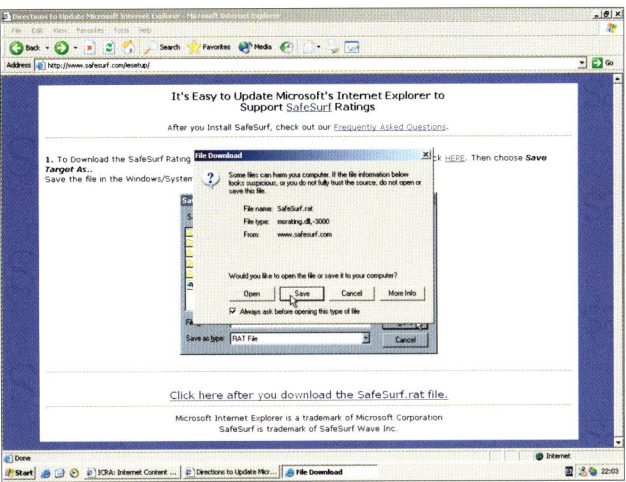

**8** At the SafeSurf web page follow the link marked **Update Explorer** where you will see the step-by-step instructions for downloading a small file called safesurf.rat, and details of how to save this in your Windows/System folder. Follow these instructions and then return to the Content Advisor window.

**6** Enter a **password** in the lower two fields (marked Password and Confirm Password), then click on OK to confirm the password setting.

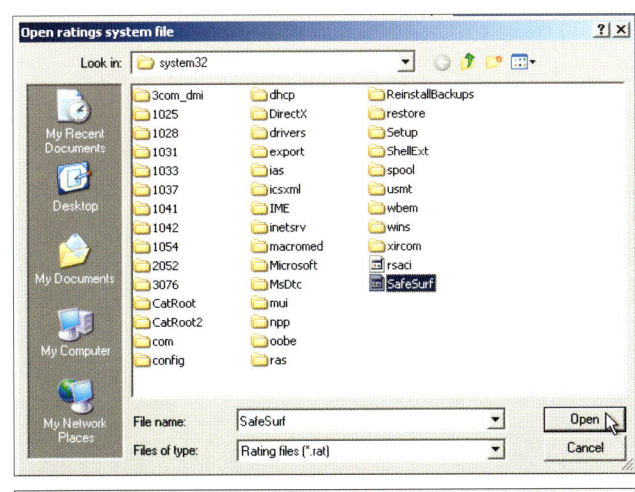

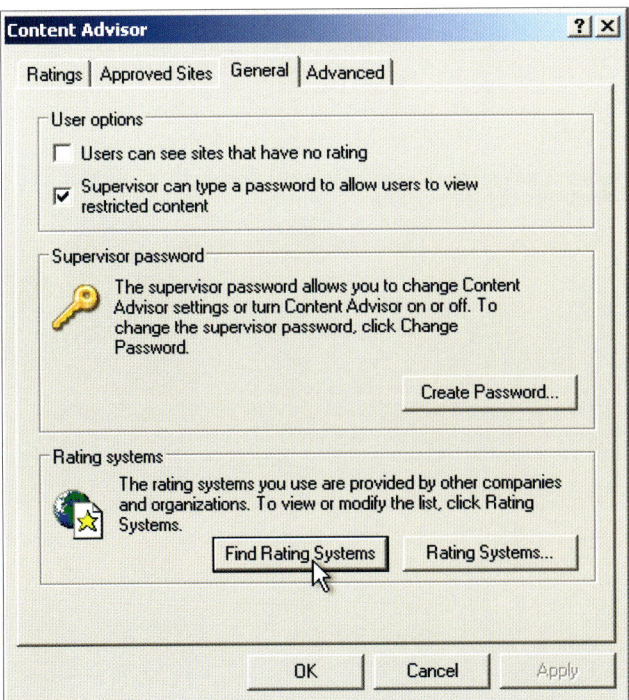

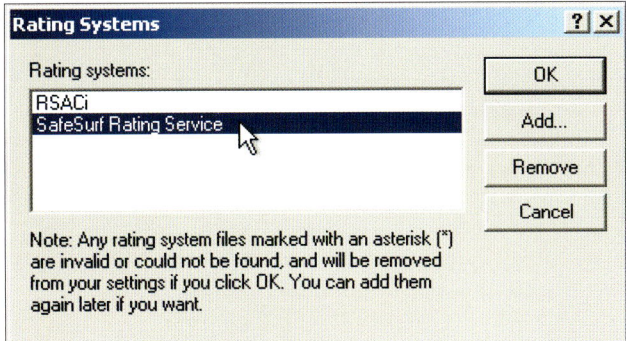

**9** Now click on the **Rating Systems** button and a window will appear that lets you add further schemes to Content Advisor. Click on the option marked Add and select the safesurf.rat file from the directory list displayed. Select Open and you should now have both the RSACi and SafeSurf rating schemes displayed in the Rating Systems window.

**7** The General tab deals with ratings schemes. By default Content Advisor knows all about the RSACi scheme, but you can add other rating schemes to make the filtering process even more effective. You may purchase a third-party software product that lets you integrate a rating scheme into Internet Explorer, or you may use a freely available scheme such as SafeSurf. In order to use SafeSurf you first click on the **Find Rating Systems** button, which will take you to a page on Microsoft's web site. This site contains a link to the SafeSurf site.

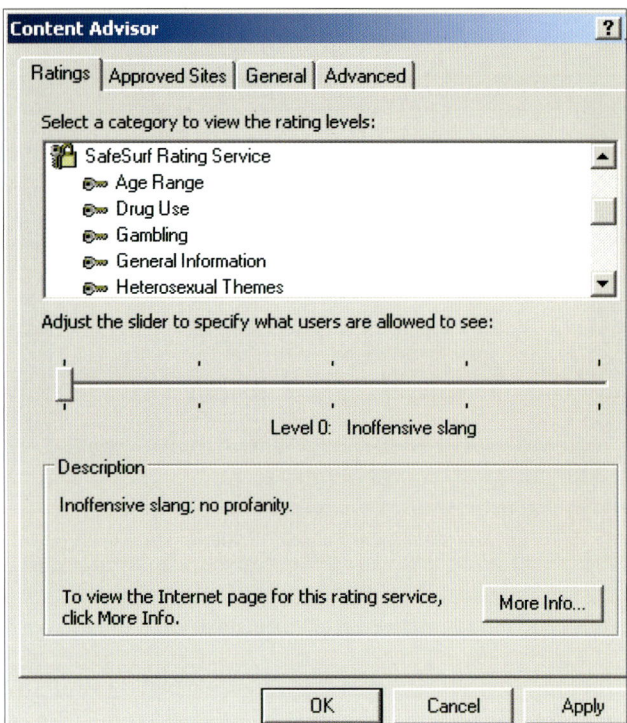

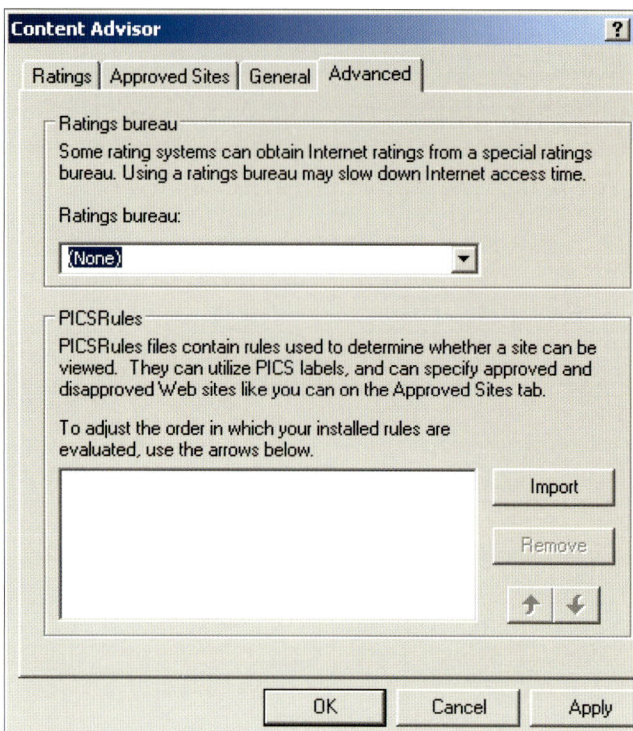

**10** Go back to the Ratings tab, and you will see that the original four categories have been joined by 12 **SafeSurf** categories that cover areas such as drug use, intolerance, profanity, homosexuality and gambling. Select any of these and use the slider bar to set appropriate rating guidelines for each. One useful addition is the Age Range category that lets you set levels for sites that have SafeSurf age ratings applied, from all ages through many steps right up to adults.

**11** The final index tab is marked **Advanced** and contains options that apply to those who have purchased software filters that use either a ratings bureau or special sets of filter rules. If either of these apply, you will find details in the manual of your filtering software. If you are using Internet Explorer Content Advisor without such programs, you can ignore this advanced section and just click on the Apply button to put your Content Advisor configuration into effect. You will then be asked to enter a password to ensure only you can disable and configure the Content Advisor.

### Watch out!

Content Advisor relies on a rating system akin to that used to rate movies, but not all sex sites are rated. Most filtering packages rely on lists that contain the web addresses of offensive or adult sites, checking against the list before allowing access. For this to be effective you need to update the filter list regularly, and even then, given the rate at which new web sites appear, there will always be sites that manage to slip through.

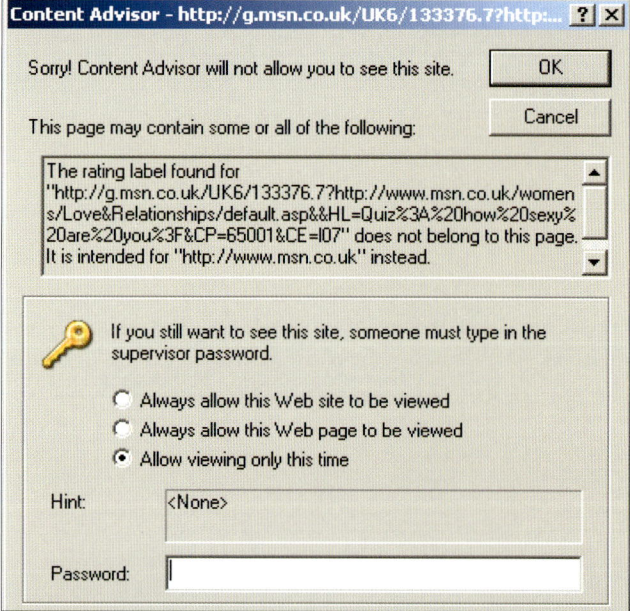

**12** When you try to access a site that is outside the rating guidelines, a **warning window** should appear before you are connected. This will explain which rating category is being breached, or if this is a non-rated page. To access the site, the supervisor password must be entered and you can choose to allow access always to the whole site, always to a specific page, or only on this occasion.

# 4

# Improving Performance

## Speeding up ................... 153
Tune it up
Disk utilities
Rev it up
Slicker software
Problem solving

## Using utilities ................ 163
Choosing utilities
System utilities
Internet utilities
Fun stuff

## Enabling technology ....... 171
Helpful hardware
Helpful software
Windows tips
The Internet
In the future
Easy access

# Speeding up

**You can get your old PC working like new without spending a fortune on new hardware or software.**

The PC you bought 18 months ago probably felt like the leading edge of technology. Yet today you're bombarded by ads ramming home the point that you can now buy more computing power, more extras and more memory for less than you paid.

### Better and cheaper
That's the way with computer technology. It changes quickly, with components getting better and cheaper all the time. Economy of scale, intense competition, and economic factors in the producing countries also force prices down.

Here's the good news: you don't need the latest go-faster PC. What you've got will almost certainly do what you want. And even if you could use some more oomph, it is possible to give your system a boost on a modest budget. The following pages look at the options. Some are free, none are too pricey. So what can you do to keep your PC in trim?

● Regularly delete the temporary files that clutter up your disk. Remove the fonts you don't use – they have to be loaded every time Windows starts up. Check the disk's health occasionally, and use a disk defragmenter every week. Your copy of Windows should have everything you need.

● Check out the latest versions of every bit of software you use. As well as bug fixes, the later versions usually offer performance improvements.

● Invest in a disk maintenance utility that extends and automates the housekeeping process with more and better tools.

● Open the hood and get out the screwdriver. Add more memory, a second hard drive, a go-faster graphics card, even a new processor. The performance gains will vary from one setup to another.

### You will need

**ESSENTIAL**
**Software** Most of the software you need to fine tune your computer system is supplied as standard with Windows, but it is also worth investing in a maintenance utility such as Norton SystemWorks.
**Hardware** A Pentium PC which has at least 64MB of RAM.

### Upgrade tip

You don't have to spend lots of money to keep your PC in tip-top condition. Stripping out unnecessary or unwanted programs, files and other extras will improve your PC's performance. It's simply a matter of getting into good habits. Windows already has a basic set of housekeeping tools to get you started.

# Tune it up

### Performance tip

If you use Microsoft Office with Windows, you can get a slight increase in performance by stopping Fast Searching (called Find Fast in earlier versions of Windows). Fast Searching is a utility that from time to time goes through the files on your hard drive and creates an index of keywords that can subsequently be used to speed a search up when an Office application goes looking for something. To enable Fast Searching, go to the Add and Remove Programs control panel and select Add/Remove Windows Components. Select Indexing Services, then click on Next. To disable the services, untick the box.

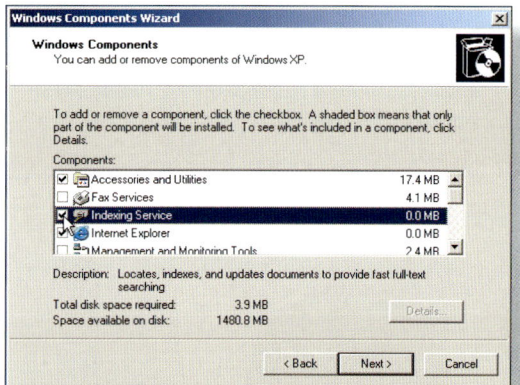

**Although Fast Searching helps you find files quickly, it does use system resources.**

## Windows comes with a number of maintenance tools – all you need for a fine tune-up.

As well as useful utilities such as Check Disk (ScanDisk in earlier versions of Windows) and Disk Defragmenter, Windows also includes programs to clean up unwanted files and Task Scheduler to plan automatically when programs are run.

### Clean sweep

To find these tools, go to the Programs menu, Accessories and then System Tools. Select Disk Cleanup to search your hard drive for unnecessary files that are clogging up space on your hard-drive. These include recently viewed Web pages that are cached away in a temporary folder for quick access if you want to see them again. The size of this cache and how often it is emptied are set through Internet Options in the Tools folder of Internet Explorer, but the default allocation is high.

Other prime targets for deletion by Disk Cleanup are temporary files set up by some programs when they run or are first installed. It is also easy to forget to empty the Recycling Bin. You can view any files before they are deleted from here. Under the Settings tab you can also select Disk Cleanup to run automatically when disk space is low.

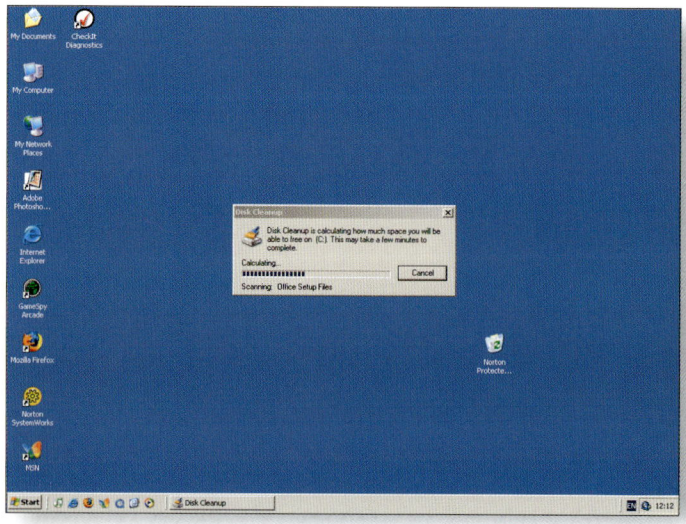

**Disk Cleanup will analyse the files on your hard drive to see what space it can make available.**

## Regular runners

Check Disk (called ScanDisk in Windows Me and 98) inspects the health of your hard drive and locks out any impaired areas so they can't be used. You should run Check Disk once or twice a month. (See pages 116–117.)

Disk Defragmenter is more useful as a tuning aid. Windows saves programs and data on a disk by filling up one block of space and then looking for the next free block to continue. This might not be next to it, so the file ends up being scattered all over the disk. Although Windows will still know which blocks of information are linked to each other, it can slow things down. Disk Defragmenter reorganises the drive so all the blocks of a file's data are, where possible, together. It also improves performance by keeping track of the programs and files you use most often. It moves these files to the fastest area of the disk so they start quicker. Use Disk Defragmenter once a week to keep things running sweetly. (See pages 118–119.)

Similarly, Task Scheduler enables you to set up programs or tasks to be run automatically at set times – usually periods when you're least likely to be needing your PC for other work. You can access Task Scheduler by selecting the Scheduled Tasks folder in System Tools or by double-clicking on its icon in the Taskbar.

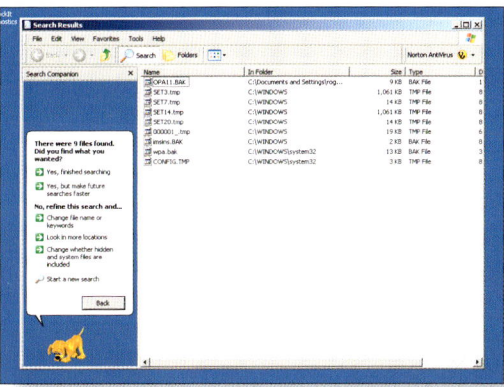

Use the Windows **Find** tool to locate unwanted files on your hard disk and then delete them.

### Cache tip

Under Windows XP, the operating system itself will choose how best to allocate the memory it has available. Typically this is optimised for running your programs. However, if you want Windows itself to use more of the cache, go to the Control Panel, select the Advanced tabs and under Performance, click on the Settings button, then Advanced tabs. In Memory Usage select System cache.

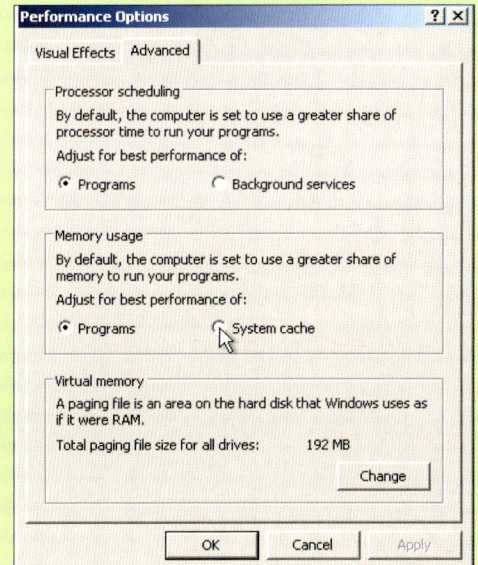

## Check the Web

Several web sites include tips and tweaks for Windows and the more you can use the faster your computing will be. Try these:

- **Computertips**
www.computertips.com/contents.htm
- **PCWin Resource Center**
www.pcwin.com/

- **Pure Performance**
www.pureperformance.com/
- **System Optimization**
www.sysopt.com/
- **Nerdy Books**
www.nerdybooks.com
- **Help with PCs**
www.helpwithpcs.com

- **Windows magazine**
www.winmag.com/
- **WinFiles**
www.winfiles.com/tips/
- **WinfoHQ**
www.winfohq.com/
- **PC-Pages**
www.pc-pages.co.uk

# Disk utilities

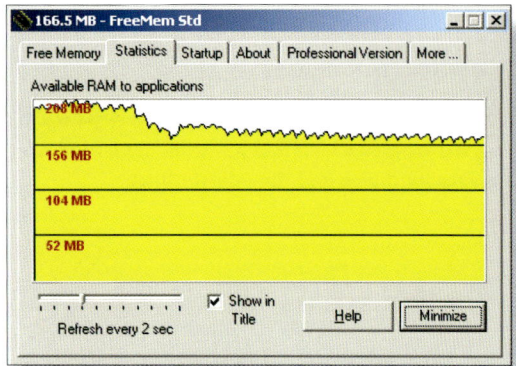

Run **FreeMem** and it will free up as much RAM as possible for your applications. The result is faster operation all round.

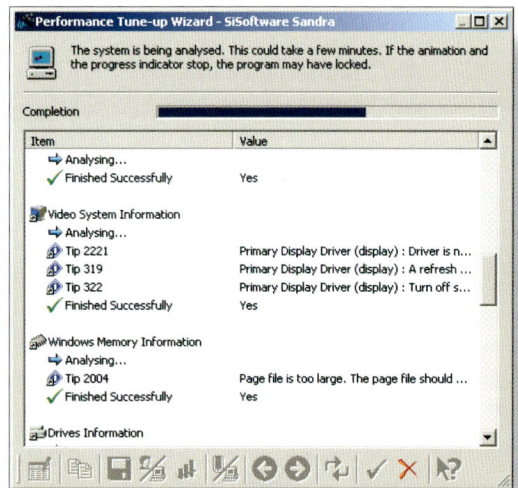

**SANDRA** identifies ways of optimising Windows' performance. The Tune-up Wizard goes through a series of tests and comes up with a list of tips and problem areas. It's then up to you to implement the solutions.

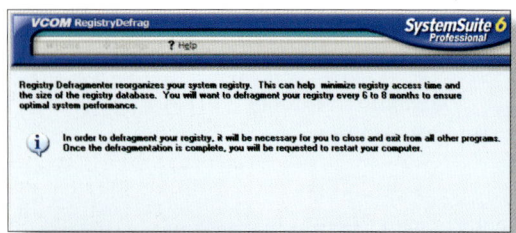

Use VCOM's **System Suite Registry Defrag** to get Windows' Registry working efficiently.

## Optimise memory and hard disk space to keep your software running at maximum speed.

Windows is very good at adapting to suit various programs and tools as they are being used. However, this process requires extra power and additional programs, which inevitably cause your PC to slow down. Fortunately there is a wide variety of utilities that will let you adjust the thousands of hidden settings in Windows and help keep your computer running smoothly.

### Memory managers

Windows XP has improved its memory management greatly compared to earlier versions, but it can always do with a helping hand. In addition, a memory manager can give an even greater boost to a computer running Windows Me or 98.

Windows uses part of the computer's memory as a cache for files stored on the hard disk. It tries to anticipate what data you will need next, and loads it into the cache so it's ready for use immediately. But this doesn't always work — sometimes Windows may allocate too much memory, and unused chunks of programs can also take up precious RAM.

FreeMem Professional, available from shareware libraries, is one of several memory managers available. It reduces the amount of RAM your programs need by switching off unnecessary background programs, such as Microsoft Office Fast Start. Fast Start preloads library files, which is meant to make the applications from Office load faster. However, the effect is nullified if the libraries fill up most of your memory and Windows has to start writing memory data to and from your hard disk, so your PC may well run better without it.

MemTurbo is a similar, but more comprehensive, program. The full version can defragment your physical RAM, reorganising it to make your system more efficient. You can run MemTurbo when you feel you need it, or the program can be set to run automatically whenever your free RAM drops to a certain level.

## System optimisers

Several utility suites are available to buy, including VCOM's SystemSuite and Norton Utilities. The Norton Utilities collection has been around almost as long as the PC itself. The current version includes useful performance enhancers such as the Speed Disk defragmenter – an advanced version of the defragmenter supplied with Windows – while System Doctor will continuously monitor your computer for problems, and can also clear out the Registry – the database used by Windows and other applications to store key configuration data. Also included in Norton Utilities is Clean Sweep, which identifies any files that may be cluttering up your hard disk and that you may want to delete.

Other tools are available to automate the removal of 'rubbish' from your hard drive, such as Wipe Info (part of SystemWorks), and McAfee's QuickClean. Because information isn't actually removed when it is deleted from a disk, these utilities will 'shred' the files by overwriting them with unintelligible data. The System Analyzer/Diagnostic and Reporting Assistant (or SANDRA) is a suite of diagnostic tools that can give you an extensive amount of information about your PC, including the operating system, peripherals and the software running on it. While they probably give you more information than you need, wizards such as the Performance Tune-up wizard will also give you tips on how to get the most from your system.

## Adjusting the interface

TweakUI is a collection of utilities developed by Microsoft. It allows you to adjust Windows' settings for 'User Interface' (UI) elements such as the desktop, folders, Internet Explorer, networks and so on. Although TweakUI doesn't do anything that can't be achieved by changing the Registry, it presents its options through a friendly interface that is much easier to use. (See pages 95–98.) Search the Microsoft site to find the release for your version of Windows. Tweak XP (at www.totalidea.com) is another system enhancer that allows you to change the UI, and it also gives easy access to various other settings to optimise your system — for example, to alter the shortcuts that appear on your Start menu.

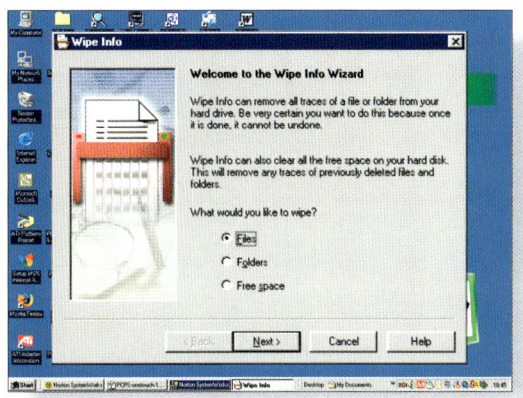

With **Wipe Info** and other cleanup programs you can decide how thoroughly files are shredded by selecting the number of times they are overwritten with unintelligible data.

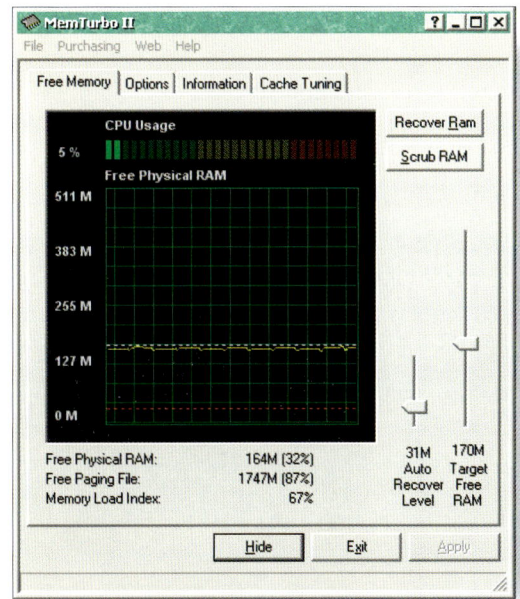

**MemTurbo** is designed to increase the available RAM on your system by flushing out unused sections of programs and fixing memory leaks – memory that was allocated then forgotten about by Windows or other applications.

# Rev it up

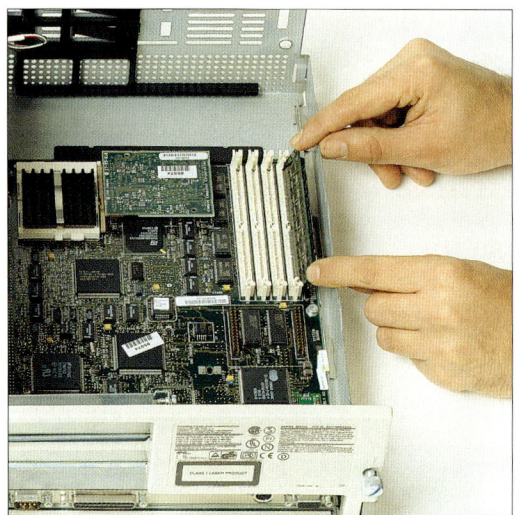

The quickest, simplest, cheapest and most effective boost you can give your PC is to add more **RAM**.

A **processor** upgrade means taking out your existing processor chip and replacing it with one that allows you to run applications faster.

### Memory tip

Be careful about paying too much for branded memory that appears to be made specifically for your PC. There aren't many different types of memory for PCs. Branded memory is made in exactly the same way and probably even on the same production lines as RAM that would be labelled industry standard.

## If you're brave enough to open up your computer, you can replace or add to the key components.

### Increase your RAM

Your PC uses RAM to store the data it's currently working on. It also needs RAM for the application you're running and the sections of Windows being used. If it runs out of RAM, it has to access some of the data it needs from the hard drive. The more RAM you've got, the faster your PC can perform.

You'll see a dramatic improvement moving from 32MB to 64MB, a noticeable gain going from 64MB to 128MB, and for particular types of work a definite result from increasing to 256MB or more.

Installing the memory should be simple enough, and there are several useful guides on the Web. Try www.kingston.com.

The only real concern in upgrading is to match the capacity and speed of the new memory strips with whatever is already inside your PC. You may be able to figure that out from your computer's handbook. If not, ask your supplier for advice.

### Upgrade your processor

The type and speed of the processor is one of the main differentiators between one PC and another. You can't usually find a replacement for the newer Intel processors, and some processor types are not upgradable at all. The fastest and most expensive upgrades available are rated at 800MHz, so if you are running anything faster than that, don't bother. But if you are running a 486 or an older Pentium (rated at 75MHz and up), you should consider it. You'll get a worthwhile speed increase. Tests suggest that moving from a 75MHz processor to a 800MHz Pentium will boost performance tenfold. Programs which use a lot of graphics, such as games or image editors, or which do a lot of number crunching, like spreadsheets and databases, will benefit greatly.

### Go for graphics

A go-faster graphics card won't do much for word processing, Web browsing or other applications that don't make a lot of use of multimedia effects. But if you want zippy games, smooth video and superfast

## Regular use

Collecting useful performance-enhancing utilities may be good fun, but it's a waste of time if you don't use them regularly to keep your PC in good shape. Set up the automated-function options wherever possible so that the utility gets used regularly; or use the Task Scheduler to schedule operations.

## Watch out!

If you have a 386 or 486-based PC, there is no point in trying to upgrade it as you won't be able to find enough replacement components.

If you're nervous, the inside of a computer can be a scary place to start teaching yourself practical electronics. And if your PC is still covered by a guarantee, even opening the hood will probably invalidate the warranty. Finally, it is wise to check out how much your bill is likely to be. If it is going to be half the price of a new computer, it's worth considering paying the extra to get a new system and a warranty on the whole thing.

screen redrawing, there's never been a better time to upgrade to one of the new accelerated 3D graphics cards. This is an easy upgrade. Just slot in the new adapter card, plug in your monitor and run the software supplied.

## Space solver

Disk drives now come with huge capacities and quite low costs – which is just as well, because modern software takes up a lot of space. Most PC cases already have a spare compartment into which the new drive slots, and there should also be spare cables already in there. The extra disk space will give Windows more room for its temporary caches, which translates into faster operation – smoother running for applications, easier switching between applications and speedier Web browsing.

**Installing a second hard drive or replacing your existing drive should be easy and inexpensive.**

## Cash in on cache

This is one for the more experienced PC owner. Increasing the size of the processor cache is one of the best upgrades you can make. The cache is used as a temporary store to relieve the processor's workload, and it comes as one or two strips of dedicated, very fast memory chips. If you can increase the cache size, your processor will be able to work faster, more smoothly and more efficiently.

The current cache size should be listed somewhere in your handbook, or may be found in the power-on setup screen. If it's 128KB or less, check whether your computer's main circuit board has plug-in cache chips. Again, the handbook should tell you, or you may be able to work out where to find the cache memory on the board and check it visually.

Then contact a specialist memory supplier — many advertise on the Internet or in the back pages of computer magazines — and find out what it can do for you. You might need to note the serial numbers on your existing cache chips, because that will help the supplier identify exactly what you need.

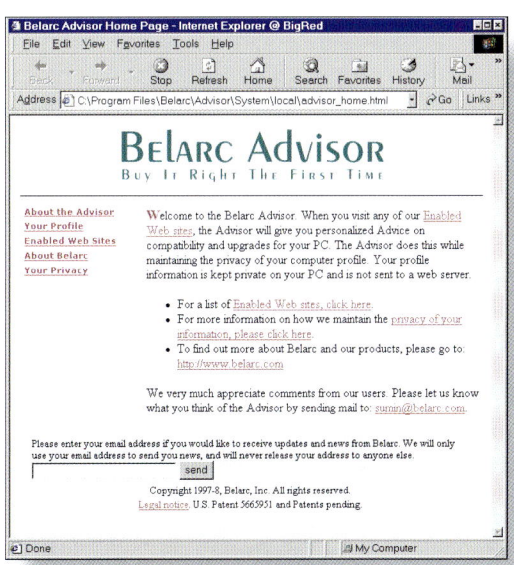

**The Belarc Advisor is a small free utility that runs a check on your PC setup and tells you where things could be improved. Get it from www.belarc.com**

# Slicker software

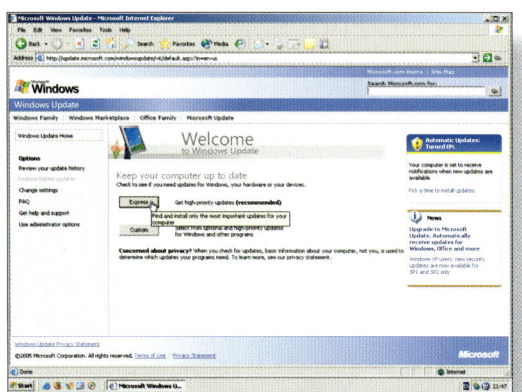

**Click on the Express Updates button at the Windows Update home page (http://update.microsoft.com) to get the priority updates for your PC.**

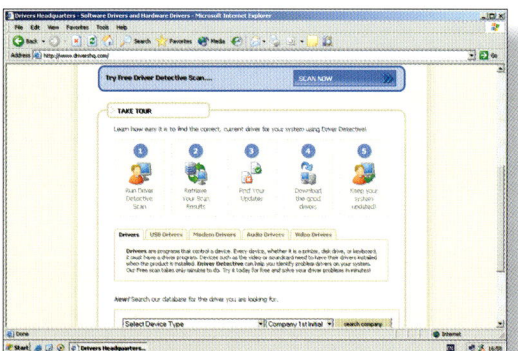

**Specialised download sites cover specific types of update. Drivers Headquarters, for example, allows you to update device drivers.**

## Patches and upgrades can be used to update your software and make it run faster.

It's not always easy to decide whether to upgrade your software. What the publisher may regard as a major improvement may, in fact, only be some improved Help files, support for recently launched and specialist devices, or extra components that may have little benefit to you.

### Degrees of change

Two basic types of software update can be found. Patches make minor changes to your existing software to improve its performance (usually at little or no extra cost), while upgrades make significant changes and are marketed as a completely new version – owners of earlier versions can usually upgrade at a useful discount.

Patches allow you to make 'running repairs' to your software. Microsoft is constantly releasing patches that fix problems in Windows and Internet Explorer – anything from crashes in specific circumstances, to gaps in security that leave computers vulnerable to attack over the Internet. It's always worth keeping your software, and particularly the operating system, updated with the

### Updating tip

It's not always easy remembering to check whether driver updates are available. Most of the subscription services, and some free services, such as Download.com, offer a weekly e-mail service with details of all the latest updates.

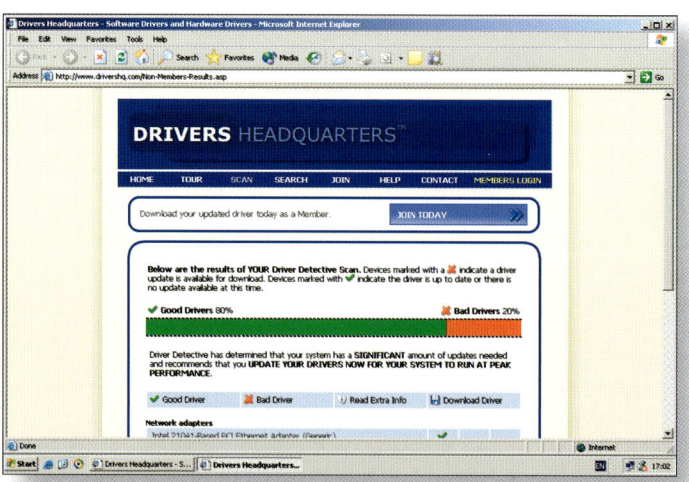

**The Driver Detective utility gives you details of the drivers you have installed. To download updates you'll need to register and pay a fee.**

latest patches, however trivial they may seem, and it costs nothing except the price of your Internet connection.

Upgrades cost money and require more careful consideration. If an upgrade fixes a major problem or adds features that will be of value, then you may want to invest. But make sure the publisher is adding something significant to its new version, and not just making superficial changes to squeeze more money out of its customers. Before investing, check the program's hardware and operating system requirements. The newest version of any application may demand the latest version of Windows, and a computer with higher specifications than you actually have.

Updates for Windows can be found on Microsoft's web site at http://update.microsoft.com. The on-line service will check what you already have, then recommend what else you need. Updates are also available from shareware libraries, such as Download.com (www.download.com) and Tucows (www.tucows.com).

## Driver updates

You should also make sure you are running the latest DLL files. At Drivers HeadQuarters (www.drivershq.com) you can scan your PC using Driver Detective, a utility that finds the version numbers of your installed drivers, and checks whether updates are available.

Where possible, download the latest drivers from the original manufacturer, though it can sometimes be hard to identify just who that is. Peripherals such as your printer and modem should be clearly marked, and you should also be able to identify manufacturers through the Device Manager in the System Properties section of the Control Panel.

### Jargon buster

**DLL** Dynamic Link Library – a collection of functions that can be used by Windows programs to enable the hardware and software to interact. Some DLLs are provided with Windows and can used by all applications. Others are written for particular applications. A missing DLL can slow a program down or even completely stop it running.

### Reference points

The version numbering used by software manufacturers can give you a clue to the significance of a new release.

Changing a whole integer, for example from version 3 to 4, denotes an important revision. It should incorporate minor changes and bug fixes, but also add significant new capabilities. Such an upgrade may have hardware requirements that fit only the most up-to-date computers.

A point release, with a change to the digit following the decimal point, signifies lesser change but could still be of interest. A move from 3.0 to 3.1 could mean major changes to the efficiency of the program and fixes for problems, without significant changes to how the product works.

Minor changes are indicated by the second and subsequent digits following the decimal point. So 4.011 is likely to have no performance advantage over version 4.01, but minor problems may have been fixed.

### Web updates

A number of free services are available, such as windrivers.com, that will notify you about updates on the Web. Typically, you sign up and the service scans your computer to find out exactly what software you have. It can then tell you if there's a more up-to-date version available, and offer you the chance to download it. You may subsequently be e-mailed when the manufacturer issues an update.

Most utility suites, such as Norton SystemWorks, include update programs, but these are specifically geared to updating the program itself, identifying and automatically downloading the latest version of the program.

# Problem solving

## Troubles tip

On Microsoft's Web site you will find a useful collection of troubleshooters for most Microsoft products. On the basis of a few key questions they can direct you to information elsewhere on the site that might help. And quite often it does. To find the troubleshooters go to http://support.microsoft.com/support/tshoot/ and find the solution centre for the product.

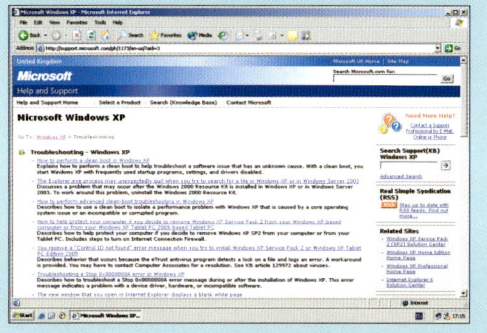

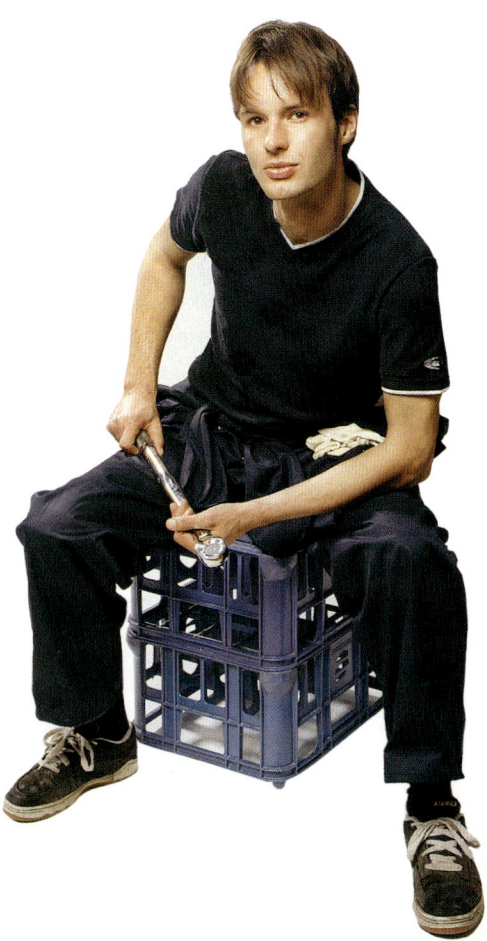

**If your computer suddenly starts to slow, don't panic. The problem could be simple and easy to fix.**

Few things are more frustrating than a computer that starts to misbehave. It's bad enough if the thing suddenly locks up, makes grinding noises or won't start up. It's worse if the occasional hiccup starts becoming a regular occurrence.

### Genius not required

Don't despair – not until you've tried some basic remedial measures. And you don't need to be a PC genius to apply a few troubleshooting principles.

First, identify the problem. If your PC appears to be wading through treacle, it's likely to be a software issue, and it's almost certainly related to Windows. If it wasn't always that sluggish, you can probably speed things up using standard Windows housekeeping tools. Strip out unneeded files, delete unnecessary fonts, defragment the hard disk (see pages 118–119) and don't have more than two or three programs running at once.

### A simple fix?

If the problem started suddenly, you might have installed some software that Windows doesn't like. Use the Add or Remove Programs tool in the Windows Control Panel to remove anything you have recently installed and see if that makes a difference. If not, a minor hardware upgrade could improve performance. The easiest and usually the most effective investment is more RAM. Put in as much as you can afford to take the PC to at least 64MB.

You could upgrade your hard disk, either by replacing the existing drive or adding a second. The latter is the easier and safer option, but you should then transfer Windows and your principal programs to the larger, faster and more modern drive.

The final step to consider is a processor upgrade. Surprisingly, this isn't the obvious way to speed up your computer. The processor isn't the only or even the most significant bottleneck in the average PC system. CPU upgrades start at little more than a chunk of additional RAM, but to get major increases in speed you'll have to spend a lot more.

# Using utilities

**Utilities extend the power of Windows and can make your applications even more versatile.**

## You will need

**ESSENTIAL**
**Software** Most of the programs featured here are available on magazine CD-ROMs or from the Internet.
**Hardware** Any type of PC running any version of Windows. Most of the utilities featured on the following pages are for Windows 98 and later, but a vast selection are available for MS-DOS. A CD-ROM drive and a modem are very useful because the two most abundant sources of shareware utilities are magazine CD-ROMs and the Internet.

As good as Windows is, it can't do everything. Just as you have to buy applications before you can use your PC for word processing, accounting or playing games, you need extra programs to help keep your PC in good working order and make it easy to use.

## What are utilities?

From their name it's obvious that utilities are useful, but not in the same way that programs like Lotus 1-2-3 and Microsoft Word are useful. While spreadsheets and word processors can be used for an almost infinite variety of tasks involving words and numbers, they're not clever enough to do really useful things like compressing their own files to save disk space. Even Windows can't do this. But there is no shortage of utilities that can.

## What do utilities do?

Utilities perform tasks that are beyond the normal scope of Windows. Some of them work in the background performing essential operations such as checking for viruses or clearing out redundant files that are cluttering up a hard disk. Others are used in the foreground in the same way as applications programs. This category includes file managers, encryption systems and utilities to catalogue graphics files and convert them from one format to another.

A graphics utility like IMSI's Hijaak differs from an application like Corel Draw in that it can't be used to create original pictures. But it can transform an existing Corel drawing into a format that is useable by a wide range of programs and computers.

# Choosing utilities

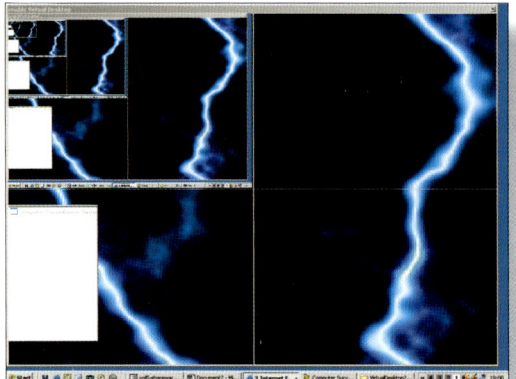

If you have several programs open it can be inconvenient to keep switching between windows. **Virtual Desktop** lets you create different desktops, open different programs in each, and switch between them using taskbar buttons.

## It's important to use utilities built for your version of Windows, and to keep them up to date.

Because many utilities work closely with the operating system – perhaps doing tasks such as uninstalling programs – it's important to make sure that the version you have is tailored to the version of Windows you use. Different versions of Windows work in very different ways and a utility program that worked well in Windows 98 may not do so in Windows XP. Windows is also being updated constantly. As bugs or faults are discovered, patches to fix them are released, as are upgrades to provide additional features. Often this means that the utilities that work alongside them must be updated too.

Previously, this might have involved getting an upgrade disk by post, but now it's all done on-line. Most utility programs have automatic update features that check you have the latest version at periodic intervals, and download any updates needed. If you don't have Internet access, many computer magazines provide CD-ROMs with patches and upgrades – but you have to remember to check for the latest versions when they come out.

Some update services, particularly those for anti-virus software, are tied to subscriptions. Once they lapse the software still works, but there's no

### Fact file

Here are the web addresses of several of the main utility publishers responsible for many of the market-leading products. Their programs are available in computer stores, through mail order, or by download from the Web.

- **Symantec**
www.symantec.com
- **VCOM**
www.v-com.com
- **PC Tools Software**
www.pctools.com
- **McAfee**
www.mcafee.com

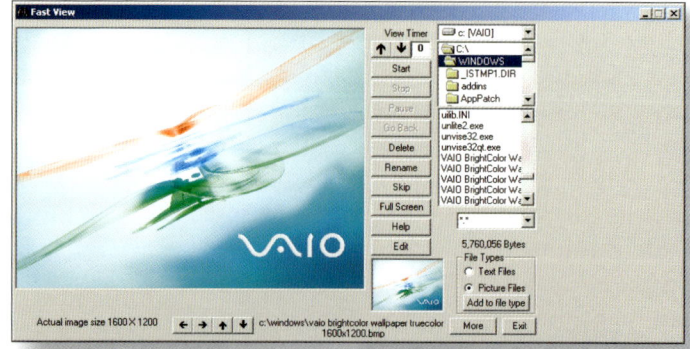

**Fast View** (from www.easydesksoftware.com) is an alternative file viewer to Windows Explorer. It can switch between text and picture files with the click of a button. You can also view pictures as a slideshow. In addition, it has a rename feature that's handy if you have a lot of clip art – you can name a file with something more meaningful than the numbers usually used.

# USING UTILITIES

automatic update of the virus definitions, so the latest bugs may not be detected. Although renewing the subscription is the simplest way to guarantee peace of mind, some updates are also available at shareware sites such as Download.com.

## Utilities for everybody

The following pages take a closer look at utilities in two categories – system helpers and graphics tools. But there are thousands of others that are less easy to categorise. OmniPage, for example, is a document management system that lets you scan, fax and e-mail from a single toolbar. It includes an OCR (optical character recognition) program that translates scanned text into an editable document, and a search tool that can find any word in any file on your hard disk. There are also other utilities designed to help you manage the desktop, such as Virtual Desktop, which allows you to create four separate desktops and switch between them.

The **Pass the Shareware** site gives some idea of the vast range of shareware utilities available – covering automation, backup/restore, file management, file viewers, icons and cursors, system maintenance and much more.

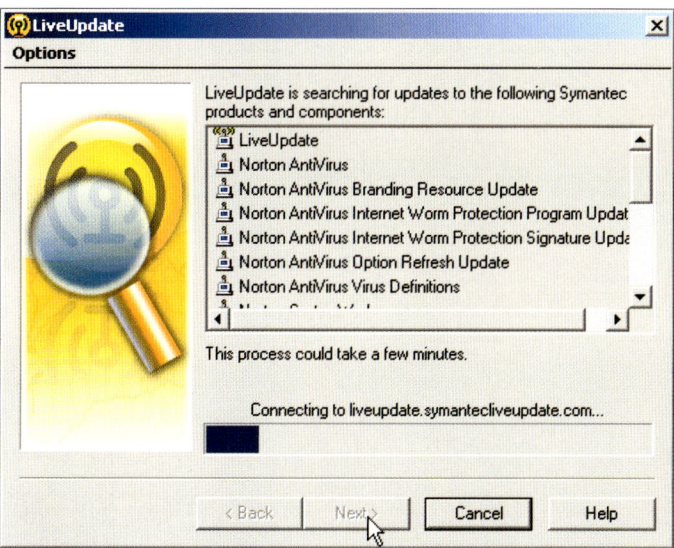

**Utility manufacturers such as Symantec are using the Internet increasingly to provide LiveUpdate services that ensure you have the latest version of their software. The update service can be launched separately from the actual utility, or can be set to run automatically at scheduled times.**

# System utilities

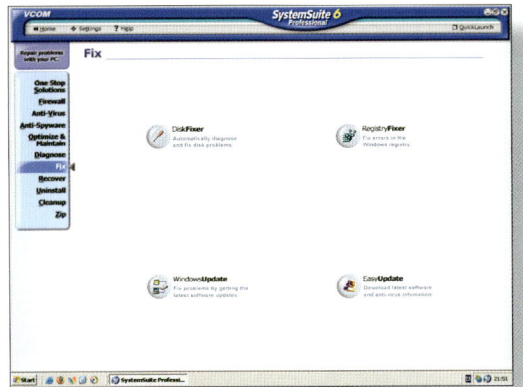

VCOM's **SystemSuite** is a multifunctional utility program. Wrapped inside one launcher is a set of 50 tools to protect your PC and keep it running smoothly, including utilities to fix disk problems, a firewall, a virus scanner, and an uninstall program.

Programs such as **AntiCrash** look out for errors and interrupt them before they cause a crash.

## DIY tips

- You can do a lot to keep your PC in good shape, using common sense and built-in utilities. Run Disk Defragmenter – from System Tools in the Accessories folder of All Programs – at least once a month to keep your hard disk in order. Use Disk Cleanup, in the same folder, to identify redundant temporary and back-up files and delete them.
- Always close down Windows properly before switching off and never delete any files from the Windows or Windows' System folders.

## System utilities can help prevent crashes and keep your computer running at peak performance.

System utilities are designed to get your computer working efficiently and then keep it in good shape. If your PC crashes because of a hardware or software fault, most system utilities incorporate a recovery system to minimise the damage.

### Utility suites

Utility suites are designed for ease of use. When you install them, they link into Windows and carry out much of their work in the background without asking you to do anything at all. Among other things, they monitor the memory and hard disk, check for viruses and make sure that other programs don't affect Windows settings. If you need to carry out a specific operation, perhaps tuning up your hard disk or solving a problem with a soundcard, you can do this from a menu.

Suites such as Norton Utilities and VCOM's Fix-it Utilities are made up of several programs that can be launched separately. But, for simplicity, they can also be started from a central control panel, and some will be loaded automatically. The advantage of this system, at least for experienced users, is that you can disable the features you don't need and

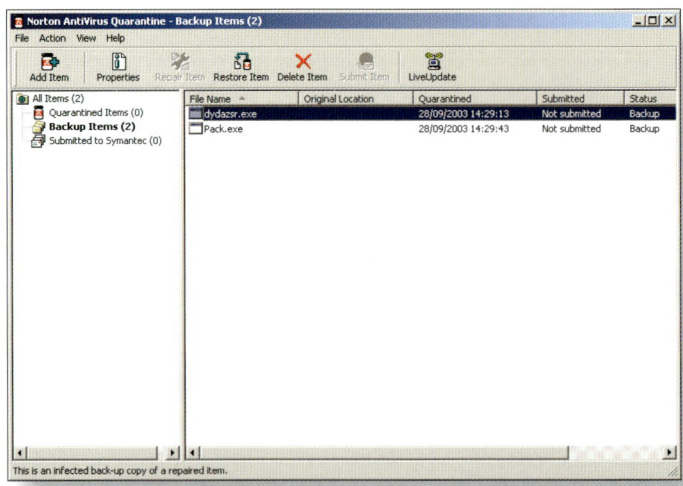

When an anti-virus program finds a bug, it takes a copy of the file and places the original in **quarantine**. The copy is repaired. If the repaired item works properly, you can delete the file in quarantine.

customise others. You can also choose which components to install, so that you are not wasting disk space on programs you will never use.

## Virus checkers

You may not want to have so many utilities programs taking over your PC, but one utility you should have is a virus checker. Standalone anti-virus programs from companies such as McAfee, Norton or Trend Micro can detect and cure a wider range of viruses than the trimmed-down versions obtained in multi-purpose packages. Free on-line services, such as TrendMicro's HouseCall, can also be used to check your PC. Go to uk.trendmicro-europe.com/consumer/housecall/housecall_launch.php and click 'Scan now' to download an anti-virus scanner. Select which disk to check and the program will scan for viruses and automatically repair any infected files.

## Uninstallers

Another utility that's best bought separately is an uninstaller. Every time you add a program, invisible changes are made to your system files. When you remove the program, it doesn't necessarily reverse all the changes it has made. This can make Windows unstable. Uninstallers such as Norton Uninstall and Ashampoo's UnInstaller track what a program does when it's installed and, if you subsequently remove it, can restore your computer to its original state.

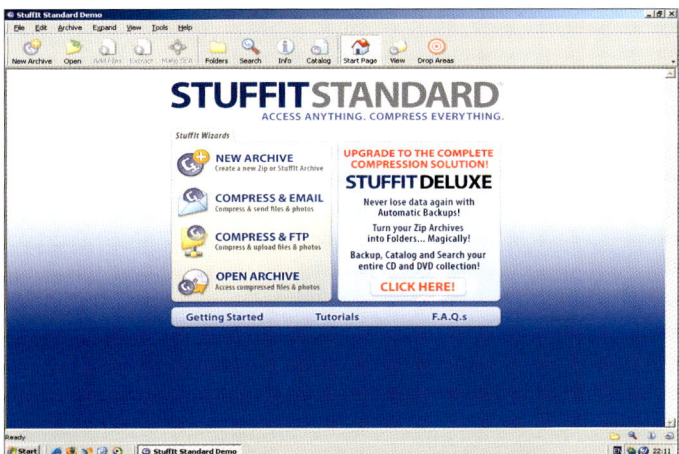

**Allume Systems' Stuffit Deluxe is a compression file manager that can compress and expand files in a variety of formats.**

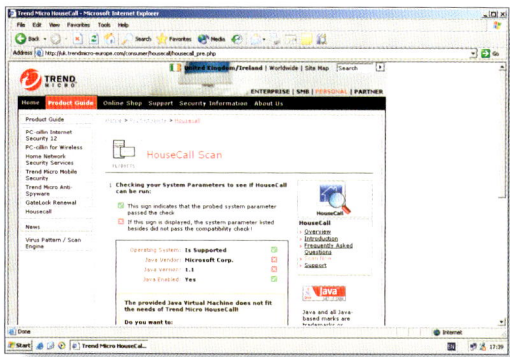

**As an alternative to a standalone program, you can scan your machine for viruses on-line. The advantage is that an on-line scanner will have the latest virus definitions. The drawback is that you have to remember to go on-line and scan your computer regularly.**

**Uninstaller programs work more thoroughly than Windows' Add or Remove Programs control panel. But to do so, they need to build a database of all the files on your computer and the links between them. The first time this is done it can take up to an hour, but it will be faster the next time.**

## Watch out!

While Windows XP and Me have their own system recovery utility using System Restore points, utility suites also often offer recovery systems for use when Windows is so badly damaged that it won't start. Most take a snapshot of your PC's settings and system files, which is saved on the hard disk or on recovery disks. In the event of problems, you start your PC with a recovery disk and this reinstates the last working version of Windows from the snapshot.

But a recovery system is not the same as a backup. Neither your work nor your programs are protected, so if your PC fails because its hard disk is physically damaged, a recovery system won't help. Keep copies of your programs and data – if you haven't got a back-up drive, you should at least make regular copies of important work on DVD, CD-ROM or floppy disks.

# Internet utilities

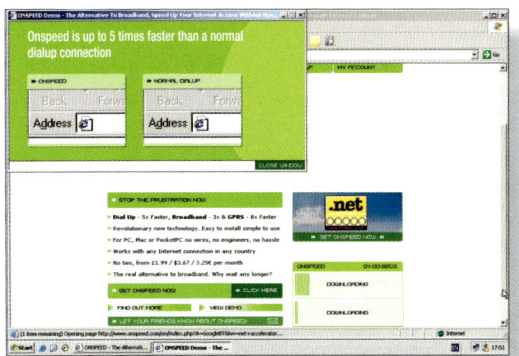

**OnSpeed** works in the background to speed up Internet browsing using a dial-up connection. It claims to make it five times faster, although not quite matching the typical home broadband connection that is on average 10 times faster than the fastest dial-up modem.

## Speed up World Wide Web browsing and protect your computer from unwanted files and viruses.

While an always-on broadband connection does a lot to speed up web browsing, it can still be frustratingly slow to connect to the Net via a traditional modem; there's the danger of virus infection; thousands of space-hungry files are downloaded to your hard disk; and it's easy to get lost on the Web trying to find what you want. It's not surprising that utility writers have leapt on the Internet bandwagon and brought out programs designed to tackle these and other problems.

### Speed enhancers

Some web pages take longer to load than the time it takes to read them. Speed enhancement programs can't make your modem faster, but they make browsing smoother by looking ahead. While you are reading a page, utilities like OnSpeed will pre-load pages – the addresses of which appear as links on your page – while using compression to make the pages download faster. Ideally, when you click on a link the new page will already have been loaded.

Download managers also download software more quickly. They do so using a mixture of compression and multiple links to the Web site.

### Jargon buster

**Cookie** A short text file downloaded to your PC when you visit a web site. It identifies you and stores information about your preferences. Cookies are meant to be used when you revisit a site, but other sites can gather information about you by analysing them.

### Browser tip

By installing an anti-virus utility and correctly setting up your World Wide Web browser you can duplicate many of the features of Internet security utilities. In the Options dialogue box of Internet Explorer click on the Security tab and you can choose whether you want to download and run ActiveX controls and Java applets. If you decide to do so, then you should set the safety level to medium so you'll be warned before they're used.

On the Advanced tab choose whether or not you want to accept cookies on your computer. The Settings button on the same screen allows you to save disk space by reducing the percentage of your disk used to store temporary Internet files.

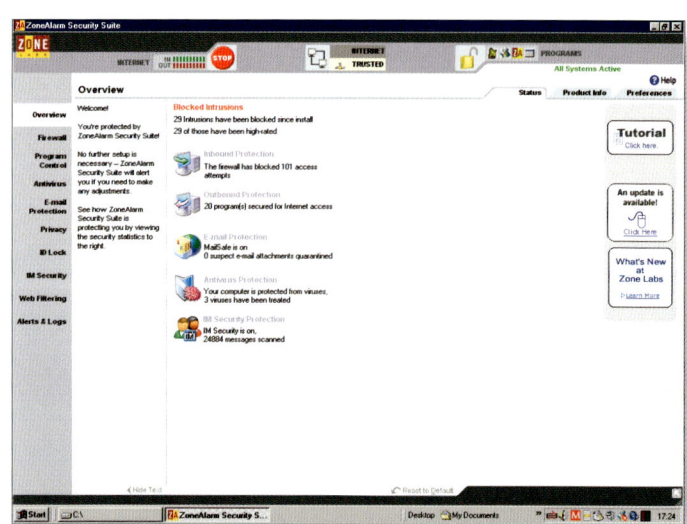

**ZoneAlarm** is a program that can detect and stop hackers accessing your information. It is available from www.zonelabs.com.

## Finding your way

Programs such as Copernic's Agent are an alternative to the search engines on the Web. With Agent you enter words and phrases of interest and then the program connects to the most-used search engines on the Internet. Where Agent differs from similar multiple-search facilities on the Web is that once you've got a site list you can sort, index and analyse it, and save it for future use.

Similar programs, such as MicroPlanet's Gravity, are available for searching and sorting newsgroups. Messages can be downloaded for off-line reading, replies can be typed while you're off line and Gravity will post them to the appropriate newsgroup the next time you connect.

## Safety and security

A good anti-virus program will protect your PC from viruses while you're on the Web but there are other Internet files that also pose threats. The concern about cookies is that those left by one site could be read by another site, although in practice cookies seldom store any personal information of significance. More problematic are ActiveX controls and Java applets. These are mini programs that a hacker can use to read data on your hard disk or cause other damage. Check whether your anti-virus program scans for these hostilities.

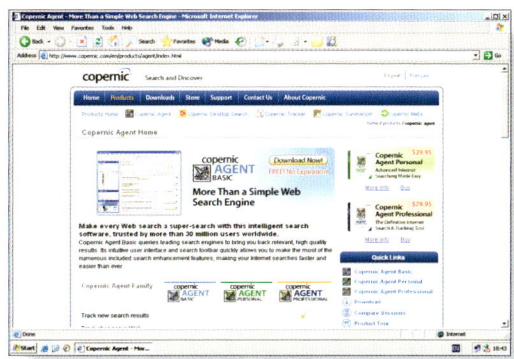

**Copernic Agent** makes Internet searches faster by querying several search engines at once. It also lets you organise the results.

### Jargon buster

**Java applets** Small programs that can be downloaded from a web site and run on your PC by a Java-compatible browser, which Netscape Navigator and Microsoft Internet Explorer both are. Java is a programming language used on the Web.

**ActiveX controls** A way of sharing information between applications. ActiveX controls can be embedded in web pages, in the same way as Java applets.

### Watch out!

● Remember too that web accelerators speed things up only if you spend long enough reading a page for the accelerator to pre-load any linked sites. If other utilities are running searches or trying to access data from web sites at the same time, the accelerator's share of the modem won't be enough for it to do its job.

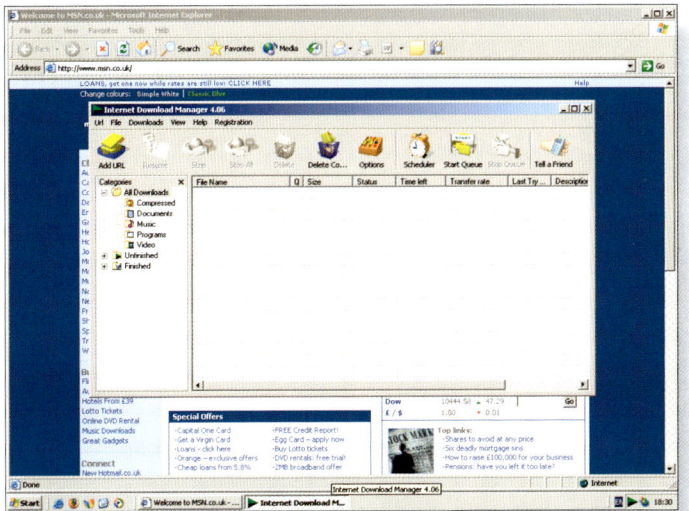

As well as making downloads faster, internet **download managers** will also resume downloads from the point where they were broken off if the connection goes down.

# Fun stuff

Several screensavers come with **Windows XP**. To change between them, right-click on the desktop, select Properties, then the Screen Saver tab. Make your choice from the list and click on Apply.

### Screensaver tip

All you have to do to install extra screensavers is copy them into the Windows\System32 folder. They then appear in the Display Properties dialogue box. Start this by right-clicking on the Desktop, then click on the Screen Saver tab and choose the one you want from the list box.

## Screensavers do a useful job at the same time as providing plenty of fun and entertainment.

The screensavers supplied with Windows aren't very exciting but hundreds can be downloaded from the Web. Modern monitors don't suffer from the screen-burn that savers were designed to prevent, but they're useful as a form of password protection and as a way of protecting your work from prying eyes. Some screensavers can also control the power-saving features of EnergyStar monitors.

### Themes and variations

Microsoft's Themes are a source of screensavers. These are sold as separate products and as part of the Microsoft Plus! packs. Each theme includes a background wallpaper, sound effects, animated cursors and a distinctive combination of colours.

You can make your own wallpaper using utilities such as ACDSee. Scan a photo or create a picture, view it in ACDSee, then right-click on it and select Wallpaper from the menu. Alternatively, copy a picture with the PrintScreen key and paste it into Windows Paint. Save it as a .bmp in the Windows folder. You can then select it as your wallpaper from Display Properties by clicking on Background.

**Desktop themes – such as The Golden Era shown here – may not make Windows easier to use but do give a very striking effect.**

# Enabling technology

**The technology is available to help everyone get the most out of computing, whatever their ability.**

If you're disabled, most of the computer operations that the rest of the computer-using world takes for granted may not be all that easy. But while some aspects of the technology may be hard to access, other aspects could cancel them out and make your life a bit easier.

## A powerful tool

Computers can be powerful tools, helping people with disabilities to deal with many parts of their day-to-day lives in ways that simply wouldn't have been possible ten or 20 years ago. Voice-controlled computers, for example, can be used to write letters or to control devices around the home. The hard of hearing or those with speech problems can use e-mail and other services to communicate, and blind or partially sighted people can have a computer read out their messages to them.

Those are just the straightforward, obvious applications. Computers can do much more when you start to add specialised equipment, allowing people with little control over their bodies to perform complex tasks.

## PCs for all

A few years ago you would have needed a very big budget for specialist equipment; now it's much easier to find products that will help overcome disabilities. Tools like speech recognition programs are more advanced, more widely available and cheaper than ever before. They can control all the functions of your PC. Devices to let your PC control the home are fairly easy to come by too, and even the basic software that comes with every computer now includes features to make it easier for everyone to use. Of course, some people will still need specialised equipment, but taking the first steps towards improving your life with a computer is now easier than ever.

### You will need

**ESSENTIAL**
**Software** The exact needs of every person will differ, but you'll need either Windows XP, Me or 98. For controlling a computer by speech, you need speech recognition software.
**Hardware** A soundcard and a microphone, either for speech control or to have the computer read messages back to you.

# Helpful hardware

## A wide range of specialised equipment is available to help disabled people with computing.

For people with disabilities, using a computer can present problems. Fortunately, many of these difficulties can be overcome by equipment that is currently available, whatever the person's disability may be.

### Fixed equipment

For people who find using a mouse difficult or impossible, a trackball may be the solution. A simple piece of equipment, the trackball stays in one place. Models are also available with larger balls, which can be even easier to use.

Another alternative is a touch-screen display, which can be bought either as a dedicated replacement for a standard computer monitor, or as an add-on. Either way, all the user will have to do is touch part of the screen to select various options.

For people unable to use their arms, there are devices such as a head-operated mouse. Several companies make these. There is also a device called the head wand, which allows you to press keys on a keyboard, or touch a screen.

Specialised keyboards are also available. These range from ones designed for children – with large, easy-to-press keys – to models controlled with a mouse stick, or designed for typists with the use of only one hand.

To control electrical devices around the home, the X10 system at www.x10.com enables a PC to switch on lights and other equipment through signals sent over the mains wiring. This system first gained popularity in the US, and is now available in the

### Equipment tip

While some disabilities will require very specialised equipment, don't overlook some of the more common devices such as trackballs and children's keyboards, which may solve some accessibility problems more easily and cheaply than a specialist solution.

### Compatibility tip

Before buying specialist equipment, remember to check that it's compatible with the hardware and software you're already using. You may need drivers for devices such as special keyboards, so you'll have to ensure that they're compatible with the version of Windows that you have installed on your computer.

UK and elsewhere. Combining a system like this with special keyboards or speech recognition software means that you can have more control over your environment as well as your computer.

## Specialist displays

For many people, viewing a computer screen is difficult or impossible. Apart from obvious solutions like a larger monitor, there are some graphics cards that can magnify one part of the screen, making it easier to read. There are also devices known as screen readers, which will read out the words on the screen for you.

But for those who are blind or visually impaired, having the computer speak to you is not the only option, and you can print out hard copies of information in Braille.

There is also a display screen called a Braille Voyager, available from HumanWare at www.visuaide.com, which allows your PC to translate the words on the screen into a form that you can feel, just like printed Braille, by raising and lowering pins beneath a smooth surface. They can even be used to edit text on the screen, but the downside is that they're also one of the most expensive add-ons for a computer – largely because they're mechanically very complicated.

**Touchscreen** displays can be bought to replace a standard computer monitor, or as an add-on.

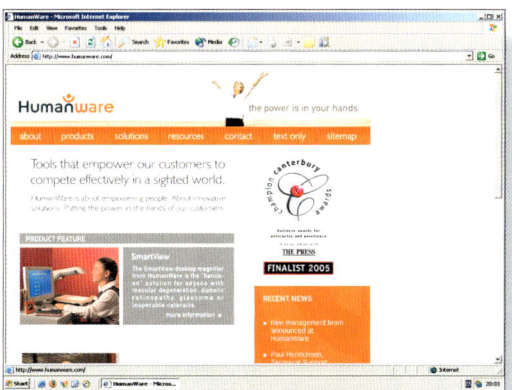

Devices are available from companies such as **HumanWare** that can translate the words on screen into a form that you can feel.

## Fact file

Unfortunately, it is unlikely that you will be able to buy special equipment at a discount. However, if you contact charities or support groups for your particular disability, some of them may be able to recommend suppliers who offer equipment at a special price.

It's unlikely that any single company will have expertise in putting together a complete solution for you, so the convenience of buying everything from one supplier is also not available. Again, contacting a charity or support group is the best way to locate someone who understands your problems and can deliver a computer that does everything you need it to.

It is possible that since your specialist equipment is necessary for medical reasons, you may be able to claim back the VAT, or set the cost against income tax. Consult your financial advisor for more information.

## Fact file

Professor Stephen Hawking famously overcame some of the difficulties of his motor neurone disease by using a speech synthesiser. But Hawking's 'voice' isn't typical of a modern speech system. The latest speech synthesisers produce a much more natural-sounding voice; the main reason that users of older models haven't updated is that their 'voice' is recognisable to the people who know them.

Jean-Dominique Bauby, the victim of a stroke that left him almost totally paralysed, wrote an account of his experience, *The Diving Bell and the Butterfly*. In his condition, he was only able to dictate by blinking his eyelid. Although he didn't use a computer to help – visitors read the alphabet to him – similar techniques can now easily be computerised, allowing communication even for the totally paralysed.

# Helpful software

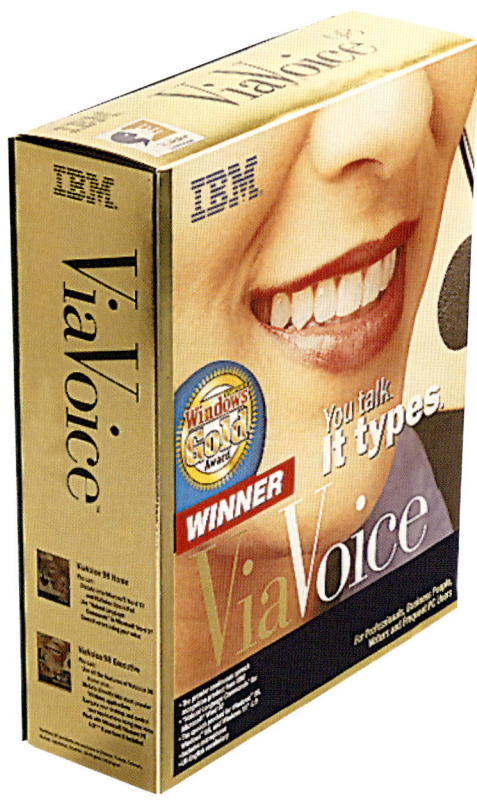

**Much of the software included as standard with PCs is designed to help people with various abilities.**

Makers of computer software are aware that people with disabilities have special needs that can be served through some simple adjustments to default settings. They even have developed programs to help make your computer easier to use.

### Talk is cheap

One of the most common software solutions for people with disabilities is speech recognition, which makes the computer respond to spoken messages. A few years ago, good quality speech software was expensive. But now it's used by many people, even by those who do not suffer from a disability, and can be bought very cheaply. Some software packages, such as Lotus SmartSuite, come with speech recognition as an option.

Some of the cheaper speech recognition programs give control over only a limited range of functions on the computer, and they may include their own word processor. Others allow you to do almost anything, and to use the programs of your own choice. So if, for example, you really have to use Microsoft Word, make sure you buy a program that will allow you to type into it with voice

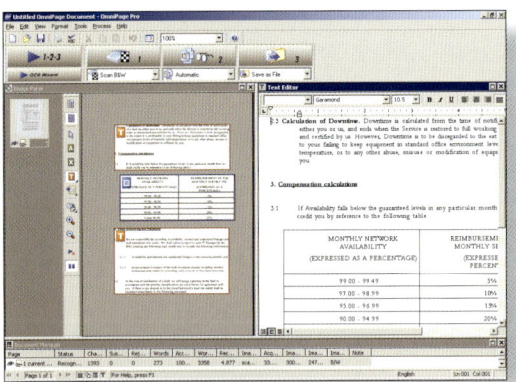

**Text recognition programs like OmniPage Pro use divided screens to make it easier to view complicated printed pages.**

### Jargon buster

**Text to speech** Text to speech is the opposite of recognition. It allows the computer to read the words that are on the screen, making it much easier for visually impaired people to use the computer.

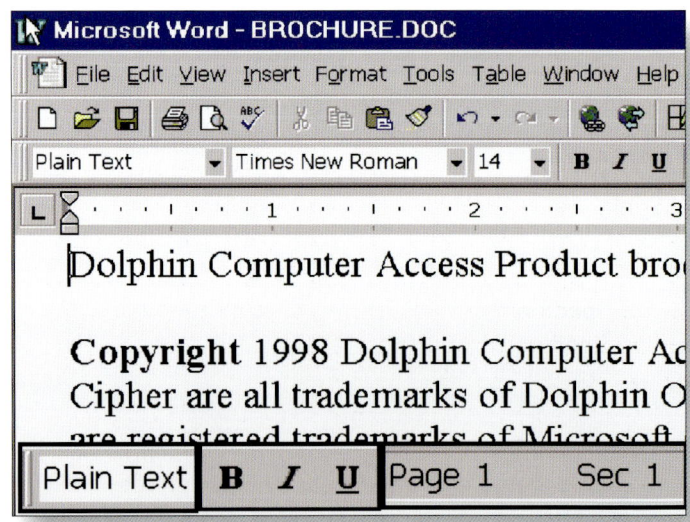

**SuperNova** can make sure key parts of the display are enhanced, so you can easily see them, whatever you're doing in a document.

## Jargon buster

**Discrete speech recognition** There are two types of speech recognition: discrete and continuous. With a discrete system, you have to pause between each word, while a continuous system lets you talk at a natural pace. Discrete systems are often cheaper, but it's possible to buy either type at a reasonable price.

recognition, such as ScanSoft's Naturally Speaking (www.dragonsystems.com). Some systems, such as ScanSoft's Real Speak, also provide text to speech facilities. Couple that with a scanner and text recognition programs like TextBridge or Caere's OmniPage (both available from www.scansoft.com) and you can use the computer to read out letters and other documents.

### All in one key

If you can type, but have difficulty, there are other programs you can consider, such as macro systems that let you assign a whole sequence of commands or typing to a single key. You could press a function key, for example, and have the PC start the word processor, and automatically insert your name and address at the beginning of a letter. One of the most popular programs for doing this sort of task is QuicKeys (www.quickeys.com).

Another useful tool, whatever sort of system you use to type, is word prediction software. Programs such as Penfriend XP (www.penfriend.biz) guess what word you're typing from the first few letters that you enter, and offer a selection of choices, which can mean you achieve the same results with fewer keystrokes.

### Braille processing

For more specialised needs there are other programs, such as the Monty Braille word processor (www.humanware.com) or the Duxbury Braille Translator, which will let you take an ordinary document and convert it to Braille for printing out, or vice versa. The visually impaired can also benefit from screen readers – programs designed to read from the computer screen. Screen magnifiers are designed to enlarge the text on the screen. Some products, such as Dolphin SuperNova (www.dolphinuk.co.uk), combine all these features in one package but, again, expect to pay more for specialised programs like this than for more general ones like the QuicKey product.

There's software available from the BBC called Betsie (www.bbc.co.uk/education/betsie) that can be added to a web site which will automatically generate a version of the site that is easier for screen-reading programs to use.

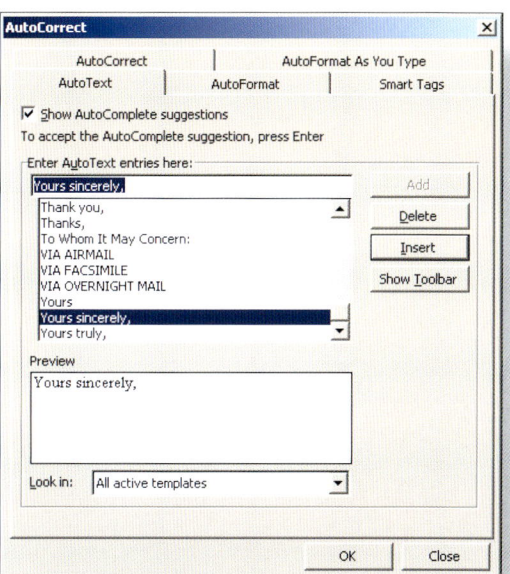

Word processors like Microsoft Word can speed up typing by predicting some phrases using the **AutoText** feature, from the Tools, AutoCorrect menu.

## Speed tip

Whatever type of system you're using to enter text into your PC, whether it's speech, a keyboard or some other type of input, you can speed up the rate at which you enter words by using macro programs such as QuicKeys to store words or phrases you use often. Before doing this, check to make sure that all the programs you're planning to use are compatible.

In some word processors, including Microsoft Word, you can set up macros that allow you to press a few keys to insert certain items automatically. The latest versions of Word include some prediction, so the program will, for example, automatically finish typing your name for you.

## Screen tip

Screen-reading software on the Internet is usually much more reliable if you choose the text only or low graphics option.

# Windows tips

## Many aspects of Windows can be configured so that they are easier to use for everyone.

From larger text to greater colour contrast, there are many ways to adjust the way Windows displays information to make it easier for anyone to use.

### Sticky business

Using StickyKeys makes it easier to select the key combinations Windows uses for special functions. Instead of having to press a key like Ctrl and hold it down while you press another, with StickyKeys you can press one after the other. Other features allow you to have the PC make a sound when a key like Caps Lock is pressed, so you know which state it's in, even if you can't see the lights. The SerialKeys option allows you to control the computer using devices other than the keyboard.

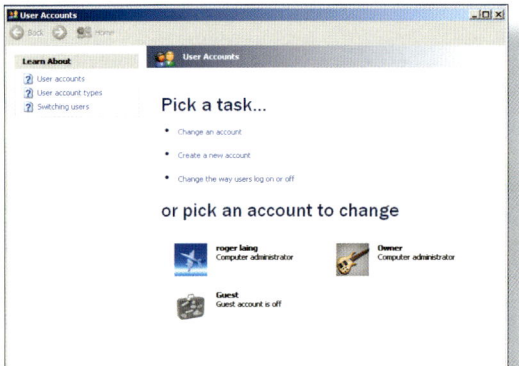

**Click on the User Accounts (previously just Users) control panel to enable profiles, with different settings for each person who uses your computer.**

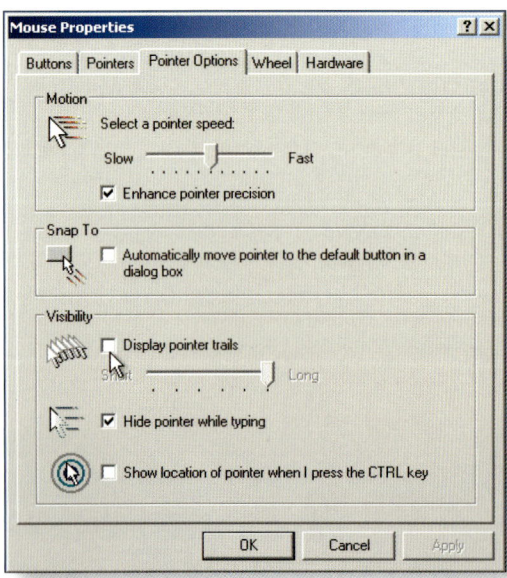

**The Mouse control panel allows you to use mouse trails and change the size and shape of the pointer to make it clearer to see.**

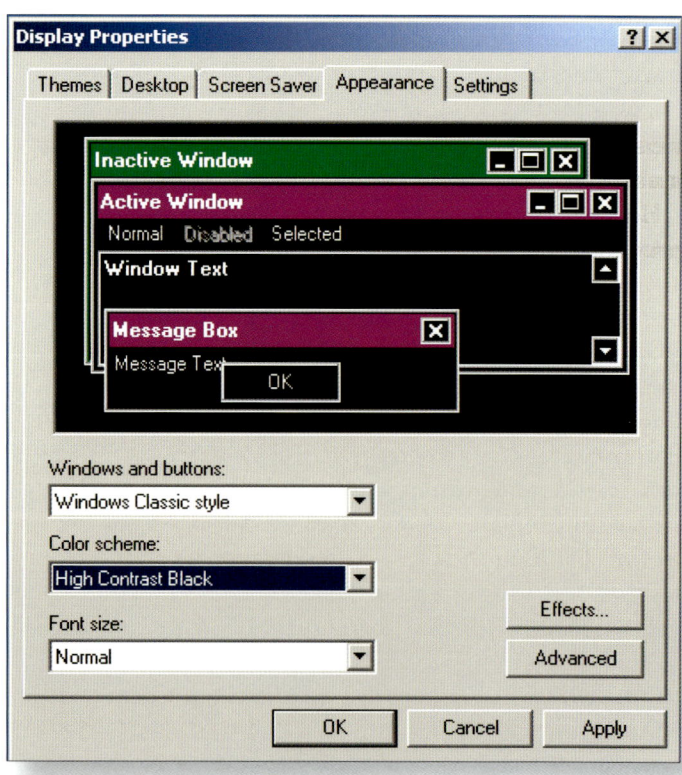

**The Appearance tab of the Display control panel allows you to choose a high-contrast colour scheme with larger fonts.**

## Larger text

For people with visual difficulties, the Display control panel can be used to make text larger, and you can also select a colour scheme that gives much greater contrast. There are other features too – mouse trails, where the mouse pointer will leave a trail on screen, and sonar, which will display a series of circles around the mouse pointer when you press a key. Both will help people who have difficulty following movement.

## Add a spot of colour

Windows has colour schemes to cope with a wide variety of visual conditions, and also pointers, so you can select a larger arrow, or one that changes colour automatically depending on what background it's moving over. The idea is to help you see it wherever it is on the screen.

There's a magnifier program, so that you can have the area of the screen around the mouse pointer magnified in a separate window.

There's also a new Accessibility Wizard, designed to help you change the settings on your PC that make it easier to use (full details are on page 181). The Wizard will guide you through creating a disk with those settings so that you can easily move them to another computer. Windows also has a version of Internet Explorer with extra options that make it easier to work with screen readers.

However, as Microsoft points out, specialist products have more features than this and may therefore be better for some people.

## Customise for users

Windows can also be configured with User Profiles. These allow you to have different settings for different users by typing your name when you start the PC. It makes it much easier for people with different levels of ability to use the same computer without having to change the settings each time.

### Watch out!

While most of the accessibility options are built-in to Windows XP, this wasn't the case in earlier versions of the operating system. If you bought a computer from an ordinary vendor without telling them that you have a disability, the Accessibility Options in Windows may not have been installed for you.

Fortunately, it's very easy to add them. Click on the Start button, choose Settings and then Control Panel. When the Control Panel window appears, double-click on the icon labelled Add/Remove Programs. Click on the tab marked Windows Setup and you'll see a list of options. Tick the box named Accessibility Tools, then click on the OK button, and you'll be asked to insert the CD or floppy disks for Windows, and the accessibility options will be added to your system. The next time you start the PC, you'll be able to use the new Accessibility Options control panel to set up the choices you need.

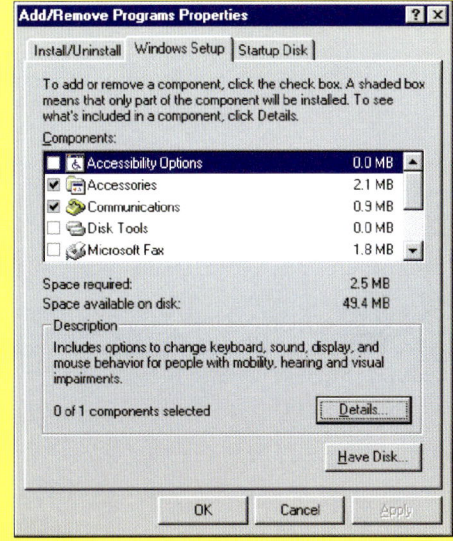

**The Windows Setup screen is the place where you can install Accessibility Options.**

**Microsoft's Accessibility site is packed with instructions that make using Windows easier.**

# The Internet

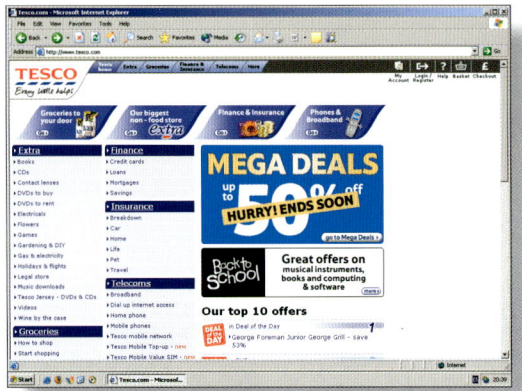

**Tesco can deliver groceries direct to your home.**

## Once you are online no disability can stop you getting as much from the Internet as anyone else.

The Internet is a great leveller, so it is not surprising to find that many disabled people have made much use of the World Wide Web. It can provide a social forum, via chat rooms or mailing lists, for meeting all kinds of people from all around the world.

### Get in touch

As well as allowing social interaction, the Internet can be a useful tool in many other ways. For example, most of the major charities and organisations working with those who have disabilities have web sites, with lists of suppliers and professionals who can help with your requirements. If you think that your disability means you can't use the computer in any of the ways covered here, you'll be able to find plenty more information on the Web. Look at the web site for an organisation concerned with your own disability and you'll be able to find contact information and, on some sites, recommendations for products that can help you.

Medical information can be very valuable too, and there's plenty of it online, from explanation of diagnoses to support groups where you can

### Jargon buster

● **Chat room** An area on the Net where messages you type are relayed to other people immediately, so you can have a conversation in real time.

● **IRC** Internet Relay Chat. The most commonly used type of chat system on the Net, although there are also chat rooms on some web pages.

● **ISP** Internet service provider. The company that provides your Internet connection. Many now make no charge, so all you will have to pay for is the telephone call.

● **Mailing list** An e-mail address that passes a copy of your message on to all the other subscribers for them to read when they collect their mail.

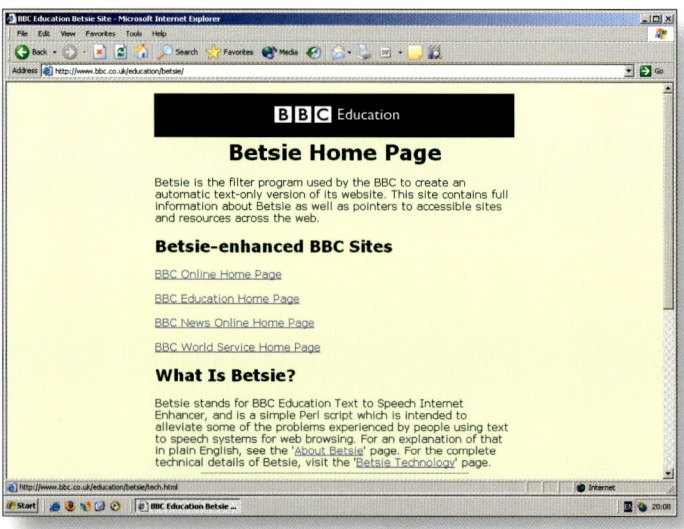

**Betsie helps make web sites easier for people with screen readers.**

exchange information or find out about new drugs that may be worth discussing with your doctor. You should find pages detailing treatments from the viewpoint of those who have tried them, and those who devised them, and you could share your own hints and tips with other users in discussion forums.

## Shop from home

On a more mundane level, how about some help with the shopping? Try visiting a supermarket site, such as Tesco at www.tesco.co.uk. Most of the major supermarket chains have a home-shopping service that lets you choose your groceries and delivers them to your door. Apart from groceries, you can buy almost anything via the Internet – clothes, books, music and gifts. Online shopping is on the up and up, and an ever-increasing variety of consumer needs can be satisfied without having to leave the house.

## Setting a standard for all

The World Wide Web is essentially a visual medium, but that doesn't mean that the visually impaired are forgotten. Many major web sites, including the BBC's news pages at news.bbc.co.uk and the RNIB at www.rnib.org.uk have special sites that are designed for access with screen-reading software. And the latest speech-enabled browsers have been designed from the outset to make them easy for people who can't see well.

The W3C, the organisation that sets the standards for the Web, is even insisting in its latest set of regulations that a properly compliant web page must have a text description of all images on the page, to make them more accessible. Of course, this is not an ideal solution, and there are still many pages that the visually impaired may find hard to use, but the situation is constantly improving.

Ultimately, the Internet can be whatever you want it to be – a library, a community centre, social club, or just a place to relax. All you need to get online is a modem, which could be one of the most enabling investments you ever make.

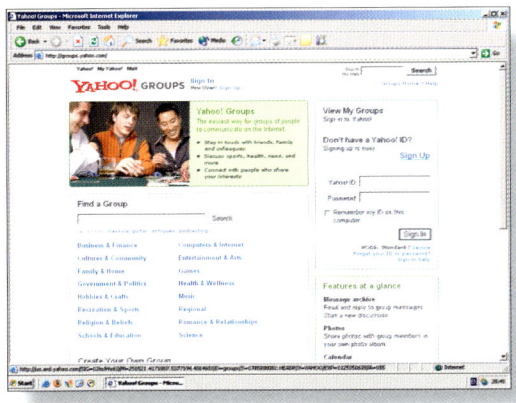

**Mailing lists** like those at Yahoo! Groups (http://groups.yahoo.com) can offer support.

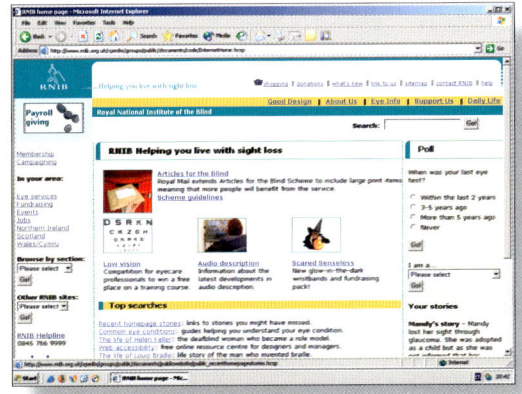

Many **charities** and support groups, including the RNIB, have a presence on the Internet where you can find valuable information.

# In the future

## Advances in technology are of just as much benefit to people with disabilities as to everybody else.

As newer versions of web browsers are developed, they will include the new standards insisted upon by the W3C (see page 179), making it much easier for screen readers to make sense of pages.

### All talk

As computers become ever more powerful, it's easier to find inexpensive speech recognition software that's efficient and doesn't involve the lengthy learning process that was necessary until recently. The programs are also more reliable, which means that having a cold or a sore throat, for example, shouldn't prevent you from controlling the computer. Natural language processing will make it much easier to learn to use the computer with your voice.

Text recognition, which enables a computer to read a printed page, is becoming much more reliable too, and better at deciphering complicated pages. People with visual problems will be able to put a magazine page, for example, into a scanner and have the computer turn it into text.

And if that text is to be read out loud, you'll be glad that the voices of computers are becoming more natural. Using the power of the latest processor chips, computers are able to work out more about what the text means, putting pauses and an emphasis in appropriate places.

### Thought transfer to your PC

Perhaps the most exciting development is in the area of mental control. This is still at the laboratory stage at the moment, but experiments around the world are letting people use the electrical power of their brain to control the pointer on a computer screen. At the University of Tübingen in Germany, a patient of Dr Niels Birbaumer has managed to write a letter using only thoughts to control the computer.

### Web tips

- If you are creating a World Wide Web page of your own, make sure that for each image you put on a page, you use the Alt option to specify a meaningful description, so that people using a screen reader can still make sense of the page.

- When you're accessing the Web, if you're visually impaired, turn off images in your browser. You'll save time on the downloads, and access the information you want much more quickly, provided web sites have been designed to be usable without images.

### Jargon buster

**Natural language processing** A development in computing that enables a computer to make sense of commands and instructions given in ordinary language. Instead of having to remember menu commands like 'file, open' you can simply say something like, 'Open the letter to Dr Jones.'

### Thought control

Some thought-control systems work by using a special skull cap with electrodes to monitor the brain's activity, while one involves placing a small glass cone inside the brain, into which nerve endings grow, allowing electrical impulses to be monitored efficiently.

These are completely new methods of doing things and patients have to be trained to control a computer in this way, but systems like these offer real hope that those who have little or no control over their bodies will, if their minds are intact, be able to communicate with the rest of the world.

# Easy access

**Windows makes it easy for nearly everyone to use a PC, no matter what their level of ability.**

Windows has an Accessibility Wizard to help make your computer easier to use. You can access it by going to the Start menu and choosing All Programs, Accessories and then Accessibility. If you can't find the Accessibility program, you can make sure it has been installed by clicking on the Add or Remove Programs control panel and then selecting Add/Remove Windows Components.

The Accessibility Wizard has over twenty steps, but it is relatively easy to use and you may not need to use all of them. These two pages take you through some of the main steps.

### Options tip

If you don't want to use the Accessibility Wizard you can still set the accessibility features through the Accessibility Options control panel. The Accessibility Options dialogue box has five tabs for Keyboard, Sound, Display, Mouse and General, and each option is clearly explained and simple to follow.

## Using the Accessibility Wizard

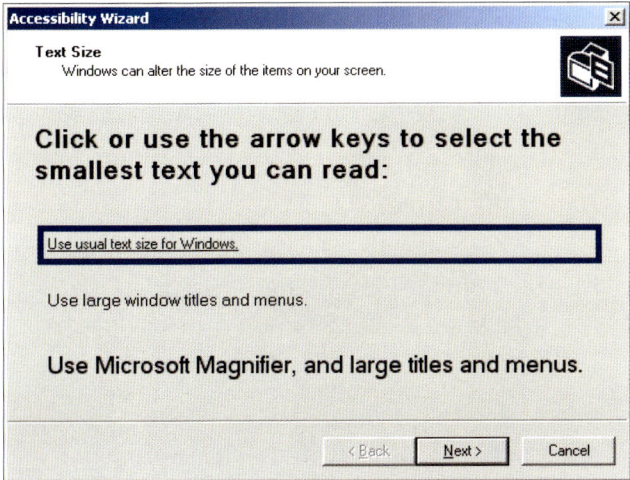

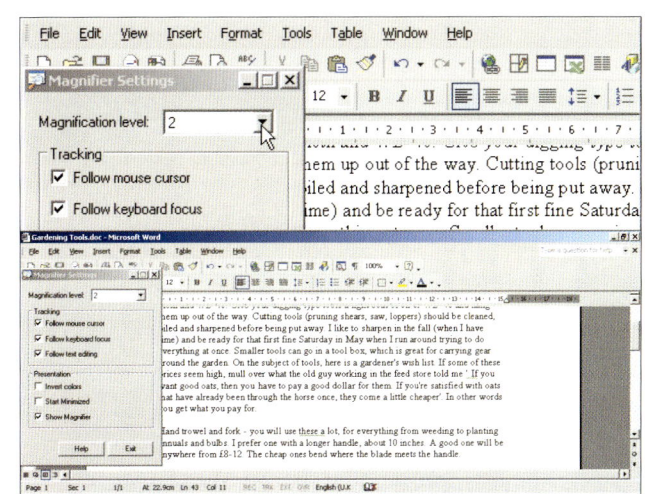

**1** The first few steps of the **Accessibility Wizard** let you decide how big things appear on your screen. You can increase the size of the font used in title bars, menus and other areas, switch to a lower screen resolution to make everything appear bigger and increase the size of on-screen buttons and icons to make them easier to see.

**2** People with severe sight problems also have the option to use the **Microsoft Magnifier**. This turns the mouse pointer into a magnifying lens. Everything it points to is magnified and displayed on another part of the screen. You can alter the amount of magnification and even change to a high-contrast colour scheme to make things stand out.

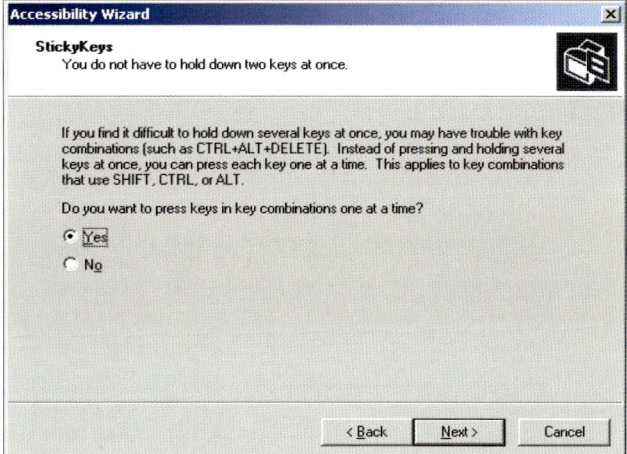

**3** The Wizard can also help you if you have **hearing problems**. You can opt to use on-screen warnings instead of system sounds, and you can activate the built-in sound and speech captions of programs like Microsoft Encarta.

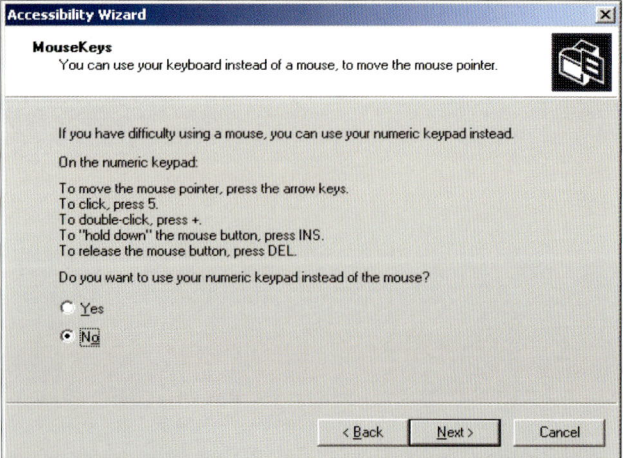

**4** If you have difficulty using a keyboard, the Wizard can help. **StickyKeys** is useful if you can't press several keys at once. With StickyKeys turned on, you can use key combinations that involve Ctrl, Alt and Del by pressing each key in turn. So to save a file using Ctrl+S, you can press the Ctrl key once and then the S key. The Wizard can also help if you have a tendency to accidentally press several keys at once.

**5** If you can't use the **mouse**, you can just use the keyboard. The arrow keys move the mouse pointer, and other keys work as the mouse buttons. If you can use a mouse, you can set the speed of its double-click and how fast the pointer moves.

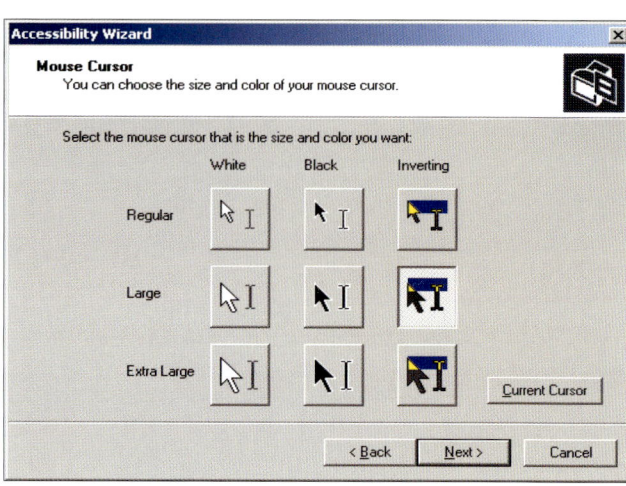

**6** The normal **cursor** (white with black edges) may not be the best colour scheme for you. You can change the colour of the cursor to black, or make it adopt variable colours that are the inverse of any object it is positioned over. You can also change the size of the cursor.

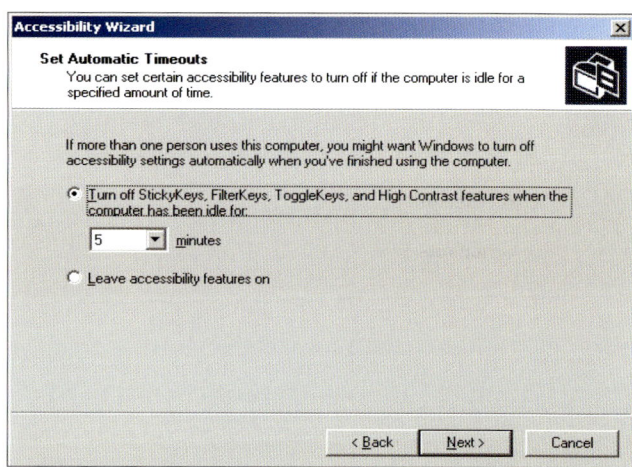

**7** If more than one person uses your PC, you can set the Accessibility features to **turn off** after a certain amount of inactivity. You can also save your Accessibility settings and load them each time you log into Windows using your own username. This way, people with different accessibility needs can all get the most out of the computer.

# Glossary
## A jargon-busting Guide

### Active desktop
Active Desktop brings your PC and the Web closer together. When Active Desktop is enabled you can take content from the Web – such as share prices, news pages and images – and use them on your desktop. To update the information you just need to go online.

### ActiveX
Technology developed by Microsoft to share information between applications. ActiveX controls can be embedded in Web pages for animation and other interactive effects.

### Active window
The part of the screen currently being used, also known as the window that is 'in focus'. When active, the title bar (the top strip of the window) will usually be a different colour from that of inactive windows.

### Adapter card
Printed circuit board that plugs into a PC expansion bus to communicate with other bits of hardware. A display adapter, for example, enables the PC to display text and images on the monitor.

### AGP
Stands for Accelerated Graphics Port. This is a new type of interface designed for the new breed of super-fast 3D graphics cards. It's great for games players.

### Analogue
A signal that varies continuously rather than being composed of discrete steps. Sound waves and clocks with hands are analogue. Clocks with LED displays are digital. A PC performs digitally, so it uses digital-to-analogue conversion (DAC) to produce sounds, display graphics and communicate along phone lines. Analogue-to-digital (ADC) converts analogue signals, such as recorded sound, into digits by 'sampling' the waveform thousands of times a second and storing snapshots of the amplitudes as numbers.

### Anti-aliasing
A technique to reduce the jagged appearance of images on screen, which is particularly noticeable when low-resolution pictures are magnified. In anti-aliasing, pixels at the edge of an image or text are given a shade of the relevant colour to give a smoother look.

### Anti-virus software
Software that scans for and removes viruses on your PC. Most anti-virus software can be set to check the PC each time you switch on and can also be used to check e-mail or downloaded programs for infected files.

### Applet
Refers to small programs, such as the Windows Calculator. Sometimes used to denote programs that can be run only from within other programs. Also refers to programs embedded in a Web page.

### Application
A program that produces useful output, such as a word processor, spreadsheet or drawing program, rather than a utility that serves to maintain or run the PC itself.

### Archive
To copy and store data away from the computer. Usually means removing data that's no longer current from the computer's hard disk (or extracting dated information from an application, such as e-mails received more than three months ago) in the same way as a library archive holds old periodicals.

### ASCII
Stands for the American Standard Code for Information Interchange. A US computing standard that details a set of numbers to represent the characters on a keyboard. It is used by almost all computers and software.

### Associate
To link a filename extension – the three letters after the dot in a filename – to a program. For example, the .xls filename extension is associated with Excel. If you double-click on the file it will load the application. If you double-click on a file that is not associated with any program a dialogue box will open asking you which application you want to use to open the file.

### Asterisk
This is used as a wild card in filenames, where it can represent one or more letters. Typing C*.txt into the Find File box will find every TXT file starting with the letter C.

### Attribute
Each file or folder on a disk can be marked (flagged) with one of four attributes, which reflect their special status. Archive files have been changed since the last back-up; Hidden files don't appear in file listings; Read-Only files can't be changed; and System files are hidden and can't be moved. In practice, these settings can be overridden.

### Autoexec.bat
One of two special text files that control the startup process of a computer. Not always necessary with Windows. (See Config.sys.)

### AVI
Stands for Audio Video Interleaved. A standard file format for mixed digital video and audio files.

### Backslash (\)
A symbol used by DOS and Windows to separate files and folders from the folders or drives that they are in. For example, C:\Windows\Help\Calc.hlp denotes the help file for the calculator (calc) which is inside the Help folder, which is itself in the Windows folder on the C: drive. Folders are sometimes referred to as directories.

### Bad sector
A physical fault on the surface of a floppy, or hard disk. Software such as Windows ScanDisk finds bad sectors and marks them off-limits, so that the operating system won't try to write to, or read from them.

### Baud rate
The speed at which a modem transmits data. The baud rate is the number of changes that occur in an electrical signal every second. This isn't the same as the number of bits per second transmitted (another, more accurate measurement of modem speed). As modems can compress data there are several bits transmitted in every baud.

### Bay
The space inside a PC's case where you fit a CD-ROM, floppy, tape back-up, or hard disk drive. Blanking plates are used to cover spare bays.

### BBS
Stands for bulletin board system. An electronic messaging and file download system available free or by subscription. Online services that also offer Internet access are taking over, but there are still many BBSs, including those maintained by hardware and software companies for downloading drivers and upgrades.

### Benchmark
A score of how well or quickly a PC, other hardware, or a program performs. Test centres use a set of specially designed tests to evaluate the performance of various components.

### BIOS
Stands for Basic Input/Output System. This is a set of essential instructions that manage the basic functions in your PC. The BIOS is stored in read-only memory (ROM) so that it starts when the computer turns on. It tests the hardware at start up, launches the operating system and controls the screen, keyboard and disk drives.

### Bit/Byte
A bit is the smallest unit of information handled by a computer. Short for BInary digiT, a bit can have one of just two values: 0 or 1. The value of a bit represents a simple choice, such as on or off, true or false. By itself a bit means little, but a group of eight bits makes up a byte – which can represent one letter, digit, or other character.

### Bits per second (bps)
A common way of describing the speed of a link between two PCs or a PC and a printer. It measures how many bits of data can be sent every second.

### Bitmap/.bmp
Images are made up of tiny dots (pixels). If you zoom in close to a bitmap image, you'll see the dots grow. Compare this with a vector image, where shapes are calculated mathematically, so they appear sharp however much you zoom in. Files that store bitmap image data are given the filename extension .bmp.

### Bookmark
Web site or document marked so you can jump to it, by name, from a bookmark list. Also used by browsers to keep a record of your favourite web sites.

### Boot
To start up your computer. When your PC boots up it carries out a sequence of instructions stored on the BIOS and loads the main operating system. A cold boot starts up the computer from scratch by turning on the power switch. A warm boot is when you restart the computer (without having first turned it off by using the power switch).

### Browser
A program used for viewing web pages – both on the Internet

and on your PC. It can also display images, play sounds and video clips, and run animations or small programs. In addition most browsers let you send and receive e-mail and link up with newsgroups.

## Buffer
A holding area in memory used for temporary storage of information. For instance, a print buffer can store data waiting to be printed so that you can carry on working with that application on something else.

## Bug
An error in a program that means it does not work properly.

## Bus
Sets of cables that connect parts of a PC – such as the processor and memory – and allow them to transfer information. There are three main buses: the data bus carries data around the PC, the address bus carries the memory location for the data, and the control bus carries a set of control and time signals to make sure all the components are working together.

## Cache
Pronounced 'cash', this is a storage area where frequently used data is kept. The information can be accessed quicker from the cache than it can from other areas. Web pages can also be cached so that when you want to look at them again they can be loaded from the computer instead of having to access the Internet.

## Capture
In Windows, you can save the current screen as an image (capture it) by pressing the Print Screen key. The image can then be pasted into a document or paint program. To capture just the active window and not the whole desktop, press Alt and Print Screen.

## Cartridge
A container that holds either ink (for inkjets) or toner (for lasers) that is used in printers. It will need to be replaced or refilled occasionally.

## Cascading menus
When you point to an item in a main menu out pops a sub-menu, or cascading menu, with further options to choose.

## Case-sensitive
Software that can detect the difference between lowercase (small) and uppercase (capital) letters. You're likely to find this in the Find and Replace function in some word processors. Searching for 'School' won't find 'school'. Most passwords are case-sensitive so be aware that typing in 'John' will not be the same as 'john'.

## CD (CD-ROM)
In the PC world, CD-ROMs (Compact Disc-Read Only Memory) can be used to store up to 650MB of data. But CD-ROMs cannot be altered. For that you need CD-R (Recordable) discs, although you can only record on them once. CD-RW (re-writable) discs can be re-recorded. You can delete and re-record information on the same discs so CD-RW drives are good for back-ups.

## Chat room
An area of the Internet where messages you type are seen by other people immediately so you can have a 'conversation' in real time. A Chat Room is a program that allows several people to chat at the same time.

## Child
A small window that appears inside a main window, often used to display options. For example, if you want to change a font, the options are all displayed in a child window.

## CMYK
This stands for cyan, magenta, yellow and key (black), the four colours used in an inkjet printer to make up any other colour.

## Code
Instructions to the computer are written in code. Source code is written by a programmer in a programming language. This is converted into machine code which consists of numerical instructions that the computer can recognise and act upon.

## Compatibility
Compatibility is a measure of how well computers, or software programs, can work with each other. The easier they can communicate with each other, share information or run the same programs, the more compatible they are.

## Compression
A method of reducing the size of a file by squashing the data it contains. Compression programs employ a number of clever tricks to do this and the results can be impressive, with some files being squeezed to less than a tenth of their original size. To use the files or programs they normally need to be decompressed first.

## Config.sys
One of two special text files that tells the computer what configuration to use for DOS systems (the old operating system used to run computers before Windows and which certain games still need to run). The other special startup file is Autoexec.bat. It is not necessary to have a Config.sys file. Without one, DOS will set itself up with basic defaults.

## Configure
To adjust software or hardware to suit your particular needs. For example, you can configure Windows so that it displays a different colour background or so that it uses a larger font that's easier to read.

## Context-sensitive help
This will display help about the specific thing you are trying to do. For example, in Word, if you are using the Find and Replace function and press the F1 key (this is almost always the Help key) the software should display advice on how to use the find and replace function.

## Control panel
This is a collection of icons that allow you to configure the basic functions of Windows and your computer. Among them are controls to define the fonts that are installed on your computer, the display settings, the type of printer that's installed, plus a mass of other options.

## Conversion
Changing (converting) from one type of program to another. For example, Word will change a file from the format used in some other word-processing programs into something it can read.

## Cookie
A small text file sent by a web server to your machine when you go to some Internet sites. It identifies you and stores information about your preferences. Cookies are meant to be used when you revisit a site, but other sites can, theoretically, gather information about you by analysing them.

## Corrupt
Where data is accidentally changed or destroyed. It can be a software problem or can be caused by a sudden power surge damaging the hard drive. Some utilities programs (such as Norton's Utilities) try to recover the data from a corrupted file.

## CPU or processor
This is the central processing unit, the brains of your PC. It is an electronic device – an integrated circuit board or chip – that contains millions and millions of tiny electronic components that carry out basic arithmetic and control functions. The speed of the processor is measured in Megahertz (MHz). The bigger the number the faster the PC.

## Crash
This is what happens when your PC goes wrong and freezes up. A crash can be caused by all sorts of problems with the software, but it normally occurs because the PC has got itself into a muddle or the software you are using has bugs in it.

## Ctrl-Alt-Del
Also known as the three-finger salute. Pressing these three keys together helps you get out of a crash. Press them once and it brings up a close box showing the programs that are running. You can then try closing the program that may have frozen the computer. Pressing Ctrl-Alt-Del twice will restart the computer.

## DAT
Stands for Digital Audio Tape, a small tape cassette used to store music or PC data. If you use a DAT for music, it provides the same quality as a compact disc. DATs are most often used to provide a back-up for computer data.

## Data/Data transfer rate
Data is a general term for anything the computer processes – it could be numbers, words or images. The data transfer rate is the speed at which data can be read from the hard disk and transferred to the processor. On a good drive this is about 33–66MB a second.

## Dedicated
This signifies a PC, printer, program, or even phone line that is used for one particular job only. If you have a network, you might find that you do a lot of printing or that you need to store a large number of files. In this case it would make sense to set aside one PC for printing or storage. It would not be used for anything else.

## Default
The choices automatically made by a program if you do not specify an alternative. For example, if you run a word processor and start typing a letter, it will use the default typeface (e.g. Arial) and the default paper size and margins. You can always change these settings later.

## Defragmentation
When a file is saved to disk, your PC does not always save it in a single area. If the disk is full, it might have to split the file and save it in sections in different places. This makes it slower to retrieve the file. Defragmentation utilities will reorganise your hard disk so

# GLOSSARY

that all the parts of a file are stored next to each other.

### Device/Device driver
Device is a general term for the parts that make up a computer system – such as a printer, serial, disk drive and modem. The software that controls each of these different parts is called a device driver, or more commonly just driver. (See driver.)

### Dialogue box
A message window that asks you to do something, such as press a button. It is called a dialogue box because it's the closest there is to a conversation between the computer and the user. It's usually used for choosing options, such as creating a name for saving files.

### Dial-up connection
This term covers the whole process of connecting to another computer over a telephone line, such as to your Internet service provider. To do this you need a modem and the dial-up software that's supplied with Windows.

### Digital/Digitise
Digital means that numbers, rather than a continuously changing signal, represent information. To digitise something is to convert an analogue signal, such as speech or sound, into a numeric form that can be processed by the computer. For example, a soundcard contains an analogue-to-digital converter to convert the sound signal from a microphone into numbers representing the volume and tone.

### DIP Switch
Sliding switch which can be moved to one of two positions – open or closed – to set options on a circuit board.

### Direct cable connection
A utility or small program supplied free with Windows that allows you to link two computers together using a cable plugged into the serial (or parallel) port on each PC. The two computers can then exchange files or share printers.

### DirectX
Needed to play some games. The software lets applications have direct access to the computer's sound and graphics hardware in order to improve performance.

### Disable
To stop something from happening. For instance, you can disable (prevent) people on a network from sharing files on your machine or having access to printers.

### DLL (dynamic-link library)
A DLL is a program file that's stored on disk and loaded only as and when an application needs it. That means it doesn't use up any memory until it is needed. Large applications, such as a complex word processor, might use several DLLs: one to carry out the spell check; one to manage printing a letter; and a third for formatting the text. DLL files have the extension .dll. The same DLL might be used by several programs so be careful before deleting any.

### DMA
Stands for Direct Memory Access. This is a fast method of accessing the contents of memory chips. Normally, if a video card wants to read data from the main memory, it has to go via the central processor. The central processor accesses the memory location and passes the data back to the video card. With DMA the video card retrieves the data directly from the memory.

### Domain/Domain name
(1) In Windows 98 a network can have groups of users or resources. For convenience, these are referred to as domains. (2) Domain is also used to identify sections of the Internet, each of which has a domain name. The domain name is part of the site name (or URL) and ends with the TLD (top-level domain) category. Some you'll encounter frequently are .com (commercial), .co.uk (UK commercial), .ac.uk (UK academic).

### Dongle
(1) A physical device – such as a key – which has to be attached to the computer for a particular software program to run on that machine. (2) It can also be a physical lock to keep a computer secure (such as locking the front of a cabinet which has the PC inside it).

### DOS
The standard operating system before Windows. DOS – which stands for Disk Operating System – was just a piece of software that managed the storage of files on the disk. It kept track of where the files were, how big they were, and when they were created. It also provided time and date functions and the ability to start other software programs. DOS was controlled through typed-in commands. (MS-DOS just stands for Microsoft Disk Operating System.)

### Dots per inch (dpi)
The number of dots that a printer can print on an inch of paper (or on a screen – the number of dots displayed per inch). The greater the number of dots, the smaller each must be and the finer the resolution. Some laser printers print at 600 dpi but most have a resolution of 1200 dpi or more.

### Download
When you download a file from the Web you are transferring a copy of a file from a computer on the Internet (the remote computer) to your computer (the local one). This can be done either by using a modem or a network. When you send files from your computer to one on the Internet it is called uploading.

### Drag and drop
A feature of Windows which means you can move a file, image or piece of text from one place on screen by picking it up with the cursor, dragging it to where you want it and dropping it into place.

### Drill down
To start at the top of a menu or directory and work your way down through sub-menus and directories until you find the file or command you want.

### Driver
A special piece of software that sits between Windows and a particular device, such as a printer or disk drive. It translates the instructions from Windows into a form that the device can understand. Some drivers come with Windows but most new devices come with drivers supplied by the manufacturer. They need to be loaded before the device will work properly. Drivers are regularly updated as bugs appear or new functions become possible.

### DVD
Stands for Digital Video Disk (or Digital Versatile Disk). It's a CD format that even in its basic form can be used to store as much data as seven ordinary CD-ROMs (4.7GB). Double-sided DVDs can store 17GB. The main attraction of DVD is to distribute feature films and sophisticated interactive multimedia titles. Films are encoded for each country to prevent piracy and to view them you need an appropriate MPEG 2 decoder. DVD drives can also be used to read ordinary CD-ROMs.

### Dynamic
Generally, it is used to mean something that changes immediately it is needed, such as a web page where the information is updated in real-time.

### E-mail
Electronic mail – messages and files that are sent from one computer to another through the Internet.

### E-mail address
Like the address on a letter it's a unique location where users receive their e-mail. The address is usually in the form of yourname@domainname – for example yourname@isp.co.uk.

### Emoticon
Emotional Icons, better known as smileys. Created by pressing keyboard characters they look like faces displaying a particular emotion. So J is I'm smiling at a joke while L is I'm sad.

### Encryption/Decryption
Encryption is the conversion of data into a secret code. Files are encrypted using a password and must be unscrambled (decoded) using the same password (also known as a key). Decryption is taking a message or file that has been coded (encrypted) and changing it back into its original form.

### .exe
The filename extension – short for executable – that tells you that a file is a program and can be run by double-clicking on its icon.

### Expansion card
A circuit board that can be plugged in to expand the functionality of your PC. For example, if you want to connect your PC to a network, you will need a network card that controls the way signals are sent over the network cable. You can fit several expansion cards to a PC by plugging them into empty expansion slots.

### Explorer
A program that's supplied with Windows that lets you manage all the files stored on a disk. With Explorer (officially called Windows Explorer) you can copy files, move files from one folder to another, create new folders, and rename or delete files and folders.

### Export
To move information from one program to another. Generally, this will involve converting a file from one format to another format so that it can be read by a different program. For example, if you have written a letter in Microsoft Word and want to give it to a friend who uses Word Perfect for Windows, you need to export the Word document to a Word Perfect format file using the File/Save As option in Word.

### Extension
The three-letter code at the end of a filename that generally indicates the type or format of the file. A filename might be Partyinvite with the extension .doc. This shows the file is a document. Similarly, .bmp means a bitmap file, and so on.

### FAQ
Stands for Frequently Asked Questions. A FAQ (pronounced fak) is a document that answers questions on specific topics. FAQs are frequently posted on the Internet to save technical support staff having to deal with the same questions over and over again.

### FAT
When you open a file, the operating system looks through the file allocation table (FAT) to find out where the file is stored. The FAT is hidden, so you cannot see it. But without it you cannot retrieve any of the information on your disk. Sometimes the FAT gets corrupted. To remedy this problem, run ScanDisk or another disk recovery program.

### Fatal error
Often shown by the blue screen of death, a fatal error causes the system or program to crash – with no hope of recovery.

### File format
The way data is stored in a file. For example, every document created in Word for Windows is stored as a Word file with special codes to tell Word how the margins are set up, the fonts that are used, and whether images are included.

### Filter
Filters work in several programs so as to pick out the bits of information you want from those you don't. For instance, an e-mail filter will stop messages from certain addresses getting through. In graphics programs, filters can be used to add special effects.

### Firewall
A firewall is a security device to protect networks (and individual PCs) from outside threats such as hackers. Instead of each computer linking directly to the Internet, they have to go through a separate server (proxy server) which decides which messages or files it is safe to let through.

### Flag
A flag is a marker or signal that something's important or needs some follow-up action. For example, in Outlook Express you can flag a message that comes in to show it needs an urgent reply.

### Flame
Red-hot passions can be aroused by messages in e-mail forums or other online chat rooms. To flame is to send rude or insulting e-mails to someone whose opinion you don't agree with. Those who do this are called flamers.

### Flicker
Images on screen flicker (appear to move) when the picture is not being refreshed often enough or quickly enough. Most screen displays need to be refreshed at 50–60 times per second in order to appear flicker-free.

### Font
A set of characters all of the same style (such as italic), weight (such as bold) and typeface (design). For example, labels in Windows are normally displayed in a font called Helvetica or Arial. Fonts are used by computers for their screen displays and by printers for producing printed pages. Windows has TrueType fonts that can be printed and displayed in almost any size, and printer fonts that can only be printed in predefined sizes.

### Footprint
The area covered by a piece of equipment, such as a PC or printer. Notebooks need to be small and light enough to carry around so they will have a smaller footprint (that is take up less space) than desktop PCs.

### Forum
Forums covering particular areas of interest (such as cookery, computing, chess, etc) are set up by newsgroups or online services. In the forums, you can post messages and get replies as well as find files, downloads and other related material.

### Freeware
Computer software that is given away free of charge and often made available on the Web or through newsgroups.

### FTP
This stands for File Transfer Protocol and is the way of moving files backwards and forwards across the Web. Using an FTP program – such as Terrapin or CuteFTP – you can take the files, pictures, and text for your web pages and 'upload' them, via an FTP server, to your web space.

### Function key – F keys
PCs have at least 12 function keys at the top of the keyboard. These are keys that are linked to specific tasks, such as refreshing the screen. However, the keys may have different uses according to different applications, although most use the F1 key to display help information.

### GIF file
Stands for Graphics Interface Format. Indicated by the file extension .gif, it is a commonly used format for storing images and bitmapped colour graphics. It was originally developed for the CompuServe online system, but is now one of the most popular formats for images stored on the Internet.

### Giga/Gigabyte (GB)
Giga before something means one billion (which, US style, is 1,000 million not a million million as it is in the UK). So the latest PCs with a processor speed of 1 Gigahertz (1GHz) go through 1,000 million cycles a second. A gigabyte (1GB) is 1,000 megabytes. The storage capacity of most hard drives today is measured in gigabytes.

### Graphics card
A graphics card produces the picture you see on your screen. It is also known as a graphics adapter, graphics accelerator, video adapter or display adapter. Most cards have special processors to boost performance and have their own memory in which to cache (store) the display. Some graphics cards are best for 2D work (standard applications) while others have been specially designed for 3D effects in games and multimedia titles. Although combined 2D/3D accelerated graphics cards appear to offer the best of both worlds, they may not be quite as fast as cards dedicated to either 2D or 3D.

### GUI
Stands for Graphical User Interface. This is a way of representing files, functions and folders with little images called icons. With a GUI such as Windows you can point and click on an icon, using the mouse, rather than typing in the filename, thereby making it easier to use a PC.

### Hacker
Originally, this meant someone who loved messing around with computers. Now it's the name for people who try to break into computer systems illegally.

### Handshaking
A series of signals that are sent between two communication devices – such as two modems linked by telephone – to establish the way in which they should send and receive data.

### Hardware
Any physical unit – hard disk, monitor, mouse, printer, electronic circuit – that is part of a computer system.

### Helper applications
Programs, such as sound or movie players, that are launched by the browser to play multimedia content downloaded from the Web. They are different from plug-ins because they are not part of the browser and can be run as stand-alone programs (e.g. RealPlayer).

### Heuristics
Heuristic programs are ones that learn from what's happened in the past. For example, heuristic scanning (also known as rule-based scanning) is where the scanning program compares files or programs with the virus files it knows, and decides the probability of them being infected.

### Hierarchical file system
A way of storing and organising files on a disk so that each file or folder is located within other folders. The main directory (folder) for the disk is called the root. The 'route' to get from there to a particular file or folder is called the path.

### Hit
Originally the way traffic to a web site was measured. The number of hits was an indication of how popular a site was. Downloading a file from a web page is a hit, but as each page can contain lots of files (such as picture files) it can take quite a few hits to download a full page. Now the number of visits (that is individual users) to a web site is used as a better measure of how busy a site is.

### Home page
A home page can be the first page you see when you log on to the Internet or the start page on any web site.

### Hot swapping
Means you can connect peripherals such as modems or CD-ROM drives to the computer and work with them immediately, without having to switch off the PC or restart.

### HTML
HyperText Markup Language, or HTML, is the special markup code used for creating web pages and saying how they should look. It's also used for creating hypertext links (see hyperlinks). A web page has .html as the file extension. There are software programs, such as FrontPage, which are HTML editors that will help you set up and change web pages.

# GLOSSARY

### Hyperlinks
Also known as hypertext links or hotlinks. Click on these to move to different parts of the page or to other web pages. The link is usually underlined or in a different colour to make it stand out from the text around it. Pictures can also be links. When the cursor passes over a link it changes from an arrow to a pointing hand.

### HTTP
This is the method – protocol – by which web pages are moved around the Internet. If you look in the address bar of your browser, http is usually seen as the first part of any web address, e.g. http://www.msn.com.

### HyperTerminal
A program included with Windows that enables you to dial up another computer, using a modem, and transfer files. It's not for accessing the Internet. It's more useful for accessing bulletin boards.

### Illegal operation
This is when a program does something that the computer thinks it shouldn't. Examples of illegal operations include protection faults where a program tries to use a protected block of memory used by another program or Windows itself, and exceptions, which are error conditions trapped by software. Stack faults occur when a program fills up the amount of space reserved for temporary data storage.

### Image map
A photo or a drawing on a web site that you can click on to link to different parts of the web page or site.

### Initialise
To set up a disk or tape for use. Usually, this includes testing the surface of the storage medium for faults, writing a startup file and setting up an index for file information.

### Inoculation
Used by anti-virus programs to check for suspicious changes in files. Programs are inoculated – that is protected against virus infection – by recording characteristic information about them. This information is compared each time the program is run. If there are any significant changes, the file may be corrupt or infected.

### I/O
Stands for Input/Output, that is, as it suggests, information that comes in and goes out of your computer. I/O cards control the data flow to and from devices such as your hard drive and mouse.

### IRC
Stands for Internet Relay Chat. This allows Internet users to chat with others online, in real-time. Through an IRC server, you can join various chat groups. Text you type is sent via the server to all other users in that group or channel. Generally, groups are dedicated to particular topics which are usually reflected in their name.

### IRQ conflict
Arises when two peripheral devices use the same number IRQ (Interrupt Request). The interrupt is a request for attention from the central processor. If two devices share the same interrupt – say the mouse and the modem – the processor may react to the wrong device and the system won't work properly.

### ISA
Stands for Industry Standard Architecture, a design standard that enabled expansion cards to be plugged into 16 bit expansion slots (known as ISA slots) on PCs. Now replaced with PCI and PCI Express.

### ISDN
Stands for Integrated Services Digital Network. This is a standard way of transmitting digital data over a telephone network at high speed – much faster than normal modems.

### ISP
Stands for Internet Service Provider. A company that offers users a connection to the Internet.

### Java/JavaScript
Java is a programming language used extensively on the World Wide Web. Small Java programs called Java applets are downloaded from a web site and run on your computer by a Java-compatible web browser, such as Netscape Navigator or Microsoft Internet Explorer. The use of Java enables more interactive content than is possible through HTML.

### JPEG
A standard you may come across if you use graphic images. JPEG is a complex way of storing images in a compressed format so they take up much less disk space. The file extension is .jpg.

### Jumpers
A small plug or wire on a device that can be moved to alter the way the device is configured.

### Kilobyte (KB)
A measure of the capacity of a storage device or size of a file. Usually written as KB, a kilobyte is equal to 1,024 bytes (210 in binary notation).

### KHz
A measure of the frequency of a sound. One KHz (or kilohertz) is equal to 1,000 cycles per second. The higher the number, the higher pitched the sound. You will see KHz mentioned in the specification of a soundcard. This can define two separate functions. The first is the range of frequencies the soundcard can output. The second is the frequency at which the soundcard takes samples of a sound when recording it onto your disk. A soundcard looks at the level of a sound thousands of times each second and so builds up a picture of it. The more times it takes a sample, the more accurate the recording.

### LAN
Stands for Local Area Network. This is a way of connecting several computers together within an office or building so that you can exchange files or messages with another user on another computer that is connected to the network. A wide area network is similar to a LAN, but links computers that are miles apart, even those in different countries.

### LCD screen
Portable computers do not have room for a bulky monitor. Instead, they often use an LCD (Liquid Crystal Display) screen. There are three types of LCD screen available: monochrome, DSTN (Double Super Twisted Nematic) colour and, at the top of the range, TFT (Thin Film Transistor) colour. A TFT screen is capable of displaying clear, bright and sharp images with tens of thousands of different colours. However, TFT screens are expensive to manufacture and they require a lot of electrical power to run.

### Macro
A series of commands or operations that enable you to automate common tasks in various programs, such as Word or Excel.

### Media player
A utility program supplied free with Windows that allows you to run multimedia files including sound or video files.

### Megabyte (MB or Mbyte)
A measure of the data capacity of storage devices, including hard drives, that is equal to 1,048,576 bytes (220 in binary notation). Megabytes are also used as the measure of the storage capacity of main memory (RAM).

### Memory
Generally, this means some device where information can be stored and retrieved. In practice, it usually refers to the fast electronic components known as RAM, or Random Access Memory, that stores data and is connected directly to the processor. Electronic memory chips remember data only for as long as electricity is supplied.

### Memory expansion
This means adding more electronic memory chips to your computer. Your PC needs memory to run software programs and Windows needs as much memory as possible. Many top-end PCs today come with 1GB of RAM.

### MHz
A measure of the frequency of a timing signal that's equal to one million cycles per second. The higher the MHz (megahertz) number, the faster the clock that's generating the signal. This normally refers to the main clock that sets the timing signal for the processor chip in your PC. The faster the timing signal, the faster the processor will run.

### Minimise
To shrink an application window down to an icon. Minimising an application allows you to run several applications at the same time.

### Modem
The name comes from MOdulator/DEModulator. A modem is a device that converts electronic signals from your PC into sound signals that can be transmitted over a phone line. To receive information the modem works in reverse and converts the sound signals back into digital electronic signals. Modems are also used to connect to the Internet. They can be internal or external. External modems are plugged into your serial or USB port. A modem's speed is measured in bits per second (bps) and the top dial-up models currently transfer data at 56Kbps (56,000 bits per second), which is roughly equivalent to three pages of A4 text a second.

### Motherboard
The main printed circuit inside your PC. It usually has the major components, such as the processor and memory, together with connections for expansion boards.

### MPEG
Stands for Moving Pictures Expert Group. A set of standards for compressing audio and video files.

# GLOSSARY

### Multi-tasking
The ability of Windows to run several programs at once. You could be typing a letter in a word processing program while sending an e-mail. In fact, the processor handles each program one at a time but does so quickly enough to make it appear they are running concurrently.

### Newsgroups
One of the features of the Internet. They are free-for-all discussion forums.

### OCR
Stands for Optical Character Recognition. This is software that takes a scanned text image and converts it into ordinary text. The scanned text can then be loaded into a word processing program – such as Word – for editing.

### OEM
Stands for Original Equipment Manufacturer. A company that produces equipment, such as a computer, using basic parts made by other companies. Only the biggest computer companies make everything themselves.

### Orientation
The way in which a piece of paper is held. Portrait orientation is with the longer edge vertical, and landscape orientation is with the longer edge horizontal.

### Pages per minute (ppm)
The number of standard A4 text pages a printer can print out each minute. With colour printers there are usually two speeds – one for colour printing and one for black and white.

### Parallel port
The socket at the back of your PC that lets you connect it to a printer. A parallel port sends data to the printer over eight parallel wires. Some other devices, such as ZIP drives, can connect through the parallel port.

### Partition
A way of dividing a hard disk into chunks. Each partition is treated by the operating system as though it is a separate drive. For instance, if you buy a large 160GB hard disk, you may find it convenient to split it into four 40GB partitions called C:, D:, E:, and F:.

### Patch
A small software program, often accessible as a piece of code that can be downloaded over the Web, which is issued by manufacturers to correct a bug that is causing persistent problems in a larger program.

### PCI
Stands for Peripheral Component Interconnect. A high-speed connection on the motherboard of your PC that can be used by components that need to exchange large chunks of information fast. PCI is a faster way of transferring information than a 16 bit ISA expansion slot.

### PDA
Stands for Personal Digital Assistant. This is a general term for any small, electronic personal organiser, as is the term palmtop computer.

### PDF
Stands for Portable Document Format. Many hardware and software manuals are now distributed in electronic format, invariably Adobe Acrobat .pdf. This can only be opened and printed using a reader program which can be downloaded for free from the Adobe web site.

### Peer-to-peer network
A simple network in which no single computer is in control. Each acts as a server to the others in the network and shares their resources.

### Peripheral
Any add-on item that connects to your computer, such as a printer or Zip drive.

### Pixel
The smallest single unit on a display, or on a printer, the colour or brightness of which can be controlled. A monitor normally has a resolution of 72 pixels per inch, whereas a laser printer has a resolution of 600 to 1200 pixels (also called dots) per inch.

### Plug and play
A development that is a combination of hardware and software, designed to make PCs far easier to upgrade. The way it works is complex, but the result is simple. Plug in a peripheral and when you reboot, Windows will automatically configure it to work with your system.

### Port
A physical connector for linking input and output devices to the computer.

### PPP
Stands for Point-to-Point Protocol. A set of commands that allows a PC to use the TCP/IP protocol over a phone connection. Normally, TCP/IP will work only over a network, but the PPP system fools it into working over a phone line.

### Protocol
A set of codes and signals that allows two different PCs to communicate. A simple protocol ensures that data is correctly transferred from a PC to a printer along a printer cable. Other protocols ensure that a PC can communicate via the Internet or over a network. A protocol is like a spoken language. If you cannot get two PCs to exchange information, it's likely that they are using different protocols.

### QuickTime
A video system originally used on Apple computers but also available for PCs. It is commonly used by interactive multimedia software such as encyclopaedias. The player for QuickTime is free and is usually bundled along with programs that require it.

### RAM
Stands for Random Access Memory. This memory allows access to any location, in any order. The memory chips in your PC are RAM – any location can be accessed by specifying its address. Magnetic tape – used for long-term storage – is not random access; you must read through all locations before you reach the one you want. RAM is short-term only. While the PC is switched on, it can store part of the operating system and run applications and other work, but all the contents will be lost when the PC is switched off. The more RAM a PC has the faster it will be.

### RAM drive
An area of memory made to look and act like a disk drive. It has its own drive letter and you can create and store files on it.

### ROM
Stands for Read Only Memory. This is a memory device that has had data written onto it at the time of manufacture. You cannot store your own information in ROM. It's contents can only be read, for example a CD–ROM.

### Refresh rate
Measures how many times a second the picture on a monitor is updated in order to maintain a constant flicker-free image. The image on the screen is visible because tiny dots of phosphor shine but the glow lasts a few tenths of a second only. The dots have to be hit by an electron picture beam to get them to glow again. This process is repeated 60 to 70 times per second.

### Registry
A database at the heart of Windows which contains information about every program stored on the disk and the users, networks and preferences. You'll never see the registry, but it's worth knowing it's there in case you see an error message such as Object Not Found in Registry. This means a program has not been correctly installed.

### Remote access
To use your PC from another location, via a phone link. You need two PCs, each with a modem, and special remote access software. This allows you to dial one PC and access the files and folders on its hard disk as if you were there.

### Resolution
Measure of the number of pixels that are displayed on your screen. The more pixels per given area, the sharper the image and the higher the resolution.

### Rich text format (RTF)
A way of storing a document that includes all the commands that describe the page, type, font and formatting. The RTF format allows formatted pages to be exchanged between different word processors.

### Safe mode
A special operating mode of Windows, that is selected if Windows detects a problem when starting. Safe mode will not load many of the (potentially troublesome) drivers, to enable you to try to identify the problem and fix it.

### SCSI
Stands for Small Computer System Interface (pronounced scuzzy). This is a high-speed parallel interface standard. Originally used with Apple Macintosh computers, it now appears in a lot of PCs.

### Serial port
A port to which you can connect serial devices such as a mouse or modem. Through it, data is sent and received one bit at a time, over a single wire. Data in a PC is usually transferred around the computer in parallel form eight or 16 bits wide. However, if you want to use a modem, for instance, you need to send it the data so that it can be converted into sound signals that can be sent one at a time over a telephone line.

### Server
A dedicated computer that provides a function to a network, such as storing images or printing data.

### Shareware
Software which is available free for you to sample. If you keep it, you are expected to pay a fee to the writer. Shareware

is often confused with public-domain software which is completely free.

## Shockwave
A programming language designed to bring animation to web pages. To view its effects you need a plug in, otherwise some web pages you visit won't display properly.

## Software
Any program, or group of programs, that tells the hardware how it should perform, including operating systems, applications and utility programs.

## Soundcard
An add-on device that plugs into an expansion slot inside your PC and generates analogue sound signals. Soundcards are used to play back music and sound effects, such as from a Wav or Midi file, or CD-ROM. A wavetable card is most realistic; it has samples of real instruments used to create music, rather than a synthesiser.

## Status bar
A line at the top or bottom of a screen which gives information about the task currently being worked on, such as the position of the cursor, the number of lines, filename, time and so on.

## Swap file
A hidden file stored on the hard disk that Windows uses to hold parts of programs and data files that don't fit in memory. Windows moves data between the swap file and memory as needed. The swap file is a form of virtual memory.

## TCP/IP
Stands for transmission control protocol/internet protocol. This is the network protocol used to send information over the Internet. It describes how information must be packaged and addressed so that it reaches the right destination and the computer can understand it.

## Terminate and stay resident (TSR)
A program which loads itself into main memory and stays there even when the user exits it. It is then immediately available at the press of a hotkey. Commonly used for utilities and for drivers such as a CD-ROM driver. However, TSRs often cause difficulties when installing new programs. To see which TSRs are running, press Ctrl-Alt-Del and close all the programs you can.

## Thumbnail
A miniature graphical representation of an image. Used by graphic designers as a quick and convenient method of viewing the contents of graphics or DTP files without opening them.

## Touch screen
A computer display that has a grid of infra-red transmitters and receivers positioned on either side of the screen, which is used to control the cursor. When you want to make a selection or to move the cursor, you point to the screen, breaking two of the beams, and this gives the exact position of your finger.

## TWAIN
Stands for Technology Without An Interesting Name. It is the standard way for scanners to communicate with a PC. All scanners come with a TWAIN driver, which makes them compatible with any TWAIN-supporting software.

## Upgrade
To improve the performance or specification of your computer by adding more RAM, a larger hard disk or another kind of improvement. Software can also be upgraded from an old version to a more recent one.

## URL
Stands for Uniform Resource Locator. A URL is the technical name for an Internet address. For example, the URL of the Microsoft home page is http://www.microsoft.com.

## USB
Stands for Universal Serial Bus. This is a recent standard for connecting peripherals, such as scanners, printers, cameras and mice. You can add up to 127 devices through a single port. USB also supports hot plugging, that is, connecting or disconnecting devices without switching off the PC.

## Utility program
Utility programs, or 'utilities', help you get more out of your PC. They provide file management capabilities, such as sorting, copying, comparing, listing and searching, as well as diagnostic and measurement routines that check the health and performance of the system.

## Vapourware
Products which exist in name and marketing hype only and are never likely to appear!

## Virtual memory
Neat trick to give your PC more memory than it physically has. Free space on your hard drive is used as a temporary storage area and information is swapped in and out of memory as needed.

## WAP
Stands for Wireless Application Protocol. WAP mobile phones can view simple web pages to look at e-mail, check share prices, or get the latest news.

## WAV
This is the format that Windows uses for storing most sound files. They can be recognised by the .wav extension.

## WYSIWYG
Stands for What You See Is What You Get. The user sees a document exactly as it will appear in the final version. An example is a word processing or DTP program where the display on screen is the same as the image or text that will be printed, including graphics and special fonts.

## Zip file
A file format used to save disk space. A single Zip file is used as a container for one or more compressed files. These must be expanded to their original size before they can be used. The format was originally devised for use by utilities called PKZip and PKUnzip, but is now so common that virtually all compression and decompression programs can handle the format. Compressed files are shown by the file extension .zip.

## Zip Drive
A high-capacity disk drive from Iomega which can store from 250MB to 750MB of data on sturdy, pocket-sized removable disks. Because of their capacity they are useful for backing up day-to-day data.

# Index

## A
Acrobat .pdf 50
anti-virus software 68, 99, 102–3, 168–9
art pad 20

## B
background monitoring 51
backing up
   configuration files 61, 127–30, 137
   creating a startup disk 64, 125–6
   types of backup 18–19, 112–13, 123–4, 136–7
   using Microsoft Backup 60–61, 112–13, 121–2
   when to back up files 136–7
Backup 60–61, 112–13, 121–2
boot floppy disk 64, 125–6
Braille processing 175
buying a PC
   buyer warnings 12
   choosing a new PC 8
   look and feel 10
   recognising PC parts 9
   shopping list 13
   shopping methods 7
   software bundles 11
buying a printer
   choosing a printer 15–16
   consumables 17
   dot-matrix printers 16
   inkjet printers 14, 16
   laser printers 14, 16–17
   printer jargon 14
   specialist printers 17

## C
cable Internet link 32
cameras
   digital 20
   video 20
CD-ROMs 9, 19, 22, 28
censoring adult Web sites 147–50
chipset 24
cleaning computers *see* spring cleaning
configuration, backing up 61, 127–30, 137
copyright 140
cover discs 29
CPU (central processing unit) 24
crashed (dead) PCs 65
crash protection 51, 166–7

## D
databases 30
data protection
   backing up 136–7
   copyright 140
   customising settings 138–9
   encryption 135, 143–6
   password protection 134–5, 137–8
   power surges/cuts 141–2
   security against theft and fire 132–3
defragmentation 119, 154–5
desktop case 10
desktop publishing 31
Device Manager error codes 76
digital cameras 20
disabilities *see* enabling technology
disabling programs 120
Disk Cleanup 62–63
Disk Defragmenter 52, 118–119
disk drives 18, 112–13, 123–4, 137, 159
disk utilities 156–7
DIY maintenance
   anti-virus software 68
   diagnostic and recovery software 64–5
   error messages 69–72, 76, 81–2
   peripherals 66–7
   troubleshooting 59, 62, 63
   using back-up 60–61
DOS applications 89–92
driver conflicts 63
drivers, updating 46–7, 73–4, 161
DVDs 9, 19

## E
e-mail 32, 144
enabling technology
   Accessibility Wizard 181–2
   advances in technology 180
   changing settings 176–7
   disabilities 171
   helpful hardware 172–3
   helpful software 174–5
   the Internet 178–9
encryption software 135, 143–6
error messages 69–72, 81–2
expansion slots 23, 24
extended warranties 44–5

## F
FAQs 46–7, 58
fault finders 51–2, 64–5
finding lost files 93–4
forums, online 47, 57–8

## G
games 38
graphics card 9, 24, 67, 73–4, 158–9
GUIs (graphical user interface) 28

## H
hard disk 9, 24, 116–19
hardware care 114–15
hardware conflicts 63, 77–8
help 41–58
   diagnostic software 51–2
   Knowledge Base 55–56
   manuals 50
   online support 46–7, 57–58
   peer-to-peer forums 57–8
   user groups 48
   utilities 49
   warranties 42–5
   Windows Help 25–6, 53–4
heuristics 104
hyperlinks 54

## I
illegal operation 72
improving performance
   disk utilities 156–7
   replace/add to components 158–9
   screensavers and wallpaper 170

slicker software 160–61
speeding up 153, 154–5, 162, 168
using utilities 163–9
inside your PC 24
integrated software 11
Internet
censoring adult Web sites 147–50
copyright 140
help with disabilities 178–9
jargon buster 33
modem 9, 23–4, 32–3, 85–8
newsgroups 47, 57–8
online support 43, 46–7
problems with connection 85–8
service provider 32, 34–5
shareware Web sites 164–5
updates and upgrades 160–61
updating drivers 46–7, 73–4, 161
user groups 48–9
utilities 168–9
viruses updates on the Internet 103
Web encryption 144
World Wide Web 36–7

## J

Jaz drive/disks 18–19, 113, 124, 137
joystick 20, 23

## K

keyboard 10, 21, 22, 67, 115, 175, 176–7

## M

mail box 32
manuals 50
memory 9
*see also* RAM
message headers 57
modem 9, 23, 24, 32–3, 85–8
monitor 10, 22, 67, 173, 177
monitor ports 23
motherboard 24
mouse 10, 22, 67, 115, 172
multiple users 138–9, 145–6, 177

## N

newsgroups 47, 57–8
notebook PCs 21

## O

office suites 11, 31
online forums 47, 57–8
online support 43, 46–7
organisers 30

## P

parallel ports 23
passwords 134–5, 137, 138
patch 47, 160
peripherals 20, 66–7
portables 21
ports 23
power lead 23
power supply 24
power surges/cuts 141–2
presentation software 31
preventing problems
backing up 60–61, 112–13, 121–2, 127–30, 136–7
censoring adult Web sites 147–50
copyright 140
creating a boot floppy disk 64, 125–6
data protection 131
disabling programs 120
hard disk health 116–17
hard disk tuning 118–19
hardware care 114–15
increasing storage capacity 123–4
multiple users 138–9, 145–6, 177
power surges/cuts 141–2
privacy 134–5, 143–4
security against theft and fire 132–3
spring cleaning 111, 114–15
printers 14, 15, 16–17, 66–7, 114–15
privacy 134–5, 143–4
processor 9, 158
PS2 ports 23

## Q

QuicKeys 175

## R

RAM (Random Access Memory) 9, 24, 158
recovery disk 51
Registry 127–30
replace/add to components 158–9
restricting usage 143–4
REV drive 18–19, 59

## S

safe mode 63
satellite Internet link 32
ScanDisk 116–17, 154–5
scanner 20
screensavers 170
search engines 37
security against fire and theft 132–3
serial ports 23
service provider 32, 34–5
shareware 164–5
smart disk 51
software
anti-virus 68, 99, 102–3, 168–9
bundles 11
choosing 29–31
disabilities 174–5
problems 81–4
slicker software 160–61
tools 64–5
solving problems
Device Manager error codes 76
error messages 69–72, 81–2
fault finders 51–2, 64–5
finding lost files 93–4
hardware conflicts 63, 77–8
help from other users 57–8
Internet connection 85–8
manuals 50
online support 43, 46–7
PC warranties 42, 44–5
peripherals 66–7
running DOS applications 89–92
software problems 81–4
software tools 64–5

Startup menu 79–80
system conflicts 75–6
technical help 41–58
troubleshooting 62–3
updating drivers 73–4
user groups and utilities 48–9
using back-up 60–61
viruses 68, 99–108
Windows Help 53–4
soundcard 9, 23, 24, 67, 73–4
speakers 9, 22, 67
speech recognition software 174–5
speeding up 153, 154–5, 158–9, 162, 168
spreadsheets 30
spring cleaning 111, 114–15
starting up
    choosing software 29–31
    games 38
    inside your PC 24
    the Internet 32–7
    looking at parts of the system 22–3
    Windows 27–8
    Windows Help systems 25–6
Startup menu 79–80
StickyKeys 176, 182
storage
    back-up 19
    expansion 18
    increasing capacity 123–4
    jargon buster 19
    removable 18–19
surge suppressors 141–2
system conflicts 75–6

## T

tape drives 19, 113, 123–4, 137
technical help 41–58
3D accelerators 24
tower case 10
troubleshooting 62–3
TweakUI 95–8

## U

uninstallers 120, 167

uninstalling programs/software 118–19
updates and upgrades 153
    anti-virus software 68, 103
    Direct X 67
    drivers 46–7, 73–4, 161
    hardware 158–9
    software 47, 160–61
UPSs (uninterruptible power supplies) 141–2
USB ports 23
user groups 48
utilities
    choosing 164–5
    Configuration Backup Utility 127–8
    disk utilities 156–7
    Emergency Recovery Utility 128–30
    Internet utilities 168–9
    system utilities 166–7

## V

video cameras 20
viruses
    anti-virus maintenance 108
    anti-virus software 68, 99, 102–3, 168–9
    definition of a virus 100–1
    types of virus 104–7

## W

wallpaper 170
warranties 42–5
Windows 27
    consistent system 27
    software 28
    Windows Help system 25–6, 53–4
word processing 30
World Wide Web 36–7
WYSIWYG 28

## Z

zip drives/disks 18–19, 113, 123–4